Auto/biographical discourses

In this important study, Laura Marcus explores autobiography as a genre and as an organising concept in nineteenth- and twentieth-century thought.

Drawing on a wide range of writings, both literary and theoretical, she shows how autobiography and biography have been crucial in debates over subject and object, public and private, fact and fiction – debtes now refigured in feminist theory.

The book explores the significance of autobiography and biography in eugenics and theories of 'genius', the 'new biography' of Lytton Strachey, Virginia Woolf and others, autobiography and historical consciousness from Wilhelm Dilthey to the present, recent theories of subjectivity and genre and contemporary autobiographical writings and feminist theories of life-writing.

Laura Marcus is a lecturer in English
at Birkbeck College, University of London

Auto/biographical discourses

Criticism, theory, practice

Laura Marcus

Manchester University Press
Manchester and New York

distributed exclusively in the USA and Canada by St. Martin's Press

Copyright © Laura Marcus 1994

Published by Manchester University Press
Oxford Road, Manchester M13 9NR, UK
and Room 400, 175 Fifth Avenue, New York, NY 10010, USA

Distributed exclusively in the USA and Canada
by St. Martin's Press, Inc., 175 Fifth Avenue, New York, NY 10010, USA

British Library Cataloguing-in-Publication Data
A catalogue record for this book is available from the British Library

Library of Congress Cataloging-in-Publication Data
Marcus, Laura.
    Auto/biographical discourses : theory, criticism, practice / Laura Marcus.
        p.   cm.
    Includes bibliographical references and index.
    ISBN 0–7190–3642–9
    1. English prose literature—History and criticism—Theory, etc. 2. Authors,
English—Biography—History and criticism—Theory, etc. 3.
Autobiography. I. Title.
    PR756.A9M37   1994
828'.80809492—dc20   93–47153
ISBN 0 7190 3642 9 *hardback*
ISBN 0 7190 5530 X *paperback*

Photoset in Linotron Ehrhardt
by Northern Phototypesetting Co. Ltd, Bolton

Printed in Great Britain
by Biddles Ltd, Guildford and King's Lynn

Contents

For William
who suffered and was there

Acknowledgements

I would like to thank my parents and grandparents for their support and interest in my work over the years. I am grateful to David Ellis, Bernard Sharratt and Michael Holquist for stimulating my interests in auto-biography: more recently, Paul Thompson has introduced me to the world of oral history and life-stories. Claire Buck, Annie Coombes, Elizabeth Cowie, James Donald, John Ellis, Bill Marshall, Howard Mills, Lynda Nead and Nancy Wood have been stalwart friends on the long march to completion. My thanks also to other friends and former colleagues at the Universities of Southampton, Sussex and Westminster. Birkbeck College has provided a stimulating and supportive environment for research and discussion: my thanks to my colleagues in the English Department and the Centre for Interdisciplinary Research in Culture and the Humanities, and, in particular, to Tom Healy and Steve Connor for their commitment and concern for their colleagues and for intellectual life. I have had the best of friends and readers in Michael Baron, John Barrell, Steve Connor, Peter Middleton, Jan Montefiore, Francis Mulhern, Michael Sheringham and Carol Watts, and the most helpful and patient of editors in Anita Roy at Manchester University Press. Isobel Armstrong and Rachel Bowlby read and commented on the whole manuscript at different stages: their suggestions, encouragement and friendship made, and make, all the difference. William Outhwaite helped, with extraordinary generosity, and at the expense of his own writing (and sleep), in more ways than I can enumerate. This book is for him, with all my love and my deep gratitude.

Introduction

Autobiography has been a topic of central interest for literary and cultural theory in the past few decades, enlivened and in many cases transformed by feminist, working-class and black criticism and historiography. Autobiography was a central case for feminist criticisms in the 1980s, exposing processes of exclusion and marginalisation in the construction of literary canons. Not only were women autobiographers self-evidently outside the 'Great Men' tradition with which many autobiographical critics operated; generic definitions served to exclude forms of 'life-writing' such as diaries, letters and journals, often adopted by women and those outside mainstream literary culture. The extensive feminist literature on women's autobiography over the last decade or so introduces many writers previously excluded from discussion, while revealing how 'androcentric' the autobiographical tradition and autobiographical criticism have been.

More traditional literary critics have tended to distance themselves from earlier approaches to the study of autobiography – although holding on to some of the major claims made for the 'genre' – on the grounds that their studies constitute a radical new departure in the field and that autobiography has only recently been recognised as an important form of literary creation. Yet an examination of earlier autobiographical criticism reveals a number of preoccupations and suppositions which are often continuous with those present in recent criticism. Whereas autobiographical writing as a genre has proved very difficult to define and regulate, as the following chapters will show, there is a distinctive genre of autobiographical *criticism*, and a substantial part of this book is concerned with the forms taken by this critical genre in the nineteenth and twentieth centuries.

A central issue is the way in which a number of 'seminal' autobiographies have come to dominate autobiographical criticism. This is related in the first instance to accounts of an autobiographical 'tradition'. For example, the positing of Augustine's Confessions as the first 'true' autobiography has become firmly linked with the view that autobiography is both introspective and centrally concerned with the problematics of time and memory. Moreover, the view that Augustine is the founding father of the autobiographical form becomes synonymous with the claim that autobiography is in essence an aspect of Christian Western civilisation, and could only take shape and develop within this context. Rather than opting for an alternative origin and source, one might interrogate this critical desire for points of origin, and explore how the various claims made for specific moments of departure are aligned with other judgements about historical developments within literature and culture, and, perhaps most crucially, with beliefs about the nature of selfhood and identity.

The concept of an autobiographical tradition is further related to the concept of mentors and models invoked in autobiographical criticism. We have accounts, for example, of 'pre-autobiographical' texts which offer 'model' conceptions of the personality: 'exemplary ways of being human', in Karl Weintraub's description. Such conceptions, it is claimed, are subsequently challenged by the ideas of individuality which emerge together with the growth of auto-biography itself.[1] The move then made within forms of auto-biographical criticism such as Weintraub's is towards the location of 'exemplary' texts which offer the 'fullest' accounts of individuality (seen as historically specific but uncontested within each period), while themselves becoming 'models' for the autobiographical genre. The idea of the model or exemplary life is thus transmuted into that of the model or exemplary text: one whose exemplariness, para-doxically, lies in its representation of the uniqueness and singularity of the individual life. And because, in the field of literary studies at least, to be seen to follow an exemplar too obediently involves the sacrifice of originality, the demand placed on the 'seminal' auto-biographical texts is that they each, in and of themselves, express an exemplary individuality. The model (of the) text is thus referred back to the model (of a) life. The need to locate the 'seminal' within the autobiographical genre has limited the context for discussion, returning critics to the same set of texts with the same set of demands.

The critical strategies outlined above also represent one example of the continuities within the history of autobiographical criticism. The claims of contemporary critics that their discussions of autobiography represent a total break with the primarily moral emphases of nineteenth-century accounts of biography and autobiography are put into question by this continued concern with autobiographical models and mentors. Other definitions and issues have also retained a certain constancy: for example, the question of what constitutes autobiography proper, in opposition to popular 'confessional' literature or memoir. The distinction most frequently made is that between autobiography as the evocation of a life as a totality, and 'memoirs' which offer only an anecdotal depiction of people and events. This discrimination is made at times on formal grounds, in an attempt to distinguish between generic categories, but also invokes discussion of the autobiographer's intentions and motivations. If the autobiographer is 'sincere' in the attempt to understand the self and to explain that self to others, then the 'autobiographical intention' becomes accepted as a serious one.

The concept of 'intention' pervades discussions of autobiography: it not only refers to an authorial motive governing the production of the text, but becomes an elaborate structure which apparently defines the ways in which the text should be received. In a number of cases, it is used to resolve the intractable problem of 'referentiality' – that is, the kind and degree of 'truth' that can be expected from autobiographical writing. Very few critics would demand that autobiographical truth should be literally verifiable – this would, after all, undermine the idea that the truth of the self is more complex than 'fact'. Thus, it is claimed, the 'intention' to tell the truth, as far as possible, is a sufficient guarantee of autobiographical veracity and sincerity. The concept of intention in literary criticism usually implies a grasping of what an author 'meant to say' – this was the critical process rejected by the New Critics – but this concept of intention is not the only one relevant to autobiography. In autobiographical criticism, the intentions and character of the person, conceptualised in a more psychological register, are made the condition of autobiographical 'truth'. Roy Pascal is only one of several critics to formulate this claim: 'The first condition is the seriousness of the author, the seriousness of his personality and of his intention in writing.'[2] Autobiography, clearly, should be neither lightly undertaken nor lightly received.

A further repeated tenet within autobiographical criticism is that the true autobiographer is in some way driven by an inner compulsion to write of the self, and that the autobiographical act must involve a degree of difficulty and struggle, both in 'grasping' the self and in communicating it. Much autobiographical criticism thus retains a strong ethical emphasis. Moreover, attention is focused upon the individual as sole producer of the life-history. Questions of the production and circulation of autobiographies are for the most part bracketed off, perhaps because the autobiography is perceived, like the life it narrates, to be 'unique' and singular. But the question of the perceived degrees of 'seriousness' of autobiographical texts is in fact not separate from perceptions of the literary market. From the early nineteenth century onwards, 'serious' autobiographical writing is viewed in contradistinction to autobiographies held to be produced with the aim of achieving notoriety and/or for mercenary motives. This is made explicit in nineteenth-century discussions, in which attacks on commercial publishing and the literary market-place are closely linked with vilifications of 'commercial' autobiographies. The mercantile aspects of writing are viewed as particularly insidious in relation to autobiographical writing, especially when this is held to be an authentic and autonomous expression of an essentially private self.

Attempts to define the 'conditions and limits' of autobiography, which appear with some frequency in recent autobiographical criticism, are ostensibly concerned with historical questions – the rise of autobiography, and with generic definitions – what marks out autobiography from other forms of writing. These are not negligible issues, but conditions and limits may also include implicit provisos about what constitutes 'valid' autobiography, and these tend to be based in part on the perceived cultural status of the autobiographer.

For the nineteenth- and early twentieth-century critic of auto-biography, the concept of genius is central to the debate. Twentieth-century approaches tend to phrase the question in terms of an 'inner' necessity which motivates and guides the writing of autobiography. The spatial metaphors of 'inside' and 'outside' which repeatedly appear in a range of critical discussions are closely linked with oppositions between self and world, private and public, subjectivity and objectivity, the interior spaces of mind and personal being and the public world, including that of the literary market-place. They inform the now accepted distinctions between autobiography proper, and memoirs or *res gestae*. Theorists of autobiography emphasise the differences or connections between these opposed 'spaces' to varying degrees: for the most part introspection is perceived as a value, but for more than one critic, the inwardness of autobiography is seen to result in obsessive self-absorption, remoteness from reality and from the world of history and progress. One route out of this difficulty involves linking historical progress with a growth in human individuality and self-consciousness. Other critics emphasise the 'dialectical' relationship between self and world, inside and outside.

For the most part, however, the value of autobiography is seen to lie in its 'insider' quality: the autonomous status of autobiography is based on its separation from forms of history-writing, where history was and is defined as an 'objective', 'documentary' approach to lives and events. Psychological and philosophical issues filled the space left by the rejection of history. Freedom from the strictures of positivist historiography has led, however, to other cognitive straitjackets. For example, idealist theories of autobiographical 'truth' as coherence, the only absolute truth being 'the whole', set in opposition to positivist theories of truth as correspondence, have perhaps led to an excessive emphasis on the need for unity within the autobiographical work. But there are other, equally important, reasons for the valorisation of unity. In philosophical terms, autobiography is seen to secure, at one level at least, the much desired unity of the subject and object of knowledge. In aesthetic terms, the elevation of autobiography to the status of a literary genre has involved its endowment with the properties of the unified work of art. In the broader terms of an Arnoldian account of 'culture', the ideal autobiography may be seen as expressing humanity's 'approaches to totality, and to a full, harmonious perfection'.[3]

A related and important concept within autobiographical criticism is that of 'introspection'. The conceptual problem of how a mind can simultaneously observe and be observed emerged as a correlate of mind–body dualism in the seventeenth century and became of central importance for science, and particularly psychology, in the late nineteenth century. Because autobiography *ex hypothesi* means that the author is identical with the autobiographical subject, it has come to be assumed that autobiography will shed light on this problematic. But whereas philosophers have assumed that consciousness is aware of its contents, theorists of autobiography have tended to emphasise the retrospective and therefore non-immediate nature of autobiographical self-awareness. Nevertheless, critics have continued to assume some form of parallelism between the two areas of enquiry. Debates over introspection are carried into discussions of autobiography, from early twentieth-century texts arguing for the 'scientific' nature of autobiographical writing to later phenomenological and existentialist theories of autobiography.

As significant as the critical emphasis on subjective truths is the view that general laws of human nature can be drawn from auto-biographical texts when a comparative focus is adopted. Hence the organisation of studies of autobiography around such supposedly universal themes as childhood, loss, conversion and quest. The themes may be 'poetic', but the critic seeks scientific credibility by approaching autobiographies as 'data'. In itself, this may not be a worthless approach; what for the most part is wholly lacking is any discussion of what has governed the selection of this data. From the autobiographies of twentieth-century poets, for example, it is pre-sumably possible to extrapolate some account of what it means to be a twentieth-century poet, but this is hardly the same as deriving from this selective material an account of universal features of life. This approach is connected to the concerns of nineteenth-century critics, discussed above, with the issue of who is entitled to write auto-biography. If autobiographies are the materials from which general laws of individual existence and identity are to be drawn, it becomes likely that the critic will select autobiographical texts which confirm the importance of certain values rather than others. For the twentieth-century critic, these are most often to be found in a repre-sentation of the 'creative' life.

This raises a number of questions about how 'literary' auto-biography is to be defined. In fact, a number of autobiographical theorists use the term pejoratively; for the historian Georg Misch and the philosopher Georges Gusdorf, for example, the 'literariness' of autobiography implies stylisation, literary conventionalism and, in Gusdorf's argument, commercialism: these militate against the original and authentic act of autobiography 'proper'.[4] On the other hand, the impetus behind much contemporary criticism has been the desire to see autobiography recognised as a specifically literary genre in its own right, although this involves a number of very different approaches and positions.

Nineteenth-century writers on the topic of autobiography are, on the whole, less troubled by definitional questions than twentieth-century critics, and are more concerned with the question of classification. But in discussions from both centuries, 'auto-biography' appears as an ideal type or form, which may bear little or no relation to individual autobiographies. Here as elsewhere, the singular collective noun may express a conceptual reification, assuming an essence before the chosen critical task of defining and consolidating resemblances has even begun. In other discussions, particular autobiographies become elected as paradigmatic texts, out of which a number of observations about the nature of the genre can be drawn. This is one reason why autobiography is a near-impossible topic to discuss as a totality. Many critics claim that this is because the boundaries of autobiographical writing are blurred. But it is also possible that critics have been using autobiographies as a point of departure from which to address problematics which are often not made explicit, and which therefore may be the sources of ambiguity rather than the autobiographies themselves.

Underlying these issues is the fundamental problem of the instability or hybridity of autobiography as a genre. On the one hand, this makes it a particularly valuable resource in a variety of argumentative strategies in such topics as subject/object, self and identity, private and public, fact and fiction. It also plays a central role in discussions of a perceived crisis of nineteenth- and early twentieth-century culture, marked by such notions as alienation, reification, the decline of community and the rise of mass society. Autobiography appears in part as a microcosmic version of many of these concerns, serving to articulate them, and for some critics, to offer at least a partial solution. Autobiographical consciousness, for example, may be held up as a mode of healthy self-awareness which could heal some of the wounds of the nineteenth-century spirit.

But autobiography is itself a major source of concern because of its very instability in terms of the postulated opposites between self and world, literature and history, fact and fiction, subject and object. In an intellectual context in which, as Raymond Williams has perceptively argued, these are seen as irreconcilably distinct, autobiography will appear either as a dangerous double agent, moving between these oppositions, or as a magical instrument of reconciliation.[5]

The proliferation of classificatory and categorising systems in autobiographical criticism testifies to the extent to which autobiography is seen as a problem which requires control and containment. In the variant in which autobiography is seen as offering a solution and not just presenting a problem, the identity of autobiography is seen as a precondition or guarantor of a remedy for the fractured identity of modernity. For some recent literary critics and theorists who oppose the application of generic classifications to autobiography, the rejection of categorising systems can also stem from a perhaps exaggerated sense of autobiography's role in bridging traditional oppositions. Here, autobiography is seen as 'transcending' rather than transgressing categories, generic and cultural. In a different model, taken up primarily by deconstructionist critics, auto-biography becomes a testimony to the artificiality of all generic classifications and the repudiation of a model of genres as natural kinds. Thus autobiography is important as the most conspicuous example of a 'genre' which exposes the heterogeneity of all literary productions – as in Mary Jacobus's description of autobiography as 'that mixed and transgressive genre'[6] and Barbara Johnson's reference to the 'monstrosity' of autobiographical writing.[7]

I have referred to the literary critical view that autobiography needs to be redeemed from its 'traditional' placing as a sub-category of history-writing. There has, however, been very little discussion of the competing claims made by, or raised on behalf of, the various human sciences, in particular sociology and psychology, and even the natural sciences, for example physiology and biology. It is here that a number of the most interesting issues arise. The emergence of an auto-biographical criticism runs parallel to the formation of the modern disciplines, including literary studies and sociology. The demand that autobiography be understood as a specifically literary form arises within the context of recent battles between the new disciplines over particular domains and definitions of language, truth and knowledge. These debates have their roots in the earlier formation of disciplines, and these disciplinary conflicts are of paramount importance in understanding what is at stake in the debates over the provenance of autobiography itself.

Often, the competing claims of different disciplines are based on similar or identical grounds. James Olney, in *Metaphors of Self*, follows a number of commentators in claiming for autobiography that it can advance our understanding of the question 'How shall I live?'[8] It could be suggested that there is a relationship between the disci-plinary struggle over autobiography and the attempts by the new disciplines to answer the same question. Recent studies of the forma-tion of the disciplines of literature and sociology in the nineteenth and early twentieth centuries have charted this dispute over which branch of knowledge offered the most profound and comprehensive guide to living; the 'two cultures' debate, literature versus science, produces further ramifications. Autobiography is of particular significance in these contexts, precisely because it can legitimately be used as a resource by psychologists, historians, sociologists and literary critics. The dead end reached by many literary critics seeking to define the real and essential nature of autobiography and its proper disciplinary place results from their failure to recognise that disciplines, as well as genres, have histories, and that their boundaries are always contestable. Autobiography functions in this book as a topic, a resource and a site of struggle.

The first section of the book explores nineteenth- and early twentieth-century approaches to autobiography, and to a lesser extent biography, in periodical literature, essays and critical texts. Chapter 1 examines nineteenth-century discussions, drawn in large part from periodicals, with a particular focus on the perceived distinctions between 'serious' and 'popular' autobiography, and on the question of the classification of autobiographical texts. This issue is further explored in Chapter 2, in which I discuss early twentieth-century autobiographical and biographical criticism against the background of the competing claims of science, psychology and literature. Chapter 3 shifts the focus to the discourse of the 'new biography' in the early twentieth century, examining some of Lytton Strachey's and Virginia Woolf's biographical writings in the context of the biographical criticism of the period, and their contributions to critical debates about biography. Chapter 4 looks at the tradition in autobiographical criticism developing out of the work of Wilhelm Dilthey, Georg Misch and Georges Gusdorf, in which autobiographies are used to support developmental histories of human consciousness.

The second part of the book explores autobiographical theory, criticism and writing of the last few decades. Chapter 5 discusses the emergence of 'autobiographical studies', most prominent in American criticism, and explores the ways in which autobiography is deployed from the 1970s in the renewed 'crises of the subject' and in the debates between humanist, formalist and deconstructionist critics. Chapter 6 discusses autobiography in relation to genre theory and literary history. Chapter 7 looks at recent developments in autobiographical criticism, including British and American feminist approaches and discussions of class, ethnicity and autobiography. The concerns of this chapter include the move to 'personal criticism' in feminist discussions – here the autobiographical enters into the critical act, and feminist epistemology and autobiography become closely linked formations. Finally, the perceived hybridity which troubled earlier critics is now celebrated, at least by some critics, as a powerfully transgressive property of the autobiographical form.

Notes

1 Karl J. Weintraub, *The Value of the Individual: Self and Circumstance in Autobiography* (University of Chicago Press, 1978), p. xv.
2 Roy Pascal, *Design and Truth in Autobiography* (London: Routledge and Kegan Paul, 1960), p. 60.
3 Matthew Arnold, *Culture and Anarchy* (Cambridge University Press, 1932), pp. 12–13.
4 See Georges Gusdorf, 'De l'autobiographie initiatique à l'autobiographie genre littéraire', *Revue d'histoire littéraire de la France* 75 (1975), 957–94.
5 On the fact–fiction distinction, see Raymond Williams, 'The Multiplicity of Writing', in *Marxism and Literature* (Oxford University Press, 1977).
6 Mary Jacobus, 'The Law of/and Gender: Genre Theory and *The Prelude*', *Diacritics* 14 (Winter 1984), 47–57. A version of this essay is reprinted in Jacobus's *Romanticism, Writing and Sexual Difference* (Oxford: Clarendon Press, 1989).
7 Barbara Johnson, 'My Monster/My Self ', in *A World of Difference* (Baltimore and London: Johns Hopkins University Press, 1989), pp. 144–54.
8 James Olney, *Metaphors of Self: The Meaning of Autobiography* (Princeton University Press, 1972), p. xi.

1

Identity into form:
nineteenth-century
auto/biographical discourses

In 1805, William Wordsworth claimed, of his autobiographical self-representations, that it was 'a thing unprecedented in Literary history that a man should talk so much about himself '.[1] By 1850, when *The Prelude* was finally published, the 'genre' in which Wordsworth was working was almost over-familiar to his readers. Elizabeth Bruss has argued that, to become a genre, a literary act must be recognisable by a particular community of readers and writers, and that its functions must be relatively stable. As the genre becomes more familiar, auto-biographers have less need to provide internal signals of the act being performed.[2]

In his recent study, *The Origins of the English Novel*, Michael McKeon discusses the difficulty of constructing an adequate model of generic development:

> speaking of the 'origins' of the novel must be understood to entail the disarming 'simplicity' of describing its emergence as a simple abstraction. The origins of the English novel occur at the end point of a long history of 'novelistic usage' – at the moment when this usage has become sufficiently complex to permit a generalising 'indifference' to the specificity of usages and an abstraction of the category whose integrity is presupposed by that indifference. . . . By the middle of the eighteenth century, the stabilizing of terminology – the increasing acceptance of 'the novel' as a canonic term, so that contemporaries can 'speak of it *as such*' – signals the stability of the conceptual category and of the class of literary products that it encloses.[3]

McKeon's account of the 'origins' of the novel illuminates the much debated question of the terminology of 'autobiography' and its history. A number of critics have argued that the first recorded usage of the term – held to be Robert Southey's in 1809 – marks a new recognition of autobiography as an autonomous genre.[4] Some have asserted that it is a marker of a new genre coming into being: others, for example Georges Gusdorf, see it as heralding a new literary-critical pedagogy, a recent parasite on a lengthy and venerable tradition which developed in the absence of specific nomenclature.

Arguments for the view that the use of the term 'autobiography' heralds the autonomy of the genre and its class of 'products' overlook a certain complexity in this history of usages. The first recorded usage of 'autobiography' in fact occurs in 1797, when the reviewer of Isaac d'Israeli's *Miscellanies* – thought to be William Taylor of Norwich – writes in a discussion of d'Israeli's use of the term 'self-biography': 'It is not very usual in English to employ hybrid works partly Saxon and partly Greek: yet *autobiography* would have seemed pedantic'.[5] It is striking that the very first use of the term is a negative one – that is, it is entertained and then rejected as an inappropriate generic term. Perhaps the 'hybridity' of 'self-biography' is seen as more appropriate for a conceptual category which itself appears to be hybrid, on the borders between art and life, inner self and outer world, fiction and history. Or more obviously, the overt reflexivity of 'self-biography' shows 'biography' to be the clearly dominant form, exceptionally turned back on itself and on the self, as in another customary term, 'the biography of a man written by himself'.[6]

Extending McKeon's discussion, this first use of the term, which is also a non-use, is symptomatic of the fact that, in contrast to the novel, the terminology of autobiography is never fully stabilised nor 'autobiography' fully accepted as a 'canonic' term. Various synonyms and circumlocutions continue to be used even when 'autobiography' is available and (relatively) accepted. The conceptual category and the class of written products it encloses remain unstable and the coining of neologisms around the neologism 'autobiography' continues to the present day, particularly in feminist and deconstructionist criticism – 'autobiothanatography', 'autography', 'otobiography'. . . .[7]

In this chapter, and indeed throughout this study, I will be exploring the view that autobiography, despite its development and recognition as a genre, remains an unstable category and yet one on which a great deal rests. The perception of autobiography's hybridity and instability incites a variety of attempts to control and contain it, primarily through generic and characterological classifications and schemata. On the other hand, autobiography is itself viewed as the form which has the potential to resolve oppositions, for example between subject and object (hence the emphasis on the fact that the autobiographical 'I' both writes and is written, is the knower and the known) and between self and world. In this sense, autobiography can be understood as a Utopian form. The paradoxes arising within autobiographical discourse result from contradictory views of the genre as dangerous/anarchic or conservative, as alienating or centring the self, as creating or binding divisions.

Further preoccupations which emerge in critical discourse on autobiography throughout the nineteenth century include the relationship between private and public selves and places, the tension between 'exemplary' and 'counter-exemplary' individuals – with Jean-Jacques Rousseau holding an uneasy place in both camps – and the distinction between the controlled (introspective) analysis of character and its involuntary disclosure. These, however, are not simple oppositions; once the analysis of self ceases to be solely for the self and/or for God, it must inevitably become a display of some kind – hence the drive to control the production and consumption of self-expression in the public sphere, and the related anxiety over the disclosure of insider secrets (in the social sphere) to outsiders.

* * *

The perception of autobiography's generic 'instability' pervades nineteenth-century periodical literature, in which accounts of specific texts are invariably prefaced by lengthy disquisitions on the questionable wisdom, propriety or usefulness of autobiography. The charges of vanity and egotism regularly levelled against practitioners of autobiography – in Isaac d'Israeli's much quoted phrase, the 'ebriety of vanity and the delirium of egotism' – by nineteenth-century reviewers and critics can to some extent be taken at face value.[8] If autobiography is seen as a sub-genre of biography, and if biography has predominantly eulogistic, 'obituary' functions, as much of it does in the nineteenth century, then there will obviously be a concern about the apparently self-eulogising nature and function of 'self-biography'. Beyond this, however, the habitual expressions of disquiet indicate an uncertainty about the relationship of 'literary product' to 'generic category' and an unease about the nature and status of autobiographical writing. One reason for this uncertainty is the fact that the eighteenth-century novel 'usurps' first-person narrative and thus renders uncertain the authenticity of the autobiographical 'I', and the distinction between autobiography and fiction. A further ambiguity is the relationship between biography and autobiography.

Mikhail Bakhtin's account of 'ancient biography and auto-biography' in his 'Forms of Time and of the Chronotope in the Novel' may throw some light on this last issue.[9] Bakhtin argues that the time/space chronotope of biography and autobiography in ancient Greece was the public square: 'There was as yet no internal man, no "man for himself" ' (I for myself), nor any individualized approach to one's own self. An individual's unity and his self-consciousness were exclusively public. Man was completely *on the surface*, in the most literal sense of the word' [p. 133]. Under such conditions, Bakhtin states, 'there could not in principle be any difference between the approach one took to another's life and to one's own, that is, between the biographical and autobiographical points of view' [p. 132]. It is only later, in the Hellenistic and Roman era, 'when the public unity of the individual begins to disintegrate', that philosophers and rhetoricians specifically pose the question: 'is it permissible to write an appraisal of one's own self?' [pp. 132–3] The question is resolved in the affirmative. But, Bakhtin continues, the true significance of the question is that it should arise at all:

> Self-glorification, after all, is but the most sharply focused, most vivid distinctive feature of a biographical and autobiographical approach to life. Thus there lurks beneath the specific question of the propriety of glorifying oneself a more general question, namely, the legitimacy of taking the same approach to one's own life as to another's life, to one's own self as to another self. The very posing of such a question is evidence that the classical *public wholeness* of an individual has broken down, and a differentiation between biographical and autobiographical forms had begun. [p.133]

Clearly, this account of, to borrow a phrase, 'the fall of public man' needs to be treated with some caution. Michael Foucault usefully reminds us, in his account of the Hellenistic and Roman world, of the necessary distinctions to be drawn between 'individualism' as (1) the individualistic attitude and an exaltation of individual singularity; (2) the positive valuation of private life; (3) the intensity of the relations to self.[10] Setting these qualifications aside for the moment, however, it remains significant that Bakhtin locates the transformations occurring in concepts of the self in relation to the splitting apart of biographical and autobiographical forms and sees a more general question 'lurk[ing] beneath the specific question of the propriety of glorifying oneself' [p. 133]. This is of central importance in the debates about biography and autobiography in the late eighteenth and nineteenth centuries. However great the problems in transferring arguments about ancient Greece to post-Enlightenment Europe, Bakhtin's questions bear interestingly on the later context, and move us beyond the overly simple account in which autobiography steadily gains a relative freedom from its parent-genre, biography, as modern 'individualism' develops, and literary classifications become more sophisticated. The uncertainty of critics and reviewers about the relationship between the two forms is the striking feature. In its turn, it alerts us to questions concealed by the ostensible concern with self-glorification. The nineteenth-century emphasis on the charges of vanity and egotism risked by the autobiographer is too insistent, hinting at more radical anxieties it serves to mask.

What are these questions and anxieties? Bakhtin's answer – that to even pose the question of approaching one's own life in the same way as someone else's suggests a fissure in 'public wholeness' – is again too general to address the particularities of eighteenth- and nineteenth-century contexts. But we might begin with the fact that ideas of the self, subjectivity and consciousness are undergoing radical revision in the period immediately prior to the point at which 'modern' autobiography is said to be inaugurated *as a result of its separation from biography* – indeed, at the point at which it 'gains' a name, albeit one which is continually under question. As a hybrid form, autobiography unsettles distinctions, including the division between self and other. In this sense, it becomes a destabilising form of writing and knowledge. The perceived instability and hybridity of 'autobiography' are inextricably linked to the problematics of selfhood and identity, with the boundaries between 'inner' and 'outer', 'private' and 'public' becoming the sites of the greatest concern. Autobiographical discourse in the nineteenth century, following on from eighteenth-century accounts of 'self-examination', reveals the extent to which the 'inner' of the self is constituted as both a sacred place and a site of danger. Introspection, moreover, divides the self. In Isaac d'Israeli's account, diaries – or, more generally, writing as self-analysis – 'form that other Self', which is both known and alien, pre-existent and constructed.[11] The perceived 'dangers' of autobiography are inextricably linked to the problematics of subjectivity, whether autobiography is seen as a way of ordering and objectifying the self, and thus importing alterity into the self that engenders it, or mirroring its vacillations and alterations.

* * *

In her recent study of eighteenth-century autobiographical discourse, *The Autobiographical Subject*, Felicity Nussbaum explores the complex conceptions of 'self' and 'character' in this period, and the ways in which autobiographical writings both consolidate and question emergent/dominant definitions of identity; definitions which are heavily inflected by class and gender interests.[12] As she notes, 'identity', 'self', 'soul' and 'person' are dangerous and disputed formations in the eighteenth century, with profound implications for the individual's legal, moral and spiritual responsibility to Church and State. Autobiography offered a private occasion, and subsequently a public forum, for attempting to resolve the problematics of identity: contradictions between the view that identity exists through time (Locke) and the idea that its existence is uncertain (Hume) are displayed and mediated through self-reflective writing. The 'self' as capital or property is essential to the newly emergent bourgeoisie, who 'formed a class that would begin to keep an unprecedented record of its individual selves' [p. 54], but autobiographical writings – including or especially women's – could also provide locations where subjects disrupted dominant conceptions of the bourgeois self. Such writings are also fundamentally engaged with categories of private and public, at times reinforcing the distinction between the two spheres, at others dangerously cutting across their boundaries. Identity and genre thus become inextricably linked in their complexities and contestations.

A further related concern which emerges in the eighteenth century, and particularly vexes critics and reviewers from the early nineteenth century onwards, is that of the propriety of 'the published self' and the status of autobiography in print culture. 'Vanity' in this context becomes intricately bound up with 'publicity'. In the following passage from the *Quarterly Review* of 1810, 'vanity' is a form of self-regard, echoing the anxieties among religious sects about the extent to which self-scrutiny in a spiritual context passes over into an overweening concern with self.

Let any man, who has in common degree mixed with the world, delineate a true picture of himself, unfold without reserve his motives of action, his feelings under different circumstances, together with the views, interests, and associations by which his life has been regulated; and he could not fail to produce a work, in which many would take a lively interest, and from which all might draw matter of instructive reflexion.

But, unluckily, there are no instances in which self-biography has fully answered this purpose, and very few in which it has done so to any tolerable degree. It may perhaps be said, notwithstanding all professions to the contrary, that no one ever published memoirs of himself, entirely for the benefit of others. Vanity, variously directed, mixed up with different elements, displaying itself under different forms, and aided more or less by accessory feelings, has, we shrewdly suspect, been the great moving spring in all these matters.[13]

This is one of many nineteenth-century reviews of autobiography to open with a discussion of the oddness, difficulty or illegitimacy of the enterprise and particularly of its failure to meet an 'ideal' – whether of self-knowledge, truth, sincerity or transparency. The passage above indicts the failure to write solely for the purpose of providing 'instructive reflexion' for others – the 'self', which is both the subject and object of autobiography, is also what 'contaminates' the text and makes authorial intention impure. Bishop Huet, the author of the memoirs reviewed, written a century earlier, is also criticised for appropriating the motive force behind confessional or spiritual autobiography ('I felt myself summoned by God to scrutinize the ingrained spots of my conscience, and most humbly and submissively lay them before his sight') when his memoirs fail to do more than detail 'the ordinary events of his life'. 'The memoir before us has not the slightest claim to the title of confession, for there is no appearance of frankness, no disclosure of secret infirmities, no acknowledgements of failings and errors', the reviewer writes. It is 'totally destitute of that free development of character, for which memoirs of this description are chiefly valuable'. In other words, there is too much of the 'life' and not enough of the 'self'.

The views expressed here are one variant of a more general concern revolving around relationships between self and other, public and private, revelation and concealment. The 'ideal' of auto-biographical 'veracity' as fortified by 'certainty of knowledge'[14] (Dr Johnson) is complicated by the view that some forms of self-knowledge should remain private. A reviewer comments on William Cowper's *Memoirs* (*c.* 1767, pub. 1816), with their vivid account of Cowper's mental illness and religious melancholia: 'if it be said that the Memoirs are the confessions of Cowper concerning himself, we answer, that what might be proper and beneficial for Cowper to write for his own private admonition, it may not be equally proper to publish to the world'.[15]

The tension between spiritual autobiography as self-scrutiny and writing for public consumption is central to these perceptions of selves and self-writing. The difficulty of preventing self-scrutiny and self-knowledge from sliding over into self-regard and self-absorption certainly vexed spiritual leaders from the eighteenth century onwards, and emerges in more recent and apparently wholly secular contexts, attesting to the way in which discussions of secular auto-biography inherited religious paradigms and value-systems. The interchange between philosophical and religious discourses in the eighteenth century is also revealed, as Nussbaum notes, in the similarity of their exhortations to self-scrutiny in and through the keeping of periodic records of the 'self' and/or 'life'. The demand for spiritual 'bookkeeping' intersects with the philosophical concern with 'character' and its development, as may be seen from the following discussions of autobiography and biography in the early nineteenth century.

The literary historian and essayist Isaac d'Israeli wrote, in one of the earliest discussions of 'self-biography':

> Our souls, like our faces, bear the general resemblance of the species, but retain the particular form which is peculiar to the individual. He who studies his own mind, and has the industry to note down the fluctuations of his opinions, the fallacies of his passions, and the vacillations of his resolutions, will form a journal to himself peculiarly interesting, and probably not undeserving the meditations of others.[16]

Although d'Israeli is not overly concerned about the 'public' display of the 'private' self, he shares with a great many commentators on self-scrutiny and self-writing a sense of the dangerous aspects of the inner self. His focus on the incoherences within identity could have led him to a greater emphasis on the threat to the stability of public selfhood, although he chooses rather to focus on the haunting aspects of the self as double, and on the integrating function of diary-time/chronology in constructing the self as Other:

> Could a Clive, or a Cromwell, have composed a Diary? Neither of these men could suffer solitude and darkness; at the scattered thoughts of casual reflection they started; what would they have done, had memory marshalled their crimes, and arranged them in the terrors of chronology?

These Diaries form that other Self, which Shaftesbury has described every thinking being to possess; and which, to converse with, he justly accounts the highest wisdom. When Cato wishes that every man had a glass window in his breast, it is only a metaphorical expression for such a Diary.[17]

In the essayist John Foster's 'On a Man's Writing Memoirs of Himself' (1805), which takes up many earlier themes concerning the value of 'self-examination' and was republished throughout the nineteenth century, memoir-writing is a programme for self-discovery and self-knowledge.[18] Foster's major emphasis is on the value of introspection, a removal from 'exterior interests', in order that the individual being 'be collected and concentrated in the consciousness of its own absolute *self*, so as to be recognized as a thing internal, apart and alone, for its own inspection and knowledge' [p. 5]. Written memory creates identity. The distinction he draws between the focus on the inner self and the recounting of 'the mere facts and events of life' anticipates the distinction drawn in more recent criticism between autobiography and memoirs; one which implies a residual belief in the possibility of introspection, despite a general scepticism in modern discussions about the validity or even possibility of the introspective method as traditionally conceived.

Two further themes from Foster's essay concern us here: the view that autobiographies reveal the laws of human nature and character and the perception of autobiography as a private act.

I recollect having proposed to two or three of my friends, that they should write, each principally for his own use, memoirs of their own lives, endeavouring not so much to enumerate the mere facts and events of life, as to discriminate the successive states of the mind, and so trace the progress of what may be called the character. [p. 1]

Foster endorses through his essay the Christian injunction to 'know thyself'. The reason he offers for the importance of recording 'states of the mind' in writing is ostensibly that character changes radically during the stages of an individual's life. Thus although Foster's emphases on the processes of memory, association and recollection remain within the sphere of mind and thought, he also stresses the value of written memoirs as records of the stages through which an individual passes. His conception of memoirs as the equivalent of religious confessions combines with both historical and 'psychological' concerns. He asserts, for example, that the value of writing memoirs is that it will fix an idea of what an individual was in this life for recall in an afterlife, 'that I may possess this idea in ages too remote for calculation' [p. 5]. This account of the importance of memoirs, however, seems to be as much that of the historian or the chronicler seeking to examine or record past and present as that of the evangelist, despite the fact that the middle sections of the essay are given over to a vigorous excoriation of atheism.

The further recurring issues that perplex Foster – whether it is nature or social influences which decide 'character', and if there is a single essence of character which remains constant throughout the stages of life – are ones which he believes a study of memoirs can help to answer. Thus the future writer of his memoirs is enjoined to describe the significant influences upon his life, in order, ostensibly, that he, the writer, may understand what has shaped him, and to establish the extent to which 'identity' remains constant despite changes in feeling and opinion. But, and despite the fact that the memoirs are intended for 'personal use', or at most, to be read by one or two friends, there is an underlying suggestion of a fantasy of access to the totality of memoirs, enabling their newly omniscient reader to make a study of how 'character' is formed. In addition to echoing eighteenth-century characterology, aspects of Foster's discussion indeed anticipate John Stuart Mill's proposal for the establishing of 'ethology', or 'the science of the formation of character':

> Human beings do not all feel and act alike in the same circumstances; but it is possible to determine what makes one person, in a given position, feel or act in one way, another in another; how any given mode of feeling and conduct, compatible with the general laws (physical and mental) of human nature, has been, or may be, formed. In other words, mankind have not one universal character, but there exist universal laws of the Formation of Character. And since it is by these laws, combined with the facts of each particular case, that the whole of the phenomenon of human action and feeling are produced, it is on these that every rational attempt to construct the science of human nature in the concrete, and for practical purposes must proceed.[19]

Autobiographical criticism is rarely neutral, however, in asking who is entitled to write autobiographically and thus to provide the records from which general laws of human nature are to be drawn. Foster specifically reassures his reader on this point, making a clear distinction between 'them' and 'us':

> I am supposing, all along, that the person who writes memoirs of himself,

is conscious of something more peculiar than a mere dull resemblance of that ordinary form and insignificance of character, which it strangely depreciates our nature to see such a multitude exemplifying. As to the the crowd of those who are faithfully stamped, like bank notes, with the same marks, with the difference only of being worth more guineas or fewer, they are mere particles of a class, mere pieces and bits of the greater vulgar or the small; *they* need not write their history, it may be found in the newspaper chronicle, or the gossip's or the sexton's narrative. [p. 14]

This passage reveals the contradiction between the pursuit of 'general laws' and the desire to restrict the writing of autobiography to the 'better' sort of person. (Illiteracy, of course, entails the automatic exclusion of those who would be unable to write their memoirs from the 'general laws' of characterology – literacy, interiority and the self as property are closely allied formations.) The relationship between various cultural representations of the individual life and the distinction between exemplary fame and inglorious notoriety is one that vexes a number of nineteenth-century commentators. Memoirs intended for publication are for the most part treated with some disdain. Without the specific term 'autobiography' coming into play, the inner/outer life, private/public dichotomy, and the hierarchy of value attached to these can be readily turned into an autobiography/memoirs distinction. Moreover, there is a hint that the writers of 'memoirs' (in the modern sense of the term), are in any case inadequate to the profundities of introspective autobiography. Thus the autobiography/memoirs distinction – ostensibly formal and generic – is bound up with a typological distinction between those human beings who are capable of self-reflection and those who are not. This opposition is still current, often correlated with class and cultural capital.

The term which most vexes a number of nineteenth-century commentators, Foster included, is 'Confessions', and its secular appropriations by published memoirists. For the nineteenth-century moralist, 'confessions' can legitimately become a form of written record, offering 'psychological' or social insights, if they remain uncontaminated by the public and popular 'literary world'. Foster's lengthy discussion of whether the individual's memoirs should be made available to others at all, even within the private sphere, and his deliberations over whether the 'secret' aspects of a life should be detailed or limited 'to a deliberate and strong expression of the *measure* of conscious culpabilities', finally suggest that the concern is not only with what is written but also the context in which it is read.

The public sphere of popular literature is clearly viewed as decadent and dangerous in its licentiousness; but the 'interior' life is itself repeatedly described in terms of danger and guilt. Foster is particularly prone to a Gothic imagery of ghostly hauntings. The opening-out of the 'private' and 'secret' self is acceptable only within specific contexts. These, however, widen progressively from the privacy of the confessional to the exchange of writings within the private sphere and finally to the fantasy of the 'private view'; the gathering in of character-testimonies before the 'student of character' in his role as moral psychologist or pathologist. Foster's references to Rousseau (whose *Confessions* served to inflame the debate) are significant in this context.

> If we could, in any case, pardon the kind of ingenuousness which he has displayed, it would certainly be in the disclosure of a mind so wonderfully singular as his. We are almost willing to have such a being preserved to all the unsightly minutiae and anomalies of its form, to be placed, as a unique in the moral museum of the world. [pp. 65–6]

A growing interest in what the written records of a life might reveal of 'human nature' develops concurrently with an anxiety over the dangers of the 'public' display of the self. It is the 'literary world' which is accused of exhibitionism and the encouragement of vice: a new 'scientific' and 'psychological' interest in the formation of human character gradually becomes perceived as the rightful inheritor of the religious confession. The forms of policing that grow and develop over what constitutes an autobiography 'proper' thus emerge from this need to find rules for what is permissible in self-description and self-display, and for legitimate contexts for the reading of 'private' lives.

I discuss Rousseau's *Confessions*, which form the background to a number of the debates explored in this chapter, in more detail in Chapter 5. For the moment, I wish to note the specific issue of autobiographical uniqueness and its relation to characterology. Rousseau opened his *Confessions*, Part 1 of which was published in 1782, with a claim to the uniqueness both of his autobiographical enterprise and of his being: 'I am made unlike anyone I have ever met; I will even venture to say that I am like no one in the whole world.' The alternative Preamble to the *Confessions*, the 'Neuchâtel preface', is rarely included in editions of the autobiography. It is of particular interest in the present context, however, because it directly addresses the value of 'comparative evidence' and the limits of biography and characterology. As John Sturrock notes, the Neuchâtel preface emphasises the moral ends of the *Confessions*; the self-knowledge he has acquired will, Roussseau argues, allow others to break out of the epistemological double-bind whereby self-knowledge is uncertain because purely internal, but is also the only basis for knowledge of others: 'I want to attempt so that if we are to learn to appraise ourselves, we have at least one piece of comparative evidence: so that everyone can know both himself, and one other, and that other will be me.'[20]

As Sturrock observes, Rousseau is also scornful in the Neuchâtel preface of the literary tradition against which the *Confessions* must be judged if their originality is to appear: 'Histories, lives, portraits, characters! What do they amount to? Ingenious fictions built on a few spoken words relating to them, on subtle conjectures in which the Author is seeking much more to shine than to discover the truth [p. 1149]. It is the *biographer's* vanity that is at issue for Rousseau: as a rival to his subject, the biographer will seek to 'shine' more brightly and will sacrifice the truth of his subject to self-regard. In autobiography, by contrast, authorial vanity is the guarantee of the subject's truth. Rousseau's arguments thus go against those of a number of the critics discussed in this chapter, for whom autobiographical vanity, resulting in self-delusion, militates against the advantages of 'certainty of knowledge'. They support, however, the claims of several nineteenth-century autobiographers that their auto-biographies were written as a means of forestalling potential biographers or of putting false claims to rights. Rousseau's hostile reference to 'Histories, lives, portraits, characters' is also an attack on characterology, perceived as the reduction of a unique and complex identity to a set of characteristics and traits shared with others.

*   *   *

James Field Stanfield's *Essays on the Study and Composition of Biography* (1813), the first book-length study of biography in English, consolidates a secular, psychological interest in biographical writing, in which classifications of human nature are drawn from life-writings, autobiographical and biographical. The auto/biographies themselves structure an uncertain identity into purposive form. In this sense, life-writings become the organisers of identity – the means of controlling both the written life and the life itself. Autobiography is to an extent included in the biographical category, and also singled out as potentially 'perfect biography'. However, the advantages, noted by Dr Johnson, of 'conscious certainty' of self in auto-biography, may be outweighed, Stanfield writes, by the distorting effects of self-interest.

The main interest of Stanfield's book to critics concerned with 'biography as an art' is its focus on the techniques of biographical writing, many of which continue to be upheld as good biographical practice. Stanfield's concerns include narrative coherence, the necessary integration of 'private' and 'public' elements in the repre-sentation of a life, impartiality combined with empathy on the biographer's part, the importance of the individual's early years and the essential biographic task of keeping the biographical subject in view at all times, rather than submerged by anecdotal detail and historical 'context'. Stanfield is very much of his own time in his emphasis on the use of biographical data for associationist and empirical psychology, although his desire to find systematic ways of classifying biographical writing remains a central feature of auto/biographical discourse.

Stanfield's study usefully embodies the link between eighteenth-century attempts to conceptualise 'character' and 'identity' and nine-teenth-century concepts of the 'career', or the 'life-course'.[21] Stanfield debates at length the relationship between a constant and universal identity, and character as socially constructed, subject to principles of individual differences and variation. In the study and composition of biography, of which 'character' is 'the very spirit and essence' [p. 275], the principle seems to be that the student of biography, and by extension of 'human nature', should work inductively from the individual case to general principles, based on a system of comparison. Yet knowledge of 'the general theory of mankind' must also precede biographical composition, to which it is as indispensable 'as grammar is to language, or anatomy to medical knowledge or to the delineation of the human figure' [p. 85]. Just as Stanfield's emphasis on the 'dialectical' relationship between part and whole in life-writing suggests a hermeneutic circularity, so the relationship between general and particular seems to follow the same pattern of circular influence. In this sense, Stanfield is able to move out of the static systemacity of a Theophrastan characterology, which in any case he wishes to combine with the focus on 'the internal springs of action' he finds in Jean de La Bruyère.[22]

The ultimate undecidability of the relationship between character as fixed and universal, and as shaped and particular, however, is a part of the general crisis around questions of character, identity and subjectivity. One response to this crisis, which Stanfield shares to a large extent, is the 'scientific' and classificatory approach of the psychologists, at its height in auto/biographical discourse in the late eighteenth and early nineteenth centuries, before Romantic emphases on the singularity of the individual life and on the romance of history as biography became dominant. The striking feature of Stanfield's discussion, however, is that he 'resolves' the problematics of identity and character, and in particular the uncertain balance between 'permanency' and 'alteration', through the 'doctrine of pursuits'; 'the succession of appropriate advances to a determinate end' [p. 312].

Difficulties in writing biography arise, in Stanfield's account, as a result of 'eccentricity of character, running into desultory pursuits, without purpose, without system, and, sometimes, even without the appearance of chronological order' [p. 3]. The vacillations and discontinuities of character are to be resolved through the secular structures of aims, motivations, drives, pursuits, vocations, directions and meliorations – in short, 'rise, progress, improvement' – which reach their apotheosis in the 'professional biography'. 'The persevering pursuit of objects', Stanfield writes, is the 'very essence of rational being' [p. 67]. The biographer's task is to delineate 'purpose, progress and attainment', a goal-directedness which may shut out for a time 'the synchronous incidents' [p. 68]. Chronology is significant in so far as development occurs in and through time, and the importance of the complete story of each stage in the pursuit of success cannot be overemphasised – bad biography, like the bad life, is in Stanfield's account anarchic, fragmentary, impressionistic and without principle. Yet chronology becomes a despised element when it is merely 'following the order of the time, day by day, like the journal of diarist . . . (and) presents nothing but a chequered display of occasional incident and habitual occurrence'. Structurally, then, the serial or synchronous autobiography is viewed as an inferior form by Stanfield and a poor model for biography, when it fails to develop 'an ART OF ADVANCING' [p. 336].

Stanfield uses Caesar as an experimental model for the construction of a 'table' or general model of the characteristic/passion of 'ambition', extrapolated from Caesar's life and lifespan. The table sets out an 'orderly series of remarks', delineating a course of action in the biographic structure from inception to the achievement of aim and object. Caesar's ambition is also seen as a single drive, 'a connected process of advancement towards one object'; the structure and subject of the ideal biography are thus streamlined into the doctrine of pursuits, and the unified progress of life and text. As Stanfield asserts: 'it becomes necessary that characters should be selected of those personages who have been successful in their career, or who, at least, have evidently proceeded in a systematic way towards accomplishment of a purpose' [p. 100]. Stanfield may use the examples of Caesar and Cicero, but his valorisation of 'professional biography' anticipates not only Samuel Smiles's collective biographies of men of the professions at mid-century – men who, as a reviewer wrote in 1879, 'are carried along by the natural bent that is absolutely irresistible'[23] – but also J. A. Froude's influential essay 'Representative Men', in which professionals are said to be the secular substitutes for the saints.[24]

In Stanfield's account, professional men take over from the classical heroes, and are described in much the same vein as Caesar: 'Pursuits are to be considered according to the succession of appropriate advances to a determinate end' and they find their clearest form of presentation in 'Professional biography, scientifically executed . . . the term Profession is meant to be extended to every class of men who pursue a regular vocation, or who are, in some exclusive way, influenced by a certain designation of purpose.' The Theophrastan concept of 'character' as the embodiment of a single character-trait or characteristic is thus combined with an account of the 'expressive lineaments' of professional aims. The 'doctrine of pursuits' organises and gives direction, aim and continuity to identity, as the concept of the professional career provides the goal-directed centring of self in and through the 'life-course' otherwise absent from theorisations of 'character'. The plotting of the life-course becomes inseparable from the life-structures specific to bourgeois masculinity.

Developing a theme which becomes central to discussions of autobiography, Stanfield includes the example of the 'literary man' in the 'doctrine of pursuits', thereby suggesting that the literary career is to be included among the professions. Two decades earlier, Isaac D'Israeli had specifically distinguished between the 'literary character' and other professional groups:

> The LITERARY CHARACTER is a denomination which, however vague, defines the pursuits of the individual, and separates him from other professions, although it frequently occurs that he is himself a member of one. Professional characters are modified by the change of manners, and are usually national: while the literary character, from the objects in which it concerns itself, retains a more permanent and necessarily a more independent nature . . . [it] has ever preserved among its followers the most striking family resemblance.[25]

Emphasising the 'consanguinity' of authors as well as their synchronicity – 'the earliest attempt stands connected with the most recent' – D'Israeli defines the 'literary character' as independent of historical or cultural forces. His definition is close to Goethe's concept of *Weltliteratur*, which has a particular bearing on the construction of the autobiographical canon in which, as in the higher dimension of *Weltliteratur*, the permanent and universal records of artistic achievement are said to be stored.

D'Israeli's concern in this text is in large part to defend authors against the charges of 'non-utility' he sees levelled against them by the 'barbarous metaphysicians of political economy', who 'have valued the intellectual tasks of the library and the studio by the "demand and the supply" '. On the one hand D'Israeli seeks to discredit such value-systems entirely; on the other, he sets out to show that literary men do accumulate value and demonstrate 'utility' in the particular terms of their calling. Autobiography plays a crucial role in this demonstration. Firstly, D'Israeli articulates a principle widely shared in the early part of the nineteenth century when he writes:

> In the history of men of genius we may often open the secret story of their own minds, for they have above others the privilege of communicating their own feelings; and every life of a man of genius, composed by himself, presents us with the experimental philosophy of the mind. [p. 23]

Secondly, he uses the language of political economy to make the case for the literary autobiographer:

> The arts of memory will form a saving-bank of genius, to which it may have recourse, as a wealth which it can accumulate imperceptibly amidst the ordinary expenditure. LOCKE taught us the first rudiments of this art, when he showed us how he stored his thoughts and his facts, by an artificial arrangement; and Addison, before he commenced his 'Spectators', had amassed three folios of materials. But the higher step

will be the volume which shall give an account of a man to himself, in
which a single observation immediately becomes a clue of past knowledge, restoring to him his lost studies and his evanescent existence.
Self-contemplation makes the man more nearly entire; and to preserve
the past is half of immortality. [p. 122]

Autobiography is thus viewed literally as a conservative form;
'self-contemplation' conserves private identity as capital, consolidates selfhood and preserves the past in and for the present. The
concept of identity as private property is made explicit, as in Locke's
assertion that 'every man has a property in his own person'.[26]
D'Israeli's statements are in large part defensively motivated by the
perceived threat of a literary market economy, in which authors are
dependent on the 'patronage of booksellers'. His suggested remedy is
for 'men of letters' (who accumulate and disseminate 'original'
literary products through their reading and writing) to act as patrons
for 'men of genius', and for authors as producers and men of letters
alike to become booksellers, purveyors of their own books or class of
books, in order 'to make them independent, as the best means to
preserve exertion'. Untroubled by financial matters – 'the details of
trade must be left to others' – authors, like autobiographers, would
find in this system that value was located internally to their literary
productions [pp. 196–7]. They would also achieve professional independence – the ideal of middle-class masculine identity. As Mary
Jean Corbett notes, with particular reference to the new periodicals
of the early nineteenth century, in which the anonymous reviewer
(the man of letters) comments on and provides lengthy extracts from
the published works of 'original authors': 'In the production of
knowledge . . . the author exercises the independent power that runs
the literary economy, in which other writers depend on his labour for
their own.'[27] It should be added, of course, that many of the anonymous reviewers of the periodicals, which were a crucial part of the
structures of literary professionalism, were women. The history of
this aspect of female authorship and women's professional status
remains to be written.

Corbett's recent study of middle-class subjectivity and women's
autobiography opens with an exploration of the ways in which
William Wordsworth and Thomas Carlyle established dominant
cultural models of 'true authorship' in their autobiographical
writings. She discusses *The Prelude* and *Sartor Resartus* in the context
of definitions of authorship during a period in which the 'literary' text

must accumulate cultural value, even as it remains apparently untainted by its status as commodity. The Romantic and, following him, the post-Romantic autobiographer writes the self into the work and thus suggests 'that authorial identity is not determined by the marketplace but is rather a function of conditions internal to the self '. Autobiography has pragmatic uses in relation to the new forces of literary production as they emerged in the early nineteenth century; 'for Wordsworth and Carlyle writing autobiography becomes a way of attaining both literary legitimacy and a desired subjectivity' [p. 11]. The question of literature as a profession is an ambiguous and vexed one, and autobiography plays a central role in its negotiation:

> the writer, unlike the physician or barrister, does actually produce a marketable object from his labours, the literary text, and in the relationship between the man and the text lies the particular problematic of early nineteenth-century literary production ... self-representation becomes the linchpin between the anonymous writer and his writing. [p. 40]

The models of authorship established by Wordsworth and Carlyle provide an uncomfortable fit for women writers. Corbett, extensively employing feminist work on the gendering of public and private spheres, finds in Victorian women's writing a 'specifically feminine anxiety' about public authorship. Whereas Wordsworth, confidently, and Carlyle, ironically, 'identify the sources of the publicly represented self in private experience', for women writers the private and the public are indeed separate domains. Work, publicity and literary 'professionalism' are radically at odds with 'women's cultural positioning on the inside, at the center of the domestic circle', although women autobiographers throughout the century found ways of negotiating the contradictions of their placement in both public and private spheres.

An exploration of the place of Literature in the structure of work is one of the agendas set by Julia Swindells, in *Victorian Writing and Working Women*.[28] Professions are 'reality definers' and organisers of dominant thought, and writing and the writer are areas 'where professional ideologies and practices are most firmly coded as norms of taste, morality and subjectivity' [p. 8]. The structures of professionalism entail a powerful ideology of gender restriction, Swindells asserts, giving the example of an article in *Fraser's Magazine* of 1847, which announces that 'Literature has become a profession.' Male

writers' fears of the reorganisation of work which professionalisation
will entail is expressed as a fear of invasion:

> If we reflect upon the great aims of literature, we shall easily perceive how
> important it is that the lay teachers of the people should be men of an
> unmistakable vocation. Literature should be a profession, just lucrative
> enough to furnish a decent subsistence to its members, but in no way
> lucrative enough to tempt speculators. As soon as its rewards are high
> enough and secure enough to tempt men to enter the lists for the sake of
> the reward, and parents think of it as an opening for their sons, from that
> moment it becomes vitiated. Then will the ranks, already so numerous, be
> swelled by an innumerable host of hungry pretenders. It will be – and,
> indeed, is, now fast approaching that state – like the army of Xerxes,
> swelled and encumbered by women, children and ill-trained troops. It
> should be a Macedonian phalanx, chosen, compact and irresistible.[29]

The image of invasion by 'hungry pretenders' also appears in
various guises in nineteenth-century autobiographical discourse to
support the view that the status of autobiography is under threat. The
issue of a new populism within autobiographical writing is frequently
linked in early nineteenth-century autobiographical criticism to the
breakdown of class and social distinctions, the emergence of con-
fident artisanal and 'criminal' classes, and the growth of the 'reading
public'. Periodical reviews stress the need for absolute distinctions to
be drawn between popular autobiography and the 'seminal' autobiographical texts, and consolidate the view that only certain 'lives'
are worthy of record.

The popularity of and popularism within autobiographies of the
period, which is seen to 'degrade' the genre, was particularly attacked
in the conservative periodicals. The pursuit of autobiography as a
trade fuelled the ire of James Lockhart, writing in the *Quarterly
Review* in the 1820s: 'It is to be hoped that Genius will not be
altogether silent, merely because Dulness lifts up her voice so loudly
in Grub-street.'[30] On the other hand, the expanding reading public is
held responsible for encouraging superior men to stoop to vulgarity,
and inferior ones:

> who, at any period, would have been mean and base in all their objects and
> desires, to demand with hardihood the attention and sympathy of man-
> kind, for thoughts and deeds that, in any period but the present, must
> have been obscure and dirty. . . . It seems as if the ear of that grand
> impersonation, 'the Reading Public', had become as filthily prurient as
> that of an eavesdropping lackey.[31]

The 'eavesdropping lackey' is a description that can also be applied, in the author's view, to those autobiographers who, having taken advantage of freer movement within society and of the social generosity of 'circles much above their station', repay this kindness by 'turning a penny to the systematic record of privacies too generously exposed'.[32] Both writers and readers, then, feed off the exposure of private lives. Autobiography proper is perceived to be the right of very few individuals: those whose lives encompassed an aspect or image of the age suitable for transmission to posterity. Lockhart states in mocking tones that 'Modern primer-makers must needs leave *Confessions* behind them, as if they were so many Rousseaus.' He expresses a fear that the age would be represented by the 'mediocre' – 'The "Times of Frederick Reynolds!" ' – such is the style by which the child that is unborn will distinguish the last quarter of the Christian era, and the first of that now in progress' and hopes that 'the virtue and patriotism of the age may be commemorated as effectually, though not quite so voluminously, as its imbecility, quackery and vice'.[33] From this perspective, autobiography has a commemorative and memorial function linked closely to that of biography.

A *Blackwood's* reviewer gives a similar account of a genre in decline which fails to fulfil the commemorative function:

Autobiography is allowed, by common consent, to be one of the most universally agreeable kinds of reading, combining utility with amusement . . . but (alas for the vicissitudes of all earthly things!) we doubt the era of its splendour is rapidly passing away. In the days of autobiographical glory, no one dreamed of bestowing his or her memoirs or confessions upon the world, who had not either obtained such a lofty reputation as might render the private conduct and feelings of its proprietor matter of general interest; or played such a distinguished part in the great drama of life, as might bestow historical importance upon their anecdotes of themselves and their fellow-performers. If any persons of inferior pretensions did then presume to intrude into the legitimate autobiographical class, they were only such as, having spent their lives amongst those master-spirits of whom we long to know everything, had beheld them in dishabille, at least in their working-day garb, and whose misnamed autobiography, in fact, consisted of gossip, – we beg pardon, reminiscences, we believe, is the technical term, – concerning their betters. But really, if stock-jobbers and contractors are to give us accounts of their profits and losses; if every unfortunate female (the sentimental modern designation of those, whom our more jocular fathers termed ladies of easy virtue) – if every swindler and thief-taker is to nauseate the public with the detail of their vulgar vices, relying upon the names of those whose pockets they have, after their respective fashions, assailed or protected, for exciting a prurient curiosity that may command a sale, the very name of auto-biography will, we apprehend, erelong be loathingly rejected in the drawing room, as fit only for the kitchen or the servants' hall.[34]

Again, the issue of autobiographical 'legitimacy' is inseparable from the autobiographer's status and public importance. This reviewer is even prepared to admit to the category of autobiography, although grudgingly, those who can offer some insider knowledge of their social superiors; this in contrast to Lockhart, for whom this is the most dangerous result of autobiography's popularity. The *Blackwood's* reviewer (Mary Margaret Busk) reserves her greatest contempt for the autobiography of 'vice', although the literal 'pick-pocket' may not be perceived as very different from Lockhart's 'eavesdropping lackey', or the man who diverts another in conversation, while simultaneously stealing his purse or absorbing his confidences for future investment. In any case, autobiography, from this perspective, becomes a parasitical act equivalent to theft, and the profits accruing from publication are the spoils of vice. If the bourgeois self is conceptualised as capital and property, the 'crime' is to attempt to usurp bourgeois identity.

The perceived threat of theft also applies in the generic sphere, for the authors of both these essay-reviews express concern that the 'lower classes' are usurping and vulgarising what they see as indubitably a high-art form. David Vincent, in his study of nineteenth-century working-class autobiography, *Bread, Knowledge and Freedom*, describes the *Quarterly Review* essay as 'the first public recognition of the emergence of a new voice in the tradition of autobiography', but suggests that it is

> a largely unrepresentative response to its implications. It is not only that the memorabilia of cabin boys and drummers were being received ... with growing enthusiasm, but that the general principle of men, and sometimes women, in obscure circumstances entering the realm of polite literature was long established and was being increasingly encouraged.[35]

In Vincent's account, the majority of Lockhart's middle-class readership 'saw in this invasion a means of assuaging both their curiosity and their fears' about the working class. They particularly welcomed what they saw as an attempt by the lower orders to borrow their mode of expression, viewing it as a further consolidation of bourgeois literary forms and an act of obeisance by imitation.

Vincent notes, however, that there is little evidence that working-class autobiographers were consciously imitating middle-class art-forms. Their traditions were those of spiritual autobiography, which was to an extent shared with the educated class, or an oral tradition which was 'very largely hidden from the gaze of polite society'. This view is reinforced by Mary Jo Maynes in her recent discussion of French and German working-class autobiographies:

> One thing is pretty clear – few of these autobiographers seem to have read either the *Confessions* or *Dichtung und Wahrheit*, although some of the more educated workers in France were familiar with Rousseau's political treatises. In other words, the models that shaped literary autobiographies cannot be taken for granted.[36]

Autobiographical criticism continues to the present day to assume that the 'seminal' autobiographies – notably Augustine, Rousseau and Goethe – provided the models for all autobiographical writings, and has paid scant attention to the possibility of other, indigenous models for self-analysis or the recounting of the past.

Vincent's and Maynes's discussions raise some crucial points about the relationship between working-class and middle-class literary forms, but it should be noted that the 'autobiographies' reviewed by Lockhart were not exclusively working-class. The popular dramatists (represented by the despised Frederick Reynolds), actor–managers and memoir-writers for whom Lockhart reserves his greatest contempt could in no sense be seen as members of the labouring class. It seems that the most reviled group are in fact those perceived to be in the literary 'trade', ironically referred to as 'auto-biographia literaria'. The 'literary' autobiography here is thus that of the professional writer; the two examples given in the *Quarterly Review* are those of popular dramatists, authors of melodramas and comedies, who measure their success, much to Lockhart's disgust, by their pecuniary rewards. Those responsible for 'debasing' literary coinage, either through the authorship of popular art-forms or their commerce within the developing book trade (the immensely success-ful bookseller James Lackington published his memoirs in the 1790s) add insult to injury, in the eyes of the conservative reviewers, by trading in and on the self as well.

The prostitute becomes one whose double perfidy consists in her sale both of herself and of her story, as Thomas Carlyle's essay 'Biography' suggests.[37] Carlyle opens the essay with a lengthy dis-

cussion of the importance of biography for history, while asserting
that most biographies fail to fulfil their promise. His exception is
Boswell's *Life of Johnson*. The passage upon which Carlyle focuses
concerns the moment in the text where Boswell describes Dr
Johnson being solicited by a prostitute. Carlyle writes of this passage:

> Strange power of *Reality*! Not even the poorest of occurrences, but now,
> after seventy years are come and gone, has meaning for us. Do but
> consider that it is true; that it did in very deed occur! That unhappy
> Outcast, with all her sins and woes, her lawless desires, too complex
> mischances, her wailings and her riotings, has departed utterly; alas! her
> siren finery has got all besmutched, ground, generations since, into dust
> and smoke; of her degraded body, and whole miserable earthly existence,
> all is away: *she* is no longer here, but far from us, in the bosom of Eternity,
> – whence we too came, whither we too are bound! Johnson said, 'No, no,
> my girl; it won't do,' and then 'we talked', – and here-with the wretched
> one, seen but for the twinkling of an eye, passes on into the utter
> Darkness. No high Calista, that ever issued from Story-teller's brain, will
> impress us more deeply than this meanest of the mean; and for good
> reason: That *she* issued from the Maker of Men. [pp. 61–2]

Carlyle's discussion is primarily concerned with how the
'memorableness' of such incidents is effected in writing; he concludes that it is a combination of the reality of the object seen and of
the quality of the observation, the possession of 'the seeing heart'. In
the next paragraph, he clarifies the choice of the Boswell passage as
exemplum.

> Here too, may we not pause for an instant, and make a practical reflec-
> tion? Considering the multitude of mortals that handle the Pen in these
> days, and can mostly spell, and write without glaring violations of
> grammar, the question naturally arises: How is it, then, that no Work
> proceeds from them, bearing any stamp of authenticity and permanence;
> of worth for more than one day? Ship-loads of Fashionable Novels,
> Sentimental Rhymes, Tragedies, Farces, Diaries of Travel, Tales by
> flood and field, are swallowed monthly into the bottomless Pool: still does
> the Press toil . . . and still, in torrents, rushes on the great array of
> Publications, unpausing, to their final home; and still Oblivion, like the
> Grave, cries, Give! Give! . . . These Three Thousand men, women and
> children, that make up the Army of British Authors, do not, if we well
> consider it, *see* anything whatever. . . . Nothing but a pitiful image of their
> own pitiful Self, with its vanities, and grudgings, and ravenous hunger of
> all kinds, hangs forever painted in the retina of these unfortunate persons.
> [pp. 63–4]

Carlyle's essay belongs in a broader context, involving the perceived relationship between history, biography and fiction, and the early nineteenth-century response to an increase in literacy and a growing literary trade and market. I want to draw from it a rather more oblique argument: the relationship between Boswell and Johnson's prostitute and Carlyle's army of British authors. Carlyle's rhetoric is near-identical in both instances; the prostitute and the author are by turns pitiful, hungry, vain and lawless, destined for Oblivion. If, to extrapolate from Carlyle's argument, the prostitute were to tell her own story, it could only join the bottomless pool; told by Boswell, it and she are redeemed. The attack on commercial publishing and the literary market-place is thus closely linked with attacks on 'commercial' autobiographies. The mercantile aspects of writing are viewed as particularly insidious when they concern the 'illegitimate' literary production and presentation of the self; exhibiting the self for sale becomes viewed as a form of prostitution. Literary overproduction, in this case of life-writings, has the corollary that general laws of human nature and character will be based on the meretricious or mediocre rather than the exemplary.

The Carlylean, or Johnsonian, episode also bears on two Romantic autobiographies, Wordsworth's *The Prelude* and Thomas De Quincey's *Confessions of An English Opium-Eater*. De Quincey's text opens with a striking illustration of autobiography's disreputable (or demi-reputable) status in the early nineteenth century. Addressing the reader, De Quincey expresses the hope that his confessions will prove 'useful and instructive', terms frequently employed by critics throughout the nineteenth century in arguing for the moral worth of autobiography. The value of his confessions as object-lesson justifies, De Quincey suggests, the sin or solecism of 'breaking through that delicate and honourable reserve which, for the most part, restrains us from the public exposure of our own errors and infirmities':

> Nothing, indeed, is more revolting to English feelings, than the spectacle of a human being intruding on our notice his moral ulcers or scars, and tearing away that 'decent drapery', which time, or indulgence to human frailty, may have drawn over them: accordingly, the greater part of *our* confessions (that is spontaneous and extra-judicial confessions) proceed from demireps, adventurers, or swindlers: and for any such acts of gratuitous self-humiliation from those who can be supposed in sympathy with the decent and self-respecting part of society, we must look to French literature, or to that part of the German, which is tainted with the spurious and defective sensibility of the French. . . .

> Guilt and misery shrink, by a natural instinct, from public notice: they
> court privacy and solitude: and, even in their choice of the churchyard, as
> if declining to claim fellowship with the great family of man, and wishing
> (in the affecting language of Mr Wordsworth)
>   – Humbly to express
>   A penitential loneliness.[38]

As Mary Jacobus has argued, 'guilt and misery' are terms commonly
applied to the fallen woman. In De Quincey's *Confessions*, the prostitute Ann of Oxford Street, the 'double' whom he meets, loses and
searches for in vain,

> stands for more than opium addiction. Ann's wandering on the London
> streets and De Quincey's never-ending quest for her become a metaphor
> for his own attempt to recover the past through memory. The retro-
> spective and confessional movement of autobiography is De Quincey's
> primary addiction, which is also the compulsion of autobiography to
> repeat.[39]

The figure of the prostitute is inextricably linked to representations of the city in the late eighteenth century; in the nineteenth
century, as I argued in my discussion of Carlyle's 'Biography', prostitution and authorship become identified. As Catherine Gallagher
writes, in relation to George Eliot's *Daniel Deronda*, 'the activities of
authoring, of procuring illegitimate income, and of alienating one's
self through prostitution seem particularly associated with one
another'.[40] Jacobus shows how De Quincey's 'fall' in turning to the
money-lenders is compounded for him by the demand that he produce letters addressed to him as proof of his identity, in order to
establish his credit-worthiness, his credibility: 'It was strange to me',
de Quincey writes, 'to find my own self, *materialiter* considered . . .
accused, or at least suspected, of counterfeiting my own self,
formaliter considered.'[41] Commodifying his identity by pawning it to
the brokers, Jacobus argues, 'De Quincey's financial dealings with
the money-lender figure the self-sale by the commodifier of a "confessional" autobiography whose very saleability requires the
guarantee of authenticity, or legal identity' [p. 226].
De Quincey imagines death for Ann: the fallen woman 'dies' in
place of the fallen writer, who is redeemed from the self-loss entailed
by the commodified, confessional text by having 'true' poetic identity
conferred upon him by the father or brother of the Romantic family,
William Wordsworth. Yet, as we have seen, Wordsworth's own autobiographical production, *The Prelude*, serves the function of con-

cealing the workings, or economics, of self-display and literary commodification by naturalising poetic identity through the convergence,
or identity, of self and text. 'Everything in Wordsworth's life', Jacobus
states, 'tends to make him "Wordsworth", the poet of the autobiographical *Prelude*' [p. 230]. Wordsworthian 'value', which must
remain untainted by textual commodification, is in its turn dependent
upon the casting-out of the prostitute (Book VII of *The Prelude*) who
stands not only, as in De Quincey's autobiography and Carlyle's
essay, for disreputable confession and commodified selfhood, but in
her 'painted bloom', for literary figuration, seduction or solicitation
by Romantic personification itself. In her excision or exclusion,
Jacobus asserts, 'Romanticism is saved for the History of Ideas or the
history of consciousness' [p. 236]. More generally, I would add,
'literary' autobiography is 'saved' from contamination by the market-
place, degraded femininity and the conditions of textual production
for the forms of 'pure autobiographical consciousness' so promi-
nently figured in the criticism and theory I discuss in subsequent
chapters.

* * *

If 'autobiography' comes into being as a category to be questioned, an
additional irony is that at the point at which its usage is becoming
more accepted, commentators are speaking of a genre in decline.
The reasons for this negative perception are complex. However,
when considering the category 'Victorian autobiography', it should be
noted that the diaries of such autobiographical luminaries as Pepys
and Evelyn (passing over for the moment formal distinctions between
diary, memoir and autobiography) were published in partial form in
the early decades and in fuller editions throughout the century.
Although their interest was obviously in large part historical, they also
took on a contemporary coloration as texts available for the first time
in published form. Thus critics discussed these and other diaries,
memoirs and autobiographies as texts comparable to contemporary
writings, setting the terms of debates and definitions over the nature
and value of autobiographies. Without a recognition of the impact of
newly available but non-contemporary writings, which appeared both
fresh *and* established, many of the critical judgements of the period
seem mysterious. If this impact is taken into account, however, it
becomes   clearer   why   Victorian   critics   so   frequently   made

comparisons between the 'robustness' of past ages, of which individuals like Cellini and Pepys are viewed as unquestionable representatives, and the aetiolation of contemporary culture and contemporary man.

The model of 'decline' addressed here is of a rather different order
than that proposed by the reviewers discussed above, whose anxieties
over the vulgarisation of the autobiographical form are linked to fears
of public transgression, symbolised by an extension of the autobiographical franchise and of the debasement of the literary coinage.
The contrast drawn between the robust past and the aetiolated
present is more indicative of the ways in which types of text and types
of men become collapsed into each other, and of a historicist
approach to autobiography which becomes more prevalent from
mid-century onwards. In such approaches, the issue of inner self in
relation to outer world become central. John Foster's demand, which
follows on from eighteenth-century texts such as Samuel Clark's
Self-Examination Explained and Recommended (1761), that the self
remove itself from 'exterior interests . . . so as to be recognized as a
thing internal, apart and alone' becomes far more overtly problematic
in a context in which introspection is perceived to be tainted by
'morbidity'. In autobiographical criticism in the latter part of the
century, the relationship to 'subjective' autobiography is often a
highly ambivalent one.

Some critics, however, continue to endorse the value of interiority
as definitive of autobiography proper. A. O. Prickard, whose essay
Autobiography was published in 1866, addresses the issue of an ideal
autobiographer's motives for writing: 'He must be well assured
within himself that there is in the tale which he is about to tell
something which lies beyond the experience of common men, and
which will justify him in calling attention to it.'[42] The exceptional
nature of this experience may lie in the realms of action or of thought
– a very familiar opposition within discussions of autobiography,
echoing the classical distinction between the *vita activa* and the *vita
contemplativa*, the lives of statesmen and the lives of philosophers, as
the two classical ideals of personality. In Prickard's essay, the view is
reinforced that autobiography deals more properly with the realm of
thought than that of action or the public life, the latter being the more
suitable preserve of biography.

Prickard sets up

a threefold division of biographies [*sic*], according to the nature of the interest which underlies them. We have, first, the lives of adventurers, travellers, and the like, in which we read with admiration and curiosity the tale of human endurance and courage. We have, secondly, the lives of those who have attracted our attention by their prominence in public life and upon the pages of history, and awakened an interest which will lead us through the annals of their private and domestic life. And, lastly, we have the lives of great thinkers, who have either moulded the opinions of the age, or have at least awakened our sympathy by the remarkable changes which their own minds have undergone. [p. 10]

Of these, the third category alone is wholly suited to autobiography, and writers in this class produce self-writings which 'are the utterance of the man's inner mind, which he has been obliged to withhold by art in his other writings' [p. 17].

In the distinction between 'mere words' and 'genuine utterance', Prickard reiterates his earlier claim that in the autobiography 'it is always the voice of a living man which speaks to us of himself, and not the uncertain record of biographers anxious for his posthumous fame' [p. 6]. This 'voice' is viewed as superior to the written records of historian–biographers, in that it is both immediate and unmediated and is also an authentic expression of interiority.[43] Whereas biographies serve as obituary notices – 'some of the interest of biographies may be traced to the fact that their original appearance tells us, or at least forces upon our notice, that some-one worthy of such a record has passed away from among us' [p. 6] – the auto-biographer 'writes as a man who has yet interests and feelings on this side of the grave, and we are drawn to him by all those ties of sympathy in which nature includes all things human which concern the living' [p. 7]. This link between literary and temporal modes is a common theme in nineteenth-century and twentieth-century genre theory, as in Goethe's claim that the epic is narrated as completely past, while the dramatic poet presents it as completely present.[44] Prickard is also using classical accounts of genre, in which epic or heroic forms are best suited to objective and impersonal presentation, in his claim that there are kinds of lives which are unsuited to an autobiographical presentation: 'the position of autobiographer is seldom a dignified one for the public man'. The life of adventure and incident is also best told biographically; tales of heroism recounted by their actor will produce an 'unwelcome parade of self'. In other words, the 'problem' of egotism again becomes the ostensible reason for drawing a sharp distinction between biography and autobiography, but a sphere for autobiographical representation is legitimated, and relieved of the charges of vanity and egotism, by the division of autobiography into 'inner' and 'outer' forms, with biography becoming the appropriate mode for the latter.

This approach is also an example of one of the ways in which autobiography becomes secured for literature, through the use of 'literary' classifications and in particular through attempts to fit different kinds of autobiography into the traditional tripartite schema of literary classification: epic, dramatic and lyric. Prickard suggests that the poetic is identical with the autobiographical: 'the poet is always to some extent an autobiographer. Speaking the language which takes its form and sequence from his own emotions, he must often record them as his own' [p. 21]. The persistence of this view throughout twentieth-century literary criticism has created obvious complications for the critic seeking to define autobiography as an autonomous *genre* – hence, perhaps, the insistence that autobiography 'proper' is essentially a prose-form – but it also adds considerable support to the belief that autobiography is by its nature a literary kind.

In Prickard's tripartite classification, the third category, the autobiography of the interior, is the legitimate autobiographical mode, with the autobiography/biography distinction mapping on to the familiar distinction between subjective and objective poetry. In his appeal to self-expressivity, Prickard endorses Romantic valuations of the poetic, and links them to a hierarchy of value within autobiography. It is significant that the poet–autobiographer is allowed far more flexibility than the public or historical individual in relation to generic categories: on the other hand, he can rarely be read as *other* than an autobiographer. In this sense, the 'poetic' autobiography breaks down generic classifications and blurs the distinction between fact, fiction and feeling, cutting across the classifications by which the dispersed and diffused body of writing within the category 'autobiography' is contained and controlled.

The classificatory approach in autobiographical criticism also emerges strongly in the philosopher and essayist Edith Simcox's (unsigned) essay in the *North British Review* of 1870.[45] Simcox employs Comtean categories to arrange existing autobiographies in 'three principal groups, corresponding roughly to Comte's three historic periods. . . . the Monumental or Elementary, the Positive, and the Analytical, or, to keep up the analogy, the Metaphysical.' Yet, as Simcox notes of her arrangement in relation to Comte, 'the chronological order is different', allowing her to substitute a decline for a progressive model of history. A decline not only of history – but of autobiography. Her historical model is worth quoting at some length:

> Existing autobiographies may be arranged in three principal groups, corresponding roughly to Comte's three historic periods, though the chronological order is different, and subject to individual aberrations. These groups may be distinguished critically as the Monumental or Elementary, the Positive, and the Analytic, or, to keep up the analogy, the Metaphysical. The first of these schools is epic in style and heroic in substance; each of its works is that of an imaginative autocrat – a story of action told with primitive energy, unmixed self-approval and spontaneous art. The second school contains artists of a sort, but no heroes. It is literal, realistic, and in form dramatic. The writers depict themselves only as a means or accessory to the representation of the age in and for which they live. They write with unsurpassed depth of conviction what everyone knows and believes; they give expression to a sublimated common-sense; and, as their observations are authentic and their judgements unimpeachable, the universal reason of mankind admires and applauds. The last variety of autobiography is more complicated. To the autobiographer, at any rate, humanity consists of the ego and the non ego. It is possible for him to view the world as subordinate to himself, or to treat himself in subordination to the world; but a third alternative is not easy to find. Decaying originality may take refuge in a sort of criticism: but criticism of the outer world does not naturally take the form of autobiography, criticism of the writer's self paralyses the course of the narrative, and criticisms of the relations between the two are not naturally suggested by the events of an ordinary life. The only remaining possibility is to chronicle thought instead of action, changes of opinion instead of succeeding experience, or else to represent the influence of imaginary circumstances upon a real mind. To surround a fictitious hero with incidents founded upon fact can scarcely be said to constitute autobiography at all. [p. 385]

The classifications are obviously related to the tripartite categories of literary genre theory: epic, dramatic and lyric, although the last is not named, and the essay does not pursue the analogy between historical periods and generic categories as such. It should also be noted that Simcox refuses a synthesising or dialectical movement between the three categories; indeed, she insists here upon the impossibility of synthesis between self and world, ego and non-ego. Thus the third stage – although it is not clear at this point whether she is referring to temporal and successive stages or to the coexistence of different kinds of autobiography – operates as the *negation* of autobiography. Romantic literature, with its idealised concept of self, both is, through its self-absorption, and cannot be, autobiography.

In contrast to Prickard's arguments, then, the third stage or class, whether it is described as 'analytic', 'subjective' or 'poetic', is for Simcox the end of autobiography. The isolated selfhood which Foster endorses, often seen as autobiography in its purest form, becomes the aspect which leads to the death, or perhaps suicide, of autobiography. Simcox's phrase 'decaying originality' repeats an earlier statement on the difficulties involved in writing autobiography, of whatever category: 'to dissect the still palpitating corpse of decaying consciousness, is a laborious, and, as it proceeds, increasingly thankless task' [p. 384], and links forward to the statement that 'the analytic or subjective school of autobiography' will be treated 'as a note of moral and literary decadence' [p. 388]. These accounts are in part drawn from Romantic views of analysis – Wordsworth's passion that 'murders to dissect'. Simcox's narrative of decline strongly echoes Carlyle's attack on consciousness in his essay 'Characteristics', in which he links unconsciousness with health, consciousness with sickness. Primitive societies are healthy societies, Carlyle asserts: 'it is not in the vigorous ages of a Roman republic that Treatises of the Commonwealth are written. . . . So long as the Commonwealth continues rightly athletic, it cares not to dabble in anatomy.'[46] A variant on this theme appears in E. S. Dallas's *The Gay Science* (1866) – Dallas refers to the modern disease as 'excessive civilisation and overstrained consciousness'.[47] Edith Simcox's essay ends by proposing 'a desponding conclusion that autobiography was one of the arts lost by over-civilization' [p. 413].

This conclusion is reached after a detailed analysis of historical periods and autobiographical writings. Basing her arguments on the existence of 'general laws' underlying historical processes, Simcox does not automatically reach out for the category of 'genius' to distinguish great from mediocre autobiographies. She is concerned with the historical circumstances which make autobiography possible, although there are also individuals who transcend historical circumstances. The worthwhile autobiography is not the story of a 'commonplace' life, but on the other hand 'every autobiography depends for its value and interest upon the measure of common human passion and experience concentrated in its pages, or on the degree of vividness with which they depict common situations and sentiments'. Through this use of 'common' to imply 'typicality' as opposed to the 'commonplace' of the quotidian, Simcox is able to make the argument that 'every autobiographer is a representative man, and not one of a representative class, but of a class of representative men' [p. 385]. (A possible interpretation of this statement is that autobiographers belong to a 'class' whose members have something of the attributes of 'world-historical individuals'.) Many of her judgements as to the worth of individual autobiographies are based on the extent to which they adequately represent their age – and indeed, whether authors are adequate to the age in which they lived. That is, there is an ambiguity in the term 'represent' between the ideas of display and of embodiment.

In the following passage, in which she singles out 'the first rank of autobiography' – which includes Cellini, St Augustine, Newman and Giraldus Cambrensis – the judgement is made in the following terms:

> their recollections have a clearness resembling that of direct poetic intuition, so that at the moment of writing, the picture of their past lives appears to themselves as a complete artistic whole, with what faults or beauties the spectator may judge, but at least an unbroken block of nature, chiselled by the force of single human will into the form we see. [p. 387]

The reference to statuary, also present in Prickard's essay, echoes the Hegelian concept of classical sculpture as 'concrete life'.[48] Immediacy, or 'direct poetic intuition', is implicitly contrasted to the aetiolated self-consciousness of the Romantic poet. The further ideal is 'when a person of marked or singular character has met with or sought out adventures equally uncommon' [pp. 386–7]. At work, then, is an ideal of the unity or matching of self and circumstance, although at times history itself seems to invalidate this possibility. Many of Simcox's judgements, and her degenerationist model of history and culture – in which the role of autobiographies and their 'representative' value is also seen to lie in the light they throw 'upon questions of moral progress. . . . In virtue of this they enable us to follow the history of the last three centuries in a sort of miniature reflector of the outer world' – anticipate the arguments of more recent critics. Roy Pascal, for example, also implies a 'death' of autobiography equivalent to Hegel's concept of the 'death of art'. Goethe is seen as the last great autobiographer, before the divorce of self and history, intellect and feeling, thought and action, occurs. The major criticism levelled by Simcox against the 'analytic' autobiographer – or the member of 'the school of introspective sentiment' – is that he projects his own world-weariness on to the external world, in an 'attempt to connect his solution of the difficulties of modern life with his individual character and temperament' [p. 410].[49]

The valorisation of 'objective' presentations of the self, linked to classical art, is reminiscent of Matthew Arnold's highly influential 1853 Preface. With the falling-off of 'the great monuments of early Greek genius ... the calm, the cheerfulness, the disinterested objectivity have disappeared; the dialogue of the mind with itself has commenced'.[50] In Arnold's account, and those of his followers, hostility towards 'egotism' is as much to the fore as it is in early autobiographical criticism, but the term is conjoined less often with 'vanity' than with introspection or morbid self-consciousness, as in contemporary reviews of Tennyson's *In Memoriam*. Victorian poetic theories at mid-century, as Isobel Armstrong has shown, anticipate T. S. Eliot's account of the 'objective correlative' in stressing the need for connection between 'states of mind and feeling' and 'outward realities'.[51] This is also the main desideratum in theories of autobiography, nineteenth- and twentieth-century. Yet Edith Simcox, Carlyle and other more recent critics, working with models of decline in a linear narrative sequence, preclude such a reconnection of self and circumstance. A separation between 'inner' and 'outer', subjective and objective, self and world, thought and action, is perceived as the tragedy of modern man and his self-representations. I discuss this in more detail in Chapter 4, with particular reference to post-Hegelian pessimism in autobiographical criticism.

* * *

It is a nice irony that *Blackwood's Edinburgh Magazine*, sharing in the cultural pessimism of which the decline model in history and autobiography is a manifestation, endorses, in the 1870s and 1880s, working-class autobiography as a counter to the autobiographies of 'men of letters', whose lives are seen as reduced to 'a brown interior, with a library table and a waste-paper basket for its central objects' and whose persons are 'the angular and bony frameworks from which flesh and blood have been clean scraped away'.[52] These comments were made soon after the publication of John Stuart Mill's *Auto-biography*, which text 'does not do much to reunite the link of common nature between the world and its men of intellect':

> Never were books written less calculated to make us respect the place which intellect holds in the world, or indeed to prove to us how much solider, brighter, more human and more true, is the life of the ploughman or labourer than that of the sage . . . who does nothing but fill the world with a demonstration of its fallacy, and holds up his own dreary self-deception for its worship . . . we are disposed to turn rather to the experiences of those who have lived for its practical realities, than those who have lived for its intellectual possibilities, its supposed higher part; to the lives of soldiers, sailors, common men and women, rather than to those of philosophers and thinkers.[53]

It would seem, however, that the reviewer is able to avoid so extreme a course – however worthy the lives of 'the humble shoemaker and baker', they are not reviewed in the middle-class press – finding within the province of middle-class literature a number of auto-biographies which reconcile and mediate between 'outrageous Mind and affronted humanity, proceed[ing] from two classes somewhat despised in the present day – to wit, women and Frenchmen'.[54] A few years later a *Blackwood's* review reiterates the view that 'literary experience may be a positive snare', while the best autobiographies are those that have chiefly a domestic or personal interest'.[55] The domestication of the genre at times goes along with the view that some of the most satisfactory autobiographies are written by women.

Women autobiographers come to embody the 'charm' and spon-taneity of autobiography emphasised by a number of critics and reviewers in the last decades of the century, although they are rarely incorporated into discussions of model or seminal autobiographies. Women, it is suggested, cannot be representative, as can men. Discussing the *Memoirs* of the scientific writer Mary Somerville, the reviewer (Margaret Oliphant) compares her 'natural' education with that of Mill; '[She] grew like a flower, as wild as any primrose and as sweet'.[56] Mill, by contrast, is represented by a number of critics as the monster to his father's Frankenstein, the unnatural product of dehumanising 'analytic training'. Anxiety over the sterility of male 'bodiless intellect', which is often represented as effeminacy and degeneration, is an aspect of the 'decline' model; women auto-biographers are at times represented as having a greater capacity for the transmission of 'life', and, in certain contexts, 'memoirs' become

more highly valued as a result of suspicions of 'analytical' autobiography. One aspect of this valorisation of 'domestic' writing is the
condemnation of women autobiographers who do produce self-
assertive autobiographies or claim exemplary status. Mrs Oliphant, in
her review of Harriet Martineau's *Autobiography*, posthumously
published in 1877, finds in Martineau's text the danger and destruction potential in autobiographical writing, against which the autobiography of the 'ideal feminine' should protect:

> It is a proof of the enormous interest we take in the records of humanity
> that neither pity nor justice interferes to prevent the habitual desecration
> of the homes and secrets of the dead. But if biography is thus dangerous,
> there is a still more fatal art, more radical in its operation, and infinitely
> more murderous, against which nothing can defend the predestined
> victim. This terrible instrument of self-murder is called autobiography;
> and no kind interpreter, no gentle critic, no effacing tear from any angel of
> the eternal records, can diminish its damning power.[57]

Mrs Oliphant's *ad feminam* criticisms of Martineau's autobiography contrast with her enthusiastic accounts of autobiographical texts, published in *Blackwood's* in the early 1880s. Her
series, 'Autobiographies', included lengthy discussions of the autobiographies of Cellini, Lord Herbert of Cherbury, Margaret
Cavendish (Duchess of Newcastle), Gibbon, Carlo Goldoni, Lucy
Hutchinson, Alice Thornton and Madame Roland.[58] It is in fact
extraordinary that half of the autobiographers Oliphant chooses to
discuss are women; even Edith Simcox, who was fascinated by
women's autobiographical writings, outlines an almost entirely male
tradition in the essay discussed above.[59]

Mrs Oliphant's series merits more substantial discussion than I
can give it here. Two aspects of her accounts of the women's autobiographies are particularly interesting – her account of women as
historians and her representation of female 'genius'. Lucy
Hutchinson's *Memoirs of the Life of Colonel Hutchinson* is a biography
of her deceased Roundhead husband, rather than an autobiography
as such, and Mrs Oliphant quietly but tellingly points to the self-
effacement of the woman memoirist: 'There is never an 'I' in the
book from beginning to end . . . [she] made this noble memorial to
[her husband] . . . and thereafter effacing herself altogether, as if she
died with him, is seen of us no more.' The *Life* was written for her
family and not for the public, but it has acquired a permanent status:
'the sons and daughters for whom it was written all vanished without a

name, leaving no track behind them; but the story of John Hutchinson has now become the property of the world'.[60] Men owe their lasting fame, Oliphant appears to be suggesting, to the literary labours of their wives who, while effacing themselves from the record, act as historians for others and, perhaps, achieve immortality for themselves.

In 'Margaret, Duchess of Newcastle', Oliphant downplays the eccentricity attributed to Margaret Cavendish, instead focusing on her autobiography as an historical record, but one in which great events are passed over in favour of 'small matters near'. Opening her account with an 'admission' that women rarely achieve genius, 'and never at all in the highest degree', Oliphant nevertheless refers to William Cavendish's 'defence of his lady's genius and truth'.[61] She gives an affectionate account of Margaret Cavendish, but her greatest admiration is reserved for Madame Roland, the Girondist guillotined in 1793, whose 'genius' is strongly asserted and whose gifts were superior to those of her husband. Madame Roland's full genius and energies are released when domestic life becomes irrelevant in the face of political turmoil: 'thus, with head and heart alike aflame, she entered all glowing and brilliant into her natural atmosphere of high sentiment and exalted thoughts'.[62] Braver and stronger than her husband, she acts as his amanuensis:

> the woman seated at the desk, from which so many eloquent pages have issued, pouring forth *d'un trait*, without a pause, that clear and noble statement of the crisis, menaced by so many dangers, the aureole of martyrdom hovering over her own bright head ... is the most affecting spectacle.[63]

Women are more often linked to unassuming and artless forms of personal writing, neither needing nor being capable of the self-vindications of public men. In the words of one *Blackwood's* reviewer:

> Women, and especially French women, are more emotional and impressionistic than the rougher sex. When they are warmed to their work, they have less hesitation in unbosoming themselves unreservedly in the public confessional, nor are they embarrassed by false shame or overstrained sensitiveness, when they are impelled to lay bare their innermost feelings.[64]

A legitimation of autobiographical self-disclosure invokes the spontaneity of its motivation, a theme that becomes prevalent in later nineteenth- and early twentieth-century discussions. Autobiography written under external compulsion, Leslie Stephen asserts in his 1881 essay 'Autobiography', would lose 'the essential charm of spontaneity'; the true autobiography is 'written by one who feels an irresistible longing for confidential expansion; who is forced by his innate constitution to unbosom himself to the public of the kind of matter generally reserved for our closest intimacy'.[65] Stephen refers to the autobiographer's 'unconscious exposure'; J. Ashcroft Noble wrote that autobiography allows the reader access to the self of an other: 'the secrets of personality cannot be kept, and a man's nature betrays itself without his knowledge of the betrayal'.[66] Autobiographies are symptomatic texts, through which, and beyond authorial volition, the secrets of human nature can be fathomed.

These themes clearly anticipate Freudian emphases on the involuntary disclosure of 'unconscious' desires and fears through 'texts' such as dreams and jokes, and through gestures and somatic symptoms. They also recall Carlyle's emphasis in *Characteristics* on the value of 'unconsciousness', which should also be understood as 'unselfconsciousness'. Unconscious revelation is viewed as less problematic than self-consciousness by a number of commentators on autobiography because the dynamic 'natural' force of the autobiographical impulse – the 'irresistible longing for confidential expansion', in Stephen's words – is perceived to transmit the self to the world without stopping to introspect in the realms of a dangerous (over)consciousness. The self is not turned back upon itself. Variants on this trope have remained central to autobiographical discourse; a legacy, perhaps, of the fact that 'confession' must always be understood as spontaneously given, a demand from within and not a response to external force. Paul John Eakin has recently characterised 'serious' autobiographies as 'the product of some imperative authorial necessity' – although in late twentieth-century criticism the 'drive' or 'impulse' towards autobiographical expression is not seen to be in conflict with self-analysis.[67] For the nineteenth-century critic, the 'autobiographical impulse' is in part a way of avoiding the twin dangers posed or courted by autobiographical practice: 'vanity' and 'morbidity'. The 'involuntary' nature of self-disclosure allows for an escape from charges of self-interest – it is striking that Stephen's essay, written towards the end of the century, takes the issue of the autobiographer's 'vanity' as its central focus and problematic. At the same time, involuntary disclosure is held to give access to 'interiority' – the inner self expresses itself – by means other than those of an 'unhealthy' self-analysis. But even though these models of auto-biography – as introspection and as expressive selfhood – are opposed, both of them limit, contain or deny the concept of the remaking and re-creation of the self and its history in the act of autobiography.

This chapter has discussed a number of the major themes that emerge from nineteenth-century autobiographical criticism. Spiritual and moral emphases, as revealed in John Foster's essay, are transmuted into 'psychological' and sociologistic concerns, with a particular emphasis on the typologies of human nature. As I have suggested, however, these 'general laws' are drawn from selected and selective sources. Popular 'memoirs' and 'ordinary' or 'scandalous' life-stories are relegated to the sphere of the literary market-place, and are addressed by reviewers only in order to demonstrate that the genre and culture are in decline, weakened and cheapened by a new populism. Literary preoccupations re-enter, however, when literary study produces or reaffirms its own typologies, and generic categories are mapped on to historical stages and psychologistic 'charac-terologies'. 'Great writers' become used as exemplars, providing all the possible models of human life and human nature, in an extension of the view that 'literary men' are particularly suited to self-analysis. The concept of the exemplary in autobiography remains a constant preoccupation, both in overtly moral and didactic terms (in which the roles of biography and autobiography lie in their national and institu-tional functions in transmitting the achievements of one generation to the next) and in an 'anthropological' context, in which 'great' auto-biographies, the expressions of 'great' individuals, become the materials from which ostensibly 'universal' laws can be drawn. In the twentieth century, these concerns appear in a sharper form, due to a more precise thrust in the treatment of psychological and sociological issues. Thus, for example, and as I discuss in the following chapter, nineteenth-century debates over 'genius' are often reformulated, in the early twentieth century, in the discourse of eugenics.

Notes

1 William Wordsworth, Letter to George Beaumont, 1 May 1805, in *The Letters of William and Dorothy Wordsworth. Vol. 1 – The Early Years – 1787-1805*, ed. Ernest de Selincourt, revised C. L. Shaver (Oxford: Clarendon Press, 1967).
2 Elizabeth W. Bruss, *Autobiographical Acts: The Changing Situation of a*

Literary Genre (Baltimore: Johns Hopkins University Press, 1976).
3 Michael McKeon, *The Origins of the English Novel: 1600–1740* (Baltimore: Johns Hopkins University Press, 1987), p. 19.
4 Southey uses the term to characterise the work of the Portuguese poet Francisco Vieura as 'auto-biography', in *Quarterly Review* 1 (1809), p. 283.
5 The review of D'Israeli's *Miscellanies* is in *Monthly Review*, 2nd series, 29 (1797), 375. *Miscellanies; or Literary Reflections* (London: T.Cadell and W.Davies, 1796) contains an essay entitled 'Some Observations on Diaries, Self-Biography, and Self-Characters', pp. 95–110. See also Coleridge's reference to Wordsworth's 'divine Self-Biography' in *The Notebooks of Samuel Taylor Coleridge*, ed. Kathleen Coburn, 2 vols. (New York: Pantheon Books, 1957), 1, no.1801, cited in Jerome Hamilton Buckley, *The Turning Key: Autobiography and the Subjective Impulse since 1800* (Cambridge, Mass.: Harvard University Press, 1984), pp. 169–70, n.36. Issues of nomenclature are interestingly discussed in Felicity Nussbaum, *The Autobiographical Subject: Gender and Ideology in Eighteenth-Century England* (Baltimore: Johns Hopkins University Press, 1989). ch. 1, *passim*.
6 Colin Campbell writes: 'The spread of words prefixed with "self " in a hyphenated fashion, such as "self-conceit", "self-confidence" and "self-pity", begin to appear in the English language in the sixteenth and seventeenth centuries, and become widely adopted in the eighteenth; "self-consciousness" itself apparently being first employed by Coleridge.' Such words reveal the growth of self-consciousness, as 'in becoming aware of the "objectness" of the world and the "subjectness" of himself, man becomes aware of his own awareness poised between the two' (*The Romantic Ethic and the Spirit of Modern Consumerism* (Oxford: Blackwell, 1987), p.73)). This has clear implications for subject/object, inner/outer relationships in autobiography.
      It is significant, however, that 'auto-', which becomes prevalent in English in the nineteenth century, is most often prefixed to scientific terms denoting action or operation: the *OED* lists 'auto-catalepsy', 'auto-coprophagous', 'auto-innoculation', 'auto-criticism', 'auto-psychology', etc. Southey's 1809 usage of 'autobiography' – 'this very amusing and unique specimen of autobiography' – suggests something of this 'scientific' emphasis. 'Autobiography' also becomes linked, as I discuss later, to both the terms and the concepts of 'autocide', 'autoscopy', 'autopsy' and 'autopathy' (self-feeling or experience). The 'scientific' resonances of autobiography are an aspect both of the relationships between autobiography and psychology, typology, etc., and of the 'scientificity' of self-observation. It could be argued that the unease about the term 'autobiography' stems from its scientific connotations.
7 See, for example, Jacques Derrida's use of the term 'otobiography' in *The Ear of the Other* (Lincoln and London: University of Nebraska Press, 1988). The first use of 'autography' is given by the *OED* as 1644, defined as 'the action of writing with one's own hand; the author's own hand-writing'. Recently the term has been revived by literary critics: see, for example, Domna C. Stanton, who uses the term 'autogynography' in *The Female Autograph: Theory and Practice of Autobiography from the Tenth to the Twentieth*

Century (University of Chicago Press, 2nd ed. 1987), and H. Porter Abbott, who wishes to use 'autography' to preserve the 'nonnarrative status' of such meditative essays and texts as Whitman's *Song of Myself*, Valéry's *Cahiers* and Kafka's *Brief an den Vater*. 'The term "autography" frees up the term "autobiography" for a role quite parallel to that of the term "novel": a loose narrative structure housing a variety of genres. . . . To read autographically is to ask of the text: How does this reveal the author?' ('Autobiography, Autography, Fiction: Groundwork for a Taxonomy of Textual Categories', *New Literary History* 19 (1988), 612–13).

 8 D'Israeli, 'Self-characters', *Literary Miscellanies*, published in his *Literary Character of Men of Genius* (London: Frederick Warne, 1822), p. 295. D'Israeli writes: 'The writing our own life has been practised with various success; it is a delicate operation, a stroke too much may destroy the effect of the whole. If once we detect an author deceiving or deceived, it is a livid spot which infects the whole body. To publish one's own life has sometimes been a poor artifice to bring obscurity into notice; it is the ebriety of vanity, and the delirium of egotism. When a great man leaves some memorial of his days, the grave consecrates the motive.' D'Israeli also refers to the 'darling egotism' of the French (p. 296). An earlier version of this passage appears in *Miscellanies; or Literary Reflections* (London: T. Cadell and W. Davies, 1796). The only differences are D'Israeli's phrase 'the extravagance of vanity and the delirium of egotism' and 'his death-bed sanctions the truth, and the grave consecrates the motive' in the earlier version.

 9 M.M.Bakhtin, 'Forms of Time and of the Chronotype in the Novel', in *The Dialogic Imagination*, ed. Michael Holquist, trans. Caryl Emerson and Michael Holquist (Austin: University of Texas Press), pp. 84–258.

10 Michel Foucault, *The Care of the Self, The History of Sexuality vol.3*, trans. Robert Hurley (London: Penguin, 1986), pp. 41–3.

11 D'Israeli, *Miscellanies*, p. 100.

12 Nussbaum, *The Autobiographical Subject*.

13 Review of *Memoirs of the Life of Peter Daniel Huet, Bishop of Avranches, written by himself*, *Quarterly Review* IV (Aug/Nov. 1810), 104.

14 Samuel Johnson, *The Idler*, 84 (24 Nov. 1759).

15 *Quarterly Review* XIV, (Oct/Jan. 1816/17), 123.

16 D'Israeli, *Miscellanies*, p. 97.

17 *Ibid.* p. 100.

18 John Foster, 'On a Man's Writing Memoirs of Himself ', in *Essays* (London: Bohr, 1805) (30th ed. 1863), pp. 1–66.

19 John Stuart Mill, *A System of Logic*, Vol. II, 7th ed. (London: Longmans, Green, Reader and Dyer, 1868), p. 449.

20 See John Sturrock's discussion of Rousseau's *Confessions* in *The Language of Autobiography: Studies in the first person singular* (Cambridge University Press, 1993), esp. Chapter 6. The Neuchâtel preface to the *Confessions* is reprinted in the Pléiade edition: Jean-Jacques Rousseau, *Oeuvres complètes*, Tome 1, *Les confessions, Autres textes autobiographiques*, ed. Bernard Gagnebin, Marcel Raymond and Robert Osmont (Paris, 1959), pp. 1148–64.

21 I am indebted to William H. Epstein's *Recognizing Biography* (Philadelphia:

University of Pennsylvania Press, 1987) for the concept of the 'life-course' and for theorisations of biography in general. Richard D. Altick's *Lives and Letters: A History of Literary Biography in England and America* (New York: Knopf, 1965) and Ira Bruce Nadel's *Biography: Fiction, Fact and Form* (London: Macmillan, 1984) have also been invaluable.

22 Short sketches of type characters exemplifying various human qualities, based on sketches by the Greek Theophrastus, became popular in the late seventeenth and eighteenth centuries, notably in Jean de La Bruyère's *Les Caractères* (1688). Felicity Nussbaum, in her study of eighteenth-century autobiography, *The Autobiographical Subject* (p. 107), notes that 'the Theophrastan character declines in mid-century, and this loss of the character as a model occurs at the same moment that the newly emergent genres of autobiographical writing and the novel freshly engage the question of its representation'. See also J. W. Smeed, *'The Theophrastan Character': The History of a Literary Genre* (Oxford: Clarendon Press, 1985). Eighteenth-century characterology has important implications for the question of universalism/particularism in auto/biographical discourse and for the relationship between auto/biography and typology.

23 [A. Innes Shand], *Blackwood's Edinburgh Magazine* CXXV (April 1879), 486.

24 James Anthony Froude, 'Representative Men', in *Short Studies on Great Subjects*, 4 vols. (London: Longmans, 1890).

25 D'Israeli, *Literary Character of Men of Genius*, pp. 12–13.

26 John Locke, *The Second Treatise of Government* (1690) (Oxford: Blackwell, 1956), p. 15.

27 Mary Jean Corbett, *Representing Femininity: Middle-Class Subjectivity in Victorian and Edwardian Women's Autobiographies* (New York and Oxford: Oxford University Press, 1992).

28 Julia Swindells, *Victorian Writing and Working Women* (Cambridge: Polity, 1985).

29 [G. H. Lewes], 'The condition of authors in England, Germany and France', *Fraser's Magazine*, 35 (March 1847), 285.

30 James Lockhart, 'Autobiography', *Quarterly Review* XXXV (1827), 148–65.

31 *Ibid.* p. 164.

32 *Ibid.* p. 165.

33 *Ibid.* p. 149.

34 [Mary Margaret Busk], 'Autobiography', in *Blackwood's Edinburgh Magazine*, CLIX, XXVI (Nov. 1829), 737–48. Busk is reviewing four memoirs from France. Two are by women (Madame du Barry and 'La Contemporaine'), recounting their experiences of Revolution and Empire, one by a government contractor during the Revolution, and the fourth that of Vidocq, thief turned thief-taker for the French police. The reviewer is presumably attacking the popularity of memoirs such as that by Constant, Napoleon's valet. Less obviously, the context may be the spate of apocryphal memoirs which appeared after the Revolution, and which raise further difficult questions of autobiographical 'legitimacy' and authenticity.

35 David Vincent, *Bread, Knowledge and Freedom: A Study of Nineteenth-Century Working Class Autobiography* (London: Methuen, 1982), p. 30.

36 Mary Jo Maynes, 'Gender and Narrative Form in French and German

Working-Class Autobiographies', in *Interpreting Women's Lives: Feminist Theory and Personal Narratives*, ed. The Personal Narratives Group (Bloomington: Indiana University Press, 1989), p. 106.

37 Thomas Carlyle, 'Biography', *Fraser's Magazine* (1832): reprinted in Carlyle, *Critical and Miscellaneous Essays*, vol. IV (London: Chapman and Hall, 1888), pp. 51–66.

38 Thomas De Quincey, *Confessions of an English Opium-Eater*, ed. Greville Lindop (Oxford University Press, 1985), p. 1.

39 Mary Jacobus, *Romanticism, Writing and Sexual Difference: Essays on* The Prelude (Oxford: Clarendon Press, 1989), pp. 224–5.

40 Catherine Gallagher, 'George Eliot and *Daniel Deronda*: The Prostitute and the Jewish Question', in *Sex, Politics and Science in the Nineteenth-Century Novel*, ed. Ruth B. Yeazell (Baltimore: Johns Hopkins University Press, 1986), p. 41.

41 *Confessions of an English Opium-Eater*, p. 25.

42 A. O. Prickard, *Autobiography* (London: Rivingtons, 1866).

43 On the distinction between 'voice' and writing in Victorian autobiography, see my 'Brothers in their anecdotage: Holman Hunt's *Pre-Raphaelitism and the Pre-Raphaelite Brotherhood*', in *Pre-Raphaelites Re-Viewed*, ed. M. Pointon (Manchester University Press, 1989), pp. 11–22.

44 'Theater und Literatur', in *Goethe the Critic* (Manchester University Press, 1960).

45 Edith Simcox, 'Autobiographies', in *North British Review*, CII (January 1870), 383–414. Simcox (1844–1901) was an essayist, philosopher and political activist. Her major works were *Natural Law: An Essay in Ethics* (1877), *Primitive Civilizations, or Outlines of the History of Ownership in Archaic Communities* (1894) and the semi-autobiographical *Episodes in the Lives of Men, Women and Lovers* (1882). Her unpublished journal, *Autobiography of a Shirt Maker* (Bodleian Library, Oxford), begun in May 1876, records her passionate love for George Eliot. She was active in the trade union movement: the title of her journal refers to the eight years of her involvement in co-operative shirt-making and her support for women workers in the clothing industry, which she described in the June 1884 issue of *Nineteenth Century*.

46 Thomas Carlyle, 'Characteristics' (1831), in *Critical and Miscellaneous Essays*, vol. II [*Thomas Carlyle's Works*, The Ashburton Edition, Vol. XVI.] (London: Chapman & Hall, 1887), p. 204.

47 Quoted by Geoffrey Hartman, in 'Romanticism and Anti-Self-Consciousness' (1962), reprinted in *Romanticism*, ed. Cynthia Chase (London: Longman, 1993), p. 53.

48 Prickard compares the autobiographer with the tableau in Greek drama: 'Just so the autobiographer stands before us as though in statuary, and pointing to his own person offers to explain to us its features. The scarred and bronzed face of the veteran soldier, the furrows worked in the forehead of an old hero of political life by indignation at impatient judgements of his contemporaries, or in that of the philosopher or divine by the wearing action of sublime thought, suggest each their own memoir, which none knows so well or should set forth so vividly as he of whose person time has made them

part' (p. 5).

Prickard's representation of the autobiographer's 'face' as his memoir bears interestingly both on the nineteenth-century fascination with physiognomy, the reading of character from the face, and on Paul de Man's theorisations of autobiography as *prosopopeia*, the putting-on of a face or mask, discussed in Chapter 5. Prickard's analogy is an example of a recurrent image in autobiographical discourse; the 'face' of the autobiographical text as the authentic image of the autobiographical self and its history. It also suggests the ways in which visual and verbal self-representations are perceived to coalesce.

49 Byron is the major target of Simcox's attack, as 'a complete example of that curious development of vanity which allows its victims to wish to be admired not for what they are but for what they are not' (p. 408). We might recall here Carlyle's 'Close thy Byron, open thy Goethe.'

50 Matthew Arnold, Preface to First Edition of *Poems* (1853), in *Selected Essays of Matthew Arnold*, ed. Christopher Ricks (New York: Signet, 1972), pp. 27–8.

51 Isobel Armstrong, *Victorian Scrutinies: Reviews of Poetry 1830–70* (London: Athlone, 1972), p. 46.

52 [Margaret Oliphant] 'New Books (No. XV)', *Blackwood's Edinburgh Magazine*, CXV (April 1874), 443.

53 *Ibid.* pp. 444–5.

54 *Ibid.* p. 444.

55 [Shand], 488.

56 [Oliphant], 446. The *Personal Recollections of Mary Somerville* were also reviewed by Edith Simcox (*The Fortnightly Review*, 15, New Series January 1874). Simcox used her review to attack the 'current prejudice against learned ladies' and the ways in which women were deprived of education in the sciences and mathematics. Mary (Fairfax) Somerville's intellectual gifts were thwarted, Simcox asserts; if they had not been, her genius would have yielded important original results.

57 Margaret Oliphant, 'Harriet Martineau', *Blackwood's Edinburgh Magazine*, CXXI (April 1877), 472. A similar comment was made by George Eliot. Martineau's autobiography, she writes, 'deepens my repugnance – or rather creates a new repugnance in me – to autobiography, unless it be so written as to involve neither self-glorification nor impeachment of others. I like that "He, being dead, yet speaketh" should have quite another meaning than that' (*George Eliot Letters*, ed. Gordon S. Haight, Vol. VI (1874–77) (New Haven: Yale University Press, 1955), p. 371.

58 Margaret Oliphant,, 'Autobiographies', No. I – 'Benvenuto Cellini', in *Blackwood's Edinburgh Magazine* (Jan. 1881). No. II – 'Lord Herbert of Cherbury' (March 1881). No. III – 'Margaret, Duchess of Newcastle' (May 1881). No. IV – 'Edward Gibbon' (August 1881). No. V, 'Carlo Goldoni' (October 1881). No. VI – 'In the Time of the Commonwealth: Lucy Hutchinson – Alice Thornton' (Jul. 1882). No. VII – 'Madame Roland' (April 1883).

59 Passages from Simcox's *Autobiography of a Shirt-Maker* reveal her deep interest in memoir-writing, especially women's. In 1898 she wrote: 'and

reading early Victorian memoirs with some purpose – towards my notion of a literary history of the period'. In 1887, she had written of her desire for 'a few more frank autobiographical details as to women's intimate natural feelings about men than the sex has yet indulged in. Historically, psychologically, intellectually – and it may be admitted from carnal curiosity too, I should like to know how many women there are who have no story to tell, how many others have some story other than the one which alone is supposed to count, and how many of those who think it worthwhile to dissect themselves are in a position to tell all they know of the result.' I am very grateful to Norma Vince for drawing these passages to my attention.

In 'Autobiographies', Simcox refers in passing to George Sand's *L'historie de ma vie* (1854) and to Charlotte Bronte's writing. Of the latter she writes:

and though Charlotte Bronte's heroines are all of one type, it by no means follows from this that all or any of them were successful representations of herself. Yet perhaps even these writers [Thackeray and Bronte] are as near to genuine auto-biography as the Journals or Recollections published from time to time by statesmen, travellers, detectives, missionaries, and self-made men or the crowd of inferior littérateurs who, wishing to write a book, take the first worthless subject that comes to hand. (p. 414)

This passage expresses a familiar hostility towards certain forms of popular memoir-writing and a valorisation of literary texts by contrast. Simcox also points to a question that has been insufficiently explored; the perceived status of Charlotte Bronte's novels, and *Jane Eyre* in particular, as autobiography. The title-page of the first edition of *Jane Eyre* (1847) shows the novel's title as *Jane Eyre: an Autobiography*, edited by Currer Bell. In his 1847 review of the novel, George Henry Lewes wrote:

Reality – deep, significant reality – is the great characteristic of the book. It is an autobiography, – not, perhaps, in the naked facts and circumstances, but in the actual suffering and experience. The form may be changed, and here and there some incidents invented; but the spirit remains such as it was. . . . This gives the book its charm: it is soul speaking to soul; it is an utterance from the depths of a struggling, suffering, much-enduring spirit: *suspiria de profundis!* (G. H. Lewes, 'Recent Novels: French and English', *Fraser's Magazine* 36 (1847), 690.

Lewes's comments are a powerful valorisation of 'true' autobiography as legitimated by feeling rather than by factual truths.

60 *Blackwood's Edinburgh Magazine*, Autobiography VI. 'In the time of the Commonwealth: Lucy Hutchinson – Alice Thornton' (July 1882), 80.
61 *Blackwood's Edinburgh Magazine*, (May 1881), 637.
62 *Blackwood's Edinburgh Magazine*, 'Madame Roland' (April 1883), 503.
63 *Ibid.* p. 505.
64 [Shand], 488.
65 Leslie Stephen, 'Autobiography', *Cornhill Magazine*, XLIII (April 1881), 410–29.
66 J. Ashcroft Noble, 'The Charm of Autobiography', in *Impressions and Memories* (London: Dent, 1895), pp. 36–45.
67 Paul John Eakin, *Fictions in Autobiography: Studies in the Art of Self-Invention* (Princeton University Press, 1985).

2
Auto/biography: between literature and science

The essayists of the late nineteenth century, writing about biography and autobiography as 'men of letters', share in a developing interest in unconscious life and creativity in late nineteenth-century psychology;[1] the 'autobiographical impulse' and 'genius' are linked through a concept of an involuntary drive to expression. The fascination with 'genius' in late nineteenth- and early twentieth-century psychology governs auto/biographical discourse in this period. In particular, it helps to explain the near-obsessive reproduction of a canon of 'great autobiographies', central to Leslie Stephen's essay 'Autobiography' and to a later essay, 'Famous Autobiographies', published in the *Edinburgh Review* in 1911.[2]

The 'famous autobiographies' of the title – which the author of the essay sets out literally to re-view – are those of Cellini, Rousseau, Gibbon, Goethe, Mill and Spencer. The need to bring these key texts to the attention of the reading public, the essayist claims, is that the 'success achieved by periodical literature narrows the demand for permanent literature in the form of books' [p. 333]. Permanence and continuity are the markers of autobiographies seen as documents of civilisation; the autobiographies of 'genius' are perceived as embodiments and personifications of the best of Western culture. Cellini, Goethe, Gibbon *et al.*, in these accounts, 'represent' and embody their age, but their relatedness is a product of the consanguinity of both 'genius' and 'genre'. Similarly, they are represented in a historicist narrative of cultural development, but also embody an 'eternal present', of the kind to which A. O. Prickard refers in his statement that in autobiography 'it is always the voice of a living man which speaks to us of himself '.[3] Where early nineteenth-century commentators at times express unease about the reliability of autobiographical narrative, critics of the later period represent 'great autobiographies' as authenticity personified, the representations of 'great lives', which, in the arguments of 'Famous Autobiographies', are the very components of the historical and social order.

They are also invoked as a crucial resource for the 'scientific' study of human character:

> The modern school of anthropologists wish for *data* of all kinds as to the physiological characteristics and the genealogy of as many distinguished people as possible. From this data they are able to draw conclusions of immense value and interest. . . . There are many people who read biography solely as anthropological *data*; not for physical measurements indeed, but as individual cases on which may be erected general laws of mind and character. [p. 345]

Discussions of autobiographies of 'genius' are clearly one of the contributions men of letters felt they could make to the psychological and ethnographic data-gathers of the late nineteenth and early twentieth centuries. Stephen, for example, presents his autobiographical 'group' (Cellini, Rousseau, Gibbon and J. S. Mill) as jointly exhaustive ideal or possible types, classifying them along the lines of the humours, male/female characteristics, and the introvert/extrovert models of human psychology which were becoming current in nineteenth-century thought.[4] The author of 'Famous Autobiographies', in making the link between autobiography and anthropology, may well have been responding to the demands made by the psychologist and sexologist Havelock Ellis, author of *A Study of British Genius* (1904).[5] In 'An Open Letter to Biographers' Ellis urges biographers to take their true function seriously: 'In every man of genius a new strange force is brought into the world. The biographer is the biologist of this new life. I come to you to learn the origins of this tremendous energy.'[6] Ellis shares with the literary critics a naturalistic model of individual genius; he refers, for example, to 'the aboriginal energy of Nature'. He also insists upon a close link between biography and ethnography, while arguing that biography, the study of great men, should not be allowed to become a secondary activity to ethnography:

> Beside biography, the life of an individual, we have ethnography, the life of a community. . . . Should a biographer willingly admit that the life of a community is better worth serious study than the life of its greatest men. . . . Is not the fashioning of a lyric to pierce the hearts of men forever as well worth study as the making of an arrow? The child of genius gathering shells on the shores of eternity as interesting as the games of savages? [pp. 114–15]

The overwhelming concern with 'genius' and its auto/biographical expressions are, at least in part, a response to ethnographic researches. The autobiographies of 'great men' become the authentic data which shores up cultural certainties and provides the points between which the map of western civilisation is drawn. They embody the cultural value with which the 'primitive' artefacts of 'savages' are contrasted. The fixity of the autobiographical canon contains autobiographical practice within 'great lives' and thus contains the potentially uncontrolled productivity of self-reflection and self-expression. 'Expressive' selfhood is limited to a finite set of autobiographical models – an autobiographical elect – and is rarely discussed as a generalisable practice. As the 'Famous Autobiographers' essayist writes: 'No man, but the greatest, can write a thoroughly good autobiography' [p. 345].

The 'serious student of biography' becomes synonymous with 'the student of human nature'; 'human nature' in turn is understood in an individualist manner as the essence of the social 'machine'. Discussing the general principles to be drawn from a study of the 'works', the essayist asserts that, with the exception of Mill, 'they are all thoroughly *natural* lives. . . . Their greatness was in no way due to excessive ambition, or to any determination or force of will.' Thus he reinforces a naturalistic account of individual genius, and, in Wolf Lepenies's phrase, 'an indirect conduct of life', in which individuals develop according to their own natures and in which their auto-biographies, and other works, are expressions of these natures.[7] As in Stephen's essay, this also serves to resolve the problem of auto-biographical egotism, and to dispute both the didactic and intro-spective purposes of autobiography, so troubling to the Victorians. Autobiographies may contain lessons, but without the intention of the autobiographer playing a necessary part in the process: '[Goethe's] writings are not to inculcate a moral or exhibit a truth; they are nothing else than the expression of his personality, without aim or purpose' [p. 335]. Moreover, 'genius' has no necessary connection with either morality or immorality. Rousseau, in this argument, is rehabilitated as the complete 'natural' man and 'natural' genius.

*   *   *

The relatively new genre of collective biography or 'prosopography', represented by, for example, Samuel Smiles's *Lives of the Engineers*

(1861–62), and more systematically, by national biographical dictionaries, such as the *Biographie Universelle*, the *Nouvelle Biographie Générale*, and the British *Dictionary of National Biography* (*DNB*) (1885–1900), also developed in intimate relation with studies of inherited ability or 'genius'. The *Dictionary of National Biography*, published between 1885 and 1900 in sixty-three volumes, was edited by Leslie Stephen, Victorian essayist, critic and biographer and father of Virginia Woolf, and Sidney Lee, initially Stephen's assistant on the dictionary and sole editor from 1891. Lee described this monumental project as providing a 'greater mass of accurate information respecting the past achievements of the British and Irish race than has been put at the disposal of the English-speaking peoples in any previous literary undertaking'.[8] It also aroused considerable debate over inclusions and exclusions, relative length, and the kind of detail deemed appropriate to the entries.

Francis Galton, the psychologist and founder of eugenics, drew heavily on existing biographical sources in his study *Hereditary Genius*, first published in 1869; Havelock Ellis, whose *A Study of British Genius* was published in 1904, used the *DNB* as his primary source. At around the same time, Ellis's less well-known contemporary, the psychologist J. McKenn Cattell, a student of Galton's, published *A Statistical Study of Eminent Men*, drawing on six biographical dictionaries – British, French, German and American – for his list of the one thousand most eminent men (including a small percentage of women) in history. Both Cattell and Ellis proceed by measuring the space allotted to eminent figures in the dictionaries; the longer the entry, the greater the degree of eminence. In a later project, Catherine Cox used Cattell's list of eminent individuals in history for her comparative study of estimated IQ, *Genetic Studies of Genius*, from John Stuart Mill, in the 190–200 range, down to a group of 100–110, including John Bunyan, Cervantes, Cobbett, Copernicus, Faraday and Sir Francis Drake.[9]

Despite the use psychologists made of biographical dictionaries in the studies of ability and genius, they repeatedly complained about the absence of data or of interpretation relevant to 'the early mental development of their subjects'. Lewis Terman, overall editor of *Genetic Studies of Genius*, referred to 'the utter inability of a majority of otherwise competent biographical writers to appraise and interpret the facts which they themselves have recorded'.[10] The debates between biographers and psychologists inflect much of the auto/

biographical discourse of the time, and are at the forefront of Lee's and Ellis's discussions.

One of Sidney Lee's major concerns is with the 'scale' or measure of personality, intended to distinguish those suitable for biographical immortalisation and those not. Lee, who appears as an unreconstructed Victorian in the debates about biography in the early twentieth century (his essay *The Perspective of Biography* was published in 1917, only one year before Lytton Strachey's iconoclastic 'group' biography, *Eminent Victorians*) insists, in his *Principles of Biography* (1911) that 'the life of a nonentity or a mediocrity, however skilfully contrived, conflicts with primary biographic principles'.[11] When it comes to sorting out the great from the lesser, however, Lee admits that 'puzzling issues' are raised. He resorts to allegory: Ariosto's fable in which, at the point of death, the medal stamped with his name which each individual wears throughout his life is dropped into Lethe, the river of forgetfulness. A few, 'a very few', of the medals are caught by swans who deposit them 'in a temple or museum of immortality'. Ariosto's swans are biographers, Lee states: 'by what motive are they impelled to rescue any medals of personality from the flood of forgetfulness into which they let the mass sink?'[12]

Lee does not entertain the possibility that the swans' selection might be wholly arbitrary. He is not altogether happy, however, with his own suggested procedures for medal-gathering. Living subjects are automatically excluded, presenting no taxonomic difficulties. 'Death' supplies the 'completeness' demanded by the 'fit biographic theme' of a career which is 'serious, complete and of a certain magnitude'. Lee proposes a scale in which magnitude is measured by volume and in inverse proportion to 'the number of times that (a human action) has been accomplished or is capable of accomplishment'. He hints, however, that this may not be an entirely satisfactory scale: 'In estimating the magnitude of human action there is need of some workable measure or gauge which shall operate independently of mere contemporary opinion.' Lee's 'Great Man' theory of history founders on the impossibility of achieving a wholly objective and 'scientific' approach to greatness.

The Victorian critic and 'man of letters' Edmund Gosse, in 'The Custom of Biography', more confidently outlined a scale for biographical measurement. The primary test in establishing the worthiness of the subject for biographical treatment is

to satisfy one's self that the subject possessed qualities, moved in conditions, assumed characteristics, so unlike those of other men as to justify his being raised from their ranks. When this primary test has been passed, it should then be for the biographer to ask, What were the extent and the value of his uniqueness? what – in short – is his relative bulk? ... There should be a certain proportion between the size of his portrait and the effect which he produced in public life.[13]

'Relative bulk' and 'genius' become related ways of calibrating eminence.

Leslie Stephen tends to represent biography, in his essays on this topic, as a servant to history, whereas Sidney Lee emphasises the need to consolidate the autonomy of biography as a genre, insisting on its separation from history, ethics and science. 'History', he writes, 'may be compared to mechanics, the science which determines the power of bodies in the mass.' Biography may be compared to chemistry, 'the science which analyses substances and resolves them into the constituent elements' [*Principles of Biography*, p. 27]. Whereas the historian deals with 'the crowd', 'the mass of mankind', the biographer 'draws apart those units who are in a decisive degree distinguishable from the neighbours (and) submits them to minute examination. ... Biography is not a peg for anything save the character and exploits of a man whose career answers the tests of biographic fitness' [pp. 27, 30].

The demand for generic purity runs throughout auto/biographical discourse. Lee's writings are a particularly clear example of the ways in which the demarcation of disciplinary and generic boundaries is intermeshed with forms of social classification and with a fear of absence of differentiation, often linked to a strong rejection of the idea that it is environment that determines character. This is a central topic in one of the earliest studies of biography, Edwin Paxton Hood's *The Uses of Biography* (1852), in which Hood justifies the need for a classification of 'lives' and wields the monumental metaphor in the following terms:

> At present, the venerable and the vile, the worthy and the worthless, the mean and the magnificent, lie heaped and huddled in promiscuous neighbourhood: the mention of biography only suggests to the mind the idea of a vast pyramid of conglomerate marble.[14]

Sidney Lee's repudiation of the mass and the crowd as objects of study in favour of the individual also connects his interest in biography with a defence of 'individuology', the science invented in the first decade of the twentieth century by the eugenicist biologist

J. Lionel Tayler, himself the author of a study of biography and autobiography.[15] Pairing the study of individuals, 'individuology', with the study of their natural groupings, 'sociology', Tayler manifests the desire to individualise and classify 'human types' that has also dominated auto/biographical discourse. In the late nineteenth and early twentieth centuries, this differentiation becomes an aspect of the demarcation of the 'new' disciplines, including psychology and sociology. It is also closely linked to the work on eugenics, genetics and theories of 'genius' promoted by Francis Galton and continued by, among others, Havelock Ellis. Tayler wrote that 'Mr Galton's researches on twins and on finger-prints prove beyond question that man, throughout his individual life, retains his individuality and his is therefore a self-acting unity which can be studied.' 'National decadence' is to be counteracted by 'type opportunity', the type system being 'founded upon the accurate grouping of individual bodily forms'.[16]

While Tayler's concept of the individual as a 'self-acting unity' has links with Lee's claim that the biographer's proper subjects are those 'units who are in a decisive degree distinguishable from their neighbours' [*Principles*, p. 27], Lee himself drew a sharp line between biography and genetic science, despite the preponderance of 'scientific' metaphors in his account of the proper study of biography. His argument was in part a response to Havelock Ellis's, 'An Open Letter to Biographers', in which the *DNB* is singled out for special attention. Ellis expresses severe disappointment at the failure of biographers to have contributed any material of real value to his study of 'the complex nature and causes of genius' in *Study of British Genius* (1904). The circumstances of birth, heredity and family relationships, and, in particular, physical and 'racial' characteristics are not treated in any 'systematic' way in the *DNB*, Ellis asserts.

Like Lee, and Harold Nicolson after him, Ellis is concerned with the disciplinary affiliations of biography. He is in accord with Lee in stating that 'a biographer is not a historian' [p. 109]. The biographer's links, he writes in 'An Open Letter to Biographers', are rather with the natural scientist and the ethnologist. Firstly, there is the connection, noted earlier, between biography and biology: 'In every man of genius a strange new force is brought into the world. The biographer is the biologist of this new life. I come to you to learn the origins of this tremendous energy, the forces that gave it impetus and that drove it into one channel rather than another' [p. 111]. Ellis also elaborates on the correspondence between biography and ethnography:

> Now both one and the other are branches of applied psychology, a strict method of scientific research. There was a time not so long ago when psychology was not a strict method of research and when any arm-chair philosopher sat down to write the history of the general soul as light-heartedly as the biographer still sits down to write the history of the individual soul. So far as pure psychology at least is concerned, these days are passed. . . . But how often does any such attempt, on however imperfect material, to bring us nearer to the heart and brain of a great creative personality form part of what the biographer presumes to call 'Life'? How many biographers so much as know that they are – may the real students forgive me! – psychologists, and that the rules of their art have in large part been laid down? [p. 115]

Ellis's strictures did have a certain impact on conceptions of biography, as we shall see in the discussion, in the following chapter, of Harold Nicolson's account of the genre. Lee's is certainly a weak defence against what he saw as the encroachments of 'biology and anthropology'. Although willing to entertain the idea that biography could contribute 'to the needs of the scientific investigation of heredity and eugenics', and 'aid the scientific enquiry into the origin and development of ability or genius', he balks at the demand of genetical study that 'every great man's pedigree' should be investigated 'with the result that undistinguished grandfathers, grandmothers, fathers, mothers, even second cousins shall receive almost as close attention as the great man himself' [pp. 31–2]. The 'dangers' of this are clear: the promiscuous, or perhaps incestuous, inter-mingling of the mediocre and the great.

The debates to which Ellis and Lee contributed are part of more extensive border disputes over disciplines and knowledges. Lee's insistence on the generic autonomy of biography is part of a broader attempt, which begins with nineteenth-century auto/biographical discourse, to isolate biography as the human science *par excellence*, the art or science (and the terms vary) of life. Lee calls upon 'science' in an attempt to legitimate the purity of biography, while at the same time sharply distinguishing biography from the sciences themselves. The means of legitimation turn out to be the vehicle of contamination, however. Lee's obsessive recourse to the 'magnitude' of personality as biography's rationale should in part be seen as an attempt to locate value internally to the biographical subject and as an end in itself.

The discourses of biography and eugenics converge in the conceptualisation of 'genius', often understood, as it is by Francis Galton, in the broader sense of high ability, transmitted largely within the
boundaries of the upper classes and legimating their rule by means of
a new 'scientific' sociodicy. Ellis's project is a more descriptive and
less overtly racist one, although Ellis also sees it as a contribution to
racial anthropology. More broadly, one can see a set of interrelations
between biological and biographical conceptions of 'life' as a dynamic
force and life-as-lived, as well as between the life of an individual and
the life of the species. 'Ontogeny' is said to repeat 'phylogeny' and the
biographical method becomes of central importance. The category of
lived experience, or *Erlebnis*, explored in Chapter 4, adds a further
reflection on the succession of important experiences which constitute a life.

*   *   *

As we have seen, a crucial element of the *rapprochement* between
autobiography and science was the search for the laws governing
human nature, but the much proclaimed 'general laws' of mind and
character often turn out to be somewhat disappointing. Of particular
interest, for example, to the author of 'Famous Autobiographies',
discussed earlier, was the question of women and, in particular, the
profound 'influence of women upon men of ability. . .not one of (the)
writers of great autobiographies stood in absolutely normal relations
with their women. . .here surely is the material for the philosopher of
biography to work upon' [p. 339]. From a study of Rousseau's and
Goethe's relationships with women, the conclusion is drawn that
great men benefit from association with robust women without intellectual pretensions.

More importantly, a model of sexual difference is employed in
many discussions to distinguish between the whole and continuous
nature of male identity and the fragmentary character of female
identity. As in the discussions at the turn of the eighteenth/
nineteenth centuries, autobiography is again being mobilised in
debates around identity and subjectivity, but this time often in
explicitly gendered terms.

There are two basic models of autobiographical production in this
period. The first has already been mentioned: it invokes the idea of
autobiography as the spontaneous expression of genius, in which the

written and the lived life are barely distinguished. The second model, which I discuss in more detail later, defines 'serious' autobiography as introspection or 'self-study', with the corollary that only 'genius' or 'greatness' is capable of such sustained achievement. Women are excluded from both models. They are excluded from the category of natural genius – sometimes on the historical grounds that there is no female equivalent of a Mozart or a Shakespeare. More precisely, they are seen as incapable of the sustained self-study, and lacking in the continuous goal-directed identity, held to be necessary for auto-biographical consciousness. A 'Lockean' conception of continuous personal identity is associated with men, while an associational con-sciousness ('Hume's 'bundle of perceptions') and a discontinuous identity become definitional of female subjectivity.

A graphic example of this gendering of identity is provided by Otto Weininger's influential *Sex and Character*.[17] This book was published in Vienna in 1903, the year in which its twenty-three-year-old author took his own life, and translated in England and the US in 1906. For Weininger, women lack the continuous, unbroken identity and hence the full memory necessary for autobiographical creation; 'this pecu-liar continuity by which a man first realizes that he exists, that he is and that he is in the world, is all comprehensive in the genius, limited to a few important moments in the mediocre, *and altogether lacking in woman*' [p. 124]. The absence of consistent, centred selfhood is also, for Weininger, a feature of Jewish identity. *Sex and Character* was, Sander Gilman writes, 'a work of intense self-hatred which, however, had an unprecedented influence on the scientific discourse about Jews and women at the turn of the century'.[18]

Sex and Character is a disturbing text in its 'scientific' vilification of women and Jews. The two aspects of specific relevance to auto-biographical discourse are Weininger's renewed appeals for a science of characterology, to be based in large part on a study of sexual differences and of 'sexually intermediate forms', and his statements about the gendered nature of identity. Weininger makes explicit the masculinist assumptions of many accounts of 'autobiographical con-sciousness'; the excesses of his desire to exclude women from 'uni-versal' categories and to deny them subjectivity shows up the androcentrism of many of his more 'legitimate' contemporaries.

Women's psychic life is discontinuous and limited, Weininger asserts; 'the female is concerned altogether with one class of recollec-tions – those connected with the sexual impulse and reproduction. . . . A real woman never becomes conscious of a destiny, of her own destiny.' She (Weininger claims he is referring to an 'absolute female', to be distinguished from 'real women', but the distinction is barely maintained) demonstrates a failure to grasp the 'law of identity' and is 'incapable of grasping the anxious desire of the man to understand the beginning, middle and end of his individual life in their relationship to each other' [p. 146]. In a passage which combines certain themes of the philosopher and historian Wilhelm Dilthey with Weininger's own characteristic misogyny, he writes: 'a female genius is a contradiction in terms . . . because woman is not a monad and cannot reflect the universe'. 'Woman' is without form, limit and individuality, and cannot separate the categories of the subjective and the objective; she is thus incapable of self-reflection and introspection, truth, logic, will and moral judgement. Her 'ego' is body, her identity is matter, her self is sexuality; 'women have no existence and no essence; they are not, they are nothing. . . . Man alone is a microcosm, a mirror of the universe' [pp. 286, 290].

Weininger makes explicit the view that women are to be excluded from the foundations of philosophy. Their discontinuous identity and lack of 'ego' in fact make them the suitable 'subjects' for a despised empiricism, itself seen as soulless and 'essentially womanish'. In the case of the male, 'all the psychic life must be considered with reference to the ego, as Kant foresaw' [p. 208]. A new 'science of mind' is required to do justice to the male transcendental ego and its new form, Weininger asserts, will be that of 'ontogenetic psychology or theoretical biography . . . a science capable of giving a rational orderly account of the whole course of the mental life from the cradle to the grave' [p. 130]. The biographical method and autobiographical consciousness are thus curiously entwined in Weininger's account as essential to a masculine philosophy and psychology.

Weininger claims that only 'great men' will be moved to write autobiography proper:

> the request for an autobiography would put most men into a most painful position; they could scarcely tell if they were asked what they had done the day before. Memory with most people is quite spasmodic and purely associative. In the case of the man of genius, every impression that he has received endures. [p. 122]

The past is always present to the great man, and hence he feels himself to be a 'man of destiny'. Again, the discourse of masculine identity, power, will and destiny has disconcerting parallels in the writing of, for example, Georg Misch, discussed in detail in Chapter 4.

The language of will is part of an emphasis on consciousness and ego; 'consciousness is the mark of greatness and before it the unconscious is dispersed as the sun disperses a mist. . . . All real existence is conscious existence' [p. 118] – and can thus only be masculine. Autobiography is the representation and product of full consciousness and memory – that is, possession of the past. The 'unconscious' is despised by Weininger, in part because it is the realm open to suggestion and thus to loss of will, which in his account is feminised. Hence women's suitability as hypnotic subjects and their tendencies to psychic automatism. Weininger's obvious fear and anxiety about female sexuality emerges in its representation as formlessness, discontinuity, sensation and unconsciousness. By contrast, male identity is represented as form, consciousness, mentation, will and control of matter.

Gilman notes that many of Weininger's ideas – bizarre as they may seem – would have been very familiar to his contemporaries, and that he restates Schopenhauer's view of women.[19] Weininger also opens up the hidden or unspoken 'other' of a number of normative judgements about identity and autobiography in this period. It is not merely that women are effaced, subsumed into a supposedly universal selfhood which is in fact gendered male because all agency and identity are seen as masculine. It is that women, or 'woman', must be presented as negation in order for the male to be affirmed, as inchoate and incoherent in order that male identity can be secured. This has a number of implications for a politics of autobiography. Firstly, Weininger's diatribes should lead us to look at all definitions or accounts of autobiography predicated on will and ego, self-affirmation and self-consciousness, with a degree of caution. Secondly, we should perhaps be wary of accounts of autobiography, including feminist approaches, which insist upon 'innate' gender differences in autobiography in terms which represent men's autobiography as ego-centred and progressive, and women's as discontinuous and associative.

* * *

Anna Robeson Burr's *The Autobiography: A Critical and Comparative*

Study (1909),[20] the first full-length study in English of autobiography, pursues the theme of scientific classification and autobiographical 'genius' on a larger scale. William Spengemann, in his
study of autobiography, briefly notes the context of Burr's text; the
early twentieth-century emphasis on the 'psychological' interest of
autobiography, which justified its treatment as a distinct genre:

> Insofar as these psychological interpretations of autobiography
> emphasized its deep structures and the author's unconscious self-
> revelations, they directed attention to the text and, simultaneously,
> blurred the distinction between factual and fictive statements, treating
> both as symbolic expressions of psychic energy. As a result, an increasing
> number of critics came to associate autobiography with fiction rather than
> with biography.[21]

Spengemann views the psychological focus in autobiographical
criticism as a midway point between historical approaches, concerned with the factual status of the genre, and those which
emphasise the textuality of autobiographies. The main critical
trajectory is thus 'from life to mind to text'.[22] This broad map is a
useful one, but overlooks a number of specific debates. The psychology of William James is the guiding spirit behind Burr's studies.[23]
She emphasises consciousness rather than the unconscious, and
valorises 'self-study' rather than 'self-revelation'. And she is dismissive of the 'literary' approach to autobiography, insisting that the
scientific or psychological interest of autobiography is of primary
significance, the literary secondary: 'the writer of his own life must
remember above all, that he is making first, a scientific document;
second a piece of literature' [p. 197], 'the endeavour to stand for what
we are, springs from a deeper motive, a more serious psychological
condition, than the *littérateur* is willing to allow' [p. 66].

Science and psychology, not surprisingly, are viewed by a number
of commentators as more suitable bodies of knowledge than literary
studies for the investigation of 'human nature'. The issue of whether
autobiographies in and of themselves fall into the category of 'art' or
'science' – which is certainly the ostensible concern of many critics –
obscures the nature of the debates between disciplines, in which
'autobiography' is as much a terrain to be fought over as an 'entity' to
be defined. Burr's attempt to approach the topic of 'subjective autobiography' 'scientifically' has ramifications which extend beyond the
limitations of her study.

In *The Autobiography*, Burr alludes to a range of psychologistic and

sociologistic theories, including Francis Galton's theories of individual difference and of genius, Comtean positivism, empiricist
versions of introspection characteristic of the late nineteenth century,
theories of human 'types' (Quételet), and of individual versus group
psychology (Gustave Le Bon, Théodule Ribot). Drawing on the work
of early dynamic psychiatry, primarily French, she makes the claim
that autobiographies provide crucial material for the psychologist.[24]
She distinguishes between her approach and that of the social
statistician who 'distrusts a study of the individual': the study of
autobiography can thus be seen as a defence of 'individuology'. Burr
insists, both in *The Autobiography* and in *Religious Confessions and
Confessants*, that the 'subjective impulse' or 'introspective tendency'
are worthy of scientific psychological analysis, and this is perhaps as,
or more, important for her than claiming attention for the autobiographical form *per se*. 'Subjective' autobiography is variously
defined; it is opposed to the objective memoir [p. 67] conceived as a
lesser form, and involves for Burr a 'scientific' impulse towards
self-study, developing out of the 'ethical' drive for self-knowledge
which she believes emerges with Christianity.

A number of the psychologists referred to by Burr were themselves
interested in questions of literary creativity; the relationship between
late nineteenth- and early twentieth-century 'experiments' in literature (including the writings of Henry James and Proust), and the new
psychology has been charted elsewhere. At the time at which the
novel was exploring what might have been seen to be the province of
autobiography – for example, states of consciousness and subjective
time – the claim is also being made that autobiography is a form
peculiarly suited to this exploration. Despite the difficulties of sus-
taining the concept of a privileged relationship between autobiographical writing and introspective mental processes, this relationship has been a recurrent theme in autobiographical criticism.
The rise of the 'introspective' novel threatened this monopoly, by
providing grounds for the suggestion that the temporality of the novel
might render it superior to autobiography in this respect. Autobiography *should* be privileged, in so far as it guarantees the identity of
observer and observed, the precondition for introspection; on the
other hand, and as more recent critics have emphasised, it can only
operate in the mode of retrospection.

The autobiography to which Burr gives most attention is that of the
sixteenth-century mathematician and physician Jerome Cardano,

who, she claims, anticipated the scientific spirit of the early twentieth century. Her tripartite structure of autobiographical 'types', which she calls 'the three great archetypes', is a variant on the Comtean model outlined earlier: Burr's categories are the historical (and objective), the religious and the scientific, represented by Caesar, Augustine and Cardano respectively. In addition to offering an evolutionary model of an autobiographical tradition, this also allows Burr to claim that autobiographers have now entered the 'scientific' stage, leaving the 'literary' behind. The significance of Cardan or Cardano's *De Vita Propria Liber* (1575) for Burr is that it marks the beginning of 'scientific self-study' [p. 81] and is the model 'introspective' autobiography. Cardano is exemplary for Burr not only because he demonstrates a mind observing its processes, but because the 'brain' is one of the finest. In this shift from mind to brain, Burr produces a variant on the concept of the autobiographer's 'auto-analysis' or 'auto-dissection', and suggests that she believes that the secrets of human personality lie in neurological structures. Furthermore, she allies theories of 'genius' with empiricist introspectionist theories.

The 'great men' thesis is also advanced through reference to Weininger's *Sex and Character*. Burr proposes a category which she calls the 'autobiographical intention', which marks out the serious and sincere autobiographer from his imitators: a 'governed impulse' towards self-understanding, which also stems from 'special, very deep-seated conditions'. This last statement Burr takes from Weiniger [*sic*], and the paragraph she quotes is drawn on throughout *The Autobiography*. Weininger wrote:

> It will now be seen why (if neither vanity, desire for gossip nor imitation drives them to it) only the better men write down recollections of their lives; and how I perceive in this a strong evidence of the connection between memory and giftedness. It is not as if every man of genius wished to write an autobiography; the incitement to autobiography comes from special, very deep-seated conditions. [Burr, p. 27]

Burr disregards the context of Weininger's discussion, and uses a highly selective version of Weininger's arguments to reinforce the perceived relationship between 'great men' and 'true' autobiography:

> The imperious lash of Truth upon the neck of the great, that fretful urging to candor, is one of the many differences between them and ourselves. . . . It is time we dropped our glib generalizations, and acknowledged the different standards of greater men. A superior sincerity, a

more penetrative candor, – these are tokens of their greatness and a
reason for their survival. [p. 53]

'Sincerity' is one criterion to which Burr repeatedly returns (a version
of the chapter on sincerity in autobiography appeared as an article in
The Atlantic Monthly of 1909). 'Sincerity', she states, 'seems to have
been promised by the large number of autobiographies seriously
conceived and executed in the interest of self-study and scientific
truth.' It might, however, be expected that a 'psychologistic' approach
would not involve distinctions between the value of texts, but would
rather view all self-analyses as relevant 'data'. This is not the case in
Burr's account:

> All literary records are of unequal value and while they are being sifted
> they must also be judged. . . . The scandalous memoir, written from an
> ulterior purpose, apart from any revelation of human life, has but a
> negligible value for us here. So also is it with the teeming thousands of
> commonplace, modern imitations, from which is absent every trace of
> serious intent. The cases remaining must conform to a certain standard,
> must establish, as it were, their right to be heard, ere their testimony can
> be accepted. For the whole value of personal testimony lies in the quality
> of the witness, and the special danger attending the study of self-
> revelation lies in treating all self-revealers alike, in giving an equal weight
> to all. [p. 13]

The 'ulterior purpose' of the 'scandalous memoir' is, presumably,
that of gaining notoriety or money; the judgement echoes those of the
nineteenth-century discussions referred to earlier, in which any
suspicion of mercenary motives on the part of the autobiographer
disallows his place in the canon, and forward to contemporary judgements, albeit only implicit, of the radical distinction between 'serious'
autobiography and its trivialising versions. She is also concerned with
the distinction between 'spurious' and genuine autobiography; the
spurious autobiography or memoir includes both 'the memoir as
fiction and the memoir transposed by another hand'. Such texts:

> walk the paths of autobiography, loitering, to use the police phrase, in a
> suspicious manner. Enwrapped as they are in veils and disguises, one has
> to be particularly careful as to identification before using their material.
> For this reason they are more subtly dangerous than the frankly spurious
> class. The spurious autobiography is the refuge of both the sciolist and
> the literary charlatan. Once thrown upon life, difficult to avow, impossible
> to recall, it lurks about the decent society of books like some base-born
> adventurer, communicating evil and distrust. . . . When the original

circumstance of its writing is forgotten, it becomes listed under
biography in the libraries. [pp. 19–20]

Again, this passage emphasises the importance of the authenticity of
the 'data' from which general laws of human nature are to be drawn.
Burr's statement suggests that, like the distinction between memoirs
and autobiography, apparently neutral but implicitly value-laden,
literary classifications begin in a domain structured by ethical and
characterological concerns. Like many autobiographical critics, Burr
moves back and forth between types of text and types of men.

The establishing of a means by which discriminations between
'serious' and 'inferior' autobiographies are made, is, Burr suggests,
one of the particular values of her approach:

> if we believe, with M. Cousin, that the great man represents the
> quintessence of his epoch, an autobiography possesses the strong advan-
> tage of superior quality. . . . The quality of our witness, as against the
> quantity of the statistician, is our first claim; the ore from this mine must
> essay to a certain degree of value. [p. 11]

Discriminations become particularly crucial in modern times, in
which 'hordes of cheap and commonplace persons have been
encouraged to mount the witness-stand' [p. 206]. The legalistic and
also religious term 'witness', employed throughout the study, refers
to those who provide 'data' for the psychologist and the student of
human nature; their 'sincerity', synonymous both with their
'greatness' and with their commitment to 'self-study', is all-
important if they are to provide the materials for the laws of human
nature.

The further purpose of Burr's study is to propose classifications,
comparisons and general laws both for the benefit of the psychologist
and to show 'how much the critic has need of the psychologist' [p. 66].
The subtitle of the book – 'a critical and comparative study' – takes on
particular resonance; Burr emphasises that she is examining the
subjective documents of autobiographical literature as *comparative
data*. This needs to be understood not in the context of 'comparative
literature', but of comparative psychology, or *Komparationslehre*: the
belief that the comparison of individuals, and individual 'differences',
will allow for the production of general laws of human nature and
human life. She is critical of earlier discussions of autobiographies
and memoirs – Sainte-Beuve is the critic she names – for treating
texts on a purely individual basis.

One central aspect of Burr's text, which forms a link with the preoccupations of other early twentieth-century autobiographical critics, is that of the relationship between 'genius' and 'pathology'. The psychologist against whom Burr argues is the Italian Cesare Lombroso (1836–1909), noted for his theories of psychopathology, criminality and regression. Lombroso's study of Cardano, Burr believes, did not do justice to the autobiography or to Cardano himself, 'dispos[ing] of him as a *halluciné* ' [p. 87]. The attention paid by Burr to Cardano's *De Vita Propria Liber* is thus in part an attempt to redeem Cardano from his status as a specimen of psychopathology, by arguing that he adopted a scientific attitude towards his own condition. In broader terms, her critique of Lombroso can be seen to form part of a general debate between progessivist and degenerative theories of human psychic and cultural development; a debate which also lies behind the theme of decline informing much of the auto-biographical criticism discussed in the previous chapter, and is an aspect of the tension between 'exemplary' and 'counter-exemplary' lives and texts. One could argue, however, that in Burr's and others' studies, the decline model is endorsed in so far as it applies to 'degenerate' and 'criminal' individuals, while the progressivist account is used to embellish the familiar theme of genius.

Burr's further argument with Lombroso concerns the issue of the 'psychology of genius' [p. 380] and the assumed relationship between genius and neurosis. Lombroso explicitly described autobiography as a pathological form. 'The literary productions of the insane are', he asserted, 'nearly always autobiographical.'[25] Ernst Kretschmer, discussing madness and genius more generally in his *The Psychology of Men of Genius*, claimed that 'mental disease, and more especially, those ill-defined conditions of the boundary of mental disease are decidedly more frequent among men of genius'.[26] Much of Burr's special pleading for the essential 'normality' of the autobiographer arises not only from the difficulty of disassociating theories of genius from theories of abnormality, but also of keeping the introspective process free from the charge of a pathological self-absorption.

A variant on this theme emerges in a later study of autobiography, P. Mansell Jones's essay 'The Paradox of Literary Introspection', published in the *London Mercury* in 1935. In a reversal of Burr's arguments, Mansell Jones argues both that the introspective process is allied to neurotic illness and morbidity, and that the majority of readers rightly prefer the memoirs of men of action to the autobiographies of self-analysts. Whereas Burr is critical of the 'objective' autobiographer who is so preoccupied with dates, events and occurrences that he neglects the 'inner Self', in Mansell Jones's account, introspective autobiographers 'neglect externals to concentrate on their minds and motives'.

> It is difficult to evade the category of an 'introspective type', whether we think of such a type as the sporadic emergence of a rare species or as produced and moulded by circumstances operating on more favourable predispositions. The introspective is not a hero or a man of action; he is not a 'genius', except perhaps posthumously, and he is never a success . . . as a man judged by ordinary standards, he is in danger not so much of appearing abnormal as of being thought *sub*normal – less than the average in application and adaption, feeble with men, incompetent with women, a bungler at 'life'.[27]

Mansell Jones's choice of French writers to illustrate his argument – these include Montaigne, Senancour and Baudelaire – demonstrates a characteristic British dismissiveness towards the French, predicated on a sense of the sentimentality and effeminacy of the *journal intime*; this is a recurrent theme in autobiographical criticism from the nineteenth century onwards.

Mansell Jones states that we have no choice but to draw our laws of human nature from morbid, introspective individuals, when we would rather construct an image of human nature from the 'inner selves' of men of action; but they are too involved with life to sit around navel-gazing or investigating their states of consciousness. He asks whether the 'inner self' is in any case an adequate guide to human nature, and, indeed, if the injunction to 'know thyself' is a wise one: 'The important question is whether what we look like from within is what we really are – whether in the last resort we are likely to know ourselves otherwise than as an engrossing or debilitated function' [p. 450].

The claim that autobiography is better 'performed' by men of action than by men of thought reverses the categories of a number of the critics discussed previously. Mansell Jones's image of the neuraesthenic autobiographer, however, echoes that of the aetiolated self critiqued by, for example, Edith Simcox, although without the context of historical 'stages' and thus of cultural 'decline'. The recurrence of this image throughout discussions of autobiography indicates a need to discriminate between the kinds and degrees of self-analysis and 'interiority'. But the metaphors used to describe the inner self in Romantic, and later, psychoanalytic theories – for example, the haunted house[28] – with their Gothic resonances, suggest that this self is perceived as never wholly free from the taint of a morbid pathology, even when the journey into the interior is viewed as necessary or desirable.

To the problems of autobiographical 'vanity', and now introspection, one should add the concern over the exhibitionism of the autobiographer. Of course, introspectionism and exhibitionism could be viewed as two sides of the same coin: it is significant that the 'inside out' image is used as a title by a number of autobiographical critics and autobiographers.[29] Autobiographical exhibitionism is the theme of a somewhat earlier essay, W. A. Gill's 'The Nude in Autobiography' (1907), which takes as its focus Rousseau's *Confessions*.[30] 'The nude' of the title refers, by analogy, to the disclosure of those facts of a life 'which people generally hide through interest or shame'. Gill asserts that the display of 'the naked truth' has come to be expected of the autobiographer, but that, as argued in the previous essay discussed, such revelations may not in fact contribute to the most comprehensive autobiographical portrayal of self: 'the nude has a peculiar and perhaps incalculable faculty of destroying proportion' [p. 74]. Its 'innate protrusiveness' destroys the proportions of the whole. Gill emphasises that autobiographies are 'works of art', and thus subject to the requirements of artistic unity and balance. Like Mansell Jones, Gill ends on a note of scepticism about the value of autobiography 'as a means of revealing a personality' and, indeed, about the idea that we know ourselves better than others do, by suggesting that the involuntary disclosure of self through behaviour is more 'revealing' than conscious autobiographical self-display:

> In life we do not get our clearest insight about a man when he is telling us about himself, but when we see him acting without any thought of us. More can be learned in this kind of overhearing than by hearing . . . and it is hardly a paradox to say that he who is least autobiographical will be more so. [p. 79]

One recurrent theme in auto/biographical discourse is the use of body images to describe auto/biographical presentations. The spatial metaphors used to figure psychic 'interiority' seem to lead inevitably to an image of the interior of the body, turned 'inside out' in an act of self-display. One curious aspect of Gill's essay is that he approaches the question of the mind/body relationship in a quasi-scientific fashion, while failing to connect his statements on this topic with his own sexual and corporeal metaphors. Thus he writes, albeit with a degree of irony, that 'an autobiography which presented a full, scientific history of a body parallel to that of a mind, and demonstrated the correlation between the two at every step, would be of supreme utility'. However, 'the comprehension of psycho-physical contacts has not yet reached that stage of minuteness; far from it' [p. 77].[31]

It is unclear how Gill is imagining such a history, but the mind/body theme is of some importance in autobiographical criticism. After all, the move unreflectively made from text to life or mind is a problematic one, which involves a transposition from one sphere to another. The metaphors employed to gloss this transposition reveal the difficulties of the enterprise, and a residual uncertainty, central to the philosophy of mind, about how far the self is to be defined in corporeal or mental terms. (Hence the way in which self-analysis is sometimes conflated with self-dissection.) And in a number of critical discussions, concern with the exposure of the sexualised body – in Rousseau's case, both metaphorical and literal[32] – is tied into criticisms of an 'unseemly' self-display, thus displacing the question of what constitutes identity in the first place.

* * *

The project of mapping psycho-physical parallelism in autobiographical discourse now seems absurdly dated, and psychoanalysis, despite Freud's own neurological interests, has emphatically shifted the debates to issues of fantasy, the complexities of retrospection and narrative structure. One largely neglected autobiographical text which invokes a materialist model of mind is H. G. Wells's *Experiment in Autobiography*.[33] Wells defines his autobiography, begun in 1932 and published in 1934, as the history of a brain, and emphasises that it 'is not an apology for a life but a research into its nature'. The 'experiment' of the title pushes the concept of experience into its associated meaning as scientific experiment, and Wells repeatedly describes his project in the terms of autopsy and dissection – 'as I dissect the dead rabbit of my former self' [p. 424]. Experiment also takes on the broader meaning of experimentation or experimentalism in ordinary life (Wells's unconventional sexual life was notorious), as well as a degree of unfinishedness in the development of the human species and of human relationships: 'We are too preoccupied and too experimental to give ourselves freely to other people, and in the end other people fail to give themselves fully to us' [pp. 22–3].

A substantial part of the two-volume autobiography is given over to Wells's experience of a scientific education, and the text should be read in part as an attempt to redefine the substance of education (or indeed *Bildung*) in ways appropriate to a new scientific age. In this sense he is redefining the nature of autobiography as a history of the individual in ways which correspond to the demands of the (scientific) researchers who use auto/biography as data: 'a biography', Wells writes, 'should be a dissection or a demonstration of how a particular human being was made and worked' [p. 25]. He also emphasises that his story is both personal and representative 'of my sort and my time. An autobiography is the story of the contacts of a mind and a world' [p. 28].

> And now, having conveyed to you some idea of the quality and defects of the grey matter of that organized mass of phosphorized fat and connective tissue which is, so to speak, the hero of the piece, and having displayed the *personas* or, if you will, the vanity which now dominates its imaginations, I will try to tell you how in this particular receiving apparatus the picture of its universe was built up, what it did and failed to do with the body it controlled and what the thronging impressions and reactions that constituted its life amounted to. [p. 37]

Additionally, for Wells, autobiography becomes the means of bridging the personal and the collective. He emphasises that his is a 'sample life' and that, although contingency played a large part, it took its shape and meaning from broader historical forces and social changes. In the last section of the autobiography, 'The Idea of a Planned World', Wells presents his life as part of a larger whole and, as his influence increased, a shaping force upon that whole. 'My individual life is a participating unit in this multitudinous brain-life, the mind of the species.' The trajectory described by the autobiography is thus a move from origins in the family unit to broader and broader forms of association. The function of writing the autobiography, which was substantially, Wells begins by saying, a form of solace, through a recapitulation of the past and an exploration of former selves, is transmuted into a writing of the self into the world.

Wells's 'experiment' is also a play with generic form. In the autobiography he writes:

> Who would read a novel if we were permitted to write biography – all out?
> Here in this autobiography I am still experimenting – though still very
> mildly, with biographical and auto-biographical matter. Although it has
> many restraints, which are from the artistic point of view vexatious, I still
> find it so much more real and interesting and satisfying that I doubt if I
> shall ever again turn back towards The Novel. [p. 503]

Earlier in his career, Wells had nominated the novel, and specifically
the Utopia, as the form which would best combine science and art,
and would act as the basis for, in Wolf Lepenies's words, 'a sociology
conceived of as literature'.[34] Lepenies argues that the hostility of the
Fabian sociologists Sidney and Beatrice Webb to H. G. Wells was
that 'he constituted in himself a treaty between a highly successful
novelist and a natural scientist and thus forewent the mediation of
sociology' [p. 189]. Lepenies places these disputes in the context of
what came to be known in Britain as the 'two cultures' debates, the
culmination of the border disputes between literature and science
that run throughout nineteenth- and twentieth-century intellectual
life.[35]

   Autobiographies play a significant role in this struggle, and in those
of John Stuart Mill, T. H. Huxley and Charles Darwin we see, in
various ways, how science is thematised through its opposition to
literature, represented as subjective experience. Mill, in his autobiography, represents his spiritual and intellectual crises as caused by
an overscientisation of his thought, and cured by immersion in a
culture of feeling to which literature is central and in which the
feminine genius of Harriet Taylor plays a crucial role. By contrast,
Darwin and Huxley, as Regenia Gagnier argues, represent themselves in their autobiographical writings in the 'character of the
objective scientist, whose *vita* or "life" consists of scientific *res gestae*
approved by one's colleagues in science'. Both Darwin and Huxley
drew contrasts between scientific and literary thought, to the benefit
of science, and 'denied themselves as subjective agents in order to
speak for objective Truth. . . . More than anything, this banishment
of the individual subject lent to science its prodigious claim to speak
for "us"'.[36]

   The positioning of autobiography also shares something of the
ambiguity of sociology as a discipline in its early formation, poised

between the registration of fact and laws of society, and the subjective experiences of the researcher and his or her subjects. The tension in sociology between descriptive science and first-hand experience runs throughout the Webbs' sociological work and emerges, in its most interesting form, in Beatrice Webb's diaries, some of the materials of which she incorporated into her autobiographies, in particular *My Apprenticeship*.[37] Lepenies states that, for Webb, 'the autobiography had become a species of compromise through which she could unite her scientific and her literary inclinations' [p. 144]. Webb herself wrote at the opening of *My Apprenticeship*:

> I have neither the desire nor the intention of writing autobiography. Yet the very subject matter of my science is society; its main instrument is social intercourse: thus I can hardly leave out of the picture the experience I had gathered, not deliberately as a scientific work, but casually as a child, unmarried woman, wife and citizen. For the sociologist, unlike the physicist, chemist and biologist, is in a quite unique manner the creature of his environment. [p. 17]

Webb's autobiography, as her diaries make clear, was the realisation of her desire, unfulfilled in the sociological works she wrote jointly with Sidney Webb, to speak in 'my own words and sentences'. In the opening paragraphs of the autobiography, however, she justifies the enterprise by its value in alerting readers of her sociological work to 'the inevitable bias' which the sociologist brings to his or her work as a result of specific class and cultural determinations, 'a bias which ought to be known to the student of his work so that it may be adequately discounted' [pp. 17–18]. Yet bias, of course, is thus made identical with experience, and despite Webb's self-effacing gestures here, experience *makes* her text.

Autobiography as a genre itself lies on the border or boundary between science and literary representations, objective and subjective orientations, experiment and experience. The question of auto/biographical discourse as fact or fiction, referential or non-referential language, maps on to I. A. Richards's distinction between the languages of science and literature.[38] Early twentieth-century critics seek to claim autobiography as material for the scientist and not the bellettrist; autobiography becomes, for its practitioners, the mediating term between philosophy and experience and then between the sciences (natural and social), and the literary. Self-analysis shifts from a spiritual context (which literature inherits, when its function becomes defined as culture's compensation in the face of religious doubt) to a scientific and positivist function. Experience and experiment, biography and biology, are alternately allied and polarised.

* * *

The recognition of this interplay between science and literature and of the fact that, as Gagnier points out, the construction of the 'scientific' perspective is also a discursive strategy, provides a further reason, if one were needed, for avoiding any simple distinction between 'literary' and 'non-literary' autobiography. There has been a tendency in autobiographical criticism to equate 'literary' auto-biography as the autobiography of a professional writer with auto-biography as an art-form – it being assumed that the professional writer will produce a superior form of autobiography. In addition, a number of critics, for example Brian Finney in *The Inner Eye* (1985),[39] relegate the autobiographies of non-literary figures to the categories of memoirs and reminiscences, conceptualised as lesser forms. The higher valuation of the 'subjective' autobiography is in part a result of the literary-critical view that 'history' involves an appeal to the realms of fact, data and verification, the 'scientific' pole of language. The influence of I. A. Richards is implicit here, in the suggestion that 'literary' autobiography is not a domain of factual truth or at least, in Finney's words, that the truths it reveals 'are broader and more complex than sheer actual veracity' [p. 44]. In Richards's terminology, it is non-referential. Thus science/history has traditionally been seen by autobiographical critics as the opposite pole of poetry/literature/autobiography.

In his distinction between verifiable and non-verifiable knowledge, Richards develops a role for art as 'pseudo-statement', determined as 'a form of words whose scientific truth or falsity is irrelevant to the purpose in hand'. The memoirs/autobiography distinction thus repeats a science/poetry opposition, and whereas memoirs are seen to employ the referential dimension of language, autobiography uses the emotive dimension. Following Richards, critics suggest that memoirs/history make statements, autobiography/poetry 'pseudo-statements'. In Finney's account, as in those of a number of auto-biographical critics, true autobiography is perceived to employ the principles of internal verification, order and harmony, the organic nature of the whole. 'Hybrid' forms are rejected or devalued. Memoirs, letters and diaries are seen as both closer to referential language functions and lacking the single 'inner meaning' of inter-nally coherent, non-referential and non-verifiable forms. These views have only recently been challenged, primarily in the work of feminist critics, who have pointed to the historical and cultural centrality for women of 'private' forms of life-writing, including letters, diaries and memoirs, and have begun to revalue these forms.

* * *

The image of scientificity which pervades many of the critical posi-tions discussed in this chapter is one which rapidly loses its apparent fixity and homogeneity when followed through. It is difficult to take seriously the apparent precision given to the notion of 'genius' by the concept of intelligence-quotient or the length of a *DNB* entry – though the historical connections between eugenics and the con-struction of genealogies of great men, to which developments in biographical method contributed, are of considerable interest. Burr's conception of the advance of autobiography to the positive stage looks similarly implausible, though a variant of it appears in Harold Nicolson's account of the future of biography, written in the 1920s and discussed in the next chapter. If ethology (in its nineteenth-century sense of the science of formation of character) and what came to be known as characterology in the early twentieth century in the work of Weininger and others have ceased to exist as separate sciences, the idea that autobiography might contribute to a somewhat less systematic reflection on character survives in literary discourse, in which the autobiographies of creative writers have often been used as data on which to ground more universal claims. This can be contrasted with more recent work in which literary identity or sub-jectivity, and indeed other identities and subjectivities, are treated more historically and in a way which is attentive to differences of class, gender and culture. Finally, Wells's gestural physicalism is in fact of less significance than his contribution to a possible set of models for the interrelation of genres and knowledges, scientific and literary, in which a concept of autobiography as a Utopian mode may be a particularly fruitful line for autobiographical theory to pursue.

A more attractive, if controversial, approach to the scientific study of the mind, and one which gives a central place to categories of memory and narrative, is found in Freudian theory. Clearly this is not the place for a substantial discussion of the Freudian *oeuvre*, but of particular interest to the present discussion is Freud's project, and more broadly the project of psychoanalysis, of turning autobiography into science.

There is a sense in which psychoanalysis is founded on the work of autobiography. Many of Freud's most significant 'discoveries' were based on his own dreams, memories and reflections. These include the workings of screen memory (in which one memory 'covers up' another, more significant one, and which has such radical implications for autobiographical memory), the Oedipus complex, the repetition–compulsion (the child who plays 'fort-da' with the spool is Freud's grandson, the child of his soon-to-die daughter Sophie).[40] *The Interpretation of Dreams*, which contains accounts of many of Freud's own dreams and which, he writes, was written as a response to his father's death, is held to be Freud's 'true' autobiography, rather than *An Autobiographical Study*, defined by Michel Neyraut as 'peri-autography', an account of the origins and development of a professional or intellectual career.[41] Jacques Derrida poses a 'simplified' question about the relationship between Freud's 'autobiography' and psychoanalytic theory: 'How can an autobiographical writing, in the abyss of an unterminated self-analysis, give to a world wide institution *its* birth?'[42]

Freud also wrote about autobiographies. His 'Psycho-Analytic Notes upon an Autobiographical Account of a Case of Paranoia' is an analysis of Judge Schreber's *Memoirs of my Nervous Illness*.[43] He analysed autobiographical fragments by Leonardo da Vinci and Goethe, using Goethe's 'Childhood Memory' (of throwing all the household crockery out of the window) to illustrate the more general response of children to the births and deaths of siblings.[44] The ultimate meaning Freud draws from Goethe's example is a 'train of thought' which runs through the child's mind in this form: 'I was a child of fortune . . . destiny removed my brother, so that I did not have to share my mother's love with him.' Freud comments on the confidence such a feeling gives, which often brings success in life with it:

'Goethe might well have given some such heading to his autobiography as: "My strength has its roots in my relation to my
mother".'[45] We might contrast this with Freud's accounts of his
response to his father's exasperated claim, after the infant Sigmund
had urinated in his parents' bedroom: 'The boy will come to nothing.'[46] A discourse about 'Great Men', with its attendant celebration
of ambition and success, is combined with an analysis of the child's
relationship to its parents and to 'primitive scenes' experienced by the
child.

In his study of Leonardo, Freud formulated a theory of
psychoanalytic biography or 'pathography'. He explores most
biographers' refusal to analyse their subjects' 'sexual activity or sexual
individuality' as a result of their idealisations of their heroes, who take
on the inflated dimensions of the child's conception of its father.[47] It
goes without saying that the model here is of biography as an affair
between men. Freud also raises issues of debunking and idealisation
which are particularly important in relation to the 'new biography',
which is the topic of my next chapter. Edmund Gosse and Lytton
Strachey, for example, could be read as acting out precisely these
structures through the biographies of fathers, literal or symbolic.

The Famous 'Wednesday night meetings' in Freud's office, beginning in 1902 and continued in the Psychoanalytic Society of Vienna,
treated such questions as incest, symbolism and myth. As Michel de
Certeau writes, 'the analyses that were produced diverted
psychoanalytic narrative from the "case study" toward biography,
culminating in the "psychological portrait" of Woodrow Wilson, a
joint effort by Freud and William Bullitt'.[48] He also explores the ways
in which Freud's relationship to his disciples inflected the theory
produced, 'which oscillates between the biographical facts that
fragment it and mythic representations that disguise the conditions
governing its production' [p. 9]. Topics of the Wednesday meetings
also included the work and lives of Lenau, Wedekind, Jean-Paul
Richter and Kleist. It was at one of these seminars that Freud
presented his paper on Leonardo (1909). De Certeau interprets the
psychobiography, and the new form of 'case history', as an important
form of critique of the bourgeois individual: 'even if social pressures
can lead it to encomiums in defense of the individual, psychoanalytic
biography is in principle a form of self-critique and its narrativity is an
anti-mythic force' [p. 15]. He elaborates on this in a second essay:
Freud reverses one by one Kantian affirmations of the rights and

obligations of an enlightened consciousness. 'In his analysis, the "adult" appears to be defined by his "minority"; knowledge, by desire mechanisms; liberty, by the law of the unconscious; progress, by originary events' [p. 24].

Numerous commentators on Freud's work have analysed the 'birth' of psychoanalysis as a form of conversion to literature. In his *Studies on Hysteria*, Freud described his responses to the fact that his case-histories read like novels:

> The fact is that local diagnosis and electrical reactions lead nowhere in the study of hysteria, whereas a detailed description of mental processes such as we are accustomed to find in the works of imaginative writers enables me, with the use of a few psychological formulas, to obtain at least some kind of insight into the course of that affection.[49]

In other contexts, he expresses indebtedness to 'poets and novelists' who know, 'of heaven and earth, more than our scholarly knowledge would dream of ': 'the novelist has always preceded the scientist'.

The 'conversion', however, is neither simple nor absolute. In his case-history 'Dora', Freud insists that he is writing science and not literature, constructing some curious oppositions between the 'man of letters' and the 'medical man':

> I must now turn to consider a further complication to which I should certainly give no space if I were a man of letters engaged upon the creation of a mental state like this for a short story, instead of being a medical man engaged upon its dissection. The element to which I must now allude can only serve to obscure and efface the outlines of the fine poetic conflict which we have been able to ascribe to Dora. This element would rightly fall a sacrifice to the censorship of a writer, for he, after all, simplifies and abstracts when he appears in the character of a psychologist. But in the world of reality, which I am trying to depict here, a complication of motives, an accumulation and conjunction of mental activities – in a word, overdetermination – is the rule.[50]

The hypothetical man of letters, Stephen Marcus writes, 'is nothing but a straw man; and when Freud in apparent contrast represents himself and his own activities, he is truly representing how a genuine creative writer writes'.[51] In his rich and detailed reading of 'Dora', Marcus places Freud's text in the context of literary modernism and argues that 'Freud's case histories are a new form of literature – they are creative narratives that include their own analysis and interpretation' [p. 81]. Placing the case history so firmly within the sphere of the literary, however, Marcus perhaps underplays the tensions that remain between the definitions and institutions of science, literature and history, and between the fictional and the referential. The 'literary' or poetic, for example, can represent both the undoing of any claims to scientific or historical status, or it can stand for unimpeachable cultural value, making, and substantiating, its own claims to historicity and truth. De Certeau reads Freud's 'manoeuvres' in the light of Freud's awareness of the instability of institutional and disciplinary legitimation: 'At times he confesses himself to be a novelist, a way of marking his sensitivity to what he knows of the semblance the institution adds to the text. At times he prevails upon his academic position as professor and works to remain "Master" of "his community" ' [p. 33]. The legacy of Freud's strategies and defences, which include the mixing and crossing of the forms and truth-claims of myth, literature, fiction, science and history, is a new logic of these forms of knowledge and belief.

Notes

1 See, for example, the work of F. W. H. Myers, one of the founders of the Society for Psychical Research in 1882. Myers, and other theorists of creativity and psychic life, are discussed in Henri F. Ellenberger, *The Discovery of the Unconscious: The History and Evolution of Dynamic Psychiatry* (New York: Basic Books, 1970).

2 *Edinburgh Review*, 'Famous Autobiographies', 214 (1911), 331–56.

3 A. O. Prickard, *Autobiography* (London: Rivingtons, 1866), p. 6.

4 Rousseau, Stephen asserts, is both introverted and emotional, and corresponds to the 'melancholic' type, while in Cellini we find the 'choleric' – extraverted and emotional.

5 Havelock Ellis, *A Study of British Genius* (London: Constable and Co., 1927).

6 Havelock Ellis, 'An Open Letter to Biographers', in 'Views and Reviews', 1, reprinted in *Selected Essays* (London: Dent, 1936).

7 In addition to this naturalistic account, the author of 'Famous Autobiographies' puts forward a historicist account of varying social and historical conditions upon which the recognition of genius is contingent. He thus claims that there are also historical circumstances bringing natural development into accord with the social machine.

8 Sidney Lee, 'A Statistical Account', *Dictionary of National Biography*, p. lxxviii.

9 For an interesting discussion of statistical approaches to 'genius', see Christine Battersby, *Gender and Genius: Towards a Feminist Aesthetics*

(London: The Women's Press, 1989), pp. 124–33.

10 Lewis M. Terman, Preface to Catherine Cox, *The Early Mental Traits of Three Hundred Geniuses*, Volume II of *Genetic Studies of Genius* (Stanford University Press, 1927).

11 Sidney Lee, *Principles of Biography* (Cambridge University Press, 1911), p. 10.

12 *Ibid.* p. 11.

13 Edmund Gosse, 'The Custom of Biography', *Anglo-Saxon Review* VIII (March 1901), 206.

14 Edwin Paxton Hood, *The Uses of Biography: romantic, philosophic, and didactic* (London: Partridge and Oakley, 1852), p. 13.

15 See, for example, 'The Study of Individuals (Individuology) and their Natural Groupings (Sociology)', in *Sociological Papers*, vol. III (London: Macmillan, 1907). Tayler also wrote a study of autobiography entitled *The Writing of Autobiography and Biography* (Hull: Printed for the author, 1926).

16 Tayler, 'The Study of Individuals', p. 112.

17 Otto Weininger, *Sex and Character* (London: Heinemann; New York: Putnam, 1906); this is a translation of the sixth German edition of *Geschlecht und Charakter*, first published in 1903.

18 Sander Gilman, *Jewish Self-Hatred: Anti-Semitism and the Hidden Language of the Jew*, (Baltimore: Johns Hopkins University Press, 1986). See also David Abrahamsen, *The Mind and Death of a Genius* (New York: Columbia University Press, 1946), and Jacques Le Rider, *Le Cas Otto Weininger: racines de l'anti-féminisme et de l'antisémitisme* (Paris: Presses Universitaires de France, 1982) and *Modernité Viennoise et crises de l'identité* (Paris: Presses Universitaires de France, 1990).

19 See Arthur Schopenhauer, 'On Women', in *Studies in Pessimism* (London: Swan Sonnenschein and Co., 1891), pp. 105–23.

20 Anna Robeson Burr, *The Autobiography: A Critical and Comparative Study* (Boston: Houghton Mifflin, 1909). Burr, who was born in Philadelphia in 1873, followed *The Autobiography* with *Religious Confessions and Confessants* (1914), but the bulk of her work, primarily fiction, did not appear until the 1920s and 1930s. There is little to suggest why Burr should have made the study of autobiography the topic of her first book, before moving on to fiction writing in her later years. She emphasises the novelty of her project (although her approaches are in many instances similar to those of the nineteenth-century critics discussed in the previous chapter) and refers very briefly and in footnotes to the publication of Georg Misch's work, asserting that the first volume of *Geschichte der Autobiographie* (1907) appeared after *The Autobiography* had been written. She thus holds on to the claim to be the writer of the first book on the topic of autobiography, or more particularly 'the rise and tendency of self-study' and 'the subjective trend in literature'. Burr thus becomes the first of many writers on autobiography to claim that their particular approach to the topic is the filling of a critical gap.

21 William C. Spengemann, *The Forms of Autobiography: Episodes in the History of a Literary Genre* (New Haven and London: Yale University Press, 1980), p. 187.

22 *Ibid.* p. 188.

23 See Burr, *The Autobiography*, p. 92, on William James and 'introspective observation'.

24 It should be noted, however, that Burr was working against the tenor of early twentieth-century American psychology in seeking to understand subjectivity and introspection through the categories of scientific psychology, at a time when psychology was being defined as 'the science of behaviour', marking the beginnings of the process 'whereby behaviourism sought to expunge introspection' (Peter Manicas, *A History and Philosophy of the Social Sciences* (Oxford: Blackwell, 1987), p. 236).

25 Cesare Lombroso, *The Man of Genius* (London and Felling-on-Tyne: Walter Scott Publishing Co., 1905), p. 175.

26 Ernst Kretschmer, *The Psychology of Men of Genius* (London: Kegan Paul, Trench, Trubner and Co. Ltd, 1931), p. 6.

27 P. Mansell Jones, 'The Paradox of Literary Introspection', *The London Mercury* 32 (1935), 446–50.

28 See Tayler, *The Writing of Autobiography*, pp. 10–11: 'Biography is only successful when it records and makes real to the reader an invisible wraith-like occupant who moves in ghostly manner, and by material signals reveals the spirit's characteristics.'

29 See E. Stuart Bates, *Inside Out: An Introduction to Autobiography*, 2 vols. (Oxford: Blackwell, 1936/37); Adrian Stokes's autobiography, *Inside Out*, in *Critical Writings of Adrian Stokes* (London: Thames and Hudson, 1978), vol. 2; and Robert Creeley, *Inside Out: Notes on the Autobiographical Mode* (discussed in John Martone, 'Augustine's Fate', *Southern Review*, 23, 3 (July 1987), 597–8.

30 W. A. Gill, 'The Nude in Autobiography', *The Atlantic Monthly*, 99 (1907), pp. 71–9.

31 Charles Rycroft speculates in a similar way in 'On Autobiography', in his *Psychoanalysis and Beyond* (London: Chatto and Windus, 1985), p. 195. 'Autobiographies are also unconsciously selective in a way that probably only doctors and psychoanalysts notice; they underestimate the part played by biological processes in the story of one's life. If anyone were to write a psychosomatic autobiography, giving equal weight to soma and psyche, not only would bodily functions play a larger role than existing autobiographical conventions allow them, but a quite different set of patterns and connections would emerge.'

32 I refer to Rousseau's account of his sexual 'exhibitionism' – see, for example, the opening of Book Three of *The Confessions*.

33 H. G. Wells, *Experiment in Autobiography: Discoveries and Conclusions of a Very Ordinary Brain since 1866*, 2 vols. (London: Gollancz, 1934).

34 Wolf Lepenies, *Between Literature and Science: The Rise of Sociology* (Cambridge University Press, 1988), pp. 145–54 *passim*.

35 The 'two cultures' debate refers here to the debate between C. P. Snow and F. R. Leavis. On 6 October 1956, Snow published an article entitled 'The Two Cultures' in the *New Statesman*; he expanded this when he was invited to give the Rede Lecture in Cambridge, and it was published as *The Two Cultures and the Scientific Revolution* [The Rede Lectrure, 1959] (Cambridge University Press, 1959). Snow argued, as a matter of regret, that the cultures

of the scientist and the literary intellectual had become entirely oppositional, and that men of letters were particularly culpable because they had turned away from ethical questions. Leavis attacked Snow's arguments, and in particular his claims to an understanding of literature and literary culture in *The Two Cultures: The Significance of C. P. Snow. Being the Richmond Lecture, 1962* (London: Chatto and Windus, 1962).

36 Regenia Gagnier, *Subjectivities: A History of Self-Representation in Britain* (Oxford and New York: Oxford University Press, 1991), p. 265.

37 Beatrice Webb, *My Apprenticeship*, 2 vols. (London: Penguin, 1938).

38 See I. A. Richards, *Poetries and Sciences. A Reissue of Science and Poetry* (1926) (London: Routledge and Kegan Paul, 1970).

39 Brian Finney, *The Inner I: British Literary Autobiography of the Twentieth Century* (London: Faber, 1985).

40 See 'Screen Memories' (1899), *Standard Edition* (referred to henceforth as *SE*) Vol. III, pp. 301–22, and pp. 453–53 of *The Psychopathology of Everyday Life*, *SE* Vol. VI; *Beyond the Pleasure Principle* (1920), *SE* Vol. XVIII.

41 Michel Neyraut, 'De l'Autobiographie', in M. Neyraut *et al.*, *L'Autobiographie. VIes Rencontres psychanalytiques d'Aix-en-Provence, 1987* (Paris: Les Belles Lettres, 1988), pp. 32–3. The term 'periautography', coined in the early 1700s, is used for short intellectual autobiographies which, like Vico's *Life* of 1728 and Freud's *An Autobiographical Study* (1925), were commissioned for collective works on eminent writers, scientists, etc. Freud's study appeared, as James Strachey points out in his Note to the English translation, in a collection on contemporary medical specialists. The focus on the professional, rather than the personal lives of the contributors, suggests that such a work 'would . . . be more accurately described (if the word existed) as an "auto-ergography" ' (Sigmund Freud, *An Autobiographical Study* (1925), trans. James Strachey (London: Hogarth Press, 1936), p.9).

42 Jacques Derrida, 'To Speculate – on "Freud" ', in *A Derrida Reader: Between the Blinds*, ed. Peggy Kamuf (Hemel Hempstead: Harvester Wheatsheaf, 1991), p. 531.

43 Sigmund Freud, 'Psycho-Analytic Notes on an Autobiographical Account of a Case of Paranoia (Dementia Paranoides) (Schreber)' (1911), in *SE* XII, 1–82 and in Penguin Freud Library (Harmondsworth: Penguin) (henceforth PFL) 9, *Case Histories*, 2, 131–223.

44 Sigmund Freud, 'A Childhood Recollection from *Dichtung und Wahrheit*' (1917), in *SE* XVII, 145–57; and PFL 14, 321–35.

45 *SE* XVII, 156; PFL 14, 333.

46 Sigmund Freud, *The Interpretation of Dreams* (1900), in *SE* IV, 216; PFL 4, 309.

47 Sigmund Freud, 'Leonardo da Vinci and a Memory of his Childhood' (1910), in *SE* XI, 59–60; PFL, 14, 158.

48 Michel de Certeau, 'Psychoanalysis and its History', in *Heterologies: Discourse on the Other* (Minneapolis, University of Minnesota Press, 1986), pp. 9–10.

49 Sigmund Freud (with J. Breuer), *Studies on Hysteria* (1895), in *SE* II, 160–1; PFL 3, 231.

50 Sigmund Freud, 'Fragment of an Analysis of a Case of Hysteria' ('Dora')
[1910] (1905), in *SE* VII, 59–60; PFL 8, 94.
51 Stephen Marcus, 'Freud and Dora: Story, History, Case History', in *Freud
and the Culture of Psychoanalysis* (New York: W. W. Norton, 1984), p. 58.

3

Bringing the corpse to life: Woolf, Strachey and the discourse of the 'new biography'

In the early twentieth century in Britain, the desire of the literary 'moderns' to mark their absolute difference from their Victorian predecessors finds one expression in the construction of 'the new biography'. Autobiography appears to be of secondary importance in this project, although a number of discussions of autobiography from the first decades of the twentieth century are of interest. Biography is partially figured, in the discourse of 'the new biography', as an autobiographical project. The biographer is perceived by a number of critics and practitioners of biography not as a neutral, objective reporter, but as having an active, and, in psychoanalytic terms, even a 'transferential' relationship to the biographical subject. In this sense, he/she is said to be in part narrating his/her own story, real or fantasised. The biographer's awareness of the complexity of the self is often viewed in this period as a consequence of autobiographical self-awareness, or at least awareness of the difficulty of knowing and grasping the self. 'Consider one's own life', Virginia Woolf wrote in her essay 'The New Biography':

> we can assure ourselves by a very simple experiment that the days of Victorian biography are over. Consider one's own life; pass under review a few years that one has actually lived. Conceive how Lord Morley would have expounded them; how Sir Sidney Lee would have documented them; how strangely all that has been most real in them would have slipped through their fingers.[1]

The failure of Victorian biography, a theme that dominates discussion of the new biography, is shown up here as inadequacy to the felt realities of 'one's own life', to autobiographical consciousness. André Maurois uses the same strategy when arguing that the self is irreducible to a 'scientific' knowledge of its parts; 'Think of your own life', he enjoined the audience of his lectures in 1928, subsequently published as *Aspects of Biography*.[2]

Virginia Woolf appears to have coined the term 'the new biography' in describing experiments in biography in the 1910s and 1920s – in particular, those of her contemporaries Lytton Strachey and Harold Nicolson. Woolf described Nicolson's play with biography and autobiography, real and imaginary portraits, in his *Some People* as the most successful example of the new biographical writing, in part because Nicolson achieves self-portraiture under the guise of biography: 'Each of the supposed subjects holds up in his or her bright diminishing mirror a different reflection of Harold Nicolson . . . It is thus, he would seem to say, in the mirrors of our friends, that we chiefly live.'[3] It was, however, Strachey's *Eminent Victorians* (1918), with its 'debunking', satirical approach to historical figures and its emphasis on biography as an art, in which the selection and shaping of 'facts' is all-important, which was the greater influence by far. Biography was seen, in Richard Altick's words, as 'the literary emblem par excellence of Victorianism, a product faithful to the old era's habit of misapplied and exaggerated hero worship, with all its attendant hypocrisy and evasiveness'.[4] 'The new biography' stood for modernity against the previous century. The significance of Lytton Strachey's *Eminent Victorians* – heralded on its publication as creating a revolution in biography and still seen as marking the break between old and new – is above all that its critique of Victorian values, institutions and 'personalities' is inseparable from its critique of nineteenth-century biographical discourse. In this sense it is an 'emblematic' work.

Strachey's arguments for an aesthetics of biography form part of a larger debate about the disciplinary affiliations of biographical and autobiographical writing in the early twentieth century, with the claims of literature and science being variously argued. Both Strachey's and Virginia Woolf 's experiments in biography place generic and gender identities and boundaries at risk, radically disrupting the concept of the life-course. Woolf 's *Orlando*, in particular, questions the very principles of biographical identity and biological unity, in its narrative of a hero/heroine who lives through several centuries as a man and a woman in turn. It breaks up the fixities on which Leslie Stephen's and Sidney Lee's models of biography depend.

The new biography

Woolf characterises 'the new biography', in her essay of that title, by its more concise form and by a new relationship of equality between biographer and subject; 'he preserves his freedom and his right to independent judgement' [p. 231]. Other commentators focused on the new element of satire, especially as it was introduced by Lytton Strachey in *Eminent Victorians*, and the influence of psychology on an understanding of 'personality'. A focus on the subjective nature of the interpretation of the 'facts' about an individual, and on the necessary shaping and selection that goes into biographical portraiture, led to an emphasis on the aesthetic dimensions of biography and the increasing similarity between the novel and biography. In Woolf's words, the biographer 'chooses; he synthesizes; in short, he has ceased to be the chronicler; he has become an artist' [p. 231]. Much was made of Strachey's technique, for example, of a form of stream-of-consciousness, in which he took phrases from letters and reported conversations and ran them into a representation of the subject's thoughts and feelings. André Maurois defined the biographer's essential task as a search for the thematic unity and harmony of the life he recounts, claiming that this is not an imposed but a natural aesthetic. The life of an individual, he asserts, is 'naturally' made up of motifs and metaphors which constitute its unity. In his highly romanticised biography of Shelley, *Ariel*, Maurois locates a 'water motif' and water imagery; Shelley's life is, in addition, a ' "wonderful natural composition", being grouped around two women, each of [whom] corresponds with a different stage in Shelley's ethical development'.[5] Maurois shares this concept of an essential theme or motif in the subject's life with the so-called 'intuitive biographers', such as Gamaliel Bradford and Emil Ludwig, who believed in the existence of a 'key to character' which illuminates every aspect of the subject's personality and career.[6]

As I have suggested, however, 'the new biography' is defined as much by its reaction against Victorianism as by any positive identity of its own. When Woolf refers to Lord Morley and Sir Sidney Lee (and by implication her father, Sir Leslie Stephen, co-editor with Lee of the monumental *Dictionary of National Biography*) in 'The New Biography', she invokes an image of traditional, conservative, 'Great Men' approaches to lives, literature and history. This homogeneous image of Victorian biography, however, needs a little more unpacking. Morley (editor of the English Men of Letters series from 1877), Lee and Stephen already saw themselves as revivifying biography through their production of brief (or briefer) lives, their rejections of eulogistic biography in favour of greater degrees of candour, and their substitution of analysis and synthesis for the mere accumulation and enumeration of 'facts'. One should also remember that Lee's and Stephen's work on national and 'collective' biography in the *DNB* raises somewhat different questions from those involved in the biography of a single subject. Those responsible for the *DNB* might need to engage with the issue of, for example, the excessive celebration of the 'mediocre' which so vexed nineteenth-century reviewers of full-length biography, but they were unlikely to be as troubled by the issue of intrusion into private and domestic life, which J. A. Froude's biography of Thomas Carlyle had posed in a particularly dramatic way.[7]

It is also worth noting that critics and reviewers from early in the century were expressing very similar criticisms of the expansive, panegyric form of 'Victorian biography' to those of the new biographers. They are scathing about the 'journeyman' approach to biography as a form of extended obituary notice or funerary monument, unremittingly eulogistic in tone. This suggests that Victorian biographical discourse is not as uniform as some critics, the 'new biographers' included, have assumed. More specifically, the Victorian critique of the expansive, eulogistic 'official' biography, intended to immortalise the achievements and virtues of the deceased, may well have been motivated by a concern that too many biographies of purely domestic and familial interest were circulating in the public literary sphere. In other words, there is concern not only with intrusion into the private sphere and the display of the private in public, but also with the inflated publicity given to private lives of little general interest and hence of the encroachment of the private into the public. Where some critics have seen a relatively smooth 'evolution' of the genre towards a greater sophistication, both aesthetically and in terms of openness to previously taboo material, we should rather see the interplay of a variety of different concerns and spheres of literary and other interests.

Monumental metaphors

Both Strachey and Woolf satirise the extent to which biographers, the historians of life, dwell on the death-bed scene. The paradoxical connection between biography and death, and the view that biography should more properly be called thanatography, receives ample

support from the metaphors in which it is couched, with both favourable and unfavourable connotations, by nineteenth- and early
twentieth-century critics. The language of monuments, statuary,
epitaphs, widows, effigies, waxworks and corpses pervades biographical and autobiographical discourse and testifies to the tension
between a posthumous memorialisation of a life and the attempt to
grasp the 'life' as it was lived. The cultural function of biography is,
W. H. Epstein asserts, to turn life into text and text back into life, but
it could be argued that the profusion and confusion of metaphors
relating to modes of life and death signals a breakdown in this system
from the nineteenth century onwards and a far less easy sense of the
relationship between biography as memorial and monuments of
marble and stone than obtains in the seventeenth century.[8] In nine-
teenth- and early twentieth-century discussions, the body of the
biographical subject becomes increasingly prominent, often giving
rise to images of decay and fragmentation. These also bear a curious
relationship to the naked bodies invoked by defenders of biographical
discretion, for whom candour becomes equivalent to stripping bare,
or in the case of autobiography, to self-exposure.

The following passage from a *Blackwood's* review of 1879 is one
example among many of the negative image of biography as a
funerary form:

> If vanity and ambition have inspired many indifferent biographies, the
> partiality of love or friendship has to answer for many more. We are all
> familiar with the emotional mourners who will obtrude the heartfelt
> expressions of their grief and affection into the brief obituary notice in the
> newspaper, which is paid as so many shillings the line. So there are
> sorrowing widows and admiring intimates who seem to consider an
> elaborate memoir of the departed as much *de rigeur* as the tombstone that
> is to commemorate his gifts and virtues.[9]

Edmund Gosse gives a similar account of the 'custom of biography' in an article published in 1901:

> We in England bury our dead under the monstrous catafalque of two
> volumes (crown octavo), and go forth refreshed, as those who have
> performed a rite which is not in itself beautiful, perhaps, but is inevitably
> and eminently decent . . . the 'life' of the deceased begins with the day of
> his death.[10]

Elaborating on the theme of 'sorrowing widows', Gosse states that
'the Widow', 'a generic term for the class of life-writers whose only

claim is that they are "on the spot"', 'is the worst of all the diseases of biography. . . . It is to the Widow that we owe the fact that a very large section of recent biography might pass for an annex to Madame Tussaud's gallery.'[11] (Gosse outlines a brief history, in which English biography is born in 1557 with the publication of George Cavendish's *Life of Cardinal Wolsey* and is led up the false path of hagiography and the production of monster biographies around 1830.) The figure of the Widow, 'the worst of all the diseases of biography', hints at a contempt for the perceived feminisation of the genre – women were seen as commissioning, though not necessarily writing, the autobiographies. It may well also include an implicit reference to Queen Victoria, whose forty-year period of mourning for Prince Albert made 'the widow' one of the central images of Victorian femininity. In his biography of Queen Victoria, Lytton Strachey describes the monumental biography of Albert commissioned by Queen Victoria from Theodore Martin, on whose five volumes Martin laboured for fourteen years:

> The mass of material with which he had to deal was almost incredible, but he was extremely industrious, and he enjoyed throughout the gracious assistance of Her Majesty. . . . In the case of Albert her passion for superlatives reached its height. To have conceived of him as anything short of perfect . . . would have been an unthinkable blasphemy: perfect he was, and perfect he must be shown to have been. . . . By a curious irony an impeccable waxwork had been fixed by the Queen's love in the popular imagination.[12]

Strachey also recounts the story of the erection of the Albert Memorial in London's Kensington Gardens, finally completed in 1872, seven years after its inception. It was this Gothic edifice, the historian R. G. Collingwood claimed in his autobiography, that provoked him into study of the philosophy of history by his inability to understand what could possibly have been in the mind of its architect.[13] The overwhelming scale and detail of the monument (169 life-size figures in the frieze and 16 colossal statues around its base) mirror the voluminous biographies of the nineteenth century, while the massing of sculptures of 'eminent men' in the frieze turns the monument into a concrete counterpart to the *Dictionary of National Biography*.

The 'monumental' aspects of biography were in fact endorsed by Sidney Lee, who, in his *Principles of Biography* (1911) and *The Perspective of Biography* (1917/18), combined his reactions against Vic-

torian biographical panegyric, hero-worship, the 'family' bias and the
'ethical' or didactic bias with an absolute insistence on the commemorative functions of biography and on the requirement that the
subject of significant biography must be a personality of 'magnitude'.
In his account biography is a necessary adjunct to 'concrete'
memorials: 'Biography is not so imposing to the general eye as
pyramids and mausoleums, statues and columns, portraits and
memorial foundations, but it is the *safest* way, as Thomas Fuller
wrote, to protect a memory from oblivion' ('Principles', p. 8); 'Biography is in any case a necessary complement, a protective corollary,
of other forms of commemoration. In its absence the commemorative
purpose, the personal significance, of a surviving portrait, or statue,
or monument, or foundation lacks any certain guarantee of a long life'
('Perspective', p. 7). This view of biography recalls Cotton's
dedicatory poem to Izaak Walton's life of John Donne, in which the
biography is described as a more 'faithful monument' than the marble
statue of Donne at St Paul's, damaged by the Great Fire.[14]

Lee's definitions of and credos for biography are unequivocally
stated: 'Biography exists to satisfy a natural instinct in man – the
commemorative instinct – the universal desire to keep alive the
memories of those who by character and exploits have distinguished
themselves from the mass of mankind' ('Principles', p. 7). 'An unfit
biographic theme is a career of trivial aim, incomplete, without
magnitude, or of below mediocrity. . . . Death is a part of life and no
man is fit subject for biography till he is dead. . . . The living theme
can at best be a torso, a fragment' ('Principles', p.12). As Suzanne
Raitt notes, 'it seems that the integrity of the living body actually
prevents the body of the biography from taking shape.'[15] In Lee's
account, textual completeness is dependent on the closure of the life
and is imaged by implication as a body whole and complete.

The macabre aspects of this metaphor emerge – knowingly or
otherwise – in Woolf's description of Victorian biography as, in 'The
Art of Biography', 'like the wax figures now preserved in Westminster
Abbey, that were carried in funeral processions through the street –
effigies that have only a smooth superficial likeness to the body in the
coffin'.[16] Here the biographical and the funereal have become so
intermeshed that the biographical subject becomes identical to the
dead, and soon to decompose, body in its coffin, from which effigies
were moulded. The smooth textual effigy – akin to the embalmed
body – is without open orifices, resistant to penetration and, by

implication, interpretation, an image Strachey was to exploit in his biographical writings. In other discussions, including those of Gosse, the wax figures take the form of tailors' or hairdressers' dummies, or commemorative busts. By contrast with Lee, it is the memorialised body that is represented as partial and fragmented, a mere torso, in which the lower body is written out in a representative act of Victorian prudery.

The lives of the obscure

In 'The New Biography', Woolf stresses the newly democratic relationship between the biographer and his subject; 'he is no longer the serious and sympathetic companion, toiling even slavishly in the footsteps of his hero. Whether friend of enemy, admiring or critical, he is an equal' [p. 231]. In her critique of Victorian 'Great Man' biography in 'The Art of Biography', she extends the issue of democracy to 'whether the lives of great men only should be recorded', while still apparently retaining a sense of the need for heroes:

> Is not any one who has lived a life, and left a record of that life, worthy of biography – the failures as well as the successes, the humble as well as the illustrious? And what is greatness? And what smallness? He must revise our standards of merit and set up new heroes for our admiration. [p. 125]

Whereas Lee asserts that the lives of the mediocre conflict with biographic principles, Leslie Stephen, in an essay on 'National Biography', states that the value of collective biography, as represented by the *DNB*, is in the reconstruction of the lives of 'second-rate people':

> The judicious critic is well aware that it is not upon the lives of the great men that the value of the book really depends. It is the second-rate people – the people whose lives have to be reconstructed from obituary notices, or from references in memoirs and collections and letters; or sought in prefaces to posthumous works; or sometimes painfully dug out of collections of manuscripts, and who really become generally accessible through the dictionary alone – that provide the really useful reading. There are numbers of such people whom one first discovers to be really interesting when the scattered materials are for the first time pieced together.[17]

Lee tends to describe the *DNB*, and biography in general, as a national mission, while Stephen's emphasis is on collective biography as a resource, particularly for historians, a gathering-up and recapitulation of previous generations' documentation of individual lives. Stephen's document-based model of history contrasts with Lee's focus on the monuments of the past, in a way which recalls Foucault's distinction between an earlier historiography which 'undertook to "memorize" the *monuments* of the past, (and) transform them into *documents'* and history today, 'which transforms *documents* into *monuments* . . . deploy[ing] a mass of elements that have to be grouped, made relevant, placed in relation to one another to form totalities'.[18] Stephen's would thus appear to be the more 'modern' version of history, although one should note that the 'textual' emphasis in his discussion excludes undocumented lives, including those of individuals who lived and died before the development of biography. Stephen, moreover, may appear less troubled by generic and characterological classifications than Lee, but he is equally concerned with the search for ordering principles. In his account the role of biography is to guide the specialist or general reader through the 'swamp' or 'jungle' of information that accumulates in a society 'in which nothing (is) ever to be forgotten'.[19]

The links between Stephen's and Virginia Woolf's essays on biography and memoirs, particularly her 'Lives of the Obscure', are striking, however, especially given the common perception that Woolf wholly rejected her father's biographical methods. In 'Lives of the Obscure' Woolf exploits the metaphoric relationship between lives and books to the point where the terms collapse into one another; 'the obscure sleep on the walls, slouching against each other as if they were too drowsy to stand upright'. The reader, however, opens up the 'nameless tombstones' and brings the dead to life:

> It is one of the attractions of the unknown, their multitude, their vastness; for, instead of keeping their identity separate, as remarkable people do, they seem to merge·into one another, their very boards and title-pages and frontispieces dissolving, and their innumerable pages melting into continuous years so that we can lie back and look up into the fine mist-like substance of countless lives, and pass unhindered from century to century, from life to life. Scenes detach themselves. We watch groups.[20]

Woolf thus subtly redefines the concept of 'collective biography' away from Lee's definitions of its nationalistic, monumental functions, and towards the group and its interrelations. 'Obscurity' ceases to be a negation, and becomes a medium 'thick with the star dust of innumerable lives', while the dissolution of boundaries is perceived as generative and not degenerative. Woolf also pursues Stephen's hint that (in his terms) 'second-rate lives' are of more interest because they are less documented than those of the 'great' when she writes of the 'lives of the obscure': 'It is so difficult to keep, as we must with highly authenticated people, strictly to the facts. . . . Certain scenes have the fascination which belongs rather to the abundance of fiction than to the sobriety of fact' [p. 123]. The histories Woolf recreates from these lives are eccentric and obscure in their implications: questions remain unanswered and secret stories unresolved. Their oblique relationship to the mainstream is precisely their fascination, although they are not outside history. The 'obscure' – and women form a large part of this category – could also be seen as the repository of a kind of collective memory, in which history is the medium, not the monument.

In an early short story, 'Memoirs of a Novelist', Woolf invents a two-volume 'life and letters' of a fictional Victorian woman writer, Miss Willatt, written by her friend, Miss Linsett.[21] The story is an account of this invented text, in which Virginia Woolf satirises the 'typical' eulogistic Victorian biography. Passing over the larger questions of 'why lives are written' as leading 'to an uncomfortable vagueness of mind', Woolf (or her narrator) narrows her inquiry down 'to ask why the life of Miss Willatt was written, and so to answer the question, who she was'. The biographer, Miss Linsett, gives an account of Miss Willatt's life which blanks out its most interesting event, a possible love affair. 'At this point we can no longer disregard what has been hinted several times: it is clear that one must abandon Miss Linsett altogether, or take the greatest liberties with her text . . . we see only a wax work as it were of Miss Willatt, preserved under glass' [p. 74].

Woolf 's narrator is both fascinated and appalled by Miss Linsett's apparent belief in the pieties she pronounces, pieties wholly at odds with the character of Miss Willett 'read' in her letters and most clearly in her portraits. These 'reveal' her (although this oppositional account, based in part on a physiognomic reading of Miss Willatt's features, must also be open to question) not as a saintly figure but as 'a restless and discontented woman who sought her own happiness rather than other people's' [p. 75]. Her interest increases as her sanctity is undone. Failing to understand her subject and having a 'natural distrust of life', Miss Linsett is more comfortable with the obligatory death-bed scene; '(death) was an end undisturbed by the chance of a fresh beginning' [p. 79].

In this story, Woolf introduces themes subsequently explored in *Orlando* and in a number of her essays, in particular those of the relationship between biographer and subject, in this story both women, and the extent to which conventional biography (and literary naturalism) kills 'life' rather than creating or expressing it. All that is most interesting and subversive about Miss Willatt is suppressed – firstly by Victorian society, which allows no outlet for a potentially rebellious spirit, other than the role of 'lady novelist', and secondly by her biographer, who denies the very existence of this spirit.

Woolf's story is a satire on Victorian hypocrisies represented by and through the Victorian media of biography and the 'lives and letters' form. It raises further questions about the representation of women's lives. Who, after all, is Miss Linsett, and what were the experiences which 'prompted [her] curious view of human life'? Lives intersect with other lives, other stories, although Miss Willatt, when she became a novelist, 'thought it indecent to describe what she had seen' and turned her pen to romantic fiction. Where does a life begin and end? Miss Linsett fills biographical lacunae with historical 'background' – 'praise of Florence Nightingale in the Crimea' – but the reader wants to know about the 'lives of the obscure' who crossed Miss Willatt's path when they came to tea: 'What did they look like, and do, what did they want from Miss Willatt and what did they think of her, in private? – but we shall never know, or hear of them again. They have been rolled into the earth irrecoverably' [p. 78]. The implied question is why these lives have not been granted biographical immortality – or, more cruelly, why one 'little life' rather than another is bound in two quarto volumes.

Woolf's short story reveals some of her complex and ambivalent attitudes towards biographical and autobiographical writings; forms which preserve aspects of past lives which would otherwise dissolve without trace and, in the very act of preservation, destroy the very features which make 'life' into the activity of living. 'Memoirs of a Novelist' both creates a space for women's culture and history and hints at its limitations:

> George Eliot and Charlotte Bronte between them must share the parentage of many novels at this period, for they disclosed the secret that the precious stuff of which books are made lies all about one, in drawing-rooms and kitchens where women live, and accumulates with every tick of the clock. [p. 75]

The story, as I have suggested, points up the 'littleness' of the lives described – a feature of her writing which some of her critics have seen as Woolf's patronising of the 'obscure' whom she also seeks to rescue from oblivion.

More problematic, perhaps, is Woolf's response to a collection of working-class women's autobiographies, 'Memories of a Working Women's Guild' (1930).[22] Woolf's discussion of the narratives has raised a number of questions about the middle-class woman writer's relationship to working women's life-histories. She suggests that, judged from the position of the literary critic – and her Preface is ambiguous about her own relationship to this position – the working women's texts cannot be literature – lacking 'detachment and imaginative breadth, even as the women themselves lacked variety and play of feature. Here are no reflections, he might object, no view of life as a whole and no attempt to enter into the lives of other people.' Where Woolf does locate the 'literary' is in the use of certain vivid phrases and descriptions which she relates to a tradition of literary realism – 'the words are simple but it is difficult to see how they could say more'. But whereas Woolf states, as quoted above, that the middle-class lives she uncovers open up fictional possibilities and incite the creation of stories, the working women are placed squarely in the context of brute fact: 'the imagination is largely the child of the flesh'.

Purity and danger

In 1927, the year prior to Orlando's publication, the Woolfs' Hogarth Press published Harold Nicolson's *The Development of English Biography*.[23] Nicolson provides both a chronological account of English biography from the fifth century to the present, and a 'theoretical' approach to the definition of 'pure' biography. While Nicolson is dismissive of Lee's writings on biography, and in particular his espousal of the 'commemorative' aspects of the genre, which Nicolson views as biography's false start and the reason for its late development, he shares with Lee both an emphasis on a national tradition of biography and a desire to 'isolate' biography from its contaminating influences and affiliations. Somewhat overplaying metaphors of heritage and horticulture, perhaps in order to retain some ironic distance from his linear historical narrative, Nicolson writes an account in which the development of biography rises and falls in proportion to the extent to which it asserts itself via a 'native realist' tradition (Boswell's *Johnson* is, as ever, the exemplar) or succumbs to classical and French imports in the shape of typologies and characterologies, Theophrastus and La Bruyère. 'Pure' biography is distinguished from 'impure' by its emphasis on historical truth and skilful construction, while 'impure' biography comes about as a result of 'either an undue desire to celebrate the dead, or a purpose extraneous to the work itself, or an undue subjectivity on the part of the biographer' [p. 10]. 'Truth' is a constant desideratum – 'the veracity of complete and accurate portraiture' [p. 11] – and Nicolson is dismissive of autobiographical writing on the grounds that the wholly 'objective' approach to personality required for 'true' biography cannot, or has not yet, been attained in autobiographical writing: 'creative biography necessitates something more than diagnosis: it necessitates a scientific autopsy; and this sense of a rigorous post-mortem is just what the autobiographist has always found it impossible to convey' [p. 15].

The transition from the funeral bier to the dissecting-table as a metaphor for biography reveals the extent to which the ideal of a stern science has entered the literary philosophy of even a bellettrist like Nicolson, who elsewhere in the book states of biography 'that it is essentially a clubbable art'. Metaphors of dissection and anatomising tend to appear in nineteenth-century criticism as a means of expressing shock and disgust at intimate revelations about 'private lives', as in the *Saturday Review*'s response to Froude's biography of Carlyle: 'a minute and exhaustive anatomical demonstration has been made of every morbid structure, the scalpel of the biographer has been ruthlessly employed to lay bare and exhibit all the ravages of disease'.[24] Here, as elsewhere, the private self is imaged as a literal bodily interiority, damaged and diseased, stripped not only of its clothes but of its flesh by the biographer's scalpel. Nicolson obviously mobilises the metaphor of autopsy for different ends; the biographical 'corpse' is contained inside science, while the biographer's relationship to the subject is surgically cleansed of affect or desire.

In 'The New Biography' Woolf refers to the new equality between biographer and biographical subject; in *Orlando*, she opens up the issue (for the contemporary reader, at least) of the biographer's (homo)erotic desire for his/her living subject. This is also gestured towards by André Maurois, in a series of lectures, published as *Aspects of Biography* in 1924, which were in large part a response to Nicolson's *The Development of English Biography*.[25] In 'Biography as a Means of Expression' Maurois uses the examples of his own biographies of

Shelley and Disraeli to explore the question of the biographer's identification with the subject:

> Biography is a means of expression when the author has chosen his subject in order to respond to a secret need in his own nature. It will be written with more natural emotion than other kinds of biography, because the feelings and adventures of the hero will be the medium of the biographer's own feelings; to a certain extent it will be autobiography disguised as biography. [p. 125]

The results of such an approach, Maurois states, need not be the 'undue subjectivity' feared by Nicolson. If the identification of biographer and subject is sufficiently complete, the biographer *will* tell the 'true' story of the subject, even though the primary desire of the biographer is for self-expression. The biographical ideal shifts from that of the historian's self-effacement to that of a passionate empathy in which, as in all the best love affairs, the distinction between self and other is effaced. It is fully appropriate that Maurois's *Ariel* should be subtitled *a Shelley Romance*.

The dangers of the biographer's passionate or perverse identifications were formulated by Freud in his one 'great man' biography, or 'pathography', 'Leonardo da Vinci and a Memory of his Childhood' (1910):

> biographers are fixated on their heroes in a quite special way. In many cases they have chosen their hero as the subject of their studies because – for reasons of their personal emotional life – they have felt a special affection for him from the very first. They then devote their energies to a task of idealization, aimed at enrolling the great man among the class of their infantile models – at reviving in him, perhaps, the child's idea of his father. To gratify this wish they obliterate the individual features of their subject's physiognomy; they smooth over the traces of his life's struggles with internal and external resistances, and they tolerate in him no vestige of human weakness or imperfection. They thus present us with what is in fact a cold, strange, ideal figure, instead of a human being to whom we might feel ourselves distantly related. That they should do this is regrettable, for they thereby sacrifice truth to an illusion, and for the sake of their infantile phantasies abandon the opportunity of penetrating the most fascinating secrets of human nature.[26]

Freud's account of biographical idealisation as resulting in the effacement of 'life' from the portrait is a familiar one; the difference is now that blame is laid not at the door of discretion, prudery or the widow, but results from the biographer's regressive identification of the 'great man' with an infantile father imago. Leonardo's 'infantile phantasies' are, of course, discovered to be 'the key to all his achievements and misfortunes', but in penetrating them, the biographer/ pathographer must purge himself of his own. It is perhaps unsurprising that Nicolson, rather than confront the complexities of fantasy, identification and projection in biographical representation, should describe Freud as a theorist of body rather than mind.

Literature and science

I have discussed Nicolson's emphasis on 'pure' biography as an aspect of the emphasis on control and containment which characterises auto/biographical discourse. It should also be noted, however, that Nicolson's (and to a certain extent Lee's) emphasis on generic autonomy helped to free biography from the ethical and social constraints formerly imposed, attempting to dispel the idea that it was the role of biography to serve and preserve reputations. Edmund Gosse's articles on biography, most notably 'The Ethics of Biography', had set out a programme for dealing with demands for discretion and restraint: Gosse's advice to the biographer was to discover 'how to be as indiscreet as possible within the boundaries of good taste and kind feeling'.[27] The theorists of the 'new biography' are ostensibly far less concerned with issues of publicity and privacy, discretion and indiscretion than Gosse: 'truths' and 'facts' are no longer known quantities to be concealed or revealed at will or whim. The questions which Maurois, Nicolson, Woolf and Strachey debate concern the relativity of truth, the interpretability of facts and the differing claims of art and science on biography. Yet it is clear that Nicolson's demands for 'accurate' portraiture, for the objectivity of facts and statements, and for intellect and not emotion in biography, are a response to the hypocrisy, falsity and sentimentality which he views as characteristic of the nineteenth century. His positivist view of science, which is combined with a fear of the 'insatiability' of 'the scientific interest', stems from a belief in its power to correct the distortions of the previous age.

The 'development' of biography which Nicolson outlines includes a near future in which 'scientific' and 'literary' biography will split apart:

> I would suggest, in the first place, that the scientific interest in biography is hostile to, and will in the end prove destructive of the literary interest. The former will insist not only on the facts, but all the facts. The scientific interest, as it develops, will become insatiable; no synthetic power, no

genius for representation, will be able to keep the pace. I foresee, therefore, a divergence between the two interests. Scientific biography will
become specialized and technical. There will be biographies in which
development will be traced in all its intricacy and in a manner compre-
hensible only to the experts; there will be biographies examining the
influence of heredity – biographies founded on Galton, on Lombroso, on
Havelock Ellis, on Freud; there will be medical biographies – studies of
the influence of character on the endocrine glands, studies of internal
secretions; there will be sociological biographies, esthetic biographies,
philosophical biographies. These will doubtless be interesting and
instructive, but the emphasis which will be thrown on the analytical or
scientific aspect will inevitably lessen the literary effort applied to their
composition. The more that biography becomes a branch of science, the
less will it become a branch of literature. [pp. 154–5]

In Nicolson's account, 'facts' will go in one direction, creativity in
another; literary biography will, he suggests, 'wander off into the
imaginative, leaving the strident streets of science for the open fields
of fiction'. His conception of a 'scientific' biography as the study of an
individual's 'internal secretions' gives a pleasing concreteness (or
fluidity) to the familiar metaphor of the inner self. Nicolson may have
been influenced here by Havelock Ellis's writings on 'sexual perversion' and homosexuality in his sketch of 'scientific biography'. In
Sexual Inversion. Studies in the Psychology of Sex Ellis explored the roles
played by heredity (hypotheses about the transmission of hereditary
traits) and embryology (the processes of sexual differentiation in the
human embryo) in the 'making' of the homosexual; he also suggested
that the study of 'internal secretions' (endocrinology) might play a
significant role in research into sexual 'inversion'.[28] More generally,
a fascination with sexuality appears to be the motivating force behind
the ostensible concern with the development of 'character' in this
period, while much of the interest in 'scientific biography', including
Ellis's, is, in more or less coded forms, an interest in sexology. Woolf,
however, contradicts at least one of Nicolson's claims in her incorporation, and to an extent satirising, of current 'scientific' theories
about sexual development, androgyny and homosexuality into the
structures of fantasy and the realms of 'creativity' in *Orlando*.[29]

Maurois, in turn, disputes the equation Nicolson makes between
the exact and the historical sciences. Biography should be written, he
states, 'with a strict care for truth – a care not only for truths of fact (so
far as the unfortunate biographer can attain them) but for that
profounder truth which is poetic truth'. Variants on this formulation

form the core of twentieth-century autobiographical criticism, echoing I. A. Richards's distinction between referential and emotive statements, verifiable and non-verifiable knowledge, and his development of a role of art as 'pseudo-statement', 'a form of words whose scientific truth or falsity is irrelevant to the purpose in hand'. Science/history, as noted in the previous chapter, is often seen by autobiographical critics as the opposite pole of poetry/literature/ autobiography, but Maurois is concerned to defend the necessary relativity of historical interpretations against a positivist image of natural science. This involves bringing history-writing into the 'literary' domains of creativity and imagination: the image of the complexity of the self, and of the elusiveness of the truth of that self, is ultimately being deployed to argue for history as a creative, not a scientific, activity. In this Maurois is supported by Lytton Strachey:

> That the question has even been, not only asked, but seriously debated, whether History was an art, is certainly one of the curiosities of human inaptitude. What else can it possibly be? It is obvious that History is not a science; it is obvious that History is not an accumulation of facts, but the relation of them. . . . Facts relating to the past, if they are collected without art, are compilations, and compilations, no doubt, may be useful, but they are no more History than butter, eggs, salt and herbs are an omelette.[30]

Fact and fiction

In her essays 'The New Biography' and 'The Art of Biography' Woolf examines the relationship between fact and fiction, 'dream and reality', 'granite and rainbow' in biographical writing. In both essays she suggests that the way forward for biography lies in the amalgamation of these oppositions, and yet that 'truth of fact and truth of fiction are incompatible'. Appearing to echo Nicolson's 'scientific' approach to the purity of generic elements, Woolf suggests in 'The New Biography' that the compounding of fact and fiction is explosive: 'though both truths are genuine, they are antagonistic; let them meet and they destroy each other' [p. 234].

'The New Biography' is an essay–review of Harold Nicolson's *Some People*, and Woolf uses the occasion to sketch out a brief history of biography, in outline very similar to that given by Nicolson in *The Development of English Biography*, and to contrast 'new' biographies with the 'parti-coloured, hybrid, monstrous birth[s]' produced by the Victorians. The central question for biography, Woolf suggests, is how to weld together 'truth' and 'personality', 'granite-like solidity and . . . rainbow-like intangibility'. Biographers are bound to tell 'the truth', as in Desmond MacCarthy's account of the biographer as an artist under oath, but the truth with which the new biography is concerned must not be like that pursued by Sir Sidney Lee:

> truth in its hardest, most obdurate form; . . . truth as truth is to be found in the British Museum; . . . truth out of which all vapour of falsehood has been pressed by the weight of research. Only when truth had been established did Sir Sidney Lee use it in the building of his monument. [p. 229]

Lee, Woolf asserts, 'failed to choose those truths which transmit personality', the biographer's central task, and one that she believes Nicolson has in part achieved: '*Some People* is not fiction because it has the substance, the reality of truth. It is not biography because it has the freedom, the artistry of fiction' [p. 232]. Yet if such a description would seem to parallel Woolf's own desire for her writing to be free of traditional generic labels, or to create new categories, she also seems to suggest in 'The New Biography' that Nicolson's neither/nor is as much an evasion as a liberation: 'Let it be fact, one feels, or let it be fiction; the imagination will not serve under two masters simultaneously . . . the mixture of the two is abhorrent' [p. 234].

In 'The Art of Biography', written more than a decade later, Woolf examines Lytton Strachey's biographical writings. Strachey's 'three famous books, *Eminent Victorians*, *Queen Victoria*, and *Elizabeth and Essex*', she writes,

> are of a stature to show both what biography can and what biography cannot do. Thus they suggest many possible answers to the question whether biography is an art, and if not, why it fails . . . In the *Victoria* he treated biography as a craft; he submitted to its limitations.[31]

In *Elizabeth and Essex*, the combining of historical fact and artistic invention, is, in Woolf's view, a failure, but an educative one:

> the trouble lies with biography itself. It imposes conditions, and those conditions are that it must be based on fact. And by fact in biography we mean facts that can be verified by other people besides the artist. If he invents facts as an artist invents them – facts that no one else can verify – and tries to combine them with facts of the other sort, they destroy each other. [p. 123]

It may seem that the distinction Woolf draws between fact and fiction is overly rigid. It would appear to be at odds with her own project to 'revolutionize biography overnight' in *Orlando*, in which she embroiders fantasy around Sackville-West family history; 'the balance between truth and fantasy must be careful', she wrote in her diary.[32] The apparent anomaly could be explained by *Orlando*'s status as mock-biography, by the function it serves of dramatising the conflict, or delineating the borderline, which she postulates between art and biography, and by its exposure of the fictions and fantasies involved in biography's pretensions to objectivity. In addition, there are important distinctions to be made between 'fiction' and fantasy'.

Nonetheless, the seeming absoluteness of Woolf's fact/fiction dichotomy does emerge as a problem for a reading of Woolf based on her transgression of barriers and boundaries. Raymond Williams wrote of 'the crippling categorizations and dichotomies of "fact" and "fiction", or of "discursive" and "imaginative" or "referential" and "emotive"': distinctions, as I have suggested, that pervade auto/biographical discourse. As Williams notes, 'the extreme negative definition of "fiction" (or of 'myth') – an account of "what did not (really) happen" – depends, evidently, on a pseudo-positive isolation of the contrasting definition, "fact"'. Both these definitions leave out the range of propositions and modulations involved in any understanding of reality, from the potential to the actual to the typical. Biography and autobiography are test-cases for Williams: they are traditionally viewed as 'difficult' forms because of the 'deformed definition' of the 'fictional' and the 'factual', a definition which denies the overlap and 'community' between so-called fictional and non-fictional prose. Secondly, these forms repeatedly cross the artificial categories of fiction/fact, internal/external, individual/society, mind/world. The dichotomies fact/fiction and objective/subjective, Williams concludes, are the theoretical and historical keys to a theory of literature 'which has controlled and specialized the actual multiplicity of writing'.[33]

Williams's account is central to understanding the dependence of autobiographical discourse on 'crippling categorizations' in its attempts to claim a specifically 'literary' status for autobiographical writing, and, more generally, to understanding the ways in which the 'multiplicity of writing' is controlled and contained by generic and conceptual classifications. It is central to many of the arguments of this book. In Woolf's case, however, I would argue that the fact/fiction dichotomy is both used and interrogated, both an aspect of her 'aestheticism' ('imaginative' truths are always perceived as of a higher order than truths of 'fact') and a marker of a realism which refuses to mediate or collapse the fact/fiction dichotomy by means of fictionalism.

In her essays on biography, Woolf argues that the way forward for the biographer is not to flout the law of factuality, but to exploit the richness, the 'proper creativeness' of 'fact' and, *à la* Gosse, to demand the right to all the facts that are available, 'so far at least as the law of libel and human sentiment allow'. Woolf is also in apparent accord with Maurois in stating that 'these facts are not like the facts of science – once they are discovered always the same':

> They are subject to changes of opinion: opinions change as the times change. What was thought a sin is now known, by the light of facts won for us by the psychologists, to be perhaps a misfortune; perhaps a curiosity, perhaps neither one nor the other, but a trifling foible of no great importance one way or the other. The accent on sex has changed within living memory. This leads to the destruction of a great deal of dead matter still obscuring the true features of the human face. Many of the old chapter headings – life at college, marriage, career – are shown to be very arbitrary and artificial distinctions. The real current of the hero's existence took, very likely, a different course. ['The Art of Biography', p.124]

It is significant that the example of 'the facts' Woolf gives, we can assume, is the 'fact' of (homo)sexuality. The erosion of the absolute nature of sexual difference implied in this passage – 'neither one nor the other ... of no great importance one way or the other' – is obviously central to *Orlando*, but may also serve here to undermine the absoluteness of other dichotomies, fact and fiction included, and to suggest that their difference may be similarly unstable. This is certainly in accord with the suggestion Woolf makes at the close of 'The New Biography' that the future of biography lies in 'that queer amalgamation of dream and reality, that perpetual marriage of granite and rainbow'. In this reading, the dichotomies on which Woolf's work is structured – granite and rainbow, masculine and feminine, fact and imagination – are seen as contingent classifications, which in some future time might be superseded.

From a different perspective, it is clear that the category of 'fact' is not a stable entity in Woolf's writings. In *Three Guineas*, published a year prior to 'The Art of Biography', Woolf explores the uses of biography and 'the facts' in constructing her epistolary polemic for women's rights and against war. Here she pits, for example, 'the white light of fact' against 'the coloured light of biography'.[34] Yet

facts are also 'double-faced', not only open to more than one interpretation but duplicitous in their claims to the status of a single truth.
Biography, similarly, is successively oracle, testimony and evasion,
concerned with 'the private life' and failing to yield up the 'truths' of
history and public documents. The text mounts its arguments on the
basis of truths, facts, dichotomies and documents whose
trustworthiness it constantly questions.

Killing the fathers: Edmund Gosse and Lytton Strachey

In both Maurois's *Aspects of Biography* and Nicolson's *The Development
of English Biography*, Edmund Gosse's *Father and Son* and Lytton
Strachey's *Eminent Victorians* represent the new autobiography and
the new biography respectively. Maurois described *Father and Son* as
an example of 'entirely satisfactory autobiography', motivated by the
novelist's desire 'for freedom, for liberation', but written with such
accuracy of portraiture and detachment of tone 'that the reader
cannot at any single moment feel shocked. *Father and Son* contains a
proof, and a very rare proof, that an unfettered examination of one's
self is possible'. Nicolson is even more effusive, describing Gosse's
text in terms similar to those Woolf used about Nicolson's *Some
People*. *Father and Son* is neither a conventional biography nor an
autobiography, Nicolson writes, but 'something entirely original; it is
a triumphant experiment in a new formula; it is a clinical examination
of states of mind over a detached and limited period'. Nicolson's
hyperbole notwithstanding, it is clearly the case that *Father and Son*
created a stir on publication and has become one of the canonical
texts of the autobiographical genre.

A number of factors contributed to its success. Firstly, Gosse
followed in his writing the precepts central to the aesthetics of the
new biography: brevity and selection. As he wrote to Frederic
Harrison on the problems of writing autobiography: 'A very great
difficulty is to select. My own view is that one ought to take certain
vivid passages as samples or examples, elaborate them into living
pictures, and entirely omit other passages of no less interest.'[35] (One
might note in passing the highly 'textualised' account of a life here,
with parts of experience becoming 'passages'.) Secondly, Gosse is
writing as an Edwardian putting the Victorian age behind his own
and, as I have suggested, the Edwardian self-image was substantially
defined by its rejection of the Victorian legacy. Hence his critics'

readiness to see the Victorian father and the 'modern' son as representative of their respective 'epochs'; as if Gosse *fils* were still the
rebellious son at the time of writing, rather than an establishment
figure in his late fifties. This is reinforced by the autobiography's
skilful manipulations of 'childhood' consciousness, creating an
impression of immediacy through dramatisation and dialogue, while
calling upon a nostalgia for a world not entirely well lost. Thirdly, the
text contributed to early twentieth-century debates between the 'two
cultures', literature and science. Gosse, in fact, positions himself on
both sides of the polarity. He employs 'scientific' or positivist terms to
describe his auto/biographical project – 'document', 'study', the
diagnoses of a dying Puritanism' – thus laying claim to the
'objectivity' to which both Maurois and Nicolson refer. His father's
'tragedy' is centred upon the clash between his religious beliefs and
the evolutionary theories to which he was intellectually drawn as a
scientist; refusing to acknowledge the truths of Darwinism, Gosse
writes, his father 'closed the doors upon himself for ever'. Yet the
values espoused by *Father and Son* are entirely those of the literary
system, and it is central to the autobiographical canon in part because
it so emphatically endorses the claims of the literary life. In summary,
the success of the text results from its control over the discourses and
dichotomies it incorporates or ironises: autobiography/biography,
literature/science, Calvinism/Enlightenment, tragedy/comedy,
past/present. In ironic contrast, Philip Gosse, at least in his son's
account, 'dies' to history in large part as a result of his absurd attempt
to reconcile his religion and his science.[36]

In his essay 'Lytton Strachey and the Art of Biography', Desmond
MacCarthy, like Nicolson and Maurois, described Gosse as Lytton
Strachey's immediate precursor: 'Edmund Gosse had been able to
record in the person of his father and in his own experience a
tragi-comic clash between an age of belief and one of scepticism, a
theme which constantly inspired Lytton Strachey's irony.'[37] Gosse's
responses to the ironies of his biographical 'successor' are recorded
in his review of *Eminent Victorians*, 'The Agony of the Victorian Age'.
Here Gosse comments on the ways in which the biographical paradigm came to dominate representations of historical periods and
processes. The 'Victorian Age', he writes, is usually represented in
terms more appropriate to the biography of an individual; 'The world
speaks glibly of it as though it were a province of history no less
exactly defined than the career of a human being from birth to death.'

Strachey, he adds, exploits this link between history and biography:

> Mr Strachey has conducted his attack from the point of view of biography.
> He realizes the hopelessness of writing a history of the Victorian Age; it
> can only be dealt with in detail; it must be nibbled into here and there;
> discredited piecemeal; subjected to the ravages of the white ant. He has
> seen that the lives of the great Victorians lend themselves to this insidious
> kind of examination, because what was worst in the pretentiousness of
> their age is to be found enshrined in the Standard Biographies (in two
> volumes, post octavo) under which most of them are buried. Mr Strachey
> has some criticism of these monsters which could hardly be bettered.[38]

Gosse's view of the aptness of Strachey's Preface may, of course, be
influenced by the fact that in it Strachey quotes almost verbatim from
Gosse's 'The Custom of Biography', a seemingly fitting tribute from
one literary iconoclast to his supposed mentor.[39] The two texts
should not be read as fully complementary, however. Gosse's
experiences as a biographer had not endeared 'family' biography and
Victorian panegyric to him. The 'caution' to which Woolf points in
her portrait–sketch of Gosse may have played its part in the sanitised
portrait of Swinburne Gosse produced, but he was under great
pressure from Swinburne's family to pass over the more scandalous
aspects of the poet's 'private' life. In 'The Custom of Biography', he
writes that 'exaggerated respect for the conventions and tenderness
lest the susceptibility of survivors should be wounded are constant
causes of biographical failure' [p. 207]. Where Gosse was caught up
in a literary milieu in which these questions were central, however,
Strachey interrogates the very terms on which the biographical
system is based. For example, rather than entering into discussion of
what 'properly' belongs to the public and what to the private sphere,
Strachey used his biography of Queen Victoria, in Perry Meisel's
words, 'to historiciz[e] the categories by which his own narration
customarily proceeds, chief among them the distinction between
public and private'.[40] In *Eminent Victorians* Strachey recounts the
'lives' of Cardinal Manning, Florence Nightingale, Thomas Arnold
and General Gordon, 'representatives' of Church, Army and the
Public Schools, whose idiosyncrasies and egotism put the very concept of the representative into crisis.

The Preface to *Eminent Victorians* became a manifesto for the new
biography and is thus worth quoting at some length:

> The history of the Victorian Age will never be written: we know too much
> about it. . . . . It is not by the direct method of a scrupulous narration that

the explorer of the past can hope to depict that singular epoch. If he is wise he will adopt a subtler strategy. He will attack his subject in unexpected places; he will fall upon the flank, or the rear; he will shoot a sudden, revealing searchlight into obscure recesses hitherto undivined. He will row out over that great ocean of material, and lower down into it, here and there, a little bucket, which will bring up to the light of day some characteristic specimen, from those far depths, to be examined with a careful curiosity. Guided by these considerations, I have written the ensuing studies. . . . I have sought to examine and elucidate certain fragments of the truth which took my fancy and lay to my hand. . . .

To preserve . . . a becoming brevity – a brevity which excludes every-thing that is redundant and nothing that is significant – that, surely, is the first duty of the biographer. The second, no less surely, is to maintain his own freedom of spirit. It is not his business to be complimentary; it is his business to lay bare the facts of some cases, as he understands them. That is what I have aimed at in this book – to lay bare the facts of some cases, as I understand them, dispassionately, impartially, and without ulterior intentions. To quote the words of a Master – *'Je n'impose rien; je ne propose rien: j'expose'*.[41]

Here Strachey articulates the ambiguity – a term of which is is particularly fond – of the relationship between the objectivity of 'facts' and 'truth', and the subjectivity of fancy, interpretation and understanding. In an essay written a decade earlier, Strachey stated that 'uninterpreted truth is as useless as buried gold; and art is the great interpreter. It alone can unify a vast multitude of facts into a significant whole, clarifying, accentuating, suppressing, and lighting up the dark places with the torch of the imagination.'[42] In *Eminent Victorians*, the relationship between fact and fancy has become more tortuous, while the 'Freudian' metaphors – the dark recesses of the self, the ocean of the unconscious with its buried treasures or traumas – now map on to a set of military metaphors which are also overtly (homo)eroticised. Comparing the Preface to the earlier review quoted above, it seems that the 'dark places' have become imaged as bodily orifices, while the 'torch of the imagination' is now a probing searchlight. The body-without-orifices of the Victorian biography is now imaged as an 'embodiment' – of an Age and an ideology – to be exposed to a penetrating investigation.

Analysing the legend of Florence Nightingale as the prototypical Angel in the House or on the Ward, Strachey writes:

Everyone knows the popular conception of Florence Nightingale . . . consecrating with the radiance of her goodness the dying soldier's couch – the vision is familiar to all. But the truth was different. The Miss

Nightingale of fact was not as facile fancy painted her. She worked in another fashion, and towards another end; she moved under the stress of an impetus which finds no place in the popular imagination. A Demon possessed her. [p. 111]

In this opening passage, the 'truth', the 'facts', about Florence Nightingale so confidently proclaimed, turn out to be even, or apparently, less rational than 'the vision' created by 'fancy' – Nightingale, far from being an Angel, is 'in fact' possessed by the Devil. Strachey also hints, in the brief passage quoted above, at the eroticism of both the popular conception of Florence Nightingale and of the soldier's 'vision', which, in the popular legend, is a 'vision' of an angelic presence 'dreamed' by the wounded soldiers from which they 'awake' to the living presence of Nightingale. Yet she, of course, is also the 'vision' of popular conception, the woman as angel. In short, Strachey creates a vertiginous structure of relationships between fact and fiction, reality and myth, which exposes or lays bare not the 'truth' of history or personality but the fictionality of positivism's premises. Fact and fiction, as Meisel notes, turn out to be 'simply rival versions of the same evidence'.

Strachey's strategy of 'lay[ing] bare', a phrase which recurs throughout *Eminent Victorians*, is accompanied (as in the tenets of Russian Formalism) by the process of estrangement, a making strange of the familiar, rather than the 'debunking' (which implies a replacement of illusions with common-sense realities) normally associated with Strachey's biographical method. Strachey 'makes strange' not only the life-courses of his eminent Victorians, showing, in Epstein's words, how ' "obscure recesses, hitherto undivined" divert the course of the miraculously lamplit pathway of the professional career' [p. 148], but also the documents, the 'official biographies', on which his 'lives' are based. Strachey, notoriously, drew on published sources alone, which he lists at the end of each life, rewriting written 'lives' and showing how supposedly 'factual' elements can be deployed to quite different ends in different narrative contexts. His emphasis on the role of texts within lives – his biographical subjects are repeatedly depicted in the act of self-portrayal and self-communion through their diaries and letters – reinforces this sense of lives fashioned in and through written texts, while collapsing the conventional distinction between wo/men of action and wo/men of letters. In depicting the self-deceptions practised by Cardinal Manning through 'the agony of self-examination' enacted in his diary-writing, Strachey also suggests that the 'inner truth' of confessional writings is no more reliable as evidence than 'outward seeming'. He thus puts into question the view, beloved of biographers, that the more 'private' the document, the closer to the truth of the self the biographer reaches. Finally, he makes strange the very emblems by which 'great men' are memorialised, refusing to allow that the past 'speak to' the present:

> The Cardinal's memory is a dim thing today. And he who descends into the crypt of that cathedral which Manning never lived to see, will observe, in the quiet niche with the sepulchral monument, that the dust lies thick on the strange, the incongruous, the almost impossible object which, with its elaborations of dependent tassels, hangs down from the dim vault like some forlorn and forgotten trophy – the Hat. [p. 108]

The distancing enacted in this passage, however, belies the connections and continuities between the Victorian age and their own of which Strachey's contemporaries were acutely aware. Cyril Connolly wrote that Strachey used the biographical essays

> to attack and undermine all that was most cherished in the morality of today . . . *Eminent Victorians* is the work of a great anarch, a revolutionary text-book on bourgeois society written in the language by which the bourgeois ear could be lulled and beguiled, the Mandarin style . . . a questioning of the values the Victorians stood for and all reflected from the eyes of their own demobilized and disillusioned children.[43]

Published in May 1918, five months before the Armistice, Strachey's text was perceived as the first book of post-war England, exposing the workings of power and authority, and the unthinking devotion to the shibboleths of God and Country, that had led inexorably to the slaughter of the First World War. Bertrand Russell, in his autobiography, recalls being reprimanded by a warder for laughing in his cell during his period of imprisonment for militant pacificism; *Eminent Victorians* was the cause of Russell's hilarity.[44]

In the context of 'the new biography' and in debates about biography today, attention tends to focus on Strachey's success or failure in depicting 'personality', as in Woolf's criticisms of caricature in *Eminent Victorians*, on the unfortunate legacy of irony he left to less proficient biographers, and on the legitimacy of his methods. Michael Holroyd, Strachey's biographer, in his lengthy discussion of *Eminent Victorians*, concentrates almost entirely on demonstrating that Strachey's contested representations always have some basis in 'fact'.[45] This would appear to be a somewhat literalist approach, given Strachey's play with the fact/fiction polarity, though it is revealing of the prevailing positivism in biography today. The greater oversight, perhaps, is the failure (in which Holroyd is not alone) to explore the potential in Strachey's uses of biography as cultural critique – the exposure of conventional value-systems which was the main emphasis of Cyril Connolly's discussion of *Eminent Victorians*.

Orlando and/as biography

Writing in her diary a few weeks before the publication of *Orlando*, Woolf reported that 'the news of *Orlando* is black'. Bookshop orders were far lower than she had hoped:

> They say this is inevitable. No one wants biography. But it is a novel, says Miss Ritchie.
> But it is called biography on the title page, they say. It will have to go to the Biography shelf. I doubt therefore that we shall do more than cover expenses – a high price for the fun of calling it a biography. And I was so sure it was going to be the one popular book![46]

Woolf's fears were groundless in this case; indeed, two months later, she expresses concern in her diary that the success of *Orlando* will bring its own difficulties, requiring her to repeat herself rather than experiment further. Her earlier anxiety over the generic labelling of the text, however, is in itself of some significance. The 'dialogue' between Miss Ritchie, the traveller for the press, and the buyers, anticipates a debate central to recent autobiographical criticism about the status of generic labels such as novel, biography or autobiography as they appear on the title page of literary texts.

Jacques Derrida has written of the 'genre-clause', by which a text marks itself as belonging to a particular genre, that 'participation never amounts to belonging': the label 'novel', for example, is not in itself novelistic. Both inside and outside the work, 'along its boundary', the designation of genre 'gathers together the corpus and, at the same time, in the (very) blinking of an eye, keeps it from closing, from identifying itself with itself'. The law of genre is both a set of interdictions guarding the 'purity' of genres and a transgressive and disruptive force.[47]

The genre-clause 'biography' on the title-page of *Orlando* is for Woolf, as her diary entry suggests, an act of 'fun' and transgression which seems to backfire at the moment at which her text enters the public realm and a more formal contract with her reading/purchasing public becomes operative. But the problem is also that bookshops, in shelving *Orlando* in one category rather than another, would deny to Woolf the generic ambiguity, the 'having it both ways', which she sought for *Orlando* and which, in relation to both gender and genre, it so astonishingly offers. The problem of classification here may also throw some light on the fact–fiction opposition Woolf insists on in her essays on biography; the law of genre demands that fact and fiction should not intermingle – '[biography] imposes conditions, and these conditions are that it must be based upon fact' ['The Art of Biography' [p. 123]] – and the codes of booksellers demand that books be placed in one category rather than another. Woolf has come up against what she describes in 'The Art of Biography' as 'a very cruel distinction' between biography and fiction. She escapes retribution in part, perhaps, because (as *Orlando* reveals) the fact/fiction dichotomy is far less absolute than Woolf maintains.

Woolf's description of the 'fun' entailed in subtitling *Orlando* 'a biography' calls attention to her overtly transgressive use of the genre-clause, her deliberate flouting of the law of genre. The use of the generic label mocks 'biography' in its more traditional guises, and in this sense *Orlando* is, as Leon Edel states, 'a fable for biographers'.[48] It ridicules many of the tenets solemnly laid down by the self-appointed guardians of the genre; where Sidney Lee insists that the living individual is not a proper subject for biography, Woolf took as her 'subject' her friend/lover Vita Sackville-West (whose name means 'life'), and made of the word 'life' a mocking-bird song in the text. She stretches the boundaries of the individual as, in Lee's terms, 'a unit' beyond breaking-point; Orlando is alive during the 300 years of text-time, first as a man and then as a woman. Woolf (or her narrator/biographer – the relationship is a complex one) satirises Victorian biography and its narrative plod from the subject's birth to his death, 'without looking to right or left, in the indelible footprints of truth; unenticed by flowers; regardless of shade; on and on methodically till we fall plump into the grave and write *finis* on the tombstone above our head'. She shows how transgressive the biography of a woman can be: 'the truth is that when we write of a woman, everything is out of place – culminations and perorations; the accent never falls where it does with a man' [p. 298]. She described the *DNB* as impervious to the complexities of lived time: 'The true length of a person's life, whatever the *Dictionary of National Biography* may say, is always a matter of dispute' [p. 291]. She mocks her narrator's pretension to objectivity, and reveals the impossibility of reconstructing the past as it was; documents burn or develop holes in crucial places, the perspectives of the present make the past obscure or even incomprehensible. And yet, of course, the drive of the text is towards a grand historical sweep and a denial of limit and closure.

Orlando, for a long time seen as Woolf's holiday from 'serious' fiction, is a text whose complexities deserve fuller discussion than I can give here. For present purposes, I intend to focus on the aspects of the text which engage most fully, if not necessarily most overtly, with contemporary discussions of biography. *Orlando* is in dialogue with Strachey's biographical writing, in particular *Elizabeth and Essex*, published in the same year, and with Nicolson's *The Development of English Biography*, in press as Woolf was writing *Orlando*. Reading *Orlando* and Nicolson's critical study of biography side by side, it is at times hard to know who is imitating or parodying whom. We might compare, for example, Nicolson and Woolf's accounts of the coming of the nineteenth century:

> Something like this happened to nineteenth-century biography. It all began splendidly. We had Moore and Southey and Lockhart; but then came earnestness, and with earnestness hagiography descended on us with its sullen cloud, and the Victorian biographer scribbled laboriously by the light of shaded lamps. [*Development*, p. 110]

> With the eighth stroke [of the clock], some hurrying tatters of cloud sprawled over Piccadilly. They seemed to mass themselves and to advance with extraordinary rapidity towards the west end. As the ninth, tenth, and eleventh strokes struck, a huge blackness sprawled over the whole of London. With the twelfth stroke of midnight, the darkness was complete. A turbulent welter of cloud covered the city. All was darkness; all was doubt; all was confusion. The Eighteenth century was over; the Nineteenth century had begun. [*Orlando*, p. 216]

Woolf's fascination with the representation of historical differences, as Rachel Bowlby notes, 'derives from the nineteenth-century literary interest in the idea of history as a matter of imaginative reconstructions rather than factual record'.[49] The kind of fantastical historicism that echoes throughout Nicolson's text may also bring history, and by extension biography, into the realms of fiction and fantasy rather than the stern scientificity which he ostensibly endorses. Indeed, his model of science begins to appear as no more than the most recent model of historical difference, modernity's way of representing itself to itself.

Woolf 's representation of the literary life at various periods in English history is more obviously a parody of the literary history Nicolson produces. The fantasy of an eighteenth century in which the traveller through time could enter a London coffee-house to exchange 'gossip and conversation' with the literary luminaries of the day [p. 72], an eighteenth century in large part drawn from the pages of Boswell and Johnson, reveals the extent to which historical recon-structions are based on literary representations of 'the age'. These exert a particularly powerful pull when they are drawn from bio-graphical writings; certainly Boswell's Johnson is represented time and again as reality or actuality incarnate. Woolf both fleshes out and empties out this fantasy of the 'age of Enlightenment':

> [Orlando] made a point sometimes of passing beneath the windows of a coffee house, where she could see the wits without being seen, and thus could fancy from their gestures what wise, witty or spiteful things they were saying without hearing a word of them; which was perhaps an advantage; and once she stood half an hour watching three shadows on the blind drinking tea together in a house in Bolt Court.
> Never was any play so absorbing . . . Dr Johnson, Mr Boswell and Mrs Williams, – those were the shadows' names. So absorbed was she in the sight, that she forgot to think how other ages would have envied her, though it seems probable that on this occasion they would. She was content to gaze and gaze. At length Mr Boswell rose. He saluted the old woman with tart asperity. But with what humility did he not abase himself before the great Roman shadow, who now rose to its full height and rocking somewhat as he stood there rolled out the most magnificent phrases that ever left human lips; so Orlando thought them, though she never heard a word that any of the three shadows said as they sat there drinking tea. [p. 213]

In 'The New Biography', Woolf writes of Johnson's voice 'booming out' from Boswell's pages and reverberating through history; in the passage above, Orlando does not hear a word spoken by the shadow-puppets of the literary-historical theatre. Similarly, whereas in the essay she writes of the liberating effects of Boswell's *Life of Johnson* – 'We may sit, even with the great and good, over the table and talk' [p. 230] – Orlando asks 'who are the "we"?' If, in Nicolson's words, biography is a 'clubbable' art, then it will automatically exclude women, or at best admit them as member's wives. Orlando, despite, or because of, her passion for literature, becomes weary of listening to great poets pontificating on the topic of women, puts on male clothing and goes in search of female company. Soon dropping her disguise, however, she stays not for sex but for stories:

> These poor creatures, she ascertained, for Nell brought Prue, and Prue Kitty, and Kitty Rose, had a society of their own of which they now elected her a member. Each would tell the story of the adventures which had landed her in her present way of life. So they would draw round the punch-bowl which Orlando made it her business to furnish generously, and many were the fine tales they told and many the amusing observations they made, for it cannot be denied that when women get together – but hist – they are always careful to see that the doors are shut and that not a word of it gets into print. All they desire – is – but hist again – is that not a man's step on the stair? All they desire, we were about to say when the gentleman took the very words out of our mouths. Women have no desires, says this gentleman . . . only affectations. . . . Without desires . . . their conversation cannot be of the slightest interest to anyone. [pp. 209–10]

A possible element in this episode is Woolf's coded reference to the 'scandalous memoirists' of the eighteenth century, such as Laetitia Pilkington, Harriette Wilson and Charlotte Charke (notorious for her cross-dressing). Woolf wrote elsewhere of the 'lives' of Pilkington and Wilson; their inclusion in this episode in *Orlando* would point to the existence of an alternative literary history, comprising the autobiographies of women.[50] The point is not simply, however, that the women's voices and stories are suppressed or silenced; Woolf would also appear to be investigating the creation of the private self in the interiority of the women's room and the struggle over definitions of female 'character' in the eighteenth century. *Orlando*, here as elsewhere, gestures towards a gendered history of 'subjectivity', in which private and public spaces are of central importance and auto/ biographies play a crucial role.

In her representation of the nineteenth century – damp, ivy-clad, grotesquely fecund, and circumscribed within the private and domestic spheres of marriage and family – Woolf depicts and sabotages the memorialising and monumentalising aspirations of the Victorian age. Playing with the images of sculpture and monumental architecture as 'concrete life' which, as we have seen, pervade nineteenth-century auto/biographical theory, the text constructs a 'garish erection',

> a pyramid, hecatomb, or trophy . . . – a conglomeration at any rate of the most heterogeneous and ill-assorted objects, piled higgledy-piggledly in a vast mound where the statue of Queen Victoria now stands! . . .

[Orlando] had never, in all her life, seen anything at once so indecent, so hideous and so monumental. [p. 222]

This monstrous edifice contains such 'execrescences' as military helmets, memorial wreaths and extinct monsters, and the passage shares with *Eminent Victorians* a destruction of monumental ambition via synecdoche – the parts (as with Cardinal Manning's hat) bring down the whole. The 'garish erection' also parallels Woolf's description of Victorian biography in 'The New Biography' as 'a parti-coloured, hybrid, monstrous birth . . . an amorphous mass . . . always we rummage among them with a sense of the prodigious waste, of the artistic wrongheadedness of such a method' [p. 230]. Although Orlando fears that nothing will ever demolish the erection, modernity effaces it – 'There was not a trace of that vast erection which she had thought everlasting; top hats, widow's weeds, trumpets, telescopes, wreaths, all had vanished and left not a stain, not a puddle even, on the pavement' [p. 283]. Yet the earlier passage tells us that the statue of Queen Victoria, itself a monument to the age, has replaced or, more accurately, gathered up, the monstrous conglomeration.

Woolf's account of Victorian biography clearly echoes Henry James's description of the Victorian novel as a 'loose, baggy monster', endorsing by contrast the coherence aesthetic of literary modernism. Beyond this, however, the theme or image of monstrosity bears a complex relationship to nineteenth-century taxonomies and classificatory systems, themselves linked to the life-science of the biographical. The monstrous erection in *Orlando* not only seems to defy taxonomy; it itself contains 'extinct monsters' as one of its elements. The principles of variation and difference on which classificatory systems are based need monstrosity (testimony to difference) and suppress it (it challenges principles of order and the integrity of species). Woolf's relationship to 'monstrosity' is similarly ambivalent. The 'waste' is prodigious, but it is amongst rubbish-heaps that items and elements 'buried in the huge past' are redis-covered.[51]

The naked truth

Orlando dramatises and satirises other metaphors running through-out auto/biographical discourse. Pursuing the terms of 'draperies and decencies', Woolf constructs a scenario in which, at the point where Orlando becomes a woman, 'Truth, Candour, and Honesty, the austere Gods who keep watch and ward by the ink-pot of the biographer' banish the three sisters Purity, Chastity and Modesty, who are engaged in a fruitless attempt to cast their veils and their draperies over Orlando's naked form. The scene recalls/parodies Edmund Gosse's injunctions for biographical truth-telling, in which it becomes the biographer's duty

> to drag his coy and retreating subject as far as can be done into the open light of day . . . to catch the fleeting spirit of the man down the winding galleries of his concealments. He does it, not to shame him, not to satisfy his own curiosity, but because the world requires another leader. Here the figure lies, clinging to a pillar, its robe thrown over its face; tear the veils away, and Ave, Imperator.[52]

In *Orlando*, Woolf extends her satire not only to the upholders of discretion but also to the trumpeters of truth, who are oblivious to the fact that the 'truths' of history and biography, selfhood and sexuality, do not simply lie beneath veils, awaiting the moment of revelation.

> The sound of the trumpets died away and Orlando stook stark naked. No human being, since the world began, has ever looked more ravishing. His form combined in one the strength of a man and a woman's grace. As he stood there, the silver trumpets prolonged their note, as if reluctant to leave the lovely sight which their blast had called forth – and Chastity, Purity, and Modesty, inspired, no doubt, by Curiosity, peeped in at the door and threw a garment like a towel at the naked form which, unfortunately, fell short by several inches. Orlando looked himself up and down in a long looking-glass, without showing any signs of discomposure, and went, presumably, to his bath. [p.133]

In this section of the text Woolf seems to be taking up, in order to satirise, the metaphysical concept of truth as *aletheia* – literally the not-concealed, the unveiled. As Marina Warner notes, the metaphor of truth as disclosure, when applied anthropomorphically, was translated into nakedness: 'the wholly naked human body, carrying with it multiple meanings of nature, integrity and completeness, transmitted by the allegorical tradition, generated a personification of truth as a female form, often entirely naked, because Truth has nothing to hide and can never be less than whole'.[53]

In Nietzsche's critique of the concept of truth as *aletheia*, the relationship between truth as surface/depth (the function of the veil is, as Mary Ann Doane writes, to create depth behind surface, to ensure the profundity of truth) is tied to moral questions of decency

and indecency.[54] The concept of 'the naked truth' in auto/
biographical discourse becomes inextricably linked to these questions. In turn these cannot be separated from the regimes of biographical inquiry, which are a central aspect of the technologies of
literary publicity developing in the nineteenth century. Hence, for
example, Henry James's vilifications of the quest for biographical
knowledge of artists and writers. In an essay on George Sand, he
refers to the indiscretion of Zola's 'exposure': 'when we meet on the
broad highway the rueful denuded figure we need some presence of
mind to decide whether to cut it dead or to lead it gently home'.[55]

Woolf, in *Orlando*, appears both to subvert Nietzsche's representations of truth as 'becoming a woman', and to take up his concept
of truth as the veiled gesture of feminine modesty, which creates the
illusion of surface/depth. In *The Gay Science*, Nietzsche writes:

> I am afraid that old women are more skeptical in their most secret heart of
> hearts than any man: they consider the superficiality of existence its
> essence, and all virtue and profundity is to them merely a veil over this
> 'truth', a very welcome veil over a pudendum – in other words, a matter of
> decency and shame, and no more than that.[56]

Woolf's satire on truth as *aletheia* is ambiguous. Is she, like
Nietzsche, suggesting that truth is 'reducible' to questions of decency
and indecency? In the discourse of biography, the truth of self or
identity is conventionally imaged through the body, especially as
clothed/naked, thus making the issue of private/public a question of
decency/indecency.   Satirising   these   representations   and
anthropomorphisms, *Orlando* raises two key questions. Firstly, what
is the place of the body in biography and, secondly, what is the
relationship between truth and (in)decency for the moderns?

In hinting at the voyeuristic pleasures enjoyed both by the
champions of biographical truth and of discretion, Woolf's writing
also points up the prurience of much auto/biographical discourse, in
which the auto/biographical subject is represented as being or
becoming naked. Two texts on early twentieth-century autobiography which illustrate this theme are W. A. Gill's 'The Nude in
Autobiography' (1907), discussed in the previous chapter, and Orlo
Williams's 'Some Feminine Biographies' (1920).[57]

Orlo Williams finds a number of reasons for women's perceived
failure to write great autobiography, all of them in some way connected to the problems of self-representation and self-presentation

in autobiography. Women, we are told, have been unable to 'objectify themselves into an absorbing whole to the extent which is essential for successful autobiography'.

> The autobiographer has to make his own looking-glass, and this feat of mental construction is beyond the reach of all but the specially gifted. . . . It is the intensity of the absorption that produces the reflection in which a strange but fascinating Doppelgänger is thrown up against the arras of the years.

Women, Williams states, are self-conscious but they have a 'greater secretiveness ... with regard to themselves ... they cling passionately to their last draperies even among themselves, and naturally regard the voluntary assumption of even the noblest state of nudity in public as an act of self-violation' [p. 306]. Incapable, moreover, of taking 'a comprehensive view', the woman's image of herself 'is more of a series of attitudes than of an elusive unity'. The difference between the male and the female autobiographer is that 'while she is busy with the make-up box, he, more astute, attends to the lighting of the stage' [p. 307]. Thus women are more suited to 'the cosmetic art of fiction' than to autobiography.[58]

Williams's imagery points up very clearly the gender differentiation of metaphors, as well as the gendering of genres. The mirror-image, when applied to men, is used to represent a concentrated reflectiveness which allows for the construction of a whole, entire and 'objective' autobiographical self. Men make their own mirrors, and disciplined self-contemplation leads to the production of a 'true' image of self. Self-reflection is represented as a 'mental' feat. By contrast, women's use of mirrors denotes vanity, narcissism and the inauthenticity of the 'attitude'. The mirror does not unify the female self, for women are seen as incapable of creating the mirrors necessary for the act of reflecting the self as a whole, and of the self-exposure required for the creation of an authentic self-image. Their mirrors, by implication, enable them merely to powder their noses, to decorate rather than to fashion themselves. Similarly, whereas male nakedness is often figured as a stripping for action, the naked female is at best a vehicle of an abstract beauty and more often either narcissistic or indecent.

In *Orlando*, Woolf uses the mirror-image in part as a way of representing the lures of femininity for women themselves and hence, in the manner of de Beauvoir, of the way 'one' becomes a woman. It could be argued that Orlando only recognises his/her new sexual identity (the question of the gendered pronoun only becomes pressing at this point) through the image in the mirror. The 'tedious discipline' of femininity, as gloomily contemplated by the eighteenth-century Orlando, involves not only an hour a day spent 'looking in the looking-glass', but an adoption of equivocation and 'roundabout ways', including a denial of the labour, 'the cosmetic art', that goes into the construction of the feminine ideal. The ideal is also a seductive one, although Orlando ultimately resists her own siren-song and turns her back on her own/her other image:

> 'Now,' she said when all was ready and lit the silver sconces on either side of the mirror. What woman would not have kindled to see what Orlando saw then burning in the snow – for all about the looking-glass were snowy lawns, and she was like a fire, a burning bush ... she smiled the involuntary smile which women smile when their own beauty, which seems not their own, forms like a drop falling or a fountain rising and confronts them all of a sudden in the glass – this smile she smiled ... and then she sighed, 'Life, a lover' and then she turned on her heel with extraordinary rapidity; whipped her pearls from her neck, stripped the satins from her back, stood erect in the neat black silk knickerbockers of an ordinary nobleman, and rang the bell. [p. 178]

Vita Sackville-West wrote to Woolf on reading (or, as Rachel Bowlby puts it, 'looking into') *Orlando*, 'You have invented a new form of Narcissism', the phrase capturing the doubling of selves in biography as in the mirror. The passage above also plays with the narcissism, and the universality, of 'Sapphism' – 'What woman would not have kindled to see what Orlando saw then burning in the snow' – and with the 'mirroring' effect of sexual sameness and textual/biographical doubling or difference, replicated in the photographs of Vita and the 'historical' portraits included in the Hogarth Press edition of Orlando.

Woolf incorporates these into the 'body' of the text in an excursus on the relationship between clothes and gender identity:

> If we compare the picture of Orlando as a man with that of Orlando as a woman we shall see that though both are undoubtedly one and the same person, there are certain changes. The man has his hand free to seize his sword, the woman must use hers to keep the satins from slipping from her shoulders. The man looks the world full in the face, as if it were made for his uses and fashioned to his liking. The woman takes a sidelong glance at it, full of subtlety, even of suspicion. Had they both worn the same clothes, it is possible that their outlook might have been the same. [p. 180]

This passage seems to echo Williams's contrast between men's and women's relationships to their mirror-images, images which suggest that the world itself is the mirror. In Woolf's account, however, it is the man who is the narcissist, for in his fantasy of power the world becomes an emanation of the self – as in the theories of some of the critics discussed in the next chapter. By contrast, the woman's 'sidelong glance' reflects a situation in which, to quote Sigrid Weigel, 'looking out of the corner of one's eye' could become a feminist resource, a necessary response to contradictory social and sexual positioning:

> Women should allow themselves to look out of the corner of just one eye in this narrow concentrated way so that they can be free to roam over the length and breadth of the social dimension with the other. . . . [Women] will only be able to correct this sideways look when the woman theme is redundant.[59]

The relationships Woolf postulates between clothes, gender identity and 'outlook' are highly ambiguous. Although she begins by proposing that 'it is clothes that wear us and not we them', the element of disguise makes the assumed relationship between gender and clothing far more complex than it would at first appear:

> Different though the sexes are, they intermix. In every human being a vacillation from one sex to the other take place, and often it is only the clothes that keep the male or female likeness, while underneath the sex is the very opposite of what it is above. [p. 181]

Marjorie Garber, in her recent study of cross-dressing and culture, *Vested Interests*, refers to this passage in *Orlando*. In her account, *Orlando*, 'an upper-class fairy tale *à clef*' constructs a fantasy in which gender transformations are a matter of choice and self-determination, thus denying the difficulty of gender confusions and shifts. 'Whatever Orlando *is*, her clothing reflects it; the crossing between male and female may be a mixture (a synthesis) but it is not a confusion, a transgression. The inside always corresponds to the outside'.[60] While agreeing with Garber about the class-specific nature of the fantasy, I think that she misreads Woolf's account of the relationship between clothes and gender. In the passage from *Orlando* quoted above, the sex is not identical with the clothing, but nor is the inverse relationship between them a constant one. In other words, the inside neither corresponds to the outside, nor is it reliably opposed to it. The fantasy in *Orlando* does include a disruption of categories, if not a crisis.

The body in the text

In their reaction against Victorian biography, exponents of 'the new biography', as well as its critics, emphasise the role of the biographer in exposing and revealing (laying bare) the 'real' self of the biographical subject, without disguising draperies. Gillian Beer notes that the body in *Orlando* is figured not only in Orlando's shifting sexual form, but in 'temperature, the heat and cold with which we most familiarly and with our whole body gauge the world. She offers us a sensory history of England. . . . By this means she suggests the presence of the individual living in the body.'[61] Modernity and now-time are represented as a series of shocks running through Orlando's body like an electric charge: 'Her own body quivered and tingled as if suddenly stood naked in a hard frost' [p. 305].

Lytton Strachey's use of the biographical body entails a network of metaphors in which the biographical act becomes an invasive one, as in the Preface to *Eminent Victorians* and in *Elizabeth and Essex*, in which Strachey claims the biographer's privilege of looking under the Queen's skirts. The task of the biographer, Strachey claims in *Elizabeth and Essex*, is to confront 'the bewildering discordances of the real and the apparent', to locate 'the form of the woman' under the image which was all her contemporaries saw, 'an image of regality, which yet, by a miracle, was actually alive':

> Posterity has suffered by a similar deceit of vision. The great Queen of its imagination . . . no more resembles the Queen of fact than the clothed Elizabeth the naked one. But, after all, posterity is privileged. Let us draw nearer; we shall do no wrong now to that Majesty, if we look below the robes.

The probing biographer will encounter difficulties at this stage, however. Firstly, while Strachey does not endorse Ben Jonson's rumour that the Queen could not be penetrated because 'she had a membrana on her, which made her incapable of man, though for her delight she tryed many' [p. 21], he proposes an updated version, mind over body, in which she suffered from 'vaginismus', a neurotic or hysterical condition which makes penetration painful or even impossible. Secondly, despite the pose of the realist, committed to uncovering 'the Queen of fact' – the naked Queen – Strachey also suggests that the sexual identity of the Queen is ambiguous – 'was she a man?' [p. 23] – and turns to a Freudianism which tells a story in which the (male) child, when confronted with a naked Queen or a naked mother, will speedily endow her with the 'manhood' she is observed to lack, made out of the materials of 'appearance': 'the huge hoop, the stiff ruff, the swollen sleeves, the powdered pearls, the spreading, gilded gauzes' [p. 13]. The relationship between male/ female, appearance/reality, fact/fiction is not resolved merely by looking below or beneath the robes.

Woolf, never unconditionally laudatory of Strachey's biographical writings, deemed *Elizabeth and Essex* a failure, the figure of the Queen becoming neither entirely real nor wholly fictitious, 'mov[ing] in an ambiguous world, between fact and fiction, neither embodied nor disembodied' ['The Art of Biography', p. 123]. Published in the same year, pursuing, in part, the same historical romance (*Orlando* opens with Elizabethan England and the Queen's visit to Knole), strongly influenced by and contributing to contemporary debates about androgyny and sexual identity, *Orlando* and *Elizabeth and Essex* are still very different experiments in biography. Their 'radicalism' derives from the same preoccupation, however; less the emphasis on 'sexuality' as such, reduced by Strachey's critics to a period-limited brand of literary Freudianism, than a concern with the body in history and with the question of how and where we live in our bodies. In stating that Strachey's Elizabeth is 'neither embodied or disembodied', Woolf remains overly focused on the question of 'character' or 'personality', failing to see that his concern with the problem and process of 'embodiment' in biography, also central to *Orlando*, is one of its most interesting aspects.

Woolf does not refer to Strachey's use of psychoanalysis in *Elizabeth and Essex*, a topic on which her views would have been interesting. Strachey's 'psychobiographical' portrait of Queen Elizabeth certainly met with Freud's approval, as a letter he wrote to Strachey attests:

> You are aware of what other historians so easily overlook – that it is impossible to understand the past with certainty, because we cannot divine men's motives and the essence of their minds and so cannot interpret their actions. With regard to the people of past times we are in the same position as with dreams to which we have been given no associations – and only a layman could expect us to interpret such dreams as those. As a historian, then, you show that you are steeped in the spirit of psychoanalysis. And with reservations such as these, you have approached one of the most remarkable figures in your country's history, you have known how to trace back her character to the impressions of her childhood, you have touched upon her most hidden motives with equal

boldness and discretion, and it is very possible that you have succeeded in making a correct reconstruction of what actually occurred.[62]

Freud's theories of sexuality provided Strachey with one answer to the question posed in *Elizabeth and Essex*: 'By what art are we to worm our way into those strange spirits, those even stranger bodies?' Woolf suggested that, in the absence of authentic information 'about those strange spirits and even stranger bodies', Strachey should not have attempted to lift or penetrate the thick veil behind which Elizabeth's life was lived, her comment hinting at a distaste for the psychobiographical project. Strachey, like Freud, suggests that 'authentic information' about the past is a chimera, and that the 'correct reconstruction' of Elizabeth's motives and mental essence is made through the 'universal story', the Oedipus legend:

> Yes, indeed, she felt her father's spirit within her; and an extraordinary passion moved the obscure profundities of her being, as she condemned her lover to her mother's death. In all that had happened there was a dark inevitability, a ghastly satisfaction; her father's destiny, by some intimate dispensation, was repeated in hers.

Yet, as Meisel notes, 'the book's psychoanalytic project is its beginning, not its end'.[63] In the complexities of cross-sexual identifications – mother/lover, father/daughter – Strachey pursues a deviation from the life-course inscribed by the Oedipus narrative itself: 'In a still remoter depth there were still stranger stirrings. There was a difference as well as a likeness; after all, she was no man, but a woman; and was this, perhaps, not a repetition but a revenge?' [p. 165] None of the stories quite fit the case, nor the case the stories, in part because Strachey is exploring, as in his 'Florence Nightingale' and *Queen Victoria*, the paradoxes generated by women with power, and the 'perversity' of the pathways crossed by power and sexuality, which have as their nexus the Queen's body, the Elizabethan body politic: 'for years she made her mysterious organism the pivot upon which the fate of Europe turned'.

Strachey also moves beyond the specifically sexual body in an attempt to articulate the role of the body in history, to touch 'the very pulse of the machine'. 'Minute, invisible movements' of the body might determine the future course of events: 'At a moment of crisis, a faint, a hardly perceptible impulsion might be given. It would be nothing but a touch, unbetrayed by the flutter of an eyelid, as one sat at table, not from one's hand, which would continue writing, but from

one's foot' [p. 73]. More brutally, *Elizabeth and Essex* returns
repeatedly to the tortured and mutilated body, upon which power is
exercised. Strachey's focus on torture as the accepted means of
gaining 'evidence' turns getting at the 'facts' into a violent and futile
affair:

> The existence of the rack gave a preposterous twist to the words of every
> witness . . . inextricably confusing truth and falsehood. . . . The wisest
> and ablest of those days . . . were utterly unable to perceive that the
> conclusions, which the evidence they had collected seemed to force upon
> them, were in reality simply the result of the machinery they themselves
> had set in motion. [pp. 55–6]

The message for biographers and historians is perhaps that all interpretative frameworks are machines that will grind out conclusions
according to their own mechanisms.

* * *

Both Strachey and Woolf open up the question of the historicity of
biography and the complexity of the relationship between past and
present. At the same time, they explore the absence of symmetry
between 'inner' and 'outer' selves and, more fundamentally, question
the conceptual categories of 'inner' and 'outer' in relation to the
subject. Woolf dramatises the dissolution of ego-boundaries, with its
resulting combination of fear and freedom. The relationships
between past and present, subject and object, are thus revealed to be
aspects of the same epistemological field, and are at the same time
called into question. The dichotomies inner/outer, subject/object,
mind/body, past/present, public/private, fact/fiction, are central to
the repertoire of auto/biographical discourse. In Woolf's parody of
biography, which subverts both 'old' and 'new', she exposes and
makes strange both epistemological categories and the figurations
through which they are thought.

We should not forget, however, that *Orlando*, in particular, is a
fantasy or dream-text, overtly transgressive of the laws of space or
time, as well as the logics of conventional biography. I have not
attempted to set it up as a new model biography, but rather to explore
its relationship to the biographical discourse of its period. More
generally, I have examined the ways in which both Strachey and
Woolf open up dominant metaphors in biographical criticism,
metaphors which cover over some of the most problematic aspects of

biographical representation. These include the biographer's relationship to his or her subject, the place of the body in biography, and the temporality of the life as lived and narrated. Yet however innovative their efforts (and there has been insufficient space to explore Woolf's numerous experiments in auto/biographical writings, not least her outstanding autobiographical work 'A Sketch of the Past'), they remain closely linked, even in their oppositional stance, to many of the forms of the nineteenth century. Their desire to renew biography suggests that they still believe that the biographical form retains possibilities and that, in Woolf's terms, it might be capable of representing a 'life' worth the living. On the other hand, it may be that Woolf came to feel, as she suggests in 'The Art of Biography', that biography is a deadly practice: 'Of the multitude of lives written, how few survive.' *Orlando*, in this reading, is a wish-fulfilment in that it turns biography into an art of life in a way that only a fantasy or mock-biography – or indeed a novel – could be. The larger question, which remains with us today, is that of the scope or limits of the biographical paradigm. It is this that I explore in a rather different context in the following chapter.

Notes

1 Virginia Woolf, 'The New Biography', in *Collected Essays*, 4 vols. (London: Hogarth Press, 1966–67), Vol. IV.
2 André Maurois, *Aspects of Biography* (London: Appleton and Co., 1929), p. 101.
3 Virginia Woolf, 'The New Biography', in *Collected Essays*. p. 233.
4 Richard D. Altick, *Lives and Letters: A History of Literary Biography in England and America* (New York: Knopf, 1965), p. 289.
5 André Maurois, *Ariel: A Shelley Romance* (London: Bodley Head, 1924). The quotation is from *Aspects of Biography*, p. 51.
6 The American biographer Gamaliel Bradford was an exponent of intuition in biography. In *Types of American Character* (1895), a Theophrastan study of such generalised individuals as 'the philanthropist' and 'the man of letters', he began to develop what he called 'psychography' (see his portraits of *Damaged Souls, Saints and Sinners, The Quick and the Dead*). His sketches of actual persons were always interpreted in the light of some special insight: 'It is a perpetual revelation to find how nature herself, as it were, takes a hand, and seems to dictate the structure and composition of the psychograph.' Emil Ludwig also employed a unifying theme in his biographies of *Goethe, Bismarck, Kaiser Wilhelm*, etc. The biographer, Ludwig asserted, 'begins with a concept of character and searches in the archives for what is at bottom corroboration of an intuition'. (See John Garraty, *The Nature of Biography* (London: Cape, 1958), pp. 113–14.)

7 For a discussion of contemporary responses to Froude's biography of Carlyle, see D. J. Trela, 'Froude on the Carlyles: The Victorian Debate over Biography', in *Victorian Scandals: Representations of Gender and Class*, ed. K. O. Garrigan (Ohio University Press: Athens, 1992).

8 See William H. Epstein, *Recognizing Biography* (Philadelphia: University of Pennsylvania Press, 1987), p. 27 ff.

9 [Shand, A. Innes]. 'Contemporary Literature (No. V): biography, travel and sport', *Blackwood's Edinburgh Magazine* CXXV (April 1879), 482–506.

10 Gosse, 'The Custom of Biography' *Anglo-Saxon Review*, VIII (March 1901), p. 195.

11 *Ibid.*, p. 206.

12 Lytton Strachey, *Queen Victoria*, in *Five Victorians* (London: The Reprint Society, 1942), pp. 161–2.

13 R. G. Collingwood, *An Autobiography* (Oxford University Press, 1939), ch. 5 *passim*.

14 Izaak Walton, *The Lives of John Donne, Sir Henry Wotton, Richard Hooker, George Herbert and Robert Sanderson*, World's Classics (London: Humphrey Milford and Oxford, 1927), p.11.

15 Suzanne Raitt, *Vita and Virginia: The Work and Friendship of Vita Sackville-West and Virginia Woolf* (Oxford: Clarendon Press, 1993), p. 33.

16 Virginia Woolf, 'The Art of Biography', in *The Death of the Moth* (London: Hogarth Press, 1981), p. 121.

17 Leslie Stephen, 'National Biography', in *Studies of a Biographer*, vol. 1 (London: Smith, Elder and Co., Duckworth and Co., 1907), p. 20.

18 Michel Foucault, *The Archaeology of Knowledge*, trans. A. M. Sheridan Smith (London: Routledge, 1989), p. 7.

19 Stephen, 'National Biography', p.9.

20 Virginia Woolf, 'The Lives of the Obscure', in *The Common Reader* (Harmondsworth: Penguin, 1938), p. 118.

21 Virginia Woolf, 'Memoirs of a Novelist', in *The Complete Shorter Fiction*, ed. Susan Dick (London: Grafton Books, 1991).

22 Virginia Woolf, 'Memories of a Working Women's Guild', in Woolf, *The Captain's Death Bed* (London: Hogarth Press, 1950). The text was originally published as 'Introductory Letter to Margaret Llewelyn Davies', in *Life as We Have Known It*, by Co-Operative Working Women, ed. Margaret Llewelyn Davies (London, Hogarth Press, 1931).

23 Harold Nicolson, *The Development of English Biography* (London: Hogarth Press, 1927).

24 *Saturday Review*, LVIII (1884), 598.

25 Maurois quotes Nicolson's *The Development of English Biography* extensively in *Aspects of Biography*.

26 Sigmund Freud, 'Leonardo da Vinci and a Memory of his Childhood' (1910), Penguin Freud Library 14, 223.

27 Edmund Gosse, 'The Ethics of Biography' (1903), reprinted in *Biography as an Art* ed. James L. Clifford (London: Oxford University Press, 1962), p.114.

28 Havelock Ellis, *Sexual Inversion*, vol. II of *Studies in the Psychology of Sex* (Philadelphia: F.A.Davis, 1920), p. 316. Ellis writes, in a discussion of explanations for homosexuality: 'It is probable that we may ultimately find a

more fundamental source of these various phenomena in the stimulating and inhibiting play of the internal secretions.' Ellis footnotes Ewan Bloch (*Sexual Life of Our Time*, ch. XIX, Appendix) who 'vaguely suggests a new theory of homosexuality as dependent on chemical influences', and Hirschfeld (*Die Homosexualität*, ch. xx), who believes 'that the study of the internal secretions is the path to the deepest foundations of inversion'. Ellis also believed 'glands' to be the key to sexual identity in general. In *Man and Woman* he writes: 'We are beginning to learn that a woman is a woman because of her internal secretions. As Blair Bell has lately formulated this principle: *Propter secretiones internas totas mulier est quod est.* And precisely in a similar way a man also is a man by the totality of his internal secretions. These secretions, which are many and emanate from various parts of the body, necessarily have different and even opposed functions in the two sexes. . . . Their multiple operation is beginning to make clear how it is that a man is often not all man or a woman all woman.' Ellis, *Man and Woman: a study of human secondary sexual characters*, fifth edition (London and Felling-on-Tyne: Walter Scott Publishing Co., 1914), vi–vii.

29 For an interesting discussion of these issues, see Barbara Fassler, 'Theories of Homosexuality as Sources of Bloomsbury's Androgyny', *Signs: Journal of Women in Culture and Society* 5, 2 (1979), 237–51.

30 Lytton Strachey, 'Gibbon', in *Portraits in Miniature* (London: Chatto, 1933), p. 160.

31 V. Woolf, 'The Art of Biography', p. 123.

32 V. Woolf, *A Writer's Diary* (London: Triad/Granada, 1978), p. 119.

33 Raymond Williams, *Marxism and Literature* (Oxford University Press, 1977), pp. 146–49.

34 V. Woolf, *Three Guineas* (London: Hogarth Press, 1938).

35 Quoted by Ann Thwaite, in *Edmund Gosse: A Literary Landscape* (London: Secker and Warburg, 1984), p. 432.

36 Philip Henry Gosse attempted to reconcile the evidence of evolution with the scriptural account of genesis by arguing, in *Omphalos: An Attempt to Untie the Geological Knot* (1857), that God must have fashioned his creation as though it had a past.

37 Desmond MacCarthy, 'Lytton Strachey and the Art of Biography', in *Memories* (London: MacGibbon and Kee, 1953), p.37.

38 Edmund Gosse, 'The Agony of the Victorian Age', *The Edinburgh Review*, 228 (July/Oct 1918), 281.

39 Gosse, 'The Custom of Biography', p. 195. Lytton Strachey, *Eminent Victorians* (London: Penguin, 1948), p.10.

40 Perry Meisel, *The Myth of the Modern* (New Haven: Yale University Press, 1987), p. 202.

41 Strachey, *Eminent Victorians*, pp. 9–10.

42 Strachey, 'A New History of Rome', *Spectator* 102 (2 Jan 1909), pp. 20–1.

43 Cyril Connolly, *Enemies of Promise* (Harmondsworth: Penguin, 1961), p. 59.

44 Bertrand Russell, *The Autobiography of Bertrand Russell* (London: George Allen and Unwin, 1967), p. 257. William H. Epstein gives an interesting account of the relationship between Strachey as conscientious objector and as biographer. Sidney Lee made a clear link between military service and

'biographic service' at the end of *The Perspective of Biography* (Cambridge University Press, 1917): 'Biography will be called on ... to perform its peculiar commemorative function on a vaster scale than ever before' (p. 23).

45 Michael Holroyd, *Lytton Strachey: a Biography* (Harmondsworth: Penguin, 1971).

46 Virginia Woolf, *A Writer's Diary*, pp. 132–3.

47 Jacques Derrida, 'The Law of Genre', in *On Narrative*, ed. W. J. T. Mitchell (University of Chicago Press, 1981). I discuss Derrida's essay in detail in Chapter 6.

48 Leon Edel, *Writing Lives* (New York and London: Norton, 1987), p. 192. I have used the World's Classics edition of *Orlando*, which has an excellent introduction by Rachel Bowlby (Oxford University Press, 1992).

49 *Orlando*, p. xxxii. See also Gillian Beer, 'The Victorians in Virginia Woolf: 1832–1941', in *Arguing with the Past* (London: Routledge, 1989), pp. 138–58, for a fascinating discussion of Ruskin, Woolf and clouds.

50 See 'Laetitia Pilkington' in 'The Lives of the Obscure' (*The Common Reader*) and 'Harriette Wilson' in *The Moment and Other Essays* (London: Hogarth Press, 1947).

51 Virginia Woolf, 'How Should One Read a Book?', in *The Second Common Reader* (Harmondsworth: Penguin, 1944), p. 201.

52 Gosse, 'The Ethics of Biography', in Clifford, *Biography as an Art*, p. 114.

53 Marina Warner, *Monuments and Maidens: The Allegory of the Female Form* (London: Picador, 1987), p. 315.

54 See Mary Anne Doane, 'Veiling over Desire: Close-Ups of the Woman', in *Feminism and Psychoanalysis*, ed. Richard Feldstein and Judith Roof (Ithaca: Cornell University Press, 1989), pp. 105–41.

55 Henry James, 'George Sand', in *Selected Literary Criticism*, ed. Morris Shapira (Penguin, 1963), p. 195.

56 Friedrich Nietzsche, *The Gay Science*, trans. Walter Kauffman (New York: Random House, 1974), p. 126.

57 Orlo Williams, 'Some Feminine Biographies', *The Edinburgh Review*, 231 (Jan./April 1920). Williams, author of *The Good Englishwoman* (1920), does give a very favourable account of Ethel Smyth's *Impressions that Remained* (1919) in 'Some Feminine Autobiographies'.

58 Williams's comment echoes Oscar Wilde's aphorism: 'A man's face is his autobiography; a woman's face is her work of fiction.'

59 Sigrid Weigel, 'Double Focus: On the History of Women's Writing', in *Feminist Aesthetics*, ed. Gisela Ecker, trans. Harriet Anderson (London: The Women's Press, 1985), p. 71.

60 Marjorie Garber, *Vested Interests: Cross-Dressing and Cultural Anxiety* (New York and London: Routledge, 1992), p. 135.

61 Gillian Beer, 'Virginia Woolf and the Body of the People', in *Women Reading Women's Writing*, ed. Sue Roe (Brighton: Harvester Press, 1987), p. 97.

62 Freud, letter to Lytton Strachey, 25 December 1928, in *Bloomsbury/Freud: The Letters of James and Alix Strachey 1924–25*, ed. Perry Meisel and Walter Kendrick (New York: Basic Books, 1985), pp. 332–3.

63 Perry Meisel, *The Myth of the Modern* (New Haven: Yale University Press, 1987), p. 216.

4

Autobiography and historical consciousness

Recent attempts in a variety of disciplines to bring out the centrality of biography and autobiography have located these genres in an inter-disciplinary context; one in which categories of experience, identity and subjectivity are reworked, often as an explicit counter to the anti-humanisms of the 1970s. As Robert M. Young has written, in an article which argues for biography as 'the basic discipline for human science', a 'key to epistemology in action':

> One of the things I like most about biography is that it celebrates . . . the history of ideas, narrative, will, character and the validity of the subject's subjectivity. In biography at its best, these are combined with structural and epochal causation and the historicity of the construction of the subject and subjectivity.[1]

The interest in biography and autobiography of which this is an example recalls many of the themes of the turn-of-the-century dis-cussions in which these forms of writing and cognition were central to the constitution of the 'human sciences'. The German historian and philosopher Wilhelm Dilthey (1833–1911) was the key figure in this process, and in this chapter I pursue the line from Dilthey and his disciple Georg Misch through to the existentialist Georges Gusdorf and to more recent cultural and historical approaches to auto-biography in the work of the Germanist Roy Pascal and the American critics Karl Weintraub and Christopher Lasch. Their liberal pes-simism, to which a 'decline' model of autobiographical history is central, and in which dominant conceptions of individualism are conflated with autobiographical representations, can be contrasted with a second line of development, upon which Dilthey's influence is more diffuse. Here it is not Dilthey's focus on the auto/biographies of historically significant individuals that is taken up, but his emphases on historicity as a medium shared by all and auto/

biography as a mode of understanding, of self and other, which takes a variety of forms and to which every individual has access. This inclusive, rather than exclusive, concept of historical consciousness is central to recent work on popular and women's history and life-histories, and I refer briefly to developments in these fields in later chapters.

Dilthey located the human sciences, or *Geisteswissenschaften*, in a broad interdisciplinary project of a 'critique of historical reason' which would do for the realm of human thought, culture and society what Kant had done for the foundations of natural science. Just as science, for Kant, was based on the fundamental conceptual categories of space and time, so the human sciences, for Dilthey, are grounded in the understanding of meaningful expressions of spirit or *Geist* – itself grounded in human life and experience or *Erlebnis*. Unlike Kant, who had given philosophy a foundational role in human thought, Dilthey insists, in a way which anticipates recent critiques of metaphysical thinking, that philosophy should be understood in its interactions with sciences such as history, psychology and anthropology. The concepts of 'life', 'lived experience' (*Erlebnis*) and the understanding (*Verstehen*) of life-expressions are the central elements in his model.

Biography and autobiography are central to Dilthey's project in at least two ways. First, these genres form one end of a spectrum running through to broader forms of history, and to some extent providing their foundations. Secondly, one of the ways in which the rather undifferentiated category of 'life' becomes concretised is through an essentially biographical concept of the life-course or life-as-lived. Unlike Henri Bergson, who opposed 'life' to conceptual knowledge, Dilthey stresses the interrelation between the two. We live out our lives in a temporal frame which integrates each experience into a broader context.

The category of 'experience' has played a large part in biographical and autobiographical criticism, and, arguably, in twentieth-century literary criticism more generally. (It would be another project to trace the use of the category of 'lived experience' (*Erlebnis*) through the criticism of, for example, F. R. Leavis and Raymond Williams.) Karol Sauerland[2] has argued that Dilthey's concept of experience has one of its major sources in literature, and in particular, the 'poetry of experience' of Goethe and others. Dilthey generalises the concept and locates it in a systematic theory of interpretation and understanding, and in this form it comes to dominate German literary studies in the early twentieth century.

Experience, which in this sense is distinct from the mere registration of facts or states of affairs (one of the senses of *Erfahrung*), is the source of worthwhile literary works and the basis of their value. Dilthey sets up his concept not just in opposition to empiricism, but also to the 'lifeless' epistemology of Kant. In contrast to Kantian synthesis, experience constitutes itself directly as a unity, in which perception, emotion and judgement are fused. This principle of unity leads directly into notions of interpretation; life interprets itself. Our interpretation of our experiences is continuous with the higher forms of interpretation in literary and historical studies; these are 'all founded in lived experience, in the expressions of these experiences, and in the understanding of these expressions'.[3] Clearly, the centrality of the concept of experience in Dilthey's thought brings it particularly close to the traditional concerns of autobiographical criticism, not least in recurrent emphases on 'the whole person'. On the other hand, the ubiquity of *Erlebnis* threatens the presumed distinctiveness of autobiography. In Dilthey's account, the latter is preserved by a concept of the cultural sphere as a differentiated structure, made up of distinct, although related, domains.

Dilthey's remarks on biography and autobiography are primarily contained in his *Drafts for a critique of historical reason*, part of a collection published in 1910, but containing earlier materials.[4] Dilthey has been seen not only as the founder of a scholarly approach to autobiography, but as the progenitor of the idea that 'autobiography occupied a central place as *the* key to understanding the curve of history, every sort of cultural manifestation, and the very shape and essence of human culture itself'.[5] One of the most frequently quoted statements in autobiographical criticism is Dilthey's remark that 'In autobiography we encounter the highest and most instructive form of the understanding of life.'[6] Autobiography is the formalisation of a self-reflection which is a necessary aspect of human existence:

> Autobiography is merely the literary expression of a man's reflection on his life. Every individual reflects, more or less, on his life. Such reflection is always present and expresses itself in ever new forms. . . . Combined with an infinite desire to surrender to, and lose oneself in, the existence of others, it makes the great historian. [p. 215]

Firstly, then, the importance of autobiography for Dilthey is that it is an extension of ordinary conceptions and mental activities. 'The person who seeks the connecting threads in the history of his life has already, from different points of view, created connections which he is now putting into words ... the task of historical presentation is already half-performed by life' [p. 215]. Self-reflection, which relates to the forming of connections across time within the individual life, is to be distinguished from introspection. Autobiography is, in Dilthey's account, a second-order expression of self-reflection and not the construction of a new ordering of experience. The issue of the particular nature of autobiography as a written form is not addressed here.

Dilthey does refer to specific autobiographical texts – those of Augustine, Rousseau and Goethe – primarily as a means towards the formulation of a developmental structure of historical understanding. The importance of these autobiographies for Dilthey – he refers to them as 'typical examples' – is that all three demonstrate the centrality of the 'connectedness of life', in their different ways making the connections between experiences, and of the parts of a life to the whole. In 'Drafts for a critique of historical reason' Dilthey discusses these autobiographies within the context of an investigation of temporality, 'the life of the mind' and 'the connectedness of life'. His broader concern is with the construction of categories particular to the 'human sciences', as opposed to the natural sciences. He focuses here on temporality as a category which cannot be separated from the *experience* of time, and it is, furthermore, the experience of time which determines the content or our lives [p. 210].

In a number of formulations very close to those of William James, Dilthey describes the experience of time as an endless flow, in which 'the present is always there and nothing exists except what emerges in it'. Like James, he argues further, and paradoxically, that

> there never is a present: what we experience as present always contains memory of what has just been present ... however much we try – by some special effort – to experience the flow and strengthen our awareness of it, we are subject to the law of life itself according to which every observed moment of life is a remembered moment and not a flow; *it is fixed by attention which arrests what is essentially flow*. So we cannot grasp the essence of this life.[7]

But Dilthey also wishes to propose categories which move beyond this experiential flux, and to find principles of organisation within human life and mind. Hence his emphasis on unity and coherence, understood in terms of the relations of the parts of a life to the whole. Consciousness or mind is unitary, he states. But, and more importantly, experience is relational.

Autobiography is invoked in this context as a means towards understanding the 'specific sense in which the parts of the life of mankind are linked into a whole'. 'Autobiographies are the most direct expression of reflection about life. Those of Augustine, Rousseau and Goethe are typical examples. How, then, did these writers understand the continuity between the different parts of their lives?' [p. 213]. I have touched upon the issue of the 'exemplary' as it arises in British nineteenth-century criticism, and the tripartite classifications of autobiographical texts. These are also found in Dilthey's remarks on autobiography, but whereas the British nineteenth-century critics and commentators referred to earlier inflect the exemplary with an ethical dimension, or conflate historical stages within an autobiographical tradition with a typological schema of human personality, Dilthey argues for a concept of 'value' exemplified *within* the autobiographical structure, rather than extrapolated from the life described.

In Augustine's *Confessions*, Dilthey states, the parts of his life need to be related 'to the realization of an absolute value, an unconditional highest good. . . . Looking back, we see the meaning of all the earlier features of his life in terms of this relationship: we find not development but preparation for the turning away from all that is transitory' [p. 213]. Of Rousseau, Dilthey states:

> whatever he had done and suffered and whatever was corrupt in him, he saw himself, and this, after all, was the ideal of his age, as a noble, generous soul who felt for humanity. This he wanted to show the world; he wanted to justify his spiritual existence by showing it exactly as it was. Here, too, the outer events of a life have been interpreted by seeking connections which are not merely those of cause and effect. To name these we can only find such words as value, purpose, significance and meaning. When we look more closely we see that interpretation only takes place through a special combination of these categories. Rousseau wanted, above all, to justify his individual existence. This contains a new conception of the infinite possibilities of giving value to life. [p. 214]

Dilthey's description of Rousseau is markedly different from that of the British critics discussed earlier, who viewed him as either mad or bad. Dilthey is concerned with the way in which autobiographers –

viewed as the representatives of all individuals – imbue their own lives
with value in their own terms and those of their epoch. He is not
looking for the exemplary as an ethical ideal to be transmitted to
others. In his account of St Augustine, quoted above, the question is
one of how 'value' is constructed by Augustine, and how life-value
emerges in the organisation of the autobiography. Similarly, in his
discussion of Rousseau, it is the autobiographer's *self-conception* with
which Dilthey is concerned, not the further investigation of
'rumours' about Rousseau's life. Yet for Dilthey self-conceptions are
also historically determined; Rousseau's ideal self matches the 'ideal
of his age'.

Of Goethe's *Dichtung und Wahrheit* Dilthey states:

> a man looks at his own existence from the standpoint of universal history
> . . . he experiences the present as always filled and determined by the past
> and stretching towards the shaping of the future: thus he feels it to be a
> development. Here we can see more deeply into the relations between the
> categories which are the tools for understanding life. The significance of
> life lies in its formation and development; because of this the meaning of
> the parts of life is determined in a special way; it is both the experienced,
> intrinsic value of the moment and its effective power.
>
> Every life has its own significance, determined by a context of meaning
> in which every remembered moment has an intrinsic value, and yet, in the
> perspectives of memory, is also related to the meaning of the whole. The
> significance of an individual existence is unique and cannot be fathomed
> by knowledge, yet, in its way, like one of Leibniz' monads, it reflects the
> historical universe. [p. 214]

These remarks occur within the context of a discussion of the
categories which comprise 'Understanding' (*Verstehen*): meaning,
value and purpose. The category of meaning is linked to the past and
to memory, 'value' exists in the present and the category of purpose
arises 'as we look towards the future'. 'None of these categories',
Dilthey states, 'can be subordinated to the other because each of
them makes the whole of life accessible to the understanding from
different points of view.' But he adds, 'only the category of meaning
overcomes mere co-existence of the subordinating of the parts of life
to each other. As history is memory and as the category of meaning
belongs to memory, this is the category which pertains most
intimately to historical thinking' [p. 216].

Thus although Dilthey does not explicitly describe the movement
from Augustine to Rousseau to Goethe as progressive or developmental, this is at least suggested by his categories. Augustine, in

Dilthey's account, refuses history in 'turning away from all that is transitory' [p. 213], while Rousseau is concerned to justify his 'individual existence' [p. 214]; he may seek a presentation of self which corresponds to 'the ideal of his age', but he does not consciously present himself in relationship to his age, as does Goethe, whose 'every moment' is doubly significant, 'as enjoyed fullness of life and as an effective force in the context of life' [p. 214]. For Goethe, Dilthey states, 'the significance of life lies in its formation and development' [p. 214] as an aspect of historical consciousness. Thus despite Dilthey's assertion that the parts which constitute the whole of the life cannot be placed within a hierarchy, he clearly also views the category of 'meaning' (past and memory) as effecting 'the connectedness of life'. In other words, historical consciousness alone makes hermeneutic understanding possible.

Goethe's declared intention in his preface to *Dichtung und Wahrheit* to 'exhibit the man in relation to his age'[8] must then be perceived as a step beyond Rousseau's Romantic individualism, and his desire to embody uniqueness rather than 'connectedness'. The view of Goethe as the apogee of autobiography, of which this is an early statement, became canonical in twentieth-century German and Germanist approaches to autobiography, entailing a pessimistic assessment of the autobiographies which followed Goethe's 'sublime' achievement and a reinforcement of the exclusion of non-canonical autobiographical texts, particularly those of working-class writers and women which became more significant in the nineteenth and twentieth centuries. *Dichtung und Wahrheit* has become, in Katherine Goodman's words, 'a theoretical and a historical hurdle'[9] for students of autobiography.

Goethe's formulations on the relationship between the self, history and society are strongly echoed in Dilthey's further formulations on biography and autobiography, entitled 'The scientific character of biography' and 'Biography as a work of art',[10] from which it becomes clear that autobiography is not an end-point for Dilthey. In 'The scientific character of biography', he seems to suggest that biography is to be considered as a development from autobiography, in that it takes *expression* into the realm of *understanding*.

I discussed in Chapter 1 the perceived distinctions between biography and autobiography in nineteenth-century accounts of the genres. Common within these is the view that certain types of lives are more suited to biographical treatment, others to autobiography.

Recent critics have tended to argue that the conceptual separation of biography and autobiography which occurred from the mid-nineteenth century onwards heralded a growing theoretical sophistication in relation to literary genres and kinds. Dilthey certainly saw the specificity of autobiography in terms which appear to prefigure contemporary theorisations; for example, he stresses the fact that in autobiography 'the person who understands it [the life] is the same as the one who created it. This results in a particular intimacy of understanding.'[11] Dilthey, however, also views biography as a development out of autobiography within conceptions of the self and history; the biographer makes the crucial move from self-understanding to understanding of an other. We must begin from individual experience and understanding of that experience, giving meaning to experience through memory which creates the connections between the separate aspects of the individual life. Autobiography is the 'literary expression of this reflection by the individual on the course of his life. When, however, this reflection on one's own life is extended to the understanding of another existence, biography arises as the literary form of the understanding of another life.'

> Every life can be described, whether small or powerful, everyday life as well as exceptional life. An interest in doing this can arise from very different points of view. The family preserves its memories. Criminal justice and its theories may grasp the life of a criminal, psychopathology that of an abnormal human being. Everything human becomes a document for us which represents to us one of the infinite possibilities of our existence. But the historical human being, whose existence is linked to lasting effects, is worthy in a higher sense of living on in biography as a work of art. Among these possibilities the attention of the biographer will be particularly attracted to those whose effects emerge from depths of human existence which are particularly hard to understand and which therefore afford a deeper insight into human life and its individual forms.[12]

A number of issues arise from this statement. While Dilthey takes as his 'typical' autobiographers three writers whose classic status is unquestionable, he does not suggest that autobiography is solely the preserve of 'important' individuals. In his assertion that the task of autobiography is already half-performed by life itself, he indeed suggests that all lives are 'lived' autobiographically, whether the autobiography emerges as a formal document or not. 'Autobiography is the understanding of oneself ', Dilthey asserts, a definition which includes reference neither to the written forms this understanding takes, nor to the status of autobiographers. He also, as in the quotation above, recognises a plurality of biographical forms, in which every aspect of each life bears historical witness. Yet he does produce a more elitist theory of history when he states that it is the 'historical human being' who 'is worthy in a higher sense of living on in biography as a work of art'.

> The life of a historical personality is a complex of effects in which the individual receives influences from the historical world, develops itself under these influences and then reacts on this historical world. The same sphere of the system of the world is the origin of these influences and the recipient of further influences from the individual.[13]

Here 'reaction' has been redefined away from the 'democratised' realm of conceptual labour into a more literal and individualised valorisation of historical efficacy. Whereas all individuals are, at some level, autobiographers, only some are the suitable subjects of biography as a 'work of art'. When Dilthey refers to the 'depths of human existence', he appears to be referring to the spiritual depths possessed by specific individuals; his own biographical studies of Schleiermacher and Hegel would support this. On the other hand, Dilthey's valuations can perhaps be differentiated from the kind of judgement recently made in a discussion of biography by Robert Blake, who stated that 'the social historian is concerned with the "common man". The biographer is not.'[14] In Dilthey's system of classifications, the status of the biographical subject is an issue not simply because 'mediocre' or 'ordinary' lives are perceived to be of less interest, but because, he believes, they cannot as effectively operate as a means of assessing or understanding the nature of the relationship between the individual and his historical context. He is, that is, concerned with the *structural* relationship between the individual and history, rather than with the magnitude of a personality as a value in itself.

Biography is also viewed as having a more difficult and demanding relationship to history-writing than autobiography, not because it involves a different kind of 'truth', but because it requires a 'double focus', thus presenting the biographer with a perhaps insuperable problem: the difficulty of maintaining a focus both on the individual and on 'contemporary history'. Dilthey argues both that 'his (the individual's) meaning in the historical context can only be assessed if it is possible to obtain a general context which can be separated from this individual', and that 'biography as a work of art must find the standpoint from which the general–historical horizon opens up and yet this individual remains at the centre in a complex of causal influence and meaning'. In other words, he is arguing both that historical forces must be viewed independently of the individual, *and* that history and the individual must always be perceived in relation to each other, with the individual at the centre of the connective structure: 'This is why', Dilthey asserts, 'the art form of biography can only be applied to historical personalities, for only in them is the power to make up such a centre.'[15] Dilthey has, however, argued that in an autobiography such as Goethe's, the desired relationship between the understanding of the self and its historical context is achieved, suggesting again that the historicist autobiography is perceived as of most value.

The broader context for Dilthey's arguments is the issue of whether biography can claim a 'scientific' status equivalent to that of history-writing. Dilthey answers this with the statement that all history begins from the 'life-expressions' of individuals:

> We have here the primary cell of history. For the specific historic categories arise here. As the life is held together by a consciousness of selfhood in its succession, all the moments of life have their foundation in this category of selfhood. Discrete elements are brought together in a continuity; as we follow the line of memories from the small child living in the present up to the man who affirms himself in the face of the world in his firm self-conscious interiority, we relate the course of influences and reactions to something which forms itself and thus develops itself as something which is somehow determined from inside.[16]

Dilthey's theories have been read as a powerful valorisation of the autobiographical form and of individual subjectivity as a central principle. This is certainly endorsed by a number of his statements. But he also, particularly in his later work, argues that the standpoint of the individual life has its limitations:

> general movements go through the individual as a transitional point; we must find new foundations for understanding them which are not located in the individual. Biography is not alone capable of setting itself up as a scholarly work of art. *We must turn to new categories, shapes and forms of life which are not exhausted by the individual life.* . . . The fixed relations of autobiography disappear. We leave the river of (the course of a) life and are taken up by the infinite sea.
> History makes us free by raising us above the limitation of the mean-

ingful viewpoint arising from our life. At the same time meaning is less certain here. Reflection on our life gives us depth, history makes us free.

But on this broad sea we take with us the orienting resources which have been developed in experience, understanding, autobiography and the biographical work of art.[17]

These remarks qualify Dilthey's statement that 'In autobiography we encounter the highest and most instructive form of the understanding of life';[18] the perspective from and of the self limits as well as orients. If autobiography is the 'primary cell' of history, it is also a first stage in the trajectory from autobiography to biography to history itself.

The second issue is that of unity and coherence in the life of the self-conscious and self-affirming individual and his work. Coherence and continuity become closely linked, and the life takes on the lineaments of the career. The 'life-course' becomes identified with the progressive model of professional, largely male, advancement. However much women might need in principle to affirm themselves in the face of a world which is not merely hostile but misogynistic, the terms in which this self-affirmation is couched are ones which are very likely to exclude women, and indeed all those outside the structures of the bourgeois career.

It is interesting, however, that Dilthey locates the principle of unity in the human mind and understanding rather than in the organising structures of textual artefacts. There is no sense in his theories that the biographer or autobiographer *imposes* a coherent narrative upon random experiences. Indeed, there is little sense of a distinction between primary and secondary creation, given that the *writing* of an autobiography is viewed as an extension of ordinary self-reflection. This has been an ambiguous legacy for subsequent theories of autobiography. The emphasis on unity and coherence is taken up in a number of conservative approaches to autobiography, and it is not clear that coherence theories of autobiographical 'truth' – Roy Pascal's study is one example – are necessarily more liberating than correspondence theories which emphasise autobiography's factuality. On a different note, Dilthey's suggestion that the distinction between autobiographical consciousness and autobiographical writing is one of degree and not of kind has been an important influence on more democratic theorists of life-writing. To paraphrase Gramsci's remark about intellectuals, everyone is an autobiographer, but not everyone has the social function of an autobiographer.

Ambiguities pervade subsequent developments of many of Dilthey's ideas, including his concept of experience. While Dilthey's valorisation of *Erlebnis* over *Erfahrung* is part of a broad current of early twentieth-century thought, it was challenged from several directions. Walter Benjamin, in particular, reverses the evaluative charge of the terms, stressing the fragmentation of *Erlebnis* in the modern world and contrasting it with a conception of *Erfahrung* broadened out from its narrowly rationalistic sense into a more speculative notion as something akin to group memory, involving the collective appropriation of tradition.[19] Maurice Halbwachs, whose important work on collective and group memory is, like Dilthey's, a reaction to Henri Bergson's intuitionist and subjectivist philosophies, may be said to have moved beyond Dilthey in his richer theorisation of history as memory, and his understanding of the individual's reflection on his past as irreducibly social. Halbwachs's ideas also have particular relevance to this running theme of inner and outer 'life' in autobiographical discourse, for he points up the meaning-lessness of any conception of pure interiority or exteriority. Individual memory only takes its form in social frameworks, while a purely external relation to the world is impossible because there are 'no perceptions without recollections'.[20]

Dilthey's project of a critique of historical reason and a systematisation of the whole of the human sciences and their pro-gressive development must necessarily seem somewhat dated. His original formulations have indeed been branded as merely irra-tionalist *Lebensphilosophie*, while the category of experience itself has been rejected by structuralist and deconstructionist theorists as an unusable humanist residue. On the other hand, the contestation of traditional approaches to autobiography by groups stressing gender, class and ethnic difference has characteristically appealed to what in the feminism of the 1970s was described as the 'authority of experience', at times used in opposition to abstract theoretical systems. Recent developments in 'identity politics' have included a return to a concept of experience, but one which is both more differentiated than its direct predecessors and critical of approaches like Dilthey's. For while Dilthey is sensitive to the differentiations in the sphere of culture, it could be argued that his attempts to objectify subjectivity preclude an adequate differentiation of the 'experiences' of different cultural groups.

Dilthey's approach also suffers from a presupposition of the self-transparency of consciousness, difficult to sustain after Freud. In Jürgen Habermas's words: 'Dilthey chose biography as a model because life-history seemed to have the merit of transparency. It does not resist memory through opacity.' Yet Dilthey's assumption of, in Habermas's words, 'the intentional structure of subjective consciousness as the ultimate experiential basis in the process of appropriating objective mind' has influenced our understanding of how individuals' self-reflection combines with and structures their relation to culture.[21] As James Clifford and George Marcus note: 'hermeneutic philosophy . . . from Wilhelm Dilthey and Paul Ricoeur to Heidegger reminds us that the simplest cultural accounts are intentional creations, that interpreters constantly construct themselves through the others they study'.[22] This in turn has implications for an autobiographical criticism which attempts to relate individual autobiographies to broader cultural forms.

*   *   *

The complex history of the writing and publication of Georg Misch's *Geschichte der Autobiographie* bears witness not only to the difficulty of Misch's historical project but to the fraught history of the twentieth century itself. The project, which sought in part to demonstrate the progressive development of the concept of the self within a universalised 'Western culture', came to English readers in 1950: Misch translated and expanded the first two volumes, published in Germany some forty years earlier, while taking refuge in England 'during the period of Nazi domination'.[23]

Misch's study of autobiography is an enormously detailed chronological account of written forms, from Egyptian tomb inscriptions onwards, with the major part of the work being devoted to medieval writings. The final sections of the work, covering post-Renaissance autobiography, were added after Misch's death; they were, in fact, the drafts of his prize-winning submission to the Prussian Academy of Sciences, dating from around 1900, on the basis of which he was able to embark on his lifetime project. The translation into English of his work and the publication of the later volumes coincides with and influenced the increasing critical interest in autobiography as a genre from the 1950s and 1960s, and the growth of 'autobiographical studies', discussed in the next chapter.

Dilthey was Misch's father-in-law as well as his teacher, and *Geschichte der Autobiographie* is dedicated to him. Dilthey's hermeneutics, with their emphasis on unity and coherence as fundamental principles, prefigure the critical and conceptual focus which has come to largely dominate the critical field of autobiography-studies. The particular inflection this focus takes in Misch's work is therefore of some significance in the study of the development of genre criticism. Finally, the original context for Misch's work – the desire to depict how concepts of self, individuality and personality have developed through history – needs to be considered both in relation to the theories of the subject informing autobiographical criticism and to recent critiques of the premises of these theories. Misch represents an ultimately conservative development of Dilthey's thought which incorporates autobiographies into a Whiggish history of the advance of the human mind.

Misch's approach appears to testify to a new theoretical self-consciousness in relation to the study of autobiography; he begins by outlining previous approaches to the topic, charting the growth of interest in the 'cultural phenomenon of autobiography' from the Renaissance onwards. Eighteenth-century empiricists, he notes, viewed autobiographical literature as an important source for knowledge of the world and of man; to this German historicism added a 'deeper' view, 'influenced by the idea of the development of human civilization'.

It is noticeable that Misch chooses to emphasise the radical heterogeneity of autobiographical forms. Unlike the nineteenth-century British critics discussed earlier, who attempted to classify autobiographical texts, with varying degrees of exactitude, in relation to the tripartite structure of literary categories, Misch asserts that autobiography is *unlike* any other form of literary composition:

> Its boundaries are more fluid and less definable in relation to form than those of lyric or epic poetry or of drama. Autobiography is one of the innovations brought by cultural advance, and yet it springs from the most natural source, the joy in self-communication and in enlisting the sympathetic understanding of others; or the need for self-assertion. In itself it is a representation of life that is committed to no definite form. [p. 4]

Misch's statement ramifies in a number of directions. It bears on more recent debates between those who seek to define autobiography in generic terms, and critics for whom the significance of autobiography is that it transcends literary conventions. It allows Misch the freedom to 'discover' autobiographical works everywhere he looks. Most importantly, perhaps, autobiography is seen to spring from 'life' itself, rather than from the formal categories of 'art'. Thus when he states of autobiography that 'hardly any form is alien to it', it becomes an entity which can incorporate a wealth of forms but is not itself definable in formal terms. Autobiographers can and have made use of all written modes, 'and if they were persons of originality they modified the existing types of literary composition or even invented new forms of their own'. 'This wealth of forms itself shows what life there is in the autobiographical *genre*', Misch adds, the term 'life' both suggesting the creative possibilities of the autobiographical mode and reinforcing the view that it is 'life' rather than 'art' which is contained therein.

Although he states that autobiography transcends classification, Misch differentiates between 'memoirs' and 'autobiography'. While 'memoirs' has a deeper meaning, he asserts, in that it refers to the classical belief that the psychological source of history is the memory, it has come to possess more superficial associations as a 'merely' historical resource, without literary pretensions or the securing of the identity of the subject and object which is the central purpose and interest of autobiography: 'It is on this identity of author and subject that is based the great interest we moderns have in autobiography. From this point of view this chameleon-like *genre* secures a unity that it does not possess in literary form. And from this element of unity proceed the substantial merits of the *genre*' [p. 7].

Misch offers a further distinction between 'memoirs' and 'auto-biography' – one that is now accepted within critical parlance – when he states that memoirs offer a passive relation to the world, their writers introducing themselves as 'merely observers of the events and activities of which they write', whereas in autobiography the life-story is central. I will return to this active/passive opposition later, focusing for the moment on Misch's category of unity. There are of course very few critical works on autobiography which do not take the self-identity of author and subject as the most salient feature of autobiography, or, as in Misch's case, use it as the essential definition of the genre itself. I would suggest, however, that its very obviousness has occluded its wider conceptual significance. For this reason, it is worth exploring in some detail as it appears in Misch's text.

The importance of author–subject identity for Misch is primarily that it secures an essential unity, echoing the broader philosophical theme of subject–object identity, for what he has, for other reasons, constituted as a genre without formal limits. But it would not be significant were it not for the fact that it allows Misch to adduce that individual lives possess the same intrinsic unity and coherence. Following Dilthey, Misch writes:

> the man who sets out to write the story of his own life has it in view as a whole, with unity and direction and a significance of its own. In this single whole the facts and feelings, actions and reactions, recalled by the author, the incidents that excited him, the persons he met, and the transactions or movements in which he was concerned, all have their definite place, thanks to their significance in relation to the whole. . . . This knowledge, which enables the writer to conceive his life as a single whole, has grown in the course of his life out of his actual experience, whereas we have the life of any other person before us as a whole only *ex post facto*: the man is dead, or at all events it is all past history. [p. 7]

The hermeneutic emphasis on the relation of part to whole recalls Dilthey, but Misch departs significantly from him when he suggests that autobiography offers a higher form of knowledge than biography; in Dilthey's account, as we have seen, biography involves an empathy with another life which is valued as highly as self-understanding. Whereas understanding (*Verstehen*) in Dilthey's account contains reference to an interpretive act, Misch is more concerned with the 'fundamental – and enigmatical – psychological phenomenon which we call consciousness of self or self-awareness (in German *Selbstbewusstsein*). . . . In a certain sense the history of autobiography is a history of human self-awareness' [p. 8].

The passage above also reveals a more general difficulty in the critical assumption that autobiography represents a life as a 'single whole'. Clearly, the autobiographer, unlike the biographer, is unable to tell the end of the story. From this perspective, the 'whole' to which the parts relate is incomplete. This is not a conclusion entertained by either Dilthey or Misch: indeed, their insistence, like that of more recent critics, on other guarantors of unity may well be an attempt at its avoidance. Thus the emphasis on subject/object identity endorses the idea of a unity of life without death: unity arises out of 'lived experience', and death has been held not to be an experience.

In addition to the unity of author and subject within the individual autobiography, Misch locates a fundamental and universal 'psychological root' underlying, and hence unifying, all autobiographies.

This he terms man's need for 'self-revelation', and he does not appear to distinguish between self-awareness and the need for self-revelation or 'self-assertion':

> it is of the very essence of human existence that we can raise to the clarity of consciousness that which moves us 'deep down'. We live in possession of ourselves, after the special manner of a being conscious of itself and capable of saying 'I'. To stand as an I, or, more exactly, as an 'I'-saying person, over against other persons and living beings and the things around us implies that we are aware of our independent existence.... Self-awareness gives us the feeling that the impetus of life is a sort of emanation from ourselves. [pp. 8–9]

In this formulation, self-awareness can be seen as synonymous with self-assertion in so far as consciousness of selfhood necessarily involves a separation of self not only from but against others. There are points in Misch's introduction in which he calls even more overtly on the language of power; for example, in defining the forms of relationship with the world manifested in autobiographies, he states that 'among the special relationships in life it is chiefly the self-assertion of that political will and the relation of the author to his work and to the public that show themselves to be normative in the history of autobiography' [p. 14]. In the light of such statements, it is possible to read the memoirs/autobiography, passive/active relationship as more than a convenient way of classifying literary forms; it becomes a statement about the individual's power, not so much, or not only, to act upon the world, but to assert the centrality of self by viewing the world as an 'emanation' from the self. The writers of memoirs, conversely, efface themselves within the histories they observe and record. It is no accident that women have tended to write 'memoirs' rather than 'autobiographies', and that the memoir-form has been consistently belittled in autobiographical criticism. Misch's discussion reveals the extent to which the autobiography/memoirs distinction is bound up with issues of power and powerlessness.

Any approach to autobiography which seeks to adduce from autobiographical texts the spirit of their age will of necessity have to engage with the issue of the representative status of individuals:

> Though essentially representations of individual personalities, autobiographies are bound always to be representative of their period.... In the exemplary form of autobiography, personality is to be seen and felt not only as the subject of the narrative but as a formative power. Thus the characteristic self-revelations provide us with an objective, indeed, a

demonstrable image of the structure of individuality, varying from epoch to epoch. [pp. 12–13]

Misch emphasises the view that the dependence of an autobiography on a pre-existent literary form, or the 'merely literary' presentation of the self, is a marker of mediocrity, and links originality with historical eminence. The issue of representativeness thus becomes inseparable from perceived distinctions between mediocre and great art; mediocre art corresponds to an 'average' cultural nexus, but the great autobiography represents the 'higher' forms of its author's age. And, as in Dilthey's discussion of biography, the extent of the auto-biographer's actual, and apparently measurable, participation in and influence on his time is a decisive factor for the perceived value of his autobiographical work and its exemplary nature.

Secondly, Misch raises the question of fact in autobiography, opting for coherence rather than correspondence as the criterion of truth. He states that 'autobiographies are not to be regarded as objective narratives':

> in general their truth is to be sought not so much in their elements as in the whole works, each of which is more than the sum of its parts. . . . even the cleverest liar, in his fabricated or embroidered stories of himself, will be unable to deceive us as to his character. He will reveal it through the spirit of his lies. Thus in general, the spirit brooding over the recollected material is the truest and most real element in an autobiography. [pp. 10–11]

This 'spirit', however, is given 'objective' status by Misch, in so far as its comprehensive and holistic nature 'produces a creative objectivation of the autobiographer's mind that cannot be other than true'. Thus although Misch wishes to depart from empiricist concepts of truth as correspondence to historical data or 'facts', the truth of the individual is given an 'objective' status and can be sublated into a universal history. In this way, he is departing from Dilthey's more concrete emphases on the value of 'lived experience' and construct-ing a Romantic version of the relation between self and world. Furthermore, Misch's holism, evidenced in his statement that the whole is more than the sum of its parts, can perhaps be differentiated from Dilthey's hermeneutic emphasis on the interrelationship between part and whole.

In Misch's account, the issue of the historian's or the critic's role in *constructing* a historical or critical trajectory simply does not arise:

autobiographies are works defined by their natural inner unity and form; taken as a whole they demonstrate the coherence and consistency in and of the development of Western man. The triumph of the West in cultural terms is perceived by Misch to be intimately linked, or perhaps to result from, Western man's ability, which increases throughout the centuries, to reflect upon himself and his situation. Unlike Dilthey, Misch is not a critic of introspection as a concept; he defines it as equivalent to 'meditation on the self, or self-communion or self-scrutiny'. And although Misch does not clearly define what he means by 'personality', it is for him a key term in defining cultural advance:

> in the Western world the most direct impulse to the growth of self-scrutiny arose from the formative influence upon life of the consciousness and evaluation of personality. This consciousness is not part of the general inheritance of peoples; it has been gradually acquired in the clear light of advancing civilization; it exists in the most manifold forms and at all sorts of levels, and the other tendencies also, practical philosophy and aspiration toward the eternal, gain this-wordly perfection through association with the sense of personality. In this way autobiography, through the meditative element in it, co-operates with the great spiritual forces in the freeing and deepening of human life. [pp. 15–16]

In his formulation of Dilthey's statement that 'reflection on our life gives us depth, history makes us free', Misch suggests that both 'depth' and 'freedom' are the rewards of autobiographical 'self-scrutiny'. In developing Dilthey's theories of autobiography, Misch has turned a relatively sensitive model of the relationship between self and culture into a self-congratulatory account of Western civilisation and a celebration of autonomous individualism as an absolute value. This approach has influenced even those critics who have foregrounded the independent contributions of working-class autobiographers, some of whom have simply generalised the Mischian model of an implicitly bourgeois individualism to emergent working-class movements of political and cultural affirmation.[24]

There is no way round the fact that the discourse of the growth of human individuality, from classical Greece through the Renaissance and the Enlightenment, is ineradicably masculinist. What autobiographical discourse has traditionally offered is a way of ordering or even constructing conceptions of human nature drawn from culturally desirable models, which rarely if ever included women. This is at least a partial explanation why the structures which excluded women were apparently more efficacious in autobiography than in most other genres. We should however avoid a model in which women are silenced. They did write, and in many cases publish, autobiographies, from the Middle Ages onwards, secular and religious, but these rarely achieve full canonical status. It is of course enormously important to re-examine these texts, and thus to redress the historically entrenched disproportion, but to rewrite the history and theory of autobiography also requires a conceptual approach which would explore the gender connotations of individualism.

* * *

We can trace three principal lines of development from Dilthey and Misch. The first is the autobiographical theory of the existential phenomenologist Georges Gusdorf, which became influential through his essay 'Conditions et limites de l'autobiographie' (1956). The second, an orthodox line of liberal cultural criticism, is represented in autobiographical criticism by Roy Pascal's *Design and Truth in Autobiography* (1960) and Karl Weintraub's *The Value of the Individual* (1978) – both strongly influenced by Dilthey's and Misch's writings on autobiography. Finally, recent thematisations of historicity and historical consciousness, particularly in working-class and women's history and life-histories, can be understood as a democratised version of these earlier questions. The progressive and developmental models of history outlined above become highly problematical in a more sceptical twentieth century; one of the themes I discuss in later chapters concerns the critical negotiations and conflicts that arise from this change of context.

* * *

Georges Gusdorf's 'Conditions et limites de l'autobiographie' was originally published in a Festschrift in Germany, reprinted in Lejeune's *L'Autobiographie en France* (1971) and translated and reprinted in James Olney's *Autobiography: Essays Theoretical and Critical*, which set the terms for many of the debates about autobiography in the 1980s. 'In the beginning, then, was Georges Gusdorf ', Olney asserts in the overview of autobiography and auto-biographical criticism with which he introduces *Autobiography: Essays Theoretical and Critical*. 'It is only with Gusdorf 's essay . . . that all the questions and concerns – philosophical, psychological, literary, and more generally humanistic – that have preoccupied students of auto-biography from 1956 to 1978 were first fully and clearly laid out and given comprehensive, if necessarily brief, consideration.'[25]

Gusdorf 's work developed within the post-1930s intellectual cul-ture of France, and combines intellectual history with Christian existentialism, and the philosophies of Kierkegaard and Heidegger. Gusdorf is concerned with the growth and development of man's self-knowledge and self-awareness which, in a later essay, 'De l'autobiographie initiatique à l'autobiographie genre littéraire', he locates primarily in a Christian context: the carving out of an inner space through the Protestant, Puritan and pietistic traditions in which the 'soul' finds itself through communion with God. In many ways this reproduces Dilthey's concern with subjective experience as a development out of pietism and the introspective tradition. In Gusdorf 's account, this is opposed to the public confessional mode of Catholicism and the orthodoxies of the eighteenth-century church in France. The history of religion is, for Gusdorf, closely aligned with the history of psychology, and the 'opening up' of an inner space within the self through spiritual self-seeking leads directly, in his account, to modern secular man's preoccupation with the psyche, the inner space within the self.

Gusdorf 's aim in 'Conditions and Limits of Autobiography', is, he states, to 'sort out the implicit presuppositions of autobiography'; to look beyond the unquestionable status and popularity of both literary autobiography and 'memoirs', in order to assess its significance. The 'conditions' for autobiography are, in his view, historical and cultural: 'the genre of autobiography seems limited in time and in space: it has not always existed nor does it exist everywhere'. Autobiography would appear to be possible only within Western society, and emerges only at the moment at which Christianity is grafted on to classical traditions, St Augustine's *Confessions* offering us 'a brilliantly successful landmark'.[26] Both historical consciousness and indivi-dualism are essential preconditions: 'at the cost of a cultural revolu-tion humanity must have emerged from the mythic framework of traditional teachings and must have entered into the perilous domain of history' [pp. 29–30]. The importance of the historic personage emerges in biography, which becomes established as a literary genre. But, Gusdorf asserts:

> biography provides only an exterior presentation of great persons. . . . The appearance of autobiography implies a new spiritual revolution: the artist and the model coincide, the historian tackles himself as object. . . . Our interest is turned from public to private history. . . . This conversion is late in coming insofar as it corresponds to a difficult evolution – or rather to an *in*volution of consciousness. [pp. 31–2]

To the 'light clear space' of exteriority and the public world, Gusdorf contrasts the 'shadowy nature of interior space'. Thus whereas biography is a straightforwardly achieved enterprise, legitimated in the public sphere ('the demands of propaganda and . . . the general sense of the age'), autobiography involves 'the complex and agonizing sense that the encounter of a man with his image carries' [p. 32]. The discovery of the self is both difficult and disconcerting. Gusdorf relates the emergence of autobiography to the invention of the mirror, while 'autobiography is the mirror in which the individual reflects his own image'. While Gusdorf's account of mirroring has been taken as a simple affirmation of autobiography's ability to reflect the self 'as it is', he in fact emphasises that 'the narrative of a life cannot be simply the image-double of that life' [p. 40]. Moreover, his invocation of the Narcissus myth suggests a more troubled view of the alienated experience of subjectivity.

Thus, in Gusdorf's account, autobiography is both an historically situated manifestation of 'self-discovery' – he appears at some points to endorse the widely held view that, in Lacan's words, the 'inaugural moment of the emergence of the subject'[27] occurs at the beginning of the seventeenth century – and the means by which the anxieties arising from this self-encounter, which 'Nature did not foresee' [p. 32] are appeased, through the autobiographical assertion of self-identity and unity across time. However, it is also important for Gusdorf's later arguments in the essay that the difficulty and complexity of the 'original' self-encounter be stressed, in order to maintain that the subject/object identity – self and image, writing 'I' and written 'I' – occurs within *incompletion*. The 'I' must be held to be unfinished in order to uphold the concept of self as process and becoming.

Preceding the discovery of actual mirrors, Gusdorf states, there is the theological mirror of the Christian Middle Ages; 'a deforming mirror that plays up without pity the slightest faults of the moral personality'. It is not until the Renaissance that 'man could have any interest in seeing himself as he is without any taint of the transcendent'. This new age practises the virtue of *individuality*; to this the Romantic era, with its exaltation of genius, reintroduces the taste for autobiography, and adds to individuality the virtue of *sincerity*, 'the heroism of understanding and telling all, reenforced even more by the teachings of psychoanalysis' [p. 34].

This, then, is the broad cultural history of autobiography which Gusdorf maps out. It is, in fact, a somewhat ambiguous account: in contrast to the progressive models of history of Dilthey and Misch, Gusdorf emphasises the loss which results from historical consciousness, including the loss of traditional societies through colonisations which are a product of the same impulses which make autobiography possible. 'The old world is in the process of dying in the very interior of that consciousness that questions itself about its destiny' [p. 29]. Thus he both produces a 'progressive' model of history and simultaneously undermines it.[28]

Gusdorf also examines the undertaking of autobiography itself, its intentions and its chances of success. The constitutive feature of autobiography is that 'the autobiographer strains towards a complete and coherent expression of his entire destiny': it 'requires a man to take a distance with regard to himself in the focus of his special unity and identity across time'. He also makes it the special prerogative of autobiography to show a life from the inside: 'I alone have the privilege of discovering myself from the other side of the mirror – nor can I be cut off by the wall of privacy' [p. 35]. But the special nature of this witness becomes of less value when it is employed for the purposes of defending one's reputation, or for self-aggrandisement. This is most often the case in the 'memoirs' of public men, which, like biography, Gusdorf views as simple, not complex, representations, whose 'methodological problems are no different from those of the ordinary writing of history' [p. 36].

By contrast:

The question changes utterly when the private face of existence assumes more importance. . . . Rousseau, Goethe, Mill are not content to offer the reader a sort of *curriculum vitae* retracing the steps of an official career that, for importance, was hardly more than mediocre. In this case it is a question of another truth. The act of memory is carried out for itself, and recalling of the past satisfies a more or less anguished disquiet of the mind anxious to recover and redeem lost time in fixing it forever. . . .

Furthermore, autobiography properly speaking assumes the task of reconstructing the unity of a life across time. This lived unity of attitude and act is not received from the outside; certainly events influence us; they sometimes determine us, and they always limit us. But the essential themes, the structural designs that impose themselves on the complex material of exterior facts are the constituent elements of the personality. Today's complex psychology has taught us that man, far from being subject to ready-made, completed situations given from outside and without him, is the essential agent in bringing about the situations in which he finds himself placed. It is his intervention that structures the terrain where his life is lived and gives it its ultimate shape, so that the landscape is truly, in Amiel's phrase, 'a state of the soul'. [p. 37]

Gusdorf's affiliations to existentialist philosophy are apparent, notably in his claim that the human being creates his own situation; but he also adds to this an emphasis on the unified essence of the self: 'my individual unity, the mysterious essence of my being'. His particular version of existential phenomenology is also manifested here. Existential phenomenology emphasises both the primacy of experience as lived and concrete experience, and the necessity of a 'phenomenological' method of descriptive analysis to apprehend such experience. Man *is* his experience, but he can also reflectively describe the lived sense of experiential phenomena. The privileged role of autobiography for Gusdorf is that, through his definition of the form, autobiography itself becomes this 'phenomenological' description or analysis; 'autobiography is a second reading of experience, and it is truer than the first because it adds to experience itself consciousness of it'. The 'truth' of the self or the life emerges in this second reading, revealing the profound elements of experience which make up individual destiny, as opposed to the 'agitation of things' in the immediate moment. 'The passage from immediate experience to consciousness in memory, which effects a sort of repetition of that experience, also serves to modify its significance. A new mode of being appears if it is true, as Hegel claimed, that "consciousness of self is the birthplace of truth" ' [p. 38].

Without this 'second reading', Gusdorf seems to suggest, a life can only appear unfulfilled or 'inwardly botched'. Thus the motive for writing autobiography appears to be less the desire for self-knowledge as such, than the need to redeem an uncertain destiny; 'the task of autobiography is first of all a task of personal salvation . . .

its deepest intentions . . . a kind of apologetics or theodicy of the individual being' [p. 39]. Gusdorf seems to assume that autobiography is almost a final gesture, written at the close of a life. This assumption is surely questionable, but testifies to the importance of the theme of existential anxiety in Gusdorf's thought, or even a Heideggerian 'being-towards-death'.

The gap between the avowed plan or commonsensical understanding of autobiography as the simple retracing of the history of a life, and its 'deepest intentions' as a form of apologia, accounts, Gusdorf asserts, for the 'puzzlement and the ambivalence of the literary genre'. In historical methodology, the belief in 'an objective and critical history worshipped by the positivists of the nineteenth century has crumbled. . . . The recall of history assumes a very complex relation of past to present, a re-actualization that prevents us from ever discovering the past "in itself", as it was – the past without us.' The same principle, the impossibility of capturing the past 'as it was' applies equally to autobiography; 'the original sin of autobiography is first one of logical coherence and rationalization':

> In short, a kind of Bergsonian critique of autobiography is necessary: Bergson criticizes classical theories of volition and free will for reconstructing a mode of conduct after the fact and then imagining that at the decisive moments there existed a clear choice between various possibilities, whereas in fact actual freedom proceeds on its own impetus and there is ordinarily no choice at all. Likewise, autobiography is condemned to substitute endlessly the completely formed for that which is in the process of being formed. With its burden of insecurity, the lived present finds itself caught in that necessary movement, that, along the thread of the narrative, binds the past to the future. [p. 41]

In separating 'actual freedom' from will and volition, freedom becomes an abstraction not held within the individual life or experience; in other words, 'freedom' and 'agency' become divorced. Although the quotation above is somewhat obscure, and appears to contradict the claim made earlier that 'man . . . is the essential agent in bringing about the situations in which he finds himself placed', it seems to be the case that Gusdorf is linking 'freedom' with 'destiny' as the 'essential themes, the structural designs' of a life. Freedom is non-volitional in so far as it constitutes the fulfilment of an essential selfhood, beyond conscious choice.

Alternatively, Gusdorf is perhaps making a claim for 'freedom' as indeterminism and process; the imposition of meaning on past events denies their multiple meanings, or indeed, non-meanings. In this reading, retrospection falsifies when it attempts to delineate a logical and causal chain of events and experiences, thus reducing the open-endedness of being. Gusdorf writes:

> One must choose a side and give up the pretence of objectivity, abandoning a sort of false scientific attitude that would judge a work by the precision of its detail . . . in autobiography the truth of facts is subordinate to the truth of the man, for it is first of all the man who is in question. . . . The significance of autobiography should therefore be sought beyond truth and falsity, as those are conceived by simple common sense. [p. 43]

Two lines of argument are being intertwined here; the first relates to the temporality of the life and of the subject, the second to the priority of subjective over objective truths. The question of an inner, subjective and non-verifiable truth of the individual being is inextricable, in his argument, from the rejection of the linear chronology of historical time; a rejection related to the ambiguities of Gusdorf's own models of history, and to his accounts of the relationship between autobiography and history. He states, as quoted above, that contemporary historical methodologies share the complex concepts of temporal process necessary for understanding the essence of autobiography. The autobiographer may write under the illusion that the past can be recaptured 'as it was' – the same illusion entertained by positivist historiography – but the 'new' history tells us this is not possible. The solution in the case of autobiography is to understand it not as an 'objective' document but as 'the parable of a consciousness in quest of its own truth' [p. 44]. Turning this back on to historical methodology, Gusdorf argues that this model is equally applicable to history and the other human sciences: 'the objective space of history is always a projection of the mental space of this historian'. Thus the significance of autobiography for Gusdorf in this context is that it allows him to assert that the methodologies of the human sciences take as their 'proper' model 'a likeness no longer of things but of the human person' [pp. 44–5].

At other points Gusdorf appears to be claiming that autobiography and history have wholly different cognitive interests and methodologies. In Dilthey's arguments, as we saw, the difference is more one of scope and range. Whereas for Dilthey historicity is an objective property, in Gusdorf's argument, as in existentialist thought more generally, it becomes a problematic. Thus, as in other autobiographical criticism, autobiography is at times defined only in contradistinction to history: that is, autobiography is what history is not.

The temporal mode of autobiography, Gusdorf reiterates, is the present. 'Confession of the past realizes itself as a work in the present: it effects a true creation of the self by the self. Under the guise of presenting myself as I was, I exercise a sort of right to recover possession of my existence now and later' [p. 44]. Theories of the temporality of the subject are to be found in the writings of Lacan and Sartre of the 1950s, and can be traced back to Heidegger.[29] For Gusdorf, the subject exists both in a presentness which is also directed towards the future, and in an atemporal mode: 'Temporal perspectives thus seem to be telescoped together and to inter-penetrate one another; they commune in that self-knowledge that regroups personal being above and beyond its own time limits.' The rejection of history is thus not simply a repudiation of positivism or simplistic concepts of verifiability but a critique of historical time as pastness or 'what was'. What positivist history, now made the equivalent of 'simple common sense', fails to appreciate is, however, recognised in the sphere of literature and aesthetics, that is, 'a truth of the man'. But:

> the literary function itself, if one would really understand the essence of autobiography, appears yet secondary in comparison with the anthropological significance. Every work of art is a projection from the interior realm into exterior space where in becoming incarnated it achieves consciousness of itself. Consequently, there is need of a second critique that instead of verifying the literal accuracy of the narrative or demonstrating its artistic value would attempt to draw out its innermost, private significance by viewing it as the symbol, as it were, or the parable of consciousness in quest of its own truth. [pp. 43–4]

Beyond history *and* literature, then, is 'anthropology', used in its broadest sense to mean the study of man. If, to extrapolate from Gusdorf's argument, history – in one of its guises, at least – is only capable of comprehending the public world of exterior events, and literary studies are bound into the appreciation of pure forms and images, the humanistic or 'anthropological' focus is the only stance adequate to meet an emergent 'consciousness'.

In the literary sphere

> creation of a literary world begins with the author's confession: the narrative that he makes of his life is already a first work of art, the first

deciphering of an affirmation that, at a further stage of stripping down and recomposing, will open out in novels, in tragedies, or in poems.

In this reading 'there are two guises or two versions of autobiography: on the one hand, that which is properly called confession: on the other hand, the artist's entire work, which takes up the same material in complete freedom and under the protection of a hidden identity'. This is not simply a question of an autobiographical content held within imaginative literature, but the fact that

> every work is autobiographical insofar as being registered in the life it alters the life to come. Better still, it is the peculiar nature of the literary calling that the work, even before it has been realized, can have an effect on being. The autobiography is lived, played before being written; it fixes a kind of retrospective mark on the event even as it occurs. [pp. 46–7]

The special case that is made for the 'artist' is that he lives his life 'autobiographically', endlessly composing its materials into the form of a work of art.

In Gusdorf's account, life, work and autobiography become conjoined in a mythic apprehension of the self.

> In the final analysis, then, the prerogative of autobiography consists in this: that it shows us not the objective stages of a career – to discern these is the task of the historian – but that it reveals instead the effort of a creator to give the meaning of his own mythic tale. [p. 48]

Thus history gives way to myth. The paradox contained within Gusdorf's theorisations in this essay is that he begins from the point where autobiography is made possible within culture because mythic apprehensions give way to historical time and consciousness. Yet he ends with the formulation that chronological order, 'which is altogether external', comes to seem illusory when set against the discovery or laying bare of 'those essential themes that will render the man and the work intelligible'. The conditions of autobiography would thus seem to entail a movement from cultural and collective mythologies to the individuation of personal mythology; a move which bypasses history altogether and reasserts the centrality of the 'mythic framework'.[30]

*   *   *

The tradition of cultural pessimism discussed in the following section, with particular reference to the work of Roy Pascal and Karl Weintraub, is one of the central strands of European nineteenth- and twentieth-century thought, running across the whole political spectrum from Marxist socialism to Fascism. A Romantic conception of the estrangement of the individual from society is complemented by a critique of capitalism and industrialism, urbanism and bureaucracy. As in the Victorian critical discourse examined in Chapter 1, the 'decline' of autobiography is given a key role as expression and symptom of this cultural malaise. Like Greek art, and in particular the epic, in Hegel's aesthetic theory, autobiographies are seen as having been plucked from their tree and consequently shrivelled and desiccated. If anything, the tone of the analyses discussed below is more pessimistic, abandoning the idea that autobiography might be able to contribute to healing the wounds of modernity.

Described by William Spengemann as 'the first extended theoretical work' on autobiography in the English language,[31] Roy Pascal's *Design and Truth in Autobiography* has been an influential text in the field of contemporary autobiographical studies, as well as literary criticism more generally. Many of his formulations are familiar from earlier criticism, but they appear here in a more comprehensive form. Pascal states that:

> autobiography proper . . . involves the reconstruction of a moment of a life, or part of a life, in the actual circumstances in which it was lived. Its centre of interest is the self, not the outside world, though necessarily the outside world must appear so that, in give and take with it, the personality finds its peculiar shape. But 'reconstruction of a life' is an impossible task. A single day's experience is limitless in its radiation backward and forward. So that we have to hurry to qualify the above assertions by adding that autobiography is a shaping of the past. It imposes a pattern on a life, constructs out of it a coherent story . . . in every case it is [the writer's] present position which enables him to see his life as something of a unity, something that may be reduced to order. [p. 9]

The echoes in Pascal's title of Goethe's *Dichtung und Wahrheit* serve as a useful pointer to the coincidence within the study of both historical and aesthetic approaches. Goethe's autobiography is certainly an exemplary text for Pascal, and like Dilthey and Misch before him, he views *Dichtung und Wahrheit* as something close to a final realisation of the potentialities of the autobiographical genre. Again, as in Dilthey's and Misch's writings on autobiography, the trajectory from Augustine to Rousseau to Goethe is viewed as the central line of development, historically, generically, and in relation to the development of individuality. Pascal also reinforces the perception of autobiography as an essentially European form which transcends national boundaries: 'of all literary forms, [autobiography] is the one least affected by national characteristics and most indicative of a common European culture' [p. 180].

Although many of Pascal's examples are drawn from recent autobiography, he asserts that with Goethe's text autobiography's 'groundplan was now laid and subsequent writers have had little more than modifications to contribute' [p. 50].[32] Writers within the period nominated as 'the classical age' (although it might be more accurate to define it as the Romantic age of autobiography) reveal for the first time:

> a devoted but detached concern for their intimate selves, a partial yet impartial unravelling of their uniqueness, a kind of wonder and awe with regard to themselves; and at the same time an appreciation that this uniqueness is also the uniqueness of the circumstances in which they lived, hence their attention to the concrete reality of their experiences. . . . With them autobiography becomes a conscious genre, not simply in the sense that what they write could only be written by a man about his own life and never by another person; but also in the sense that it serves a purpose all its own of self-discovery and reconciliation with self. [p. 51]

Pascal states that although there have been formal developments since the classical age of autobiography – for example, the essayistic autobiography and the autobiography of childhood – and an increased awareness of the problematic of autobiographical truth, there has been 'relatively little enrichment in conception of its central purpose and scope' [p. 55]. Thus we encounter the paradox, also present in Karl Weintraub's arguments, that although the late eighteenth and early nineteenth centuries are perceived as heralding the birth and development of a 'historical consciousness' which radically altered conceptions of self and history and to which we owe our contemporary understandings of life as process, the 'zenith' of both autobiographical and historical consciousness was reached at the point of its emergence. Pascal thus argues that whereas the great autobiographies of the classical age achieved a synthesis between individualism and awareness of historical circumstance, modern autobiography reveals a lack of relationship between self and history, inner and outer, 'personal and social being': 'I do not think one can evade the conclusion that the supreme task of autobiography is not fulfilled in modern autobiography' [p. 160].

The loss of this synthesis in the modern age has, Pascal believes, a number of determinations: a loss of faith in absolutes, a divorce between self and circumstance, the development of a 'cynical esti-mation of the core of the self' [p. 161]. A version of Hegelian aesthetics underlies Pascal's arguments in this context. Thus his use of the term 'classical' to refer to works more usually assigned to the 'Romantic' period enables a borrowing of the image of classical unity for Romantic autobiography; harmony is achieved between self, circumstance and the absolute. With this projection forward of categories, modernity and modern autobiography take on the negative aspects of Hegel's Romantic art. Hegel wrote that: 'We find . . . as the termination of romantic art, the contingency of the exterior condition and internal life, and a falling asunder of the two aspects, by reason of which art commits an act of suicide.'[33] Pascal's is a weaker form of this statement, but shares the same premises: as expressed in the statement, already quoted, that 'the supreme task of auto-biography is not fulfilled in modern autobiography . . . what . . . profoundly affects modern autobiography is a general lack of rela-tionship between personal and social being' [p. 160].

Pascal also writes of 'a cynical estimation of the core of the self' and a 'self-distrust' which 'suggests a malaise that is due to the nature of modern living altogether'. If modernity has produced this 'malaise' [p. 161], however, it is also modernity which has produced the concept of life as process, becoming rather than being. The ideal of a perpetual becoming, a dynamic conception of the self, must surely be at odds with the demand for a coherent, unified 'truth of being'. Although this dilemma is never made explicit in Pascal's study, a number of his arguments could be read as attempts to resolve it. The claim that autobiography should only be written in later life entails the argument that resolution can be reached in individual maturity; life is process and becoming up to the point from which reflection is undertaken. All definitions of autobiography as the story of a life told from a present standpoint, from which sense can be made of the past, contain this belief that stasis will be reached. Despite the emphasis on the present moment of telling, the very fact that it is viewed as a moment outside process suggests that it is also viewed outside his-tory. Any 'truth' of the self within the context of a belief in perpetual becoming would have to be viewed as arbitrary and provisional: an artificial arrest of process. In the autobiographical statement at the beginning of the text, Pascal speaks of his own 'need for meaning', which had to be personal and subjective: 'I . . . felt one could be content if one could feel one's self to be consistent, to have developed naturally and organically, to have remained 'true to itself ' . . . I think I am delineating a state of mind from which autobiography springs' [p. viii].

This statement could, of course, be read as an assertion that the individual's belief in the coherence of life and self is an illusory but necessary one. Autobiography would then become a strategy for creating the illusion of unity and coherence despite the fragmentations of identity. However, this is not an argument Pascal pursues, instead displacing this question on to an historically situated 'betrayal of self ' in the modern period.[34]

Thus despite the continuities in approach between Pascal and his intellectual mentors, Dilthey and Misch, which include the general theme of process and an emphasis on the truths of personality as opposed to literal historical truth, he is noticeably pessimistic in relation to issues where Dilthey and Misch may appear somewhat complacent. Where Dilthey and Misch see a harmonious inter-relation between the individual and history, though with Misch perhaps putting more emphasis on the individual, Pascal feels that modern man has lost the certainties which sustained this unity: 'It is difficult to say how far the assurance of a teleological purpose determines the confidence in the identity of the self, and how far it is the latter that produces the former. But certainly they are intimately linked, and in later autobiography both decline together' [p. 149]. At times, however, he appears to turn this decline to advantage, in so far as he can represent a lonely and heroic self 'wrestling with truth' and pledged to its innermost nature. At other moments in the text this alienated self, estranged from its *milieu*, is held to be unable to achieve the kind of wholeness necessary for true autobiography. Thus we see here another version of the familiar autobiographical dilemma in which, to parody Kant, concepts of the outside world without self-observations are empty: self-observations without concepts (of external reality) are blind.

* * *

The American historian Karl Weintraub acknowledges amongst his influences the work of Dilthey, Burckhardt, Misch and Pascal. His approach to autobiography is that of the intellectual historian and he seeks to establish two lines of historical development: firstly, the emergence of an 'historical consciousness' in Western culture, and secondly, the growth of individuality as a value. Autobiography serves two functions, not always clearly distinguished in his account: it is on the one hand described as perhaps the most significant manifestation of changing conceptions of history and individuality from classical antiquity onwards and on the other it is seen to fulfil its potential as a form from the period, which Weintraub dates around 1800, when 'Western Man acquired a thoroughly historical understanding of his existence'.[35]

The development from Augustine to Rousseau to Goethe outlined by Dilthey is clearly a model for Weintraub, as is Jacob Burckhardt's account of Renaissance culture; but he also adds, following Misch's direction, substantial discussion of medieval autobiography. Indeed, Weintraub seems to suggest that he is 'completing' or at least adding to Misch's unfulfilled project, not only in bringing the study of autobiography closer to the modern period, but also in extracting from the details of texts a sharper outline of the historical development of 'individuality'.

Weintraub argues that the value placed on autobiography arises at the time when man developed an historical sense of individual existence. Historical consciousness is linked to the growth of individuality which begins in the Renaissance; both are contingent upon the departure from a static conception of the world and a move towards an understanding of both self and world as process. Auto-biographical and historical consciousness are similarly related; following Pascal, Weintraub defines genuine autobiography as a cultural and literary form which demonstrates temporal scope, interprets the past from a present standpoint, and understands life as a process which can be viewed as a coherent and patterned whole. Although Augustine's *Confessions* and a number of medieval and Renaissance autobiographies contain these desiderata as latent or emergent properties, it is not until Goethe that they become fully exemplified. Thus, as for the other critics discussed in this chapter, Goethe marks both a beginning, a zenith and, in some sense, an end.

In his related essay, 'Autobiography and Historical Consciousness', Weintraub asserts that 'the necessary point of view' in autobiography can only occur 'somewhere beyond a moment of crisis or beyond an experience, or a cumulative set of experiences which can play the same function as a crisis' in the autobiographer's life; Augustine's conversion experience is given as a paradigmatic instance of this. Without such a 'conversion crisis', spiritual or secular, the autobiography lacks a standpoint from which the pattern and meaning of the life can be discerned:

> the autobiographical function tends to become self-orientation, and the autobiographic form is either crippled or underdeveloped . . . the very quest for meaning displaces the artistic intent to render the pattern of a life having run its meaningful course . . . [and] impedes the autobiographical art of presenting the essential wholeness of life.[36]

In relation to autobiographical criticism more generally, I would argue that conversion narratives have become the staple of the genre because they control their reception by asserting the supremacy of an enlightened present moment, perspective and consciousness. In other words, there is no possibility of an oppositional reading, because the perspective from which the autobiographer writes is represented as the only one which renders the past intelligible. Weintraub states this overtly when he writes that 'autobiography cannot be read in a truthful manner if the reader cannot, or will not, recapture the standpoint, the point of view of the autobiographer as autobiographer'.[37] And by implication, since Weintraub conflates autobiographical and historical consciousness, the same argument would apply to the historian's perspective on the past, which becomes the only meaningful one. It is not clear how the reader is supposed to choose between a range of alternative accounts of the same phenomenon.

Weintraub's arguments also reproduce the paradox, discussed above, that although life and history are perceived as 'process' – and, indeed, 'historical consciousness' is contingent upon the recognition of process – their structure only crystallises in stasis. It is important to note that Weintraub does not endorse teleological or 'unfolding' models of human development, in which the ordered structure is already present from the beginning, as in theories based on the concept of a human nature. But nor does he appear to be saying that order is merely an intellectual construct retrospectively imposed from a moment of stasis: his claim seems to be that the actual relationships between the events of the life only come together in an ordered structure as the result of a crisis, or a set of determining experiences.

In *The Value of the Individual* the model of crisis is transposed from an individual to a broader historical dimension. 'The ages of crisis', Weintraub writes, 'force upon the individual the task of doubting and reinvestigating the very foundations on which his self-conception traditionally rested.'[38] In this view, St Augustine's *Confessions*, for example, could be seen both as a result of and a reflection of the profound cultural and historical changes that occurred in the transition from a classical to a Christian culture. Yet Weintraub also endorses the view put forward by Dilthey, Misch and Pascal that the 'proper' relationship between the self and its historical world is interactive and mutually influencing. Thus the *Confessions* must be seen to bear more than a merely passive role in relation to historical transition. The interactive relationship is in one way ensured by the fact that the 'personal' crisis enacts in microcosm the 'historical' crisis of cultural transformation. More than this, however, Weintraub argues that Augustine 'was so centrally responsible for the then viable fusion of the two traditions entwined in Western civilization that it is perfectly proper to give his name to his age'.[39]

The issue of the 'representative' nature of autobiographical texts thus becomes a complex one. On the one hand, Weintraub is using autobiographies as the materials for an evidence of the gradual emergence of individuality and its correlate, historical awareness. On the other hand, autobiographers themselves take on the significance of 'world-historical individuals', and are portrayed as having a major causal impact on broader historical processes; in Weintraub's discussion of Goethe, these arguments are also used to support his claim that autobiography is essentially an historical genre. It is this which makes it possible for Weintraub to take *single* autobiographies as having this representative character. This is also a familiar strategy in more narrowly literary histories of autobiography; in these the causal efficacy of the great autobiographer is located in his or her effects on the development of the genre rather than on world history as a whole. The focus on 'individuality' as a developing theme in European history and literature slides into a valorisation of the specific role of *individuals* both as exemplary representatives of their age and as prime movers in cultural and historical evolution. There is, however, an important difference between Weintraub's recognition of historical context and of the relevance of an autobiographer's other works, and the tendency within literary history to treat the autobiographies in isolation while adducing from them a totalising history of the genre, parasitic on but not acknowledging the kinds of historical claims that Weintraub makes in an explicit form. It could also be argued that the focus on 'world-historical' autobiographers serves as a convenient justification for a somewhat narrow selection of canonical texts, endlessly recurring in both literary and historical accounts.

The last two chapters of *The Value of the Individual* focus on Rousseau and Goethe. In Dilthey's account, Goethe's 'self-conception' as expressed in his autobiography displays an awareness of individual and historical development which, it is implied, is a move beyond Rousseau's desire to embody uniqueness. Weintraub finds in Rousseau and Goethe two competing theories of the relationship between self and society, and applies an overtly judgemental approach absent from Dilthey's discussion.

Rousseau's example, Weintraub states,

> illustrates the perils arising from an adverse or hostile stance toward the circumstantial world. . . . Society and civilization had become the problem. . . . The hostile posture toward the real world thus cut the effective interplay of a self and its world, the very process in which the conception of historical *development* rests.[40]

In Goethe, Weintraub finds one solution to this dilemma. His representation of Goethe is very close to those of Dilthey and Pascal; 'It was [Goethe] who first wrote his own life as the history of an individuality. He saw his personal formation as the effective interplay of his self and his world. . . . History of self and history of the world are inextricably linked.'[41] In viewing his life in its historical dimension, Goethe establishes autobiography as a historical genre; after him, 'autobiography and the personality conception of individuality flourish'. Goethe is, moreover, seen as the guardian of the proper form of individuality; unlike Rousseau, he 'warned against the false cult of self-idolization which threatened the commitment to individuality when it became fashionable. . . . His warning contains almost all of the ammunition we need if we, moving close to the twenty-first century, in any way care to preserve a healthy dedication to individuality.' Inveighing against 'a sickly modern obsession with self-knowledge', Goethe allows us to distinguish between the introspection of the isolated and subjective self, and the individuality of the self which coexists with its world.

Weintraub's study ends with Goethe and it is not clear whether or not he would endorse Pascal's view of the 'decline' of modern autobiography. In his Postscript, he discusses the 'lessons' of auto-biography for contemporary society in overtly political terms, rather than remaining with discussion of the development of the genre: 'Our lives seem beset by the implications of social theories. The study of autobiography might provide some insight to help us cope with our problem.'[42] In this formulation, autobiography can teach us 'how to live' in the sense of choosing between, or rather liberating ourselves from, political systems or social theories, defined as 'problems' for the self. The legacies of Rousseau's 'dangerous dreams', it is implied, involve either a 'flight into atmospheric isolation' or one to ideologies and societies 'which either seem to say nothing about ideals of self or seem to be bent on eradicating any concern with the person as a selfish perversion'. The final, rhetorical question is whether 'Goethe's vision of the self as the simultaneously loving cultivation of one's world and one's self, inextricably intertwining both, grant[s] us a healthier view?'[43]

One undertheorised theme in these discussions is the relationship between autobiography and the novel, in particular the *Bildungsroman*. Lukács, in *The Theory of the Novel*, pointed to the 'essentially biographical' form taken by the novel and its 'recourse to the biographical form' as a way of limiting its 'bad' infinity.[44] His discussion of Goethe's *The Apprenticeship of Wilhelm Meister* as an 'attempted synthesis' – 'the reconciliation of the problematic indivi-dual . . . with concrete social reality' – strongly recalls a major theme of autobiographical criticism, which itself often seems to conflate Goethe's paradigmatic *Bildungsroman, Wilhelm Meister*, with his auto-biography *Dichtung und Wahrheit*. (*Dichtung und Wahrheit* is, of course, structured on the model of the *Bildungsroman* – the narrative ends with Goethe, at the age of twenty-six, departing from his native Frankfurt for Weimar – and has played a crucial role in the shaping of autobiography as *Bildungsroman*.) Franco Moretti, in his recent study of the European *Bildungsroman*, which he sees as beginning with *Wilhelm Meister*, treats apprenticeship as 'an uncertain exploration of social space', and the *Bildungsroman* as the contradictory 'symbolic' form of modernity.[45] The classical *Bildungsroman*, which Moretti identifies as a conservative form in Germany and England just before the French Revolution (to be distinguished from its more conflictual and radical version in post-Revolutionary France), is a unity of opposites: individuality, autonomy and interiority are fused with their polar opposites, normality, socialisation and objectification.

Moretti argues further that the youth which is valorised in the *Bildungsroman* stands for the meaning attached to modernity, while maturity and modernity are seen as incompatible. This may explain the post-Hegelian critics' specific emphases, and at times difficulty, in conceptualising autobiography, which is required to demonstrate, as in fact *Dichtung und Wahrheit* does, the mobility and development of *Bildung* combined with the static point of reflection achieved in maturity. An ambiguity in the concept of representativity, however, drives a wedge between autobiography and *Bildungsroman*. The former is conventionally expected to be the product of a 'great' individual, representing 'a society's major crises and acquisitions'. The *Bildungsroman* and the novel more generally, by contrast, take place in the sphere of 'everyday life'. The gendering of this sphere is a complex issue in the history of the novel; what is clear is that the model of representativity prescribed for autobiography has traditionally had little place for women.

Cultural criticism in America in the 1970s furnishes a further context for work such as Weintraub's. The texts that are significant here include David Riesman's *The Lonely Crowd* (1950, reissued 1971), Lionel Trilling's *Sincerity and Authenticity* (1971), Richard Sennett's *The Fall of Public Man* (1992) and Christopher Lasch's *The Culture of Narcissism* (1980). These studies are linked by firstly, a concern with charting the development from traditional or 'public' societies to individualistic societies, and secondly, a critique, strongest in Sennett and Lasch, of the 'narcissistic' preoccupation with the self in contemporary North American society. Although Weintraub's references are almost entirely to European writers, and he does not explicitly refer to any literature on these themes, he can be read as arguing implicitly against the critics of individualism, while concurring in their historical accounts of its emergence out of the *polis*. The distinctions he draws between a necessary focus on the self and an unhealthy self-obsession pervade autobiographical criticism: Weintraub's particular version of this theme is a response to the criticism of the privatised self so prominent in American cultural debates. His attacks on the 'narcissistic' relationship to self, expressed in the quotations above, thus become, indirectly, a means of defending a 'true' individuality against its critics; it is also worth noting in this context that he describes *Dichtung and Wahrheit*, his

exemplary autobiography, as a text 'as intensely public as any autobiography could be'.[46]

The American cultural critics named above raise issues of considerable importance for contemporary autobiographical criticism,
although it is not possible to give them more than brief attention here.
In Trilling's and Sennett's studies, autobiography is one cultural
manifestation among others of an emergent individuality, perceived
negatively by Sennett. Lasch directly addresses the question of contemporary autobiographical writing:

> The popularity of the confessional mode testifies, of course, to the new
> narcissism that runs all through American culture; but the best work in
> this vein attempts, precisely through disclosure, to achieve a critical
> distance from the self and to gain insight into the historical forces,
> reproduced in psychological form, that have made the very concept of
> selfhood increasingly problematic. . . . Yet the increasing inter-
> penetration of fiction, journalism, and autobiography undeniably indi-
> cates that many writers find it more and more difficult to achieve the
> detachment indispensable to art. Instead of fictionalizing personal
> material or otherwise reordering it, they have taken to presenting it
> undigested, leaving the reader to arrive at his own interpretations. Instead
> of working through their memories, many writers now rely on mere
> self-disclosure to keep the reader interested, appealing not to his under-
> standing but to his salacious curiosity about the private lives of famous
> people. . . . Even the best of the confessional writers walk a fine line
> between self-analysis and self-indulgence. Their books . . . waver
> between hard-won personal revelation, chastened by the anguish with
> which it was gained, and the kind of spurious confession whose only claim
> to the reader's attention is that it describes events of immediate interest to
> the author . . . it also allows a lazy writer to indulge in 'the kind of
> immodest self-revelation which ultimately hides more than it admits.'
> [pp. 16–19] [47]

Lasch thus reproduces the now familiar distinction between serious
autobiography, in which the true autobiographer is represented as a
martyr to his own life, and its 'spurious' imitations, marked by their
temporal immediacy, lack of mediation of selfhood and hybrid forms.
The quasi-religious language employed by Lasch, as in the distinction drawn between the 'anguish' of personal revelation and 'spurious
confession', is reinforced by the implicit appeal to a Protestant ethic
in which the true autobiographer engages in a form of labour on the
self, 'working through' his memories; by contrast, the 'lazy' writer
merely exposes himself to his public in an act intended to draw
attention away from his guilty inner being. There is also a striking

parallelism between the concern with 'vanity' in nineteenth-century autobiographical criticism and with 'narcissism' in recent discussions of self-representations.

Despite his attacks on autobiography, Lasch is in fact mourning a past in which both history and individuality were highly valued, and in which, by implication, true autobiography was possible. American culture is vilified for devaluing both the past and the personal realm of a true selfhood, and 'poets and novelists today, far from glorifying the self, chronicle its disintegration'. If Weintraub had moved beyond Goethe to the present day and from a European to an American focus, he might have found that the logic of his arguments led to very similar conclusions.

Richard Sennett's *The Fall of Public Man* provides a far more devastating critique of 'autobiographical culture', although the phenomenon of autobiography receives only a passing reference. In Sennett's historical schema, a proper balance and separation between public and private life irrevocably broke down around the year 1800; this date, so stressed in autobiographical criticism as marking the 'recognition' of autobiography's autonomy as a genre, is for Sennett the moment at which confusion arose between public and intimate life. 'People are working out in terms of personal feelings public matters which properly can be dealt with only through codes of impersonal meaning.'[48] The erosion of a strong public life, Sennett argues, deforms intimate relations by making them the only sphere for an investment of self.[49] An obsession with individual 'personality' and personal 'style' are indicative of post-Enlightenment narcissism.

Sennett's model of a public sphere has of course come in for a good deal of feminist criticism, since he fails to address the exclusion of women from this almost entirely male form of public life. Moreover, as Rita Felski notes, Sennett 'has a tendency to idealize the autonomous, rational and psychically repressed bourgeois individual, and he undervalues the importance of intimacy or emotion in human interaction'.[50] More positively, feminist conceptions of an alternative public sphere have stressed diversity and the recognition of difference in opposition to a spurious universality. A major contribution of feminist politics has been the incorporation of explorations of self and identity into projects of self-empowerment. Felski, who expresses reservations about the unconditional value of self-examination and the striving for authenticity, nonetheless points out 'that whether subjectivity is perceived as radical politics or self-indulgent narcissism is at least partly dependent upon the standpoint from which it is being judged and the context in which it occurs' [p. 108]. While feminists differ over the relative importance of opening up and thereby transforming the public sphere or of reaffirming the value of the private and the personal, the most striking feature of traditional male conceptions is that they valorise the controlled sub-jectivity and self-awareness expressed by the male autobiographical author, at least up to the time of Goethe, while mostly rejecting it in its female form.[51]

Sennett's only direct comment on autobiography addresses the issue of the retrospection believed by virtually all autobiographical critics to be a fundamental principle of the genre. Sennett argues that:

> Closely tied to a code of personality immanent in public appearances was a desire to control these appearances through increasing one's conscious-ness of oneself. . . . Consciousness becomes therefore retrospective activity, control of what has been lived – in the words of G. M. S. Young, the work of 'unraveling' rather than 'preparing'. If character is involuntarily disclosed in the present, it can be controlled only through seeing it in the past tense.
>
> A history of nostalgia has yet to be written, yet surely this past-tense relationship of consciousness to behaviour explains a crucial difference between 18th and 19th Century autobiography. In 18th Century memoirs like Lord Hervey's, the past is nostalgically recalled as a time of innocence and modest feeling. In the 19th Century memoir, two new elements are added. In the past one was 'really alive', and if one could make sense of the past, the confusion of one's present life might be lessened. This is truth via retrospection. Psychoanalytic therapy comes out of this Victorian sense of nostalgia, as does the modern cult of youthfulness.[52]

Sennett's emphasis on the relationship between autobiography and nostalgia sheds an interesting light on the perceived significance of memory and retrospection. His suggestive remarks are in tune with a noticeable and welcome trend away from generic history and towards a more conceptual approach to the history of culture, marked by recent works on, for example, 'self-fashioning', 'subjectivities', col-lective memory, confession and the social construction of childhood. In these diverse projects, autobiographies are figured in new and challenging ways, as material through which these social forms are constituted. But 'autobiography' loses its singular and privileged status as a discrete genre and form of knowledge, and we can no longer construct a history and a cultural field upon a select

Weltliteratur plucked from the contexts of two millennia.

Notes

1 Robert M. Young, 'Biography: the basic discipline for human science', *Free Associations* II (1988): 108–30.
2 Karol Sauerland, *Diltheys Erlebnisbegriff* (Berlin and New York: Walter De Gruyter, 1972), Part I.
3 Dilthey, *Der Aufbau der geschichtlichen Welt in den Geisteswissenschaften. Gesammelte Schriften*, vol. VII, 3rd ed. (Stuttgart: B. G. Teubner, 1958), pp. 70–1.
4 *Ibid.* I have used where possible the translation in H. P. Rickman (ed.), *Wilhelm Dilthey: Selected Writings* (Cambridge University Press, 1976). References to the original and to the translation are given here as 'Dilthey' and 'Rickman' respectively.
5 James Olney (ed.), *Autobiography. Essays Theoretical and Critical* (Princeton University Press, 1980), p. 8.
6 Rickman, p. 214. (Further page references in text.)
7 Rickman, p. 210. See also 'The Stream of Consciousness' in William James, *The Principles of Psychology*, 2 vols. (London: Macmillan, 1890).
8 See the Preface to Goethe, *The Autobiography of Johann Wolfgang von Goethe* (Chicago University Press, 1974).
9 Katherine Goodman, *Dis/Closures: Women's Autobiography in Germany Between 1790 and 1914* (New York: Peter Lang, 1986), p. vi.
10 Dilthey, pp. 246–51.
11 Rickman, p. 215.
12 Dilthey, p. 247.
13 Dilthey, p. 248.
14 Robert Blake, 'The Art of Biography', in *The Troubled Face of Biography*, ed. Eric Homberger and John Charmley (London, Macmillan, 1988), p. 81.
15 Dilthey, p. 250.
16 Dilthey, pp. 246–7.
17 Dilthey, p. 252.
18 Rickman, p. 214.
19 Cf. Martin Jay, 'Experience Without a Subject: Walter Benjamin and the Novel', in *The Actuality of Walter Benjamin*, ed. Laura Marcus and Lynda Nead, *New Formations* 20 (Summer 1993).
20 Maurice Halbwachs, *On Collective Memory*, ed. Lewis A. Coser (Chicago and London: University of Chicago Press, 1992), pp. 168–9.
21 Jürgen Habermas, *Knowledge and Human Interests* (London: Heinemann, 1971), p. 216.
22 James L. Clifford and George E. Marcus, *Writing Culture: the Poetics and Politics of Ethnography* (Berkeley: University of California Press, 1986), p. 10.
23 Georg Misch, *A History of Autobiography in Antiquity*, trans. E. W. Dickes, 2 vols. (London: Routledge and Kegan Paul, 1950).
24 Goodman, *Dis/Closures*, p. viii ff.
25 Olney, (ed.) *Autobiography*, p. 8.
26 Georges Gusdorf, 'Conditions and Limits of Autobiography', in Olney,

Autobiography, p.29.

27 Jacques Lacan, *Séminaires 2*, 1954–55; *Le moi dans la théorie de Freud et dans la technique du psychanalyse* (Paris: Seuil, 1978), pp. 15–16.

28 The troubling assumption Gusdorf makes is that the 'colonized' are not 'authentically' capable of autobiography.

29 See David Macey, *Lacan in Contexts* (London: Verso, 1988), esp. pp. 104–7.

30 The German paediatrician Ernst Bernhard (1896–1965) developed the conception of 'automythbiography', one of whose major principles was that the individual and the collective are connected by myth, that individual myth links the individual to the collective and that individual destiny has to fulfil a collective destiny in order to fulfil itself. Bernhard worked particularly on the 'myth' of the Jewish people: 'I had to repeat that myth.'

31 William C. Spengemann, *The Forms of Autobiography: Episodes in the History of a Literary Genre* (New Haven and London: Yale University Press, 1980), p. 182.

32 Roy Pascal, *Design and Truth in Autobiography* (London: Routledge and Kegan Paul, 1960) p. 50. Cf. Spengemann, *The Forms of Autobiography*, p. xvii: 'Although historical, philosophical and poetic autobiographies are still being written today, the generic evolution that produced these divergent forms and so related them to each other . . . was complete a century ago.'

33 Quoted in C. L. Carter, 'A Reexamination of the "Death of Art" Interpretation of Hegel's Aesthetics', in *Art and Logic in Hegel's Philosophy*, ed. W. E. Steinkraus and K. L. Schmitz (Sussex: Harvester, 1980), p. 93.

34 Cf. Candace Lang, 'Autobiography in the Aftermath of Romanticism', *Diacritics* 12, 4 (Winter 1982), 2–16. 'Spengemann creates the impression that there was once a golden age of autobiography when a substantial, unified self *could* be captured, reflected, or at least created in writing' (p. 5).

35 Karl J. Weintraub, *The Value of the Individual: Self and Circumstance in Autobiography* (University of Chicago Press, 1978).

36 Karl Weintraub, 'Autobiography and Historical Consciousness', *Critical Inquiry*, 1 (1975), 825–6.

37 *Ibid.* p. 827.

38 Weintraub, *The Value of the Individual*, p. 18.

39 *Ibid.* p.48.

40 Weintraub, 'Autobiography', p. 850.

41 *Ibid.* p. 847.

42 Weintraub, *The Value of the Individual*, p. 378.

43 *Ibid.* p. 379.

44 Georg Lukács, *The Theory of the Novel* (London: Merlin Press, 1977).

45 Franco Moretti, *The Way of the World. The* Bildungsroman *in European Culture* (London: Verso, 1987), pp. 3–13.

46 Weintraub, *The Value of the Individual*, p. 345.

47 Christopher Lasch, *The Culture of Narcissism* (London: Abacus, 1980), pp. 16–19.

48 Richard Sennett, *The Fall of Public Man* (Cambridge University Press, 1977), p. 5.

49 *Ibid.* p. 7.

50 Rita Felski, *Beyond Feminist Aesthetics. Feminist Literature and Social Change*

(London: Hutchinson Radius, 1989), pp. 107–8.
51 See Sidonie Smith, *A Poetics of Women's Autobiography: Marginality and the Fictions of Self-Representation* (Bloomington and Indianapolis: Indiana University Press, 1987), esp. p. 43.
52 Sennett, *The Fall of Public Man*, p. 168.

5
Saving the subject

In the second half of this book, I explore the rise in criticism and theory of autobiography in recent years. The focus is primarily on work in literary studies, although the boundaries between this area and more historical, cultural and sociological work, loosely grouped under the category 'life studies', has become more open. There remain, however, a set of relatively distinct concerns in literary theories of autobiography, which at times seem to emerge directly from confrontation with autobiographical texts whose definition has become increasingly diffuse and, at others, reflect broader literary-theoretical and philosophical currents. These concerns are, in particular, the nature and expression of subjectivity; the generic specificity of autobiography; the truth-status and referentiality of autobiography in relation to the fact–fiction dichotomy and the status of fictional entities. Although the present chapter is concerned principally with approaches to the autobiographical subject in a variety of related theoretical frameworks, and the following chapter principally with genre theory, it will become clear that the question of genre and the question of the subject are intimately related in autobiographical discourse.

For some critics, concerned to stabilise the category of auto-biography, its coherence is guaranteed by generic properties, whereas for others the unity of the writing subject is the agent of stability. Other critics deconstruct both genre and subject as coherent categories in a redefinition of autobiography itself. This can take the form of effacing the difference between autobiography and fiction, or, more broadly, between referential and fictional discourse. It is important, however, to distinguish between the very different reasons for seeking to efface this distinction. One follows I. A. Richards's distinction between 'emotive' and 'referential' discourse, privileging the former as a mode of higher imaginative truth. Another points to

the 'fictionality' of all discourse and the construction of 'the life' or
'the subject' in the writing. The self does not pre-exist the text but is
constructed by it. Again, however, a deconstructive critic who
adopted this position might find him or herself in uneasy collusion
with critics like Gusdorf and Pascal, who argue that the self 'finds'
itself in its acts of self-expression. Here, perhaps more than in any
other area of criticism and theory, oppositions and unwilling con-
vergences are shifting and unpredictable.

This chapter examines approaches to autobiography in critical
movements located primarily in France and North America, with a
particular focus on questions of subjectivity. In Chapter 1, I discussed the naming of 'autobiography' at the end of the eighteenth and
beginning of the nineteenth century in the context of a post-
Enlightenment anxiety over the nature of 'the subject'. The critical
and theoretical interest in autobiography which has gathered pace
since the 1950s can also be understood as a response to, or an aspect
of, the intense debates over subjectivity in the latter part of the
twentieth century. In every sphere of the human sciences (itself a
category placed in question), the categories of consciousness, self-
presence, subjectivity and identity became concepts to be critiqued *or*
defended.

One important strand in autobiographical criticism involves
rewriting the 'history' of autobiography, as distinct from its 'pre-
history', from the mid-eighteenth century, with Rousseau's *Confessions*, in particular, becoming the inaugural text of modern autobiography. This contrasts with the *longue durée* models as well as with
the narratives of decline after Goethe discussed in the previous
chapter. Once again Rousseau becomes emblematic for an interplay
of subjectivity and writing, as he attempts to construct his personal
identity in his writings. The question of subjectivity now combines
with an interrogation of the nature of writing, problematising both
components and the relations between them. Autobiography, defined
by the link between 'life' and the writing of the life, is both test and
limit-case for the parameters of subjectivity and literature.

We saw in the previous chapter how autobiography was conceptualised in historical and historiographical terms; it is both related to
biography and history, as in Dilthey's metaphor of the river of the
life-course running into the sea of history, and located in an initially
optimistic and then increasingly pessimistic account of the development of Western culture. We saw how these historical concerns

coexisted with a demand for unity – the psychological unity of the human mind and the aesthetic unity of the written text – and an insistence on internal coherence, whether of an age or an individual.

The work of some of the most influential North American autobiographical critics in the second half of the twentieth century, even those influenced by the models discussed in the previous chapter, is dominated by the project of 'rescuing' autobiography from incorporation into history and history-writing, and establishing it as an essentially 'literary' act. This could mean either a depreciation of the temporal dimension of individual existence or a rejection of certain modes of history-writing, such as descriptive or documentary accounts. The anti-historical move was part of an academic-political project to redefine what literary studies should be.

The interest in autobiography was also substantially inspired by a reaction against the so-called 'bloodless formalisms' of North American New Criticism in the 1940s and 1950s. The anti-formalist critical perspective involved an emphasis on personal identity and development, self-conceptions and other 'psychological' themes prominent in earlier autobiographical criticism. Once again, autobiography was used to focus other contemporary issues and critical battles: literature versus science, humanist versus formalist or deconstructionist criticism, the concept of 'the subject', the definition of 'the literary' and the value of genre theory. The heterogeneity of autobiography again renders it an unstable vehicle for projects such as that of rescuing a subjectivity seen as threatened, in different ways, by 'mass society' and by certain critical and theoretical trends. More specifically, the theoretical resources drawn on by James Olney and other American critics turned out to be similarly unstable, as concepts of 'the subject' changed with structuralism, new developments in psychoanalytic theory, and the partial eclipse of phenomenology by deconstruction.

A further, crucial element is the re-evaluation of Romanticism in the late 1960s and 1970s, with Wordsworth's epic autobiography *The Prelude* becoming a key text. M. H. Abrams's *Natural Supernaturalism* produced a reading of Romanticism and *The Prelude* as, in Jonathan Arac's words, 'a completed pattern of journeying', in which the autobiography becomes a paradigm of 'life' as quest and self-discovery, and history is monumentalised by grand narratives of fall, secularisation and restoration.[1] Ann Mellor notes that Abrams's 'trailing of *The Prelude* as the first work to present the writing of a

single man's life within the conventions of the classical epic ...
[elevated] the genre to the highest aesthetic status'. His way of
reading autobiography as a parable of individualism 'helped to shape
the genre of literary autobiography, to determine the linguistic conventions by which the viable self has been represented in contemporary critical discourse'.[2]

A reaction against Abrams's position, by Geoffrey Hartman, Paul
de Man and others, entailed a new theorisation of 'Romanticism', in
which, as Arac states, 'Romanticism' 'emerged as the name in our
culture of the entanglement that joins the philosophy of history with
the history of philosophy with the theory of narrative'.[3] This also
encouraged an attention to forms of romantic self-consciousness in
writings which were similarly influenced by philosophical concerns,
autobiography taking pride of place among these. These different
constructions of literary Romanticism (and there are of course
others) have in fact been based on a gendered concept of subjectivity
and consciousness which masquerades as universality. Literary
Romanticism has been so closely linked to the history and theory of
autobiography that a reconceptualising in gendered terms of the one
will inevitably inflect the other.

A further context for autobiographical theories in North America
was a critical milieu inflected by phenomenology. James Olney, who
has done most to promote 'autobiographical studies', revealed strong
affiliations to phenomenological criticism, and to the work of
Georges Gusdorf in particular. Listing the texts written on autobiography   since   Gusdorf's   'Conditions   et   limites   de
l'autobiographie' in 1956 – which in fact adopt a wide variety of
critical positions – Olney argued that they all concern themselves
with the 'dawning self-consciousness of Western man that found
literary expression in the early moments of modern autobiography –
those moments when secular autobiography was slowly developing
out of spiritual autobiography and when autobiography as a literary
mode was emerging out of autobiography as a confessional act'.[4]

The critical interest in autobiography did indeed derive in large
part from the belief that the autobiographical text as such – and this
raises crucial questions about generic definition – is the 'purest' form
of a literature of consciousness. Traditional hermeneutics, with its
totalising concept of understanding which links parts to wholes and
individuals to cultures, becomes inflected with a phenomenological
analysis of consciousness and underpins an intervention in the poli-

tics of the North American academy. Autobiography becomes the site upon which subjectivity will be saved, and saved for literature.

With the rise of deconstruction, autobiographical critics influenced by phenomenological criticism had a limited range of options. They could, like James Olney, reject the paths taken by post-structuralist and deconstructive critics, reassert the essential irreducibility of subjectivity and the absolute value of subjectivism, and turn to those forms of 'continental theory' (for example, the work of Gusdorf) uncorrupted by the theorists following in the wake of Nietzsche, Freud and Heidegger. Alternatively, they could take the deconstructionist turn and use autobiography as an exemplary instance of the impossibility of self-presence, the radical split between the self that writes and the self that is written, and the crucial role of language in the constitution of the subject. Deconstruction has also been, of course, very closely linked to the reformulations of Romanticism.

Either way, autobiography became largely focused on 'the subject', through the categories of presence/absence, unity/alienation, self/text, often to the exclusion of other issues and concerns. For example, the concentration on subjectivity as self-knowing led critics to assert a total separation between biography and autobiography. They also tended to exclude from discussion memoirs and other 'historical' or 'outer-directed' forms of life-writing which did not seem to exemplify self-analysis. Although autobiography – as concept or as a body of texts – is undoubtedly a crucial site for explorations or constructions of selfhood and identity, the focus on universal subjectivity, or the denial of its possibility, resulted in a neglect of ethnic and gender diversity and differential subjectivities, and a highly abstract concept of identity.

* * *

'I want at all costs to save the subjectivity of literature' (Georges Poulet).[5]

In his influential collection of essays, *Autobiography: Essays Theoretical and Critical* (1980), James Olney writes: 'autobiography, like the life it mirrors, refuses to stay still long enough for the genre critic to fit it out with the necessary rules, laws, contracts, and pacts; it refuses, simply, to be a literary genre like any other'.[6] In the pervasive image of the mirror, the heterogeneity of lives and their autobiographical representations underpins a critique of genre theory, coexisting with an affirmation of the substantiality of subjectivity and literature which deconstruction had already put in question. Unlike many of the genre theorists discussed later, whose bounded genres are animated by differentiated, and often historically determined, concepts of the self, Olney allows for generic diversity, attacking the restrictions of genre theory, in the name of a unified transhistorical subject.

In placing, and giving reasons for, the 'new' interest in autobiography in the 1960s critics have tended to assume the demise of the New Criticism as one of the primary conditions for the emergence of 'autobiographical studies', pointing to the New Critics' exclusions of authorial and readerly subjectivity, their insistence on the formal, objective features of the autonomous literary artefact, and their downgrading of prose, particularly non-fictional prose, by contrast with poetry.[7]

Stephen Shapiro's article of 1968, 'The Dark Continent of Literature: Autobiography', is a good example of the academic-political response to this perceived vacuum.[8] Shapiro directly addresses the issue of the pedagogic and even salvational value of autobiographies for the student of literature: the issue at stake is 'our conception of the purpose and educational value of literature and criticism'. Using autobiography as a way of attacking the New Critical focus on aesthetic distance and pure form, Shapiro writes:

> I suspect that critics of literature avoid autobiography, despite its distinguished tradition and undeniable importance to readers, because, like their colleagues in philosophy and the social sciences, literary critics are indulging in the currently prestigious 'professional' scorn for merely human problems, preferring to research the mysteries of methodology. But even here they err, for autobiography, human as it may appear to be, is a mode of art complex enough to delight the heart of the most mechanical textual engineer. Wellek and Warren and their followers misconceive the problem of fiction and imagination, and they dodge the value of literature as a reality-testing, personality-shaping institution. [p. 424]

The twofold argument here is firstly, that the introductions of autobiographies into the literary syllabus will re-humanise the discipline, and secondly, that autobiographies should in any case be studied as literary texts because of their complex narrative structures.

Autobiography, Shapiro asserts, is a literature of responsibility. The demand for the inclusion of autobiography in the literary curriculum was a way for the concerned academic in 1968 to let in 'the real world', while arguing for the student's need for authority figures, models and mentors. Academics

> who wish to live within the timeless Lichtensteinian border of the sonnet may well be failing in their job as educators because they refuse to confront the dialectical relationships between past and present selves and between the individual and his society that constitute the central concern of autobiography. [pp. 453–4]

The claims of non-fictional prose are directly opposed here to those of the lyric poem, the paradigmatic literary form for the New Critics.

Thus autobiography is imbued with a number of transformative functions, not the least of which is its potential to transform literary studies, and to return social and historical contexts to the discipline of literature: autobiographies should therefore 'be taught *as literature*'. The import of Shapiro's arguments is that the New Critical stranglehold in North American literary institutions led to an evasion of social and political responsibilities and left students unable to deal either with 'the vortex of Cold War life' or with the incursions of mass society and the mass media on personal experience. At this time, he asserts, 'we cannot afford to ignore the heritage of autobiographies' [p. 454]. Shapiro's claims for the transformational potential of autobiography may now seem a little naïve, but his article illustrates the ethical investment in autobiography as a humanistic and humanising object of study.

New Criticism may indeed have placed a low value on autobiography, but its rehabilitation in the 1970s cannot be seen as a straightforward reclamation of the literature of self or subject suppressed or put into abeyance by an overly scientised critical community. The affiliations of many of those critics who seemed to be newly engaged with autobiography are closely related to various critical trends of the 1960s and early 1970s: myth criticism, most notably the work of Northrop Frye, theories of Romanticism, structuralist approaches to literature and the 'criticism of consciousness' of the Geneva school.

Georges Poulet, who taught at Johns Hopkins University between 1952 and 1958, was perhaps the chief representative in America of Geneva school 'criticism of consciousness', characterised by its development of 'specific techniques of analyzing a poet's consciousness, his relation to time and space, the imaginary world constructed

in his writings' and its assumption of 'a history of these consciousnesses within a history of the human mind'.[9] J. Hillis Miller, in an
essay first published in 1966, points up the shared and differing
assumptions of six Geneva school critics: Marcel Raymond, Albert
Beguin, Georges Poulet, Jean Rousset, Jean-Pierre Richard and Jean
Starobinski. They share the conviction that 'literature is a form of
consciousness ... the embodiment of a state of mind. ... They
replace a concern for the objective structure of individual works with
a concern for the subjective structure of the mind revealed by the
whole body of an author's writing.'[10]

Miller notes that Poulet differs from other phenomenological
critics (who, to a greater or lesser extent, emphasise subject–object
relations) in his adherence to the Cartesian *Cogito*, in which the mind
knows nothing but itself; 'an act of self-consciousness in which the
mind is aware of nothing but its own native affective tone'. Poulet
wrote:

> I should readily consider that the most important form of subjectivity is
> not that of the mind overwhelmed, filled, and so to speak stuffed with its
> objects, but that there is another [kind of consciousness] which some-
> times reveals itself on this side of, at a distance from, and protected from,
> any object, a subjectivity which exists in itself, withdrawn from any power
> which might determine it from the outside, and possessing itself by a
> direct intuition ... as self-consciousness or pure consciousness.[11]

As Miller notes, Poulet's criticism can be defined as 'consciousness
of consciousness'. The history of literature is understood as a history
of the human consciousness, 'an investigation of the ways writers in
different historical periods have come to self-consciousness and the
mind has become aware of its own "indescribable intimacy" '.[12]

Two texts published in 1972 and influenced by phenomenological
criticism are the philosopher William Earle's *The Autobiographical
Consciousness: A Philosophical Inquiry into Existence*[13] and James
Olney's *Metaphors of Self: The Meaning of Autobiography*.[14] Earle's
study provides a defence of 'subjective cognitive consciousness':
knowledge essential to the knower. 'Ontological autobiography',
Earle asserts, 'is a question of a form of consciousness rather than of
literature' [p. 10].

Where Earle differs from Misch and from Gusdorf and other
phenomenological thinkers is in his rejection of the idea that the
value of 'ontological autobiography' lies in its contribution to an
understanding of a general or universal human consciousness. Its

significance for him is its crucial function for the singular individual. Arguing against the extension of the generalising methods of the natural sciences, Earle is clearly seeking to save subjectivity for philosophy, and the subjectivity of philosophy. Autobiography becomes identical with self-reflection, and Earle sees the retrospective nature of autobiography as a sign of its unfulfilled potential:

> If autobiography usually is indeed retrospective, that may lie in the circumstance that it is not ontological, that it has not pushed its reflections far enough to uncover the sort of being it is that *can have* an autobiography, namely a self with a past but also a present and a presumptive future. [p. 39]

James Olney's first study of autobiography, *Metaphors of Self*, is also concerned with autobiography as a mode of consciousness rather than of writing. Eschewing formal and historical approaches to the development of autobiography as a genre, Olney is concerned with the 'philosophy' and 'psychology' of autobiographical self-expression; he argues, *pace* Poulet, that 'a man's lifework is his fullest autobiography' [p. 3] and that a professedly autobiographical work serves only to magnify and focus the meanings of the lifework. As in one of Gusdorf's formulations, he asserts that the apparently 'objective' space of history, science or philosophy is always a projection of the 'inner space' of the observing or conceiving self; all forms of knowledge are in some way autobiographical. Thus his theory of autobiography is used to confirm a transcendental subjectivism, and to deny the possibility of objectivist accounts of reality.

Metaphors adopted by the self are a way of mediating and objectifying the inner self as an *experience* of that self and, via the mediation of metaphor, the experience of self can be communicated to others. Metaphor also becomes the term used to describe 'all the world views and world pictures, models and hypotheses, myths and cosmologies' created by human beings to order reality. Thus metaphors are used to represent both outside reality and the self. Olney does not conclude from this that the self is nothing but a metaphor; the upshot of his complex process of metaphorical reflection appears to be a substantial self of a traditional idealist kind.

Despite Olney's assertion that autobiography is not a literary genre amongst others, his focus on metaphor contains the germ of a literary reductionism in which all knowledge is ultimately metaphorical. Thus although he makes his case in terms of consciousness rather than linguistic practice, he is close to Northrop Frye's suggestion that 'the verbal structures of psychology, anthropology, theology, history, law, and everything else built out of words have been informed or constructed by the same kinds of myths and metaphors that we find, in their original hypothetical form, in literature'.[15]

If all forms of knowledge are reducible to literary-discursive structures, the distinction between literary and non-literary, referential and non-referential, breaks down, leaving an undifferentiated impulse to create, which Frye calls desire and Olney, following Bergson and Jung, calls 'vital energy' or 'libido'. Thus two theories of creativity are at work: one in which it is the artist who structures our knowledge of the world, the second in which all human conceptualisation is a creative and aesthetic act. The broader point is that Olney conceives of the metaphor-making process as a way of humanising (or perhaps colonising) an alien world; metaphors 'are that by which the lonely subjective consciousness gives order not only to itself but to as much of objective reality as it is capable of formalizing and controlling' [p. 30]. Autobiography is being used to advance an aesthetic of consciousness and cognition, in which metaphor, far from being a purely rhetorical figure, is the means by which self, art and world are interrelated.

In his introduction to *Autobiography: Essays Theoretical and Critical*, 'Autobiography and the Cultural Moment', Olney asserts that Gusdorf's 'Conditions et limites de l'autobiographie' (1956) marked the beginnings of critical and theoretical interest in autobiography. The fact that a number of commentators were coming to similar conclusions about the nature of autobiography, Olney argues, reflects something 'deeply embedded in the times and in the contemporary psyche'. Critics have been led to autobiography 'at the same cultural moment' by their shared preoccupation with what Gusdorf called 'le problème de la connaissance de soi' [p. 21]. The self has been born or reborn, discovered or rediscovered, in recent autobiographical criticism; thus its rescue from critical darkness involves far more than the mere establishment of a topic for academic study. The securing of the self in autobiography secures and extends the 'territory' of literature, and confirms literature as the discourse of subjectivity:

> It was this turning to *autos* . . . that opened up the topic of autobiography
> specifically for literary discussion, for behind every work of literature
> there is an 'I' informing the whole and making its presence felt at every
> critical point . . . this is what I understand James M. Cox to mean by his

'recovering literature's lost ground through autobiography'. . . . The encroachments of history on literature will only end, he implies, when we succeed in fastening the *autos* down. . . . It is my understanding that Cox is as determined as Gusdorf or anyone else to secure the self and thereby to secure added territory for literature. [pp. 21–2]

Olney's further concern with the securing of the self is to guard it against deconstructive critics, who, he believes, have attempted to dissolve the self, and consequently autobiographical criticism, as soon as it has come into being. Reaching for the man behind the work was discouraged in New Critical approaches to literature. The underlying narrative of Olney's discussion is again that autobiography and the *Zeitgeist* that produced Gusdorf provided a liberation from New Critical strictures, a liberation threatened only by the anti-humanisms of the new critical generation.

Olney included one of his own essays in the collection, entitled 'The Ontology of Autobiography'. Here he allows for the potential of the autobiography which seeks to recover the past through memory (his example is Richard Wright's *Black Boy*) but he is clearly more committed to the value of 'consciousness in itself, pure and untouched by either time or history', or to the autobiographer, such as Yeats, who 'transcends' history in the 'higher world of forms, paradigms and archetypes'. Paul Valéry's poem *La Jeune Parque*, Olney writes:

is nothing other than pure atemporal consciousness or awareness or active sensibility or better yet, it is consciousness of consciousness . . . there is in *La Jeune Parque* no return to the past but only a more intense awareness of conscious existence – 'la conscience consciente' in the present. As in the marvellous phrase describing the universe in Yeats' *Vision* ('a great egg that turns inside-out perpetually without breaking its shell'), Valérian consciousness turns inside-out perpetually but keeps its inner-outer shell wonderfully intact. [p. 252]

In his use of Yeats's image, Olney identified the (conservative) autobiographical ideal, the turning inside-out (the showing forth of the inner self) without the shattering or transgression of the inner and outer as absolute categories. The 'whole' self apparently remains intact – although the self in Olney's account is represented purely, and as pure, consciousness, untrammelled by either memory or body. Despite his sympathetic reading of *Black Boy* as 'historical' autobiography (the autobiography of memory), Olney clearly viewed the 'eternal present' of autobiographical consciousness as a higher form, a 'more immediate reality, surely, than any part of the past that memory can recall, even when it does so with the least degree of impurity it can manage'.

* * *

'We cannot escape the problem of identity, but only displace it and stage it as a problem' (Philippe Lejeune).[16]

Structuralist analysis has made a lasting contribution to the study of autobiography, allowing not only for the exploration of formal properties of autobiographical texts – including pronominal forms, questions of address and temporal relations, and markers of 'literary' and 'historical' discourses – but also, as Lejeune suggested, enabling a reconstruction in these terms of conceptions of identity.

The questions central to structural linguistics, on which narrative analysis has drawn, are also key for the study of autobiography. These include the categories explored by Émile Benveniste, in his *Problems in General Linguistics*, of person and temporality, pronouns and tenses in narrative.[17] Benveniste distinguished between enunciation (*énonciation*) and the utterance (*énoncé*): to simplify, between the act of uttering and what is uttered. By extension, this model is used to refer in theories of autobiography to the subject of the enunciation (the present 'I' of the narration) and the subject of the utterance (the 'I' whose history is being recounted and who exists at a temporal as well as ontological distance from the narrating self). By contrast, the idealised autobiography of pure consciousness, pure presentness, represents the refusal of this split and yet another version of the ideal fusion of subject and object. It should be noted, however, that Benveniste's focus on present utterance and on the subjective present which organises past and present shares something of the phenomenological emphasis on the 'now'.

A crucial element in Benveniste's theorisations of subjectivity and language was his claim that 'I' is 'the person who utters the present instance of discourse containing the linguistic instance *I*' [p. 252]. The special status Benveniste accords the 'I' – it paradigmatically refers to the speaker, as opposed to 'he' which can refer to any person or none, and is necessarily part of a discourse uttered by 'I' – is of particular salience to autobiography, often defined as the literature of the first person. The focus on the 'pronoun-boundedness' of identity, developed by Benveniste in the late 1950s and 1960s, was taken up in the 1970s by Lejeune. The autobiographical contract (*pacte*), Lejeune states, affirms the ' "identity" between the names of the author, narrator and protagonist' and guarantees the non-fictive status of the autobiography to the reader.

Lejeune grounds his discussion of possible autobiographical devices in a brisk definition of the genre: autobiography is 'a retrospective prose narrative produced by a real person concerning his own existence, focusing on his individual life, in particular on the development of his personality'. This definition, he writes, involves elements from four different categories:

1. Linguistic form: a) narrative; b) prose.
2. Subject treated: individual life, personal history.
3. Situation of the author: author (whose name designates a real person) and narrator are identical.
4. Position of the narrator: a) narrator and protagonist are identical; b) narration is retrospectively oriented.

A degree of latitude is possible in relation to the first two categories, Lejeune asserts, but two of the conditions 'are a matter of all or nothing, and these are, of course, the conditions which oppose autobiography . . . to biography and to the personal novel: these are conditions (3) and (4a). Here there is no transition or latitude. Either there is identity or there is not.'[18]

Lejeune notes that the concept of 'identity' raises numerous problems, and the primary function of his discussion is to clarify its usages and meanings. He approaches the issue in three ways; how 'identity' between the narrator and protagonist is expressed in the text; the way in which the identity of the author and the narrator–protagonist is manifested in first-person narratives – the context for a contrast between autobiography and novel; the distinction between the concept of *identity* and that of *resemblance* – the context in which to contrast autobiography and biography.

On the question of the 'identity' of narrator and protagonist, Lejeune states that while in autobiography it is most often marked by the use of the first person, this is not an essential condition. He refers to examples of second- and third-person narration in autobiography, which 'make it impossible to confuse problems of grammatical person with problems of "identity" '. Having established the distinction between grammatical person and the 'identity' of the individuals to whom the uses of the grammatical person refer, Lejeune returns to the question of the first person in autobiographical nature. Basing his discussion in part on Benveniste's analyses of the 'first person', Lejeune refers to the idea that there is no concept of 'I': 'the personal pronouns have reference only within a discourse, in the very act of utterance'.[19] Secondly, within utterance, the first person expresses the *identity* of the subject of the speech act (*énonciation*) and the subject of the utterance (*énoncé*). However, although in *spoken* discourse there should theoretically be no confusion between the 'I' speaking and the 'I' spoken of, there are situations in which uncertainty can exist; Lejeune gives as examples the use of quotation in speech, and 'speaking at a distance', in which, in the absence of dialogic possibilities, as on the radio, the situation becomes equivalent to that of writing. Thus the speech-act is not the final stage of reference – 'it raises in turn an identity problem, which, in the case of direct oral communication, we solve instinctively on the basis of extra-linguistic data. When oral communication is disturbed, identity can become problematic.'[20]

Lejeune departs from Benveniste's account in stating that, whereas it is true that the 'I' is a shifter, it is also related to the 'lexical category of proper nouns [names] designating people: there are almost as many names as there are individuals'. Invoking theories of language acquisition, Lejeune argues that 'the individual person and his discourse are connected to each other through the personal name, even before they are connected by the first person'. 'The deep subject of autobiography is the proper name', Lejeune asserts.[21] His claim has important implications for the relationship between auto-biography and authorship, which I explore in the next chapter. In the context of theories of subjectivity, Lejeune's statement, and his displacement of Benveniste's focus on the 'I' of discourse onto the proper name, are part of his desire to replace the isolated *Cogito* with a socially defined marker of personal or authorial identity, and the phenomenological focus on a psychic convergence of authorial/ textual and readerly consciousness with 'a contract of identity [between autobiographer and reader] that is sealed by the proper name'.[22] The acquisition of the proper name is not just a formal matter, however: 'it is doubtless as important as the "mirror stage" '. Whereas the 'I' is a shifter, the proper name is not so much a functional principle of classification as a personal property.

Lejeune's early work on autobiography, including this essay, is, unlike his more recent research, inattentive to questions of gender.

The definition of autobiography quoted above (the use of the masculine pronoun aside) excludes the 'diurnal', non-retrospective forms that constitute a major part of women's life-writings. He also fails to note, along with a number of other theorists, that women and men have rather different relationships to the 'proper name'. As Sandra Gilbert and Susan Gubar write:

> For women in our culture a proper name is at best problematic; . . . even as it inscribes her into the discourse of society by designating her role as her father's daughter, her patronymic effaces her matrilineage and thus erases her own position in the discourse of the future. Her 'proper' name, therefore, is always in a way *im*proper because it is not, in the French sense, *propre*, her own, either to have or to give. With what letters, then, can a woman of letters preserve herself?[23]

One answer to Gilbert and Gubar's question is that men and women autobiographers have had very different relationships to authorial and autobiographical space, and that an analysis of these relationships is a crucial aspect of autobiography's histories.

Lejeune himself wrote a refutation of some of the more absolute claims he makes in this essay, particularly in relation to strict generic definitions and the either/or nature of fiction and autobiography, biography and autobiography. Certainly, Lejeune's more recent work has opened out from its earlier affiliations to structural linguistics into a wider-ranging approach to the field of autobiography and life-writings.[24] But in 'The Autobiographical Pact', 'Autobiography in the Third Person', and discussions of tenses and temporalities in Vallès, Sartre and others, he analyses the textual dimensions and generic markers of autobiography in important ways. Rather than enclosing autobiography in formalistic and legalistic categories, a complaint that has come both from humanist critics such as Gusdorf and Olney and from deconstructionists such as Derrida, Paul de Man and Michael Ryan, Lejeune has in fact produced a model which is unusually flexible, particularly in relation to the contested and unproductive claims made about the essential nature of the autobiographical subject. As Michael Sheringham writes:

> The great advantage of Lejeune's definition is that it ties autobiography to *reference* but not *resemblance* [of text to 'life', copy to model]; to the interaction of textual 'I' and extra-textual counterpart, but not to any specific kind of relationship between them. The pressure to tie autobiography to a particular form of intentionality is greatly reduced; at the

same time anything which occurs in the space defined by the relations of author, text and reader becomes 'of the essence'.[25]

*   *   *

'Any slightly advanced analysis of the play of pronouns and persons in enunciation', Lejeune wrote, 'is faced with the dizzying necessity of constructing a theory of the subject.' In his discussion of the problematic of subjectivity, and with specific reference to the use of the third person in autobiography, Lejeune referred to what we might think of as the Scylla and Charybdis of identity, 'impossible unity' or 'intolerable division'. The pronouns of identity ('I', 'you', 'he/she') frequently appear in autobiographical texts as strategies for articulating or engaging the tension between unity and division. In Chapter 7, I discuss a number of autobiographical texts exploring these issues.

Jean Starobinski, who, in his essay 'The Style of Autobiography', incorporated elements of structuralism into his phenomenological criticism, argued that autobiography, both as 'act' and as a specific type of narrative, is dependent on the split between past and present selves.[26] Autobiography, Starobinski claims, can only be justified as a project distinct from history by the structures of conversion or transformation – a view advanced by a number of critics in the previous chapter. Without the change or 'deviation' brought about by conversion, autobiography would become history and 'a narrator in the first person would hardly continue to be necessary'.

Starobinski draws here on Benveniste's distinction between *énonciation historique*, a 'narrative of past events' marked by the exclusive use of the third person, and *discours*, in which the source of the enunciation and the auditor are marked as present. As Geoffrey Nowell-Smith puts it, 'History is always "there" and "then", and its protagonists are "he", "she" and "it". Discourse, however, always also contains, as its points of reference, a "here" and a "now" and an "I" and a "you".'[27] This distinction, variants of which occur from classical theories of rhetoric onwards, has been used to differentiate between literary forms, the poles of impersonal narrative and of writing which foregrounds the narrator, and is a central aspect of the construction of the 'subject' in language. More recently, these questions of narrative voice and subject position have been taken up in discussions of history-writing, most notably in relation to the appropriate way of recounting historical atrocities and dealing with the problems of historical agency.[28]

Starobinski states that the categories of subjective and objective do not map directly, or in any obvious way, on to the uses of the first and third persons in autobiography. The exclusive use of the third person in autobiography (examples would range from Caesar to Henry Adams and Gertrude Stein) 'accumulates and makes compatible events glorifying the hero who refuses to speak in his own name. Here the interests of the personality are committed to a "he", thus effecting a solidification by objectivity.' By contrast, the exclusive use of pure monologue, in lyrical fiction perhaps more than autobiography, entails a depersonalisation and 'fading' of the speaking subject: 'one need only examine the writings of Samuel Beckett to discover how the constantly repeated "first person" comes to be the equivalent of a "non-person" ' [p. 77]. The autobiography in which 'I' is both subject and object, standing in for past and present selves, serves both to confirm the prerogatives of the present 'I', which describes how it became what it is out of what it was, and shows up the 'ambiguous constancy' of the 'I'. The narrator may assert the difference between present and past identity, differences marked in the discourse by shifts in tense, or by 'the contamination of the discourse by traits proper to history', but 'the personal mark (the first person, the "I"), remains constant . . . Pronominal constancy is the index of this permanent responsibility' [p. 79].

The structures of conversion, referred to above, presuppose the fixity of the past in its pastness and the present in its presentness, although the danger of conversion-narrative is, of course, that in the process of confession, the present, 'reformed' self will be overwhelmed by the past it ostensibly seeks to put behind itself. For Starobinski, however, the present is always affirmed, in his stress on consciousness, his conception of the historical past as an intentional object of consciousness and his focus on the 'permanent responsibility' of the 'I' which, as *énonciation* rather than *énoncé*, consolidates the sovereignty of present consciousness.

In his major study of Rousseau, *Jean-Jacques Rousseau: La transparence et l'obstacle* (1957), Starobinski explored the relationship between present consciousness and past identity in *The Confessions*.[29] Contrary to the 'standard history' constructed in autobiographical criticism, in which the claim is often made that autobiography was perceived as a referential genre prior to the enlightened present, most critics would in fact have agreed that accuracy of recall is less important than the reconstruction of the past in the present of memory and/or writing. Starobinski rejects any idea that Rousseau's *Confessions* inaugurated autobiography as a genre committed to 'historical' truth, despite Rousseau's claim that 'I have displayed myself as I was':

> What is of primary importance is not historical veracity but the emotion experienced as the past emerges and is represented in consciousness. The image of the past may be false, but the present emotion is not. The truth that Rousseau wishes to communicate is not exactitude of biographical fact but accuracy in depicting his relation to his past. He paints a dual portrait, giving not only a reconstruction of his history but also a picture of himself as he relives his history in the act of writing. Hence it scarcely matters if he uses his imagination to fill gaps in memory. The quality of one's dreams, after all, reflects one's nature . . . We have moved from the realm of (historical) *truth* to that of *authenticity* (the authenticity of *discourse*). [p. 198]

Starobinski asserts that the law of authenticity tolerates, and indeed requires, 'that the writer give up looking for a true self in an unvarying past, and seek instead to create a self through writing'. The claim is further that Rousseau implicitly distinguishes between a reflective sincerity which entails scrutinising and reflecting upon a pre-existing self and hence introducing 'an irrevocable division into consciousness', and authenticity, which 'is nothing other than sincerity without distance or reflection'. Inauthenticity is said to be a product of man's faculty of reflection, 'the dangerous privilege of living at some distance from himself '.

What Starobinski finds in Rousseau is that complex conflation of temporal distance and the distance created by self-reflection, of the present in which Rousseau writes *The Confessions*, the 'past presents' in which the events he records took place and his own problematic attempt to be present to himself as an undivided consciousness. The paradox entailed in Rousseau's concept of authenticity is that the self is defined as both presentness and presence, and yet, of course, *The Confessions* displays the self strung along the long chain of narrative and biographical time.

Rousseau is impelled into narrative, Starobinski writes, by his awareness that his self-knowledge, the 'transparency' of himself to himself, is unavailing unless it is communicated to others, unless it becomes, in Rousseau's words, 'transparent to the reader'. What then, Starobinski asks, was Rousseau to do?

Open up 'all the folds' of his 'soul'. He displays, spread out over biographical time, the truth that feeling takes in at a glance. The unity and
simplicity of that truth are unravelled in a multitude of instants lived one
after the other in order to show how a single law governs and therefore
gives unity to his character. He must show how he came to be the person
he is. [p. 188]

There is a crucial question here about the relationship between
identity, narrative and biographical time, taken up recently in discussions of *autography*, now defined as an act of self-situating or
signature unencumbered by the representation of 'the life'.[30] Discussions of Rousseau's texts have focused on the dual role of language both as that which creates the self and as 'supplementary' to the
assumed immediacy of self-knowledge. In Starobinski's account of
Rousseau, writing is 'supplementary' primarily because it exists for
those readers who are required to bear witness, to authorise, the
'truth' to which they can only have access through narrative.

Starobinski's account is qualified by the readings of Peter Brooks
and other critics, who have claimed that narrativity provides the only
access to subjectivity in *The Confessions*, marking it as the first modern
narrative. Brooks writes:

The question of identity . . . can be thought only in narrative terms, in the
effort to tell a whole life, to plot its meaning by going back over it to record
its perpetual flight forward, its slippage from the fixity of definition . . . In
claiming the need to *tout dire* Rousseau makes explicit that the con-
tradistinctions encountered in the attempt to understand and present the
self in all its truth provide a powerful narrative machine. Any time one
goes over a moment of the past the machine can be relied on to produce
more narrative – not only differing stories of the past, but future scenarios
and narrative of writing itself.[31]

The implications of this account for autobiographical theory are
twofold. Firstly, Brooks provides a powerful model for the narrative
dimension of identity, used by a number of critics to support the
concept of the self's fictionality. Secondly, he points to the addictive
aspects of autobiography/confession; as de Man noted of Rousseau,
there can never be an end to excuses which 'generate the very guilt
they exonerate, though always in excess or by default . . .
[Rousseau's] *plaisir d'écrire* leaves him guiltier than ever'.[32]

Rousseau referred to writing as that 'dangerous supplement', and
it is the concept of 'the supplement' around which Jacques Derrida
built his earlier philosophical writings. Rousseau's writings in

general, and *Essay on the Origin of Languages* and *The Confessions* in particular, develop a conception of writing as 'supplementary' to speech, in which the immediacy of spoken communication is contrasted with the dangerous mediations and displacements of writing. As in Rousseau's general account of civilisation, complexity is linked to artifice, decadence and the loss of the natural and, in Derrida's words, 'a feared writing must be cancelled because it erases the presence of the self-same [propre] within speech'.[33] Yet Rousseau cannot make these arguments except in terms of a broader conception of language which includes both speech and writing – a conception which also rules out any idea of non-linguistic communication. Although it is interesting to recall that Rousseau gave public readings from *The Confessions* many years prior to their (posthumous) publication – and indeed the extant text closes with an account of the effect, or lack of effect, produced on his audience by one such reading – Derrida is not primarily concerned with the distinction between the oral and the written, but with the impossibility of the kind of self-presence to which Rousseau aspired.

The intricacies of Derrida's writings on Rousseau cannot be explored in detail here. Many of Derrida's works, however, are highly relevant to autobiographical theory as he reformulates the very concepts of autobiographics: the border between 'the life' and 'the text', the significance of the authorial or 'proper name' and of the signature, the status of the 'I', the relationship between a writer's written 'corpus' and his or her body, the biographical and biological, the links between auto/biography as life-writing and the problematic of mourning and memorialisation. I discussed the way some of these concerns emerged, often in metaphorical form, in nineteenth- and early twentieth-century discussions of auto/biography: Derrida now places them in the contexts of philosophical and literary writing, while allowing some of their more uncanny effects to emerge.

In his work on the signature, for example, Derrida shows how, just as the signature appears marginal to the literary work, autobiography appears in a marginal relationship to literature, while the signature's key role in relation to autobiography extends in reality to literature itself. The use of the proper name refers paradigmatically to the living person, but it also outlives him/her and thus could be said to prefigure his/her death. In short, while many of the concerns listed above would seem to bear on questions of subjectivity and identity, Derrida's contribution is not, in this context, to a theorisation of the

subject of autobiography as such, but to a *redistribution* of the autobiographical. Derrida is clearly open to the charge that by decon-
structing the concept of the subject, he cannot offer an adequate
theory of agency; yet his questioning of the borders and boundaries of
the institutions in which the autobiographical is held is a radical one.

Derrida's discussion of Nietzsche's *Ecce Homo*, in *The Ear of the
Other*, provides a striking example of the redistribution or relocation
of the autobiographical and reformulates the problematic of autobiography in several ways.[34] Firstly, he uses Nietzsche's own philosophical concepts (the 'eternal return' and affirmation) to trouble
generic models of the relationship between addresser and addressee
in autobiography and of the 'proper' auditor of autobiography. *Ecce
Homo* is frequently invoked by autobiographical critics as an example
of a text whose non-narrative form of 'introspection' excludes it from
the autobiographical canon; it has thus come to exemplify the
dangerous extreme of autobiographical interiority.[35] In Derrida's
account, which echoes something of this judgement, but with a
reversal of its values, Nietzsche's text allows for a concept of autobiography in which the *autos* does not function as a possessive pronoun attached to the *bios* (the story of one's life); it refers rather to the
process by which 'I tell my story to myself', 'I hear myself speak'
[p. 49].

Focusing on the *exergue* in *Ecce Homo*, inserted between the Preface
and the body of the text, Derrida points to Nietzsche's use of a form
of thanatography – 'It was not for nothing that I buried my forty-
fourth year today; I had the *right* to bury it; whatever was life in it has
been saved, is immortal'[36] – and his act of auto-narration – 'And so I
tell my life to myself.' Nietzsche writes the dying body: he identifies
the onset of his own illness with the death of his father at the same age
and present himself as 'already dead', with the definitive catalogue of
his works representing his immortality and embodying the dead
Nietzsche. As Michel Beaujour has noted, *Ecce Homo* is the textual
site where the corpus and the body of Nietzsche respectively change
status.[37]

This 'self-portrait', to use Beaujour's phrase, is also a self-
narration. Alluding to Nietzsche's numerous references to ears of
various sizes in the text ('des oreilles fines' means both small and
acute), Derrida appears to be exploring Nietzsche's play with the
concept of 's'entendre-parler', glossed by Christopher Norris as
'hearing oneself speak and immediately grasping the sense of one's

own utterance'.[38] This concept is one of the targets of Derrida's critique of 'phonocentrism' and self-present speech. Nietzsche's act of auto-narration – 'I tell my life to myself ' – involves, in Derrida's account of the text, sending the text out into the world to be 'signed' and returned via ('on the back of ') the concept of the 'eternal return' to its meanwhile deceased sender. Hence the act of auto-narration entails a detour via the Other – its 'signatory'. Derrida's broader concerns are the difficult issue of a text's reception and the way a text is used or abused by its readers. What responsibility, for example, does Nietzsche bear for the use of his philosophy in Nazism, and to what extent is 'he' responsible for the cognate 'Nietzschean' which represents the cultural agglomeration of 'the life' and 'the work'?

Derrida's question about the boundaries of Nietzsche's *oeuvre* or corpus is part of a broader scepticism, strikingly represented by Nietzsche himself, about the status of the human subject. Nietzsche's critique of traditional philosophical concepts of the subject, and particularly of the Kantian subject which prescribes for itself, or perhaps internalises, universally valid moral law, has been widely read, via Heidegger and poststructuralist thought, as abolishing any operative concept of subjectivity. This philosophical current con- verged with psychological theories, notably Freudian and Lacanian psychoanalysis and their offshoots, and sociological models which stressed cultural and historical difference and documented the erosion of the ego-strong bourgeois subject. The radicalism of Nietzsche's critique of the subject ran as a red thread from the European *fin-de-siècle* to the global postmodernity of the 1970s and 1980s.

Proclamations of the 'death of the subject' were commonplace and autobiographical theory, in particular, was used to articulate the deconstruction of traditional concepts of a unified subjectivity. Louis Marin and Eugene Vance developed a 'grammar of identity', in which Benveniste's assertion that the 'I' merely 'designates the one who speaks' in any given act of utterance is interpreted as meaning that 'the 'I' is a fiction, since its only context of reference is the particular instance of discourse in which it appears'.[39] Candace Lang, in the article in which this quote appears, denounced James Olney's 'insensitivity' to such issues as the distinction between author, narrator and protagonist, his reliance on problematic dualities such as individual/society, self/other and fact/fiction and his conception of a unified human nature pre-existing textual expression. By the end of this period Jean-Luc Nancy was asking 'Who comes after the subject?'[40] What seems to have emerged from this process is a stronger sense of the plurality and the social construction of subjectivities and, possibly, a shift from concepts of 'subjectivity' to those of 'identity' and 'difference', concepts less philosophically burdened and more overtly attuned to culture and history.

During the 1970s and 1980s Nietzsche was a key figure for deconstructive approaches to autobiography. As Michael Sprinker wrote:

> If autobiography can be described as the self's enquiry into its own history – the self-conscious questioning by the subject of itself – then Nietzsche offers the most fearful warning for any autobiographical text: 'The danger of the direct questioning of the subject *about* the subject and of all self-reflection of the subject lies in this, that it could be useful and important for one's activity to interpret oneself *falsely*'. In the present century no one has taken this admonition more seriously than Freud.[41]

If, at one level, Nietzsche's claim would seem to invalidate the very project of autobiography – although perhaps less so than in other contexts in which he denies the very concept of the subject – a more positive reading was made by a number of literary critics, for whom the possibility that all experience might be fictive became a legitimation of a literary appropriation of autobiography, a blurring of the boundaries between non-fictional and fictional writings and an escape from the fruitless endeavour to draw hard and fast distinctions between fact and fiction in self-writings. The complexity of autobiographical 'truth' in psychoanalysis confirms this; Freud's discovery (or assumption) that patients 'lie' is turned to advantage. The fictions which patients manufacture are perceived as enabling the truth of the therapeutic effect and the operation of the unconscious is only seen in the fictions which we invent in order to represent the unconscious.

Paul Jay's *Being in the Text* traces autobiographical self-representation from Wordsworth to Barthes via Carlyle and Nietzsche as a process of increasing fictionalisation 'within a changing epistemology of the subject – in both the psychological and literary sense of the word'.[42] Nietzsche

> does not deny the fact of the subject's existence; [he] simply insists that the central fact about subjectivity is that its previous formulations have the status of a fiction, and that our own (particular and historical) role in creating that fiction must be acknowledged as more properly – and

importantly – a 'fact'.

Nietzsche's argument in *The Will to Power* is that what we call the subject 'is the fiction that many similar states in us are the effect of one substratum' [p. 28]. The 'self' is a product of our discursive practices.

Nietzsche's scepticism extends to his historiographic prescription that the historian should aim at creativity rather than objectivity, in a move which has important implications for thinkers like Dilthey who envisaged a relationship between autobiography and history based on an inner–outer division. As Jay noted, the crises of historicism and autobiography are products of the same epistemological shift; a sense of the subjectivism of all scholarship led some nineteenth-century thinkers, notably Nietzsche, to aestheticism and a valorisation of fictionality as a way of 'dissolving', in Hayden White's account, the ironic consciousness of the problematic nature of language and the disconcerting effects of self-consciousness.[43]

One result of this 'dissolve' is an uncontested fictionalism, in which the elevation of creativity as the highest principle legitimates any poetic utterance. The implications for autobiographical theory have tended to be first, a celebration of the 'literary' autobiography concurrent with an erasure of the 'history' of disciplinary and conceptual distinctions such as fact and fiction, fiction and history, and second, a demand that autobiography perform the magical act of mediating the antithesis between fiction and reality. These issues are taken up in the next chapter.

*   *   *

Paul de Man, the most important theorist of deconstruction in the United States, has also been closely associated with rereadings of Rousseau, Nietzsche and Romanticism generally. The revaluation of Romanticism in the last two decades is in turn closely linked to academic interest in autobiography. The deconstructive reading of 'Romanticism' emphasised its ironies, its self-consciousness and the complexities of its imbrications of philosophy, history and literature, in contrast to the New Critical and modernist devaluations of Romanticism as *naïveté*. For deconstruction, both Romanticism and autobiography are defined substantially through their problematisation of the subject/object relationship. In more traditional criticism, the identity of writer and subject in autobiography is taken as providing one form, at least, of the unity of subject and object so dear to philosophy. Thus it is the subject/object identity which privileges autobiography above other forms of knowledge: conversely, the existence of autobiography guarantees at least a region in which this identity is possible. In recent criticism, autobiography is privileged for a different reason: the split it embodies between subject and object, self and other, first and third person – 'Je est un autre.' Autobiography imports alterity into the self by the act of objectification which engenders it.

To some extent, 'Romantic autobiography' becomes the model of autobiography in general, in its deployment of self-consciousness, self-division and the impossibility of giving priority to 'self' in the self–language relationship. The difficulty here is that Romanticism is both a period concept, a 'moment' in the history of consciousness and, in other literary-critical models, a way of reading. The Romantic reading could be defined as the reading of a text (any text?) as 'personal': that is, as a form of autobiography.

Paul de Man's influential essay 'Autobiography as De-Facement' combines a critique of contemporary theories of autobiography with de Man's own 'theorization' of autobiography, drawn out of a reading of Wordsworth's *Essays upon Epitaphs*.[44] De Man begins, like a number of other critics, with a statement of the impossibility of constructing autobiography as a genre. Whereas de Man and James Olney would seem to share the view, expressed by Olney, that 'autobiography refuses to be a genre like any other', the crucial difference is that Olney can allow for generic heterogeneity because for him the self is secured, whereas for de Man 'subjectivity' is an effect of language. He argues that the assumed referential status of autobiography reveals the fictionality of all referentiality: although we assume that the life produces the autobiography, it is equally possible that the autobiographical project produces and determines the life.

De Man's essay is an important intervention into genre-theory and I discuss some of the issues it raises in more detail in the following chapter. In the present context, the most important aspects of de Man's discussions are his identification of autobiography's figurative aspects and his reading of Wordsworth's *Essays on Epitaphs* in relation to 'the larger question of autobiographical discourse as a discourse of self-restoration'. De Man calls attention to the use of *prosopopoeia*, the trope whose definitions include personification (from *prosopon poiein*, to confer a mask or a face), a rhetorical figure by which an inanimate or abstract thing is represented as a person, and, applied to a person or thing, in which some quality or abstraction is embodied. An early usage, given by the *OED*, is 'the feigning of a person when we bring in dead men speaking, or our selves doe take their person upon us or give voice unto senseless things' (1609).

De Man takes up in particular a definition of prosopopeiea as 'the fiction of an apostrophe to an absent, deceased, or voiceless entity, which posits the possibility of the latter's reply and confers upon it the power of speech' [pp. 75–6]. This figure is the culminating point of a series of tropes running, in a reading of Wordsworth's *Essays Upon Epitaphs*, from the seeing sun – 'the sun looks down upon the stone, and the rains of heaven beat against it' – to the speaking stone of the epitaph – 'epitaphs so often personate the deceased, and represent him as speaking from his own tombstone' – to the giving of voice and finally of face to the subject of autobiography. Prosopopeia is the trope of autobiography, de Man writes,

> by which one's name, is made as intelligible and memorable as a face. ... The dominant figure of the epitaphic or autobiographical discourse is, as we saw, the prosopopeia, the fiction of the voice-from-beyond-the-grave; an unlettered stone would leave the sun suspended in nothingness. [p. 77]

In de Man's alignment of autobiography and epitaph, the speaking subject is not only an hallucinatory effect, but also emerges at the end of a long chain of tropological substitutions and metonymic displacements.

The subject is also a projection by and of the reader of the epitaphic/autobiographic inscription:

> the autobiographical moment happens as an alignment between the two subjects involved in the process of reading in which they determine each other by mutual reflexive substitution. ... The specular moment that is part of all understanding reveals the tropological structure that underlies all cognitions, including knowledge of self. [pp. 70–1]

De Man's attempt to shift discussions of autobiography from questions of genre to those of rhetorical and tropological structures entails reformulating the question of recognition – of the 'genre' and of the subject.

I now want to turn to Mary Jacobus's essays on *The Prelude, Romanticism, Writing and Sexual Difference*, as a way of reading 'Autobiography as De-Facement' and of opening up multiple ways of understanding 'prosopopeia' and 'specularity' in de Man's discussion of autobiography.[45] Specularity relates to the doubleness of the self: reflexive consciousness, the 'two consciousnesses' which perplex self-presence, are of two paired and interrelated kinds. The hand that writes and the eye that reads, the 'writer reading himself ', are linked to the doubled consciousness of past and present. This doubling of the autobiographical self is responsible for what Jacobus terms the 'missed encounter' of self with self, exemplified in the central image of *The Prelude*, the crossing of the Alps – 'a missed meeting, a missed meaning' [p. 6]. 'Specularity' thus refers to the mirroring relationship between writing and written selves, present and past consciousness; I take up its psychoanalytic connotations later in this chapter.

De Man's ambiguous reference to 'the two subjects involved in the process of reading' also allows, however, for a model of the reading process in autobiography. De Man's emphasis, here and elsewhere, on the *performative* moment of the text includes the idea that reading performs that which in the text always escapes us. Jacobus shows how the themes of epitaph, funerary writing and prosopopeia (the putting-on of a face or mask, the fiction of address from and to the dead) are linked to the reading relationship: 'What speaks in autobiography is a dead man; the master-trope or "figure" of autobiography both gives and takes away (undoes or obliterates) a face.' Playing on the image of a face 'working' in the physical expression of grief, Jacobus writes:

> The face of nature and the inscription of the Sublime . . . is also the face of the autobiographer, apocalyptically inscribed in the very signs of its undoing, its 'working' at the scene of imagined death. By a sleight of hand, what undoes a face becomes what makes it 'work', both affectively, and as a figure for death. When we speak, then, of the powerful 'workings' of the text – of the characters of danger and desire – it is the affect in our own reading, our identification with the displaced epitaph, that constitutes or 'works' the text of a brooding autobiographical subject, whose face the texts put on in the image of ours. We read our own auto-biographies (our own affect) in the epitaph or epitomised biography – the monumental writing – which constitutes *The Prelude*. [p. 20]

In this model, the autobiographer comes into being as a specular image of the reader, a projected image of the reader's affective identifications. Moreover, whereas the 'Romantic' focus on auto-biographical self-reflection and self-reflexivity would seem to create an absolute division between biographical and autobiographical representations, Jacobus is in fact describing a structure in which 'biography', in the form of epitaphs to dead or lost selves in *The Prelude*, is transformed by the 'work' of reading into an auto-biographics of reader and writer.

The modes of epitaphic inscription discussed by Wordsworth in *Essays Upon Epitaphs* do indeed allow for a certain interchange of the biographical and autobiographical; the epitaph can take the form of biography or 'feigned' autobiography (the prosopopeic). Wordsworth expresses a preference for the empathetic form of the 'biographical' epitaph over the 'tender fiction' of prosopopeia in which the deceased is represented 'as speaking from his own tombstone. . . . This shadowy interposition also harmoniously unites the two worlds of the living and the dead by their appropriate affections.' The 'bio-graphical' form, in which survivors speak directly, is preferable, how-ever, 'because, excluding the fiction which is the groundwork of the other, it rests upon a more solid basis'.[46] The feminisation of pro-sopopeia as the 'tender fiction' is thus an aspect of its perceived hybridity, its crossing of two worlds and two genres, to be contrasted with the 'solid basis' on which epitaph proper rests. This gendered reading is confirmed by a number of Romantic texts in which, in Cynthia Chase's words, 'prosopopeia is . . . thematized or personified as a woman, and in one way or another "abjected" or cast out'.[47]

On the other hand, as Jacobus argues, prosopopeia is perceived by Romantic rhetoricians to be the highest form of a personification otherwise devalued. Eschewing the 'personification of abstract ideas' in the 1800 'Preface' to *Lyrical Ballads*, Wordsworth is nonetheless enabled by the use of prosopopeia to construct an image of true authorship and naturalised poetic identity in his autobiographical representations: 'Prosopopeia gives voice to the face of Wordsworth, inviting us to identify the autobiographical front of *The Prelude* – its masquerade of identity – with the figure of the poet. Figuratively speaking, it masquerades as a self that is 'literal and unrhetorical', concealing the representational and economic structures which pro-duce such a person' [p. 235]. This concealment, as I discussed in Chapter 1, covers over the the self-advertisement attached to auto-biography with the growth of literary commodification, and 'saves' autobiography for the history of consciousness.

Jacobus's final variant on the nexus of prosopopeia and specularity in autobiography is one in which 'genre puts a face on theory'. Conservative forms of genre theory, however, employ 'qualities of distinctiveness, individuality, and integrity commonly associated with the concept of "character" – a concept which buttresses our sense of separateness of subjects against the dangers of (inter-)mixing'. The issue of generic 'purity' is of central importance to autobiographical theory. Playing with concepts of gender, genre and genealogy, Jacobus argues that autobiography – and her discussion again focuses on *The Prelude* – is a 'bastard' genre or, indeed, 'a distinctively revolutionary non-genre':

> Is genre theory, then, no more than 'a figure of reading or of understanding', a means of stabilizing the errant text by putting a face on it, and so reading into it a recognizable, specular image of our own acts of understanding? In this light, theories of genre become inseparable from theories of the subject, and hence inseparable from theories of writing. However mixed the genre or mixed-up the 'self ', the source of writing . . . is held finally to be a more or less integrated and coherent author, the individual named 'Wordsworth', who guarantees the stability, and finally, the legitimacy of the text. [pp. 201–2]

In this model, the reader's 'recognition' of the face of the text is an act of generic ascription whereby textual and epistemological instability or hybridity are neutralised, and, in the conflation of generic type and of character, the text is both given a recognisable generic home and at the same time stabilised as the utterance of a coherent subject, authorised by the proper name.

Mary Jacobus provides extremely rich and subtle reformulations and extensions of de Man's terms for autobiography, primarily in relation to Wordsworth. The broader question of how far de Man's model of autobiography is 'generalisable' in the way he suggests is important, however, in part because more traditional forms of Romantic theory have also constructed 'Romantic autobiography' as the enduring model – as in M. H. Abrams's account of quest, conversion and final reclamation of self in *The Prelude*. To what extent should de Man's account of the autobiographical project as, in Paul Smith's words, 'a privileged kind of impossibility, always given over to uncertainty, undecidability, and, finally to death', be allowed to stand as a model of autobiography *tout court*?[48] What are de Man's grounds for basing his argument on *Essays Upon Epitaphs* and for claiming so close a relationship between epitaph and autobiography?

Deconstruction points up the imaginary identifications by which words are transformed in the act of reading into emanations of persons. Autobiographies have conventionally been granted a secondary status in relation to a writer's 'imaginative' works but they are also privileged to the extent that they represent the 'person' of the author. The discussions of Derrida and de Man, among others, demystify these assumptions and, as we have seen, 'disperse' the autobiographical. It remains unclear, however, whether auto-biographical writing is to be seen as a separate category at all, and Derrida, certainly, has been most interested in locating a quite specific 'autobiographics' in, for example, the writings of Freud and Nietzsche and, indeed, in his own work.[49] De Man asserts the ultimate undecidability of the autobiography–fiction distinction and becomes, in Paul Jay's words, 'a kind of laboratory for demonstrating in an ultimate kind of way the crux of a literary theory about referentiality generated outside the realm of autobiographical studies *per se*'.[50]

It is also worth noting that de Man's essay shares the striking preoccupation of recent autobiographical criticism with the theme of death. Implicit in the search for totality in more traditional auto-biographical criticism is the paradox that autobiography *ex hypothesi* cannot be written from the standpoint beyond the grave which would secure this totalising vision of the life. By extension, for the auto-biographer to aim at this totalizing vision would itself be to aim for death. One might argue that this preoccupation is present, even in a displaced form, in the emphasis in criticism on the autobiographical effect to capture past states of affairs – as in Nietzsche 'burying' his forty-fourth year. This theme recalls Freud's (and Schopenhauer's) account of the death-instinct or 'drive' as the attempt of the psyche 'to restore an earlier state of things'.[51]

Of recent theorists, Derrida, de Man and Louis Marin have constructed theories of autobiography in which death, as much as life, motivates or determines autobiographical discourse. For de Man, the predicament of the autobiographer is that, as Jay states, 'in the act of self-figuration (autobiographical composition) the bio-graphical self is displaced by a trope: it is "disfigured" and in the process "dies", so that literary self-representation becomes for de Man the creation of a kind of epitaph'.[52] Louis Marin, in his article 'Montaigne's Tomb, or Autobiographical Discourse', offers a reading of autobiography centred on the necessity/impossibility of writing one's own death. He focuses on the episode in Montaigne's essay in which Montaigne describes an 'experience' of 'coming close to death' in terms of death and rebirth. Marin comments:

It is not possible to write, to transmit, to communicate death as one's own death. It is impossible and yet it is essential, for it is the ultimate experience in which each man singularly identifies himself in his particular truth, in his propriety (*Dans son propre*). And yet, through the narrative of the singular accident simulating death, there has been something like a writing of death as my death, in the proximity of the edge of death. What then is it to write oneself? And has one the right to communicate to others what one knows about oneself?[53]

Marin's argument appears to be that the simulation of death is a way of writing an experience which can be said to be the only experience which is properly one's own and unique: thus its communication constitutes the writing self as an individual subject. And yet death cannot be said to be an *experience*, as Wittgenstein noted in the *Tractatus*: 'Death is not an event of life. One does not experience death.'[54] More generally, however, the distancing from self implied by the autobiographical project has been, as we have seen, assimilated to a kind of self-dissection, in which 'experience' can also take on the sense of 'experiment'.

Behind the death or quasi-death of the autobiographical subject lies the familiar theme of the 'death of the subject'. One should not, however, assume too readily that the former theme is simply a front for the latter, given the more precise concerns which emerge in deconstructionist criticism. Noteworthy among these is a return to a concern with the 'monumental' aspects of autobiography; de Man writes, albeit ironically, that autobiography is incompatible with 'the monumental dignity of aesthetic values' [p. 68]. The majority of twentieth-century theorists have rejected the 'Victorian' notion of autobiography as an epitaph or monument to a past life and a *memento mori* for future generations, in favour of a stress on the communication of 'life' and lived experience. Deconstruction, however, with its suspicion of the categories of subjectivity and experience, seems to point back to an image of autobiography as funerary architecture – which in Georg Misch's 'monumental study' was the birthplace of autobiography.

As we saw in previous chapters, death is a constant preoccupation in much nineteenth- and early twentieth-century auto/biographical discourse. It is interesting that it should recur in a cultural context in which death has been largely rendered invisible and in which the relationship between auto/biography and memorial would seem to have been severed. There are a number of aspects to the focus on autobiography and, or as, death in deconstructionist criticism: a romantic legacy in which self-consciousness is allied to self-dissection and even self-murder; a linking of autobiography to allegory and allegorical personification as defined by Walter Benjamin, in which nature, alienated from man, becomes emblematic (torso, ruin, fragment, monument), and history's failures are 'expressed in a face – or rather in a death's head';[55] a focus on mourning, melancholia and memory, particularly in Derrida's work;[56] a desire for autobiography to 'speak' the 'impossible' phrase 'je suis mort';[57] a theory of writing as neither an expression of nor supplement to the self but a substitution for the autobiographical subject, so that the self 'dies' to the letter; a concept of autobiography as the tomb from which the subject 'speaks', in a further denial of voice as presence. The conventions of posthumous publication of previous ages are taken up as the conditions for present writing and self-inscription.

In the mid 1970s, Georges Gusdorf described the deconstructionist critic of autobiography as a kind of embalmer, conducting 'the autopsy of the exquisite cadaver of liberal man'[58] and dancing on the graves of God, Man and the Author. I have attempted to show that the thanatographical interests of deconstruction exist in a certain tradition of writing about autobiography. It is now worth noting that it is not only traditional humanists who have reacted against the death-dealing discourses of deconstruction. Autobiography has become of central importance, as I discuss in detail in Chapter 7, to those groups for whom self as agency is a crucial political and personal postulate. The argument of many feminist critics with deconstruction, although they might support its critique of, in Ann Mellor's words, 'the unified, agential, coherent self sought by the author of *The Prelude* and assumed in most social contract and rational choice theories' [p. 154], is that it would seek to deny a voice to any subject before women have fully found their own. Women have not yet gained full recognition of their subjectivity, which should therefore not be foreclosed.

The recent development in feminist theory of what has been called 'personal criticism' is part of the move to reclaim agency and subjectivity. An autobiographical moment is made central to the activity of criticism, thus both foregrounding the identity of the critic and reconceptualising the nature of criticism itself. In Nancy Miller's words, personal criticism 'entails an explicitly autobiographical performance within the art of criticism'.[59] This aspect of a broader 'return of the subject' may be seen as a positive reclamation of agency, identity and subjectivity, or as reflecting, as Kobena Mercer has argued, a sense of crisis, doubt and uncertainty about 'identity' – a defensive response 'to the sheer difficulty of living with difference'.[60] Miller situates her account of personal criticism in a dissatisfaction with deconstructionist thought:

> It seems to me that the efflorescence of personal criticism in the United States in the eighties – like the study of autobiography – has in part to do with the gradual and perhaps inevitable waning of enthusiasm for a mode of Theory, whose authority, however variously – depended on the theoretical evacuation of the very social subjects producing it. (The upset and uproar surrounding the revelations about Paul de Man's biography figure, I think, both limits and costs of this fiction).[61]

Miller's (throwaway) comment about the 'de Man affair' is, I would suggest, worth pursuing. It would be difficult to exaggerate the crisis, the trauma, at least in the Humanities, that resulted from the discovery in 1987 that the most celebrated theorist and practitioner of deconstruction in North America had, between 1940 and 1942, written a substantial number of articles for newspapers and a journal under the control of the occupation authorities in Belgium. Debates over the anti-Semitic/pro-Fascist content of de Man's wartime journalism have been both intensive and extensive – at times taking on something of the tone of a trial for war-crimes.[62]

A further set of debates arising from the discoveries concern the questions, central to personal criticism, of 'speaking out', of declaring who one is and where one has come from and a fear or anxiety about concealing oneself behind the 'abstractions' of theory. Put crudely, it would seem that the anxiety is that if one does not speak out, situate oneself or, in Mary Ann Caws's words, manifest 'a certain intensity in the lending of oneself to the act of writing', it is because one has something to hide.[63]

The question of autobiography has acquired a central role in the controversies over de Man and deconstruction – it is, indeed, 'over-determined'. One crucial issue, for both de Man's accusers and his defenders, is the break or continuity between the de Man who wrote the wartime journalism and the de Man of the later literary theory – in the terms of autobiographical discourse, the relationship between past 'I' and present 'I'. Secondly, as we have seen, de Man's writings contain very substantial reflections on the modes of autobiography, confession and apologia – reflections which assert their generic

'impossibility' or the bad faith they manifest, as in his account of
Rousseau's pleasure in the production of confessions intended as
penitential discourse. These elements in de Man's writing now tend
to be read either as veiled confessions or as dissimulations – a special
pleading by one for whom autobiography had indeed become an
impossible act.

Autobiography is, de Man suggested, 'a figure of reading' rather
than writing; it is certainly the case, rightly or wrongly, that it is now
difficult not to read de Man 'autobiographically'. Metaphors of
defacement, disfiguration and hanging figures have been traced back
to a version of the primal scene or originary trauma in de Man's life:
the discovery of the body of his mother, who had committed suicide
by hanging. Autobiography becomes defined as a telling of obsessions – a compulsion to repeat – in the obsessional way which is the
only way in which they could be told.[64]

We might also add another lurid figure here: the trope of prosopopeia which, as we have seen, is a central figure in de Man's
tropological system. In some sense, of course, the 'voice' is always
hallucinatory in de Manian theory, for the figurative nature of language is privative, eternally depriving us of voice and condemning us
not to silence but to muteness. 'Silence', de Man wrote in 'Autobiography as De-Facement', 'implies the possible manifestation of
sound at our own will'; muteness, by contrast, is an affliction [p. 80].

Many of the agonised debates over the de Man revelations centre
upon the question of whether de Man himself was, in the terms just
given, 'silent' or 'mute'. In one of his essays on de Man, 'The Art of
Mémoires', written after de Man's death but before the discovery of
the journalism, and centred on de Man's 'Autobiography as De-
Facement', Derrida wrote of the 'forgetting of the pronoun, singularly of the first-person pronoun, the "I". The effacement of the
"I" in a kind of a priori and functional forgetting could be related to
. . . "Autobiography as De-Facement" . . . memory effaces remembrance (or recollection) just as the "I" effaces itself.'[65] In 'Paul de
Man's War', written as a response to the wartime journalism and to
the kinds of claims about the 'dangers' of deconstruction it had
provoked, Derrida refers to de Man's silence: 'it was publicly broken
on at least one occasion and thus cannot be understood in the sense of
a dissimulation . . . what could the ordeal of this mutism have been,
for him?'[66]

In *Testimony: Crises of Witnessing in Literature, Psychoanalysis and*

History, co-written with Dori Laub, Shoshana Felman includes her responses to the discovery of the journalism and its aftermath in a chapter entitled 'After the Apocalypse: Paul de Man and the fall to silence'.[67] Taking up the terms of 'forgetting' and 'silence', Felman also moves from the concept of 'silence' to that of 'muteness': 'It's de Man's theories', she writes, 'that inscribe the testimony of the muted witness', and 'History as holocaust is mutely omnipresent in the theoretical endeavour of de Man's mature work' [p. 140]. De Man's voice is now heard in or from his writings, Felman seems to suggest, as a kind of prosopopeia, as

> he addresses posthumously (or in anticipation) the question so per-sistently asked today both by his critics and by his admirers, of why he had not satisfied the former's sense of justice and/or cleared the latter's conscience, by giving both the satisfaction – or the reparation – of a public confession or a public declaration of remorse that would have at least proven his regret, his present repentance of past errors. [p. 141]

Felman's deeply troubling strategy is to make de Man 'speak' post-humously in and through the words of Walter Benjamin and Primo Levi – more obviously victims of fascism.[68]

For reasons that merit further investigation, a great deal of intel-lectual work at the moment appears to be concerned with 'speaking out' or 'remaining silent'. Felman writes about the ways in which 'testimony has become a crucial mode of our relation to events of our times . . . our era can precisely be defined as the age of testimony' [p. 5]. This shift, if that is what it is, from the self-consciousness of autobiography (which may conceal a cultural demand for confession) to the ethical responsibility to testify, has important implications for conceptions of the status and value of self-writings and for concepts of experience and our relationship to it. It would seem to entail a move away from self-reflection towards a sense that we are all witnesses of history's tragedies and may be summoned to testify to our knowledge of them.

* * *

'. . . psychoanalysis was the mirror of the age. One always returned to Freud, for after all, he had invented a therapeutic method which explored the *narrative* that a life might be – identity as autobiography' (Elizabeth Wilson).[69]

'The main reason why psychoanalysis has done little to transform autobiography is . . . that autobiography is not an act of analysis but a lived activity of synthesis' (Philippe Lejeune).[70]

Both autobiography and psychoanalysis paradigmatically involve the reconstruction of a life in narrative and the shaping of events into a meaningful framework. Autobiographies in the modern period tend to make childhood memories a significant part of the narrative: psychoanalysis sees childhood as formative. Narrative, in the sense of the recounting of stories and the drive to narrate, is an important dimension of both spheres, but so is the charge attached to images and memories which stand out against the backdrop of the past. In both, fictions are often seen as more important, and revealing, than facts, while uncovering the past is viewed as a complex and difficult process. Psychoanalysis is a theory of the making of an individual, and of a gendered individual in particular; autobiography, like the *Bildungsroman*, is a privileged site for representing this process. What Freud called the 'family romance'[71] is often central to autobiography: Michel Neyraut describes it as 'a sort of revolving stage where all potential destinies are evoked . . . so as to try out all the combinations which could be produced by the encounter of these figures. The family romance is not a luxury of the imagination; it is the condition of an identity.'[72]

These affinities, however, are not enough to create a symmetry between the two practices, and from the early twentieth century onwards there has been a sense of missed opportunities and failed relationships. It would be another project, and one that I hope to undertake in the future, to trace fully the interrelated histories of psychoanalysis, biography and autobiography, and their attendant theories, in the twentieth century. In the present context, I can only sketch in some of the lines of development. I discussed Freud's interest in biography in Chapter 2, and in Chapter 3 referred very briefly to the development of psychobiography. The domain of psychobiography gathers up the issues of genius and pathology, 'Great Men', the creative impulse and sexuality which we have already encountered. In the twentieth century, the Great Man often appears in the avatar of the Great Dictator. Not surprisingly, the variant of psychoanalytic theory which formed the basis of psychobiography was 'ego-psychology' which, as Saul Friedländer puts it, 'is less concerned with the vicissitudes of the instincts than with the adaptive and structuring function of the ego'.[73] Most influential in the United States – and derided by Jacques Lacan as 'the psychology of free enterprise' – ego psychology animated psychobiographies such as Erik Erikson's studies of Luther and Gandhi and Bruce Mazlish's study of James and John Stuart Mill.[74] Erikson's work on identity and the life-cycle was also invoked for the writing, and theorising, of autobiography. Mazlish wrote in 1970: 'autobiographies, to convince us, ought ideally to deal with the self as a developing entity, developing through an Erikson-like life cycle and in correspondence with a changing world'.[75] Such emphases on adaptation, reality-testing and compromise formation arise in a number of discussions of autobiography in this period and to the present day.

This association between ego psychology and psychobiography accounts for some of the hostility to biography on the part of Lacanian theorists also writing in the 1970s, for whom ego psychology was a voluntaristic dilution of Freud's most important theories which neglected the unconscious in favour of an autonomous ego in contact with objective reality. Whereas autobiography could be redeemed for the project of refiguring subjectivity in language, with all its complexities, play and distortion, biography seemed fatally contaminated by positivist history and/or a psychology which focused on mechanisms rather than meanings and in which the ego was represented as a psychic hero.

In John Sturrock's 'The New Model Autobiographer' (1977), biographers are characterised as tradesmen tied to chronological narrative.[76] In familiar fashion, Sturrock argues that autobiography and biography should in no way be linked. He discusses Michel Leiris's Freudian-inspired autobiography *L'Age d'homme* and speaks of 'psychoanalysis, from which autobiography has everything to learn' [p. 54]. Leiris, 'an exemplary autobiographer... has preserved above all a faith in the cognitive powers of language; he believes that language has secrets, to penetrate which is to learn something about the world' [p. 58]. Jeffrey Mehlman's *A Structural Study of Autobiography* (1912) also made Leiris's autobiographical writings central – indeed, much psychoanalytical autobiographical theory has been inspired by Leiris's work.[77] Mehlman's is a Lacanian reading of Leiris, Proust and others, coloured by a phenomenological focus on key images, or indeed obsessions, in the autobiographer's work: 'in confronting texts', he writes, 'the search for repetitions, aberrant details, seeming contradictions, surprising omissions has, I believe, allowed me to generate between texts the kind of unexpectedly insistent structure for which Freud, and Mauron, use the term *'unconscious'* [p. 16]. Freud described his lecture tour of the United States in 1910 as 'bringing the plague to America'; Mehlman aims similarly to introduce into the United States 'a re-evaluation of textual values parallel to that operated by Lacan within Freud's text' [p. 19].

Sturrock and others have invoked a parallel between auto-biography and psychoanalysis in the service of their attack on chronological narrative and linear time:

> the analysis will shuttle to and fro between past and present, and its continuity will be fixed, not by the sequence of events in the past, but by the sequence of mental events in the present. The order in which the past is restored answers to the intimate needs of the patient. [p. 54]

(The specifically therapeutic efficacy of autobiographical self-analysis is a further element here.) This approach has not gone unchallenged. More recently, Paul John Eakin has suggested that critiques of an alleged conservatism mistake 'symptom for cause . . . we would do better to interpret the linearity of conventional biographical form as itself a response to the fundamental temporality of human experience'.[78]

Michel Beaujour, in his study of self-portraiture, *Miroirs d'encre*, contrasts autobiography with a non-chronological mode of self-representation exemplified by Montaigne's *Essais*, Nietzsche's *Ecce Homo* and Leiris's *L'Age d'homme*, whose material is ordered around psychically cathected themes and images, such as Cranach's paintings of Lucrece and Judith for Leiris. The heterogenous and complex form of the self-portrait derives from the same source as the medieval encyclopedic 'speculum' which represents the current state of knowledge, as in the *speculum mundi*, the mirror of the world. As the speculum is opposed, in medieval literature, to the allegorical narrative, so the modern self-portrait contrasts with autobiographical representation: 'the *mirror* does not aim at narration but rather at an intelligible representation of things or of the subject who knows them' [p. 31].

Beaujour argues that the mirror is an essentially open spatial form, whereas narrative, whether allegorical or biographical, is closed. One might question whether it is as easy, or indeed desirable, as Beaujour implies to escape from narrative form, even in works such as those cited above or in Barthes's 'autobiography' *Roland Barthes by Roland Barthes*, in which the ostensibly narrative element is provided by photographs and the 'text' takes the form of fragmented explications of images, concepts, words, memories, in Barthes's 'book of the Self '. Reversing the usual understanding of visual and verbal representations – 'the time of the narrative (or the imagery) ends with the subject's youth', Barthes defines the photographic imagery as biography, which is 'closed at the onset of productive life', i.e. the life of writing.[79]

Psychoanalysis (Freudian and post-Freudian) and autobiography share a double rhetoric of narrative/verbal and visual representations, the text and the mirror, the interpretative or hermeneutic and the specular. The mirror and mirroring relations are taken up in a number of autobiographical theories inflected by psychoanalysis. Lacan's account of the 'mirror stage', his model of human development predicated on the child's recognition/misrecognition of a mirrored self-image, a fragmented body and identity reflected back as whole and entire, has been particularly influential. Paul de Man's account of autobiography, discussed above, clearly draws on Lacan's concepts of specularity and doubling (*dédoublement*).

Elizabeth Grosz draws a useful distinction between the two accounts of the ego that emerge in Freud's theories, the 'realist ego' and the 'narcissistic ego'.[80] The 'realist' ego, innate, pre-given and identified with the self, adapts instinctual drives to the demands of external reality, effecting a rational compromise between the two. This model emerges in the ego psychology discussed above. The 'narcissistic' ego, by contrast, is an amorphous entity, enmeshed in drives, fantasies and intersubjective relations. Lacan bases his account of the ego on Freud's narcissistic model, but adds to Freud's essay *On Narcissism* a specifically visual and specular dimension. As Grosz states: 'the ego is represented as a psychical map, a projection of the surface of the body ... the psychical representation of the subject's perceived and libidinalized relation to its body' [p. 31]. Specularity is composed of the doubling effect of the mirror; the external perception of the self (autoscopy), the mother–child relationship, 'in which the mother takes on the position of specular image and the child that of incipient ego'; and the conflict between the experience of 'self ' (it is unclear who or what the experiencing self is) as a schism and the reflected image as a unified whole. 'It is the dual, ambivalent relation to its own image that is central to Lacan's account of subjectivity' [p. 39]. The ego is orientated around two poles: affirmative self-recognition and the paranoic knowledge of a split subject.

What are the implications of these theories for autobiography? As I have suggested, the 'realist ego' is invoked not only in psychobiography but in theories of autobiography predicated on the construction or development of an autonomous, self-affirming identity. By contrast, the deconstructionist models I have discussed take up the model of the narcissistic ego to describe the mirror of autobiography in terms of splitting, projection and doubling. Either the autobiography serves to create the illusion of a unified self out of the fragments of identity, or the text reveals, in its fissures, its doublings and its incompleteness, the fragmentations of the subject and its lack of self-coincidence. There are autobiographies which are clearly written out of paranoia, such as Schreber's and Rousseau's; more generally, autobiography has been defined as a paranoid form. Although I remain unsure of the value of such accounts of auto- biography, which seem to conflate infantile development, adult sub- jectivity, psychopathology and the social institution of autobiography, I have also wanted throughout this book to call attention to the prevalent imagery of fragmented bodies and the anxiety about the borders and boundaries of self in auto/biographical discourses, which seem to suggest a cultural, and perhaps psychic, ambivalence about self-representation and the place of the body in auto/ biography.

For feminist critics the question of autobiographical mirroring has been particularly crucial. This has entailed, however, a redefinition of the mother/mirror relationship, narcissism and specularity. Luce Irigaray has been one of the most influential theorists in this context: in *Speculum of the Other Woman* she offers women an alternative distorted mirror to the flat mirror which reflects the masculine subject.[81] As Grosz writes: 'her "mirror", the speculum, surrounds, and is surrounded by, the contours and specificity of the female body. It is not a device of self-distance but of self-touching, an implicated rather than disinterested self-knowledge. It represents the "other woman", not woman as in man's other, but another woman, alto- gether different from man's other' [p. 173].

Men's relationship to their mirror-images (and this account of an untroubled and authoritative male subjectivity does seem at odds with the Lacanian model described above) are defined auto-scopically, with the man looking at himself from the outside while retaining his position as a subject. His solipsistic dream of autonomy and of self as pure thought or consciousness is secured by the specularised female body: 'that all-powerful mirror denied and neg-lected in the self-sufficiency of the (self) thinking subject, her "body" hence forward specularized through and through'. As Rosi Braidotti comments: 'Wholly reflected by the looking glass of the female body, the thinking subject no longer sees his mirror; nor does he see that his thought, all thought, rests on a fiction, this illusion of himself as a totality.'[82] Reason, presented by man as 'natural' enlightenment, reflects, in Irigaray's account, the male subject's self-image in a mirror-game of speculation: self-reflection. Woman's body, maternal body, matter, are rejected and denied.[83]

The linking of mothers and mirrors was developed in a rather different context in D. W. Winnicott's work and taken up by Nancy Chodorow and others. Object-relations theory in psychoanalysis sees the self as formed, not in a simple opposition between 'I' and 'not-I', but in relationships of recognition, initially from the mother and subsequently in mirror-images, actual or metaphorical: in Winnicott's words 'in individual emotional development *the precursor of the mirror is the mother's face*'.[84] This model, as it is developed in certain feminist theories, is seen to entail a differential conception of male and female development. The reciprocal relationship between daughter and mother is held to be more direct than that between son and mother, due to gender identification as well as a weaker pressure to separate, and women are therefore likely to feel more closely tied than men to their environments and in particular to other people. In this account, women are understood to be less autonomous and more likely to experience identity as relational.

One of the strongest threads running through, and tying together, the substantial recent work on women's autobiography has been the critique of individualism developed in psychoanalytic feminism. As Jessica Benjamin states:

> According to current developments in psychoanalytic feminism, the salient feature of male individuality is that it grows out of the repudiation of the primary identification with and dependency on the mother. That leads to an individuality that stresses, as Nancy Chodorow has argued, difference as denial of commonality, separation as denial of connection;

and that is made up of a series of dualisms, of mutually exclusive poles, where independence seems to exclude all dependency rather than be characterized by a balance of separation and connection. The critique of this form of individualism is the contribution of the evolving integration of object relations that began with Chodorow's work. Central to this critique of dualism . . . is the awareness that the idealization of a particular form of one-sided autonomy permeates the Western notion of the individual as thinking subject, as explorer of the world.[85]

The concept of the (male) autobiographical self as solitary consciousness, and as explorer and coloniser of dark continents, recurs in a number of the accounts of autobiography discussed previously. The gender balance of autobiographical history cannot be corrected simply by adding more women to the list; basic suppositions about subjectivity and identity underlying autobiographical theories have to be shifted. Thus feminist critics have explicitly rejected accounts of the 'birth' of human consciousness in the originary moments of Western individualism, often turning to psychoanalytic theories to explore psychic identity and models of intersubjectivity in autobiographical texts, including the concept of 'relational' selves proposed by theorists such as Nancy Chodorow.[86] It seems to me crucial, however, that we stop equating autobiographies by men with their idealised representations in conventional autobiographical criticism, and look again at the autobiographical texts, not least in terms of the way they represent the construction of masculinities.

Many of the debates in feminist autobiographical criticism constitute an ethics of (gender) difference, arguing for a new valuation of self in relationship, embodied and empathetic consciousness, identity as likeness to an other rather than as the self-same. As with all such models of difference, it is surely important to distinguish between the 'innate' and the 'cultural'; it may not be advantageous for women to be redefined in terms of an exemplary altruism or lack of self-assertiveness. Jessica Benjamin provides an important warning-note, in her account of theories of maternal identification, when she writes of the dangers of a 'one-sided revaluing of women's position; freedom and desire might remain unchallenged male domain, leaving us to be righteous and deeroticized, intimate, caring and self-sacrificing' [p. 85]. Benjamin argues for a further development of the theory of maternal identification which can take on the problem of women's desire as her own, *inner* desire. Her proposed model is that of autonomy in relationship, an intersubjective relationship where 'subject meets subject' [p. 98].

To what extent can autobiographical writing and theory act as sites for the exploration of such questions? The mother–daughter relationship is clearly a key element in a number of women's autobiographies, which variously explore the complexity of the maternal mirror. (Twentieth-century examples would include Nancy Friday's *My Mother, My Self*, Carolyn Steedman's *Landscape for a Good Woman* and Maxine Hong Kingston's *The Woman Warrior*, discussed in my final chapter, Nathalie Sarraute's *Childhood*, Maya Angelou's *I Know Why the Caged Bird Sings* and Virginia Woolf's 'A Sketch of the Past'.)

Bella Brodzski and Celeste Schenck, editors of *Life/Lines: Theorizing Women's Autobiography*, write of the need for 'a feminist reappropriation of the mirror. . . . After Irigaray, the question remains: how have *women* articulated their own experience, shaped their own texts artistically, met their own reflections in the problematic mirror of autobiography?'[87] By denying women writers a place in the history of autobiography, 'critical work in the field, for all its insistence on mirroring universals, has presented a distorted reflection of the history of the autobiographical genre' [p. 2].

Women's autobiographies may also expose the double-edged nature of the psychic construction of femininity. On the one hand, autobiography is a vehicle for the expression of the female self. On the other hand, if women's autobiographies are read 'symptomatically', they can reveal the ways in which, in Simone de Beauvoir's phrase, one 'becomes' a woman. The narrative character of autobiography seems to have a particular affinity with the developmental accounts informing psychoanalysis, while the 'incompleteness' of the process of feminisation is seen to be mirrored in the fractured structures, or sometimes specific contents, of women's autobiographical writings. Thus Cora Kaplan, for example, has argued in a reading of nineteenth-century women's autobiographies that the recurrent accounts of childhood damage and neglect in these texts operate as symbolic accounts of the reluctant accession to femininity – itself a form of permanent damage.[88]

Modernist women's autobiographies, and in particular those of Gertrude Stein and Virginia Woolf, have become important texts for the exploration of women's subjectivities. Brodzski and Schenck assert that Stein

> knows what modern theorists have come to tell us about autobiography: that for women it is relational; that for modernists it is defamiliarized; that

for theorists it is impossible to capture the self otherwise than in pieces, fragments, refractions. . . . Being *between two covers* with somebody else ultimately replaces singularity with alterity in a way that is dramatically female. [p. 11]

Woolf's 'A Sketch of the Past' is a powerful account of her childhood which uses psychoanalytical models to understand and describe her earliest memories of her mother and maternal space, the anxiety attached to looking at her own image in the looking-glass, and her responses to her mother's death.[89] Commenting on the act of memoir-writing as she writes the memoir, Woolf uses her sense of the complexity of such 'moments' in her own life to show up the folly of assuming, as the conventional biography does, that a mere account of events can reveal anything of the person to whom they happened. Both Stein's and Woolf's texts, although by very different means, explore the impact of another's life on one's own, although they do so in ways that trouble any simple model of essential female 'altruism'.

Feminist critics of autobiography have also questioned psychoanalytic models of subjectivity and argued for a 'historicizing of the female subject'. Several essays in Shari Benstock's collection *The Private Self* stress culturally and historically specific and shared concepts of selfhood.[90] The repeated use of the concept of 'self-fashioning' implies a conscious, although culturally determined, construction of identity in literature and broader cultural spheres. The materials drawn upon include diaries, letters and journals; the perceived fragmentation of history allows for a departure from emphases on the continuity of life experience, and 'diurnal' forms become valorised accordingly. The 'new historicist' approach to auto-biographical writings substitutes genealogies, or discrete historical sequences, for a developing and continuous history. More generally, it could be argued that women's distantiation, like that of other subordinated groups, from the traditional grand narratives of Western culture has rendered particularly attractive the more critical approaches to history offered by new historicism and by Foucauldian archaeology. The specific contribution of these approaches, apart from the attention given to gender issues themselves, is a sharper sense both of the oppressive potential of discourses and of the possibilities of resistance within them.

The critique of individualism discussed above in connection with psychoanalytic theory also emerges, of course, in other contexts. Studies of working-class life-writings and those written by men and women from ethnic minorities have stressed both the importance of collective identities and the diversity of individual and group affiliations. The ranges of recognised autobiographers and forms of life-writing have expanded in tandem, while 'autobiography' as conventionally defined is often judged to be a limited and inappropriate means of representing these non-hegemonic subjectivities and identities. Autobiographical theory now has to address itself to much more complex models of ethnic, gender, sexual and class identities, as I show in my final chapter. This also raises problems of stereotyping by categorisation and what Trinh T. Minh Ha has called 'planned authenticity', in which a group may be required to accentuate its difference as defined by a dominant culture.[91] From these perspectives, the battles between humanists and deconstructionists over the ideal subject appear irrelevant compared to the theoretical innovations and changes in cultural awareness required to accommodate all these real writing subjects. Some of the theoretical approaches discussed in this chapter, however, may yet have a part to play in these crucial processes of re-evaluation.

Notes

1 M. H. Abrams, *Natural Supernaturalism: Tradition and Revolution in Romantic Literature* (New York: Norton, 1971). Jonathan Arac discusses Abrams's work, and his readings of *The Prelude* in particular, in *Critical Genealogies: Historical Situations for Postmodern Literary Study* (New York: Columbia University Press, 1987), pp. 57–81.

2 Ann Mellor, *Romanticism and Gender* (New York and London: Routledge, 1993), p. 152.

3 Arac, *Critical Genealogies*, p. 25.

4 James Olney (ed.), *Autobiography: Essays Theoretical and Critical* (Princeton University Press, 1980), p. 13.

5 Georges Poulet (ed.), *Les Chemins actuels de la critique: Suivi d'un choix bibliographique établi et commenté par D. Noguez* (Paris: Union générale d'éditions, 1968), p. 251.

6 Olney (ed.), *Autobiography*, pp. 24–5.

7 For discussion of 'the new criticism' see John Crowe Ransom, *The New Criticism* (Norfolk, CT: New Directions, 1941); Murray Krieger, *The New Apologists for Poetry* (Minneapolis: University of Minnesota Press, 1956); John Fekete, *The Critical Twilight* (London: Routledge & Kegan Paul, 1978).

8 Stephen A. Shapiro, 'The Dark Continent of Literature: Autobiography', *Comparative Literature Studies* 5 (1968), 421–54.

9 René Wellek, *The Attack on Literature and Other Essays* (Brighton: Harvester, 1982), pp. 100, 112.

10 J. Hillis Miller, 'The Geneva School', in *Theory Now and Then* (Durham:

Duke University Press, 1991), pp. 15–17.

11 Letter to Miller, 25 November 1961, quoted in 'The Geneva School', p. 23. Frank Lentriccia comments on Poulet's statement: 'In Poulet a strange and frightened Cartesianism at once seeks and claims an isolated, privileged, and transcendent space of human consciousness – as the goal of critical reading – and yet appears to grant, at the same time, the coercive power of objectivity over the interior subject and the shocking vulnerability of interiority to a voracious exteriority.' See *After the New Criticism* (University of Chicago Press, 1980), p. 69.

12 Miller, *Theory Now and Then*, p. 23.

13 William Earle, *The Autobiographical Consciousness: A Philosophical Enquiry into Existence* (Chicago: Quadrangle Books, 1972).

14 James Olney, *Metaphors of Self: The Meaning of Autobiography* (Princeton University Press, 1972).

15 Northrop Frye, *Anatomy of Criticism* (Princeton University Press, 1957), p. 352.

16 Philippe Lejeune, *On Autobiography*, ed. Paul John Eakin, trans. Katherine Leary (Minneapolis: University of Minnesota Press, 1989), p. 44.

17 Émile Benveniste, *Problems in General Linguistics* (Florida: University of Miami Press, 1971) (translation of *Problèmes de linguistique générale* (Paris: Gallimard, 1966)).

18 Lejeune, 'The Autobiographical Pact', in Eakin (ed.), *On Autobiography*, p. 5.

19 *Ibid.* pp. 8–9.

20 *Ibid.* pp. 9–10.

21 *Ibid.* p. 20.

22 *Ibid.* p. 19.

23 Sandra Gilbert and Susan Gubar, 'Ceremonies of the Alphabet: Female Grandmatologies and the Female Authorgraph', in *The Female Autograph*, ed. Domna C. Stanton (Chicago University Press, 1987), p. 24.

24 See Lejeune's essays, 'Autobiography and Social History in the Nineteenth Century', 'The Autobiography of Those Who Do Not Write', and 'Teaching People to Write their Life Story', in *On Autobiography*, ed. Paul John Eakin. Other works include *Le moi des demoiselles. Enquête sur le journal d'une jeune fille* (Paris: Seuil, 1993), '*Cher Cahier . . .*' *Témoignages sur le journal personnel* (Paris: Gallimard, 1989).

25 Michael Sheringham, *French Autobiography: Devices and Desires* (Oxford: Clarendon Press, 1993), p. 20.

26 Jean Starobinski, 'The Style of Autobiography', in *Autobiography*, ed. James Olney, pp. 73–84.

27 Geoffrey Nowell-Smith, in *Theories of Authorship: A Reader*, ed. John Caughie (London: Routledge, 1981).

28 See, for example, the essays in *Probing the Limits of Representation: Nazism and the 'Final Solution'*, ed. Saul Friedländer (Cambridge, Mass.: Harvard University Press, 1992) and essays by Cathy Caruth, Vincent Pecora and others in *Literature and the Ethical Question*, ed. C. Nouvet, *Yale French Studies* 79 (New Haven: Yale University Press, 1991).

29 Jean Starobinski, *Jean-Jacques Rousseau: Transparency and Obstruction* (Uni-

versity of Chicago Press, 1988).

30 See, for example, Domna C. Stanton (ed.), *The Female Autograph: Theory and Practice of Autobiography from the Tenth to the Twentieth Century*, 2nd ed. (University of Chicago Press, 1987).

31 Peter Brooks, *Reading for the Plot: Design and Intention in Narrative* (Oxford: Clarendon Press, 1984), p. 33.

32 See Paul de Man, 'The Purloined Ribbon', in *Allegories of Reading: Figural Language in Rousseau, Nietszche, Rilke and Proust* (New Haven: Yale University Press, 1979), pp. 278–301.

33 Jacques Derrida, *Of Grammatology*, trans. Gayatri Chakravorty Spivak (Baltimore: Johns Hopkins University Press, 1976), p. 270.

34 Jacques Derrida, *The Ear of the Other: Otobiography, Transference, Translation* (Lincoln and London: University of Nebraska Press, rev. edn. 1988).

35 See, for example, Roy Pascal, *Desire and Truth in Autobiography* (London: Routledge, 1960), p. 187: 'because of the utter lack of environment, of other people, there is no clear inward personality'.

36 Nietzsche, *Ecce Homo*, ed. and trans. Walter Kauffman (New York: Random House, 1967), p. 221.

37 Michel Beaujour, *Miroirs d'encre* (Paris: Seuil, 1980), p. 320.

38 Christopher Norris, *Derrida* (London: Fontana, 1987), p. 71.

39 See Louis Marin, 'Montaigne's Tomb, or Autobiographical Discourse', *Oxford Literary Review*, 4, 3 (1981), 43–58 and Eugene Vance, 'Augustine's Confessions and the Poetics of the Law', *Modern Language Notes* 93 (1978), 618–34. The quotation is from Candace Lang, 'Autobiography in the Aftermath of Romanticism', *Diacritics* 12, 4 (Winter 1982), pp. 2–16.

40 Jean-Luc Nancy, introduction to *Who Comes After the Subject?* ed. Eduardo Cadava, Peter Connor and Jean-Luc Nancy (New York: Routledge, 1991).

41 Michael Sprinker, 'Fictions of the Self: The End of Autobiography', in *Autobiography*, ed. James Olney, p. 334.

42 Paul Jay, *Being in the Text: Self-Representation From Wordsworth to Roland Barthes* (Ithaca: Cornell University Press, 1984), p.21.

43 See Hayden White, *Metahistory: The Historical Imagination in Nineteenth-Century Europe* (Baltimore: Johns Hopkins University Press, 1973).

44 Paul De Man, 'Autobiography as De-Facement', in *The Rhetoric of Romanticism* (New York: Columbia University Press, 1984), pp. 67–81.

45 Mary Jacobus, *Romanticism, Writing and Sexual Difference: Essays on* The Prelude (Oxford: Clarendon Press, 1989).

46 William Wordsworth, 'Essays Upon Epitaphs', in *Wordsworth's Literary Criticism*, ed. Howard Mills (Bristol: Classical Press, 1980), pp. 95–6.

47 Cynthia Chase, Introduction to *Romanticism*, ed. C. Chase (London: Longman, 1993), p. 30.

48 Paul Smith, *Discerning the Subject* (Minneapolis: University of Minnesota Press, 1988), p. 103.

49 See Jacques Derrida, 'To Speculate – On Freud', *The Ear of the Other* and *Glas*, trans. John P. Leavey jun. and Richard Rand (Lincoln: University of Nebraska Press, 1986).

50 Paul Jay, 'What's the Use? Critical Theory and the Study of Autobiography', in *Biography* 10, 1 (1987), 45.

51 Sigmund Freud, 'Beyond the Pleasure Principle', in *On Metapsychology*, Penguin Freud Library 11, pp. 332, 336. See also Peter Brooks's discussion of Walter Benjamin's account of death as 'the sanction of everything that the story-teller can tell' (Benjamin, 'The Storyteller', *Illuminations* (New York: Harcourt Brace and World, 1968)). Brooks writes: 'What we seek in narrative fictions is that knowledge of death which is denied to us in our own lives' (Peter Brooks, *Reading for the Plot: Design and Intention in Narrative* (Oxford: Clarendon Press, 1984), p. 22).

52 Jay, 'What's the Use?', p. 42.

53 Marin, *Montaigne's Tomb*, p. 55.

54 Ludwig Wittgenstein, *Tractatus Logico-Philosophicus* (London: Routledge and Kegan Paul, 1922), 6.4311.

55 See Walter Benjamin, *The Origin of German Tragic Drama*, trans. John Osborne (London: New Left Books, 1977), p. 166.

56 See, in particular, Jacques Derrida, *Mémoires: for Paul De Man* (New York: Columbia University Press, 1989).

57 See the discussions in Jacques Derrida, *The Ear of the Other*. The reference is also to Edgar Allan Poe's *The Facts in the Case of M. Valdemar*, Poe's account of mesmerism, in which M. Valdemar speaks the phrase 'I am dead.'

58 Georges Gusdorf, 'De l'autobiographie initiatique à l'autobiographie genre littéraire', *Revue d'histoire littéraire de la France*, 75 (1975), 958.

59 Nancy K. Miller, *Getting Personal* (New York and London: Routledge, 1991), p. x.

60 Kobena Mercer, 'Welcome to the Jungle: Identity and Diversity in Post-modern Politics', in *Identity: Community, Culture, Difference*, ed. Jonathan Rutherford (London: Lawrence and Wishart, 1990), pp. 43–71.

61 *Ibid.* p. 20.

62 De Man's early journalism has been reprinted as *Wartime Journalism: 1939–1943*, ed. Werner Hamacher, Neil Hertz and Thomas Keenan (Lincoln and London: University of Nebraska Press, 1988). A companion volume by the same editors, incorporating responses by academics to the discovery and contents of the journalism, was published as *Responses: On Paul De Man's Wartime Journalism* (Lincoln: University of Nebraska Press, 1989). See also David Lehman, *Signs of the Times: Deconstruction and the Fall of Paul de Man* (London: André Deutsch, 1991) and the special edition of *Diacritics* 20, 3 (Fall 1990).

63 The phrase from Mary Ann Caws, written in a rather different context, is in her *Women of Bloomsbury: Virginia, Vanessa and Carrington* (New York and London: Routledge, 1990), pp. 2–3.

64 See Neil Hertz, 'More Lurid Figures', *Diacritics* 20, 3 (Fall 1990), 2–27.

65 Jacques Derrida, 'The Art of *Mémoires*', in *Mémoires*, pp. 55–6. The line 'Memory effaces remembrance (or recollection) *just as the I effaces itself* (J.D.'s italics) is a quotation from De Man's essay 'Sign and Symbol in Hegel's *Aesthetics*' (1982).

66 Jacques Derrida, 'Like the Sound of the Sea Deep Within a Shell: Paul De Man's War', in *Mémoires*, p. 227.

67 Shoshana Felman and Dori Laub, *Testimony: Crises of Witnessing in Litera-*

ture, Psychoanalysis and History (New York and London: Routledge, 1992).

68 See the excellent article by Dominick LaCapra, 'The Personal, the Political and the Textual: Paul De Man as object of Transference', in *History and Memory*, 4, 1 (Spring/Summer 1992).

69 Elizabeth Wilson, *Mirror Writing: An Autobiography* (London: Virago, 1982), p. 136.

70 Philippe Lejeune, *L'autobiographie en France* (Paris: Colin, 1971), p. 104.

71 See Freud, 'Family Romances' (1909[1908]), in *SE* Vol. IX, pp. 236–41, and in *Moses and Monotheism*, *SE* XXIII, pp. 11–15.

72 Michel Neyraut et al., *L'Autobiographie*. VIes rencontres psychanalytiques d'Aix en Provence, 1987) (Paris: Les Belles Lettres, 1988), p. 10.

73 Saul Friedländer, *History and Psychoanalysis*, trans. Susan Suleiman (New York and London: Holmes and Meier, 1978), p. 16. Friedländer continues: 'The choice of ego psychology is justified by the needs of our object of study . . . Although the contribution of Jacques Lacan, for example, is of considerable importance, I would argue that psychohistory requires other methods of investigation.'

74 See Erik Erikson, *Young Man Luther: A Study in Psychoanalysis and History* (New York: Norton, 1962); *Gandhi's Truth: On the Origins of Militant Non-Violence* (New York: Norton, 1969); Bruce Mazlish, *James and John Stuart Mill: Father and Son in the Nineteenth Century* (New York: Basic Books, 1975).

75 Bruce Mazlish, 'Autobiography and Psycho-analysis: Between Truth and Self-Deception', *Encounter* 35 (1970), 32.

76 John Sturrock, 'The New Model Autobiographer', *New Literary History* 9 (1977), 51–63.

77 Jeffrey Mehlman, *A Structuralist Study of Autobiography: Proust, Leiris, Sartre and Lévi-Strauss* (Ithaca: Cornell University Press, 1974). See also the special edition of *Yale French Studies*, *On Leiris*, ed. Marc Eli Blanchard, *Yale French Studies* 81 (New Haven: Yale University Press, 1992). More recently, Leiris as ethnographer has become the focus of interest, and critics have explored the problematic relationship between autobiography and ethnography in his work. See, for example, Marianne Torgovnik, *Gone Primitive* (University of Chicago Press, 1990), and James Clifford, *The Predicament of Culture* (New Haven: Harvard University Press, 1988).

78 Paul John Eakin, *Touching the World: Reference in Autobiography* (Princeton University Press, 1992), p. 86.

79 Roland Barthes, *Roland Barthes by Roland Barthes*, trans. Richard Howard (London: Macmillan, 1977).

80 Elizabeth Grosz, *Jacques Lacan: A Feminist Introduction* (London: Routledge, 1990), ch. 2, *passim*.

81 Luce Irigaray, *Speculum of the Other Woman*, trans. Gillian C. Gill (Ithaca: Cornell University Press, 1985).

82 Rosi Braidotti, *Patterns of Dissidence* (Cambridge: Polity, 1991), p. 255.

83 Irigaray, *Speculum*, p. 148.

84 D. W. Winnicott, *Playing and Reality* (London: Penguin, 1971).

85 Jessica Benjamin, 'A Desire of One's Own: Psychoanalytic Feminism and Intersubjective Space', in *Feminist Studies/Critical Studies*, ed. Teresa de

Lauretis (London: Macmillan, 1988), p. 80.
86 See Nancy Chodorow, *The Reproduction of Mothering: Psychoanalysis and the Sociology of Gender* (Berkeley: Univesity of California Press), 1978.
87 Bella Brodzki and Celeste Schenk (eds.), *Life/Lines: Theorizing Women's Autobiography* (Ithaca: Cornell University Press, 1988), p. 87.
88 Cora Kaplan, *Sea Changes* (London: Verso, 1986).
89 Virginia Woolf, 'A Sketch of the Past', in *Moments of Being*, ed. Jeanne Schulkind (London: Triad/Panther, 1978).
90 Shari Benstock (ed.), *The Private Self: Theory and Practice of Women's Autobiographical Writings* (London: Routledge, 1988). See especially the essays by Felicity Nussbaum, Elizabeth Fox-Genovese and Mitzi Myers.
91 Trinh T. Minh Ha, *Woman, Native, Other: Writing Postcoloniality and Feminism* (Bloomington: Indiana University Press, 1989), p. 89.

6

The law of genre

Much of the recent interest in autobiography in literary studies has stemmed from a theoretical concern with the broader question of genre. In the previous chapter, questions of subjectivity constantly led into questions of genre – indeed, it could be claimed that the discourse of 'subjectivity' is a genre. And, as Jonathan Loesberg writes:

> Because autobiography is also clearly a generic distinction, the debate over the generic status of the form constantly makes complex and disrupts the debate over the existence and the locus of the self, the self, which is, after all the concern and possibly the root of whatever the genre auto-biography is.[1]

Discussions of the autobiographical genre are also inseparable from debates about factual and fictional discourse, authorial intention and reference. These concerns in autobiographical discourse are related to the questions of authorship and authenticity touched upon in Chapter 1.

The use of genre criticism in autobiographical discourse has been contentious ever since autobiography began to be substantially theorised, from the 1950s onwards, as a specifically 'literary' genre. As we have seen, James Olney and others have argued that the attempt to fit autobiography out with formal and linguistic pacts and functions violates the freedom and fluidity of self-expression and self-representation. Autobiography lies between 'literature' and 'history' or, perhaps, philosophy, and between fiction and non-fiction; it becomes an acute expression of the already contested distinction between fact and fiction. Theorists veer between constructing auto-biography as, in Tzvetan Todorov's terms, a 'historical' and a 'theo-retical' genre. Furthermore, genre theory itself was being totally restructured during these decades. Northrop Frye's highly

influential *Anatomy of Criticism* (1957), for example, synthesised a
number of different approaches to genre and literary system,
including formalism, neo-Aristotelianism and archetypal criticism.
Alongside other critics' distrust of generic labelling, which at times
picked up Romantic rejections of classical formalism, was a drive to
create a totalising and totalised model of literary kinds. Frye's aestheticism – a powerful support to the 'fictionalist' school of autobiographical criticism – coexists with, while markedly differing from,
the formalist and structuralist concern with 'literature as system' and
with genre as the privileged point of intersection between the individual work and literary history.

Finally, it has become all too clear that definitions of the autobiographical genre and theories of autobiography in general, derived
almost entirely from texts by male authors, and a very selective group
of male authors at that, acquired an intrinsic androcentric bias. As
Sidonie Smith writes:

> The theories seem to derive from certain underlying assumptions: that
> men's and women's ways of experiencing the world and the self and their
> relationship to language and to the institution of literature are identical;
> or that women's autobiographies, because they emanate from lives of
> culturally insignificant people are themselves culturally insignificant; or
> that women's autobiographies, because they may not inscribe an
> androcentric paradigm of selfhood are something other than real auto-
> biography; or that autobiography is fundamentally a male generic
> contract.[2]

A number of feminist critics have pursued the etymological link
between 'genre' and 'gender', and have shown how the mechanisms
and institutions of genre function to repress women's personal
writings, seen as contaminating the purity of 'true' autobiography.
Women have been positioned outside the laws – of genre and of
selfhood – within which the 'pacts' of fiction *and* of history operate.
Failing as 'universal' subjects, their lives and identities cannot provide the bases from which the laws of human nature will be drawn.
Hence the different status accorded to the representative man's
self-reflection as a self-making which can stand for the terms of
identity of his culture and epoch, and the women's self-writings, seen
as 'merely' autobiographical, subjective and personal, failing to
ramify beyond their immediate context, other than to confirm
women's narrow self-regard for their inchoate natures.[3] There is
further work to be done on the seeming paradox whereby auto-

biography, often defined as the literature of subjectivity, has, in its canonical form, so massively excluded women's writing, when that writing – whether in the form of spiritual autobiography, personal letter, or 'scandalous memoir' – has been a key factor in the historical construction of the spheres of interiority and subjectivity.

Nancy Miller has argued that gender is itself a genre:

> The difference of gender as *genre* is there to be read only if one accepts the terms of another sort of 'pact'; the pact of commitment to decipher what women have said (or, more important, left unsaid) about the pattern of their lives over and above what any person might say about his, through genre. I say 'his' deliberately, not because men in fact lead genderless lives, but because the fact of their gender is given and received literarily as a mere donnée of personhood, because the canon of the autobiographical text, like the literary canon, self-defined as it is by the notion of a human universal, in general fails to interrogate gender as a meaningful category of reference or interpretation.[4]

In Miller's argument, genre becomes defined more positively as a context for reading, rather than a prescription for writing; gender is a genre in that it implies an understanding of the conditions under which the text operates and should be received. Thus genre provides the necessary framework for 'an interaction between reader and text' [p. 61] in which gender is central. Miller argues that genre distinctions implying a hierarchy of literary forms need to be broken down. She makes a case for reading women's autobiographies and novels in tandem, as opposed to reading autobiography into the fictions or finding fictions in the autobiography.

This argument against hierarchisation is paralleled by a widespread growth of interest in forms of personal writing, such as diaries, letters and journals, used not simply to supplement biographical knowledge of a significant figure but as texts in their own right. Such forms are almost totally outlawed by generic definitions of autobiography as a continuous prose form reconstructing the whole of a 'significant' life. These ostensibly 'private' forms (which were, in fact, often written for circulation or publication) are being redefined as some of the most important modes of self-expression or self-construction for women, and ones that need to be included in any account of autobiography.

It is striking how value systems shift when the focus of attention moves away from an established literary corpus. Philippe Lejeune, for example, begins his theoretical career with the texts of high culture and rejects biography as a viable or valuable model for autobiography. By the time he begins to explore the (usually unpublished) life-writings of nineteenth-century middle-class writers, however, he sees that biography is the dominant form, developing out of the collective form of the family record book. Moreover, Lejeune's researches lead him to rethink literary traditions; 'in France, we are fascinated by Rousseau's *Confessions*, to the point of seeing in them a sort of archetype of the modern autobiography. But these texts [the nineteenth-century life-writings] would no doubt exist just as well without Rousseau.'[5] In other words, both literary form and literary models are contingent. Generic assumptions, as Lejeune's discussion reveals, are also social restrictions.

Julia Swindells's study of nineteenth-century literature and autobiography, *Victorian Writing and Working Women*, explores the distinction between the *textuality* of autobiographical writing and life-histories and a certain conception of 'the Literary'. The latter, at least in the nineteenth century, sanctions certain moral and aesthetic values which Swindells sees as alien to the class and cultural situations of the working women writers she discusses. Thus the moralising code of 'the Literary' encompasses the genres fiction, melodrama and romance, which the women use to structure their life-histories –

> as if 'the literary' itself is the key (possibly the only) means of construction of self. . . . The heroine, the victim, the martyr are the only means of representing an experience unprecedented in discourse (the working woman by the working woman) but they are also the signifiers of lack, of what is missing. [pp. 140, 153]

The articulation of the autobiographical subject as the heroine of a romance, for example, signals the entry by the autobiographers into 'literary' values, and Swindells emphasises the tension between the literary, with its constructions of subjectivity, and other gender and class interests of working women. Swindells's is a valuable discussion, although it leaves open the question of what narrative and representational structures would be more appropriate, and less distorting, vehicles of self-expression or self-construction for working-class women.

In *Subjectivities*, Regenia Gagnier describes what she calls 'the literary subject', in contrast to class and gender subjectivities, as 'a mixture of introspective self-consciousness, middle-class familialism and genderization, and liberal autonomy'. She is referring here to the Victorian subject of literature – creative yet self-controlled, individuated yet familial, goal-directed yet free. She thus historicises the constructions of subjectivity and the concept of the literary, while both subjectivity and the literary take on generic form. Genres are no longer seen as sub-divisions of the unified category 'literature'; rather, the literary, in its various historical and cultural forms, is itself a genre or habitus of culture. This is crucial to studies of auto-biography in at least two ways. Firstly, as Swindells and others have described, specific literary or narrative forms have provided, often problematically, structuring models for life-experience and its repre-sentation. Secondly, with the recent explosion of interest in life-histories and life-studies of all kinds, the literary, here represented by traditional autobiography, must necessarily appear as one genre among others in a broad interdisciplinary project.

In the next part of this chapter, I examine some critical and theoretical accounts of the generic status and the generic history of autobiography. A number of feminist theorists have produced lucid and sharp critiques of many of the critics I discuss, with particular reference to their masculinist perspectives. My primary intention here is to analyse critical discourse and its cultural assumptions and to explore autobiography (as a conceptual category rather than a body of specified texts) in its relationship to certain critical and theoretical institutions: genre, literary history, authorial intention, fictionality, authorship.

The work of genre

The concept of genre is, as we have seen, much disputed. Rather than dispense with it entirely, as a number of critics have suggested – Robert Elbaz refers to generic classification as 'an ideological grid forced upon consciousness' – we might turn to Fredric Jameson's argument that 'genres are essentially literary institutions or social contracts between a writer and a specific public, whose function is to specify the proper use of a particular cultural artifact', or to Tzvetan Todorov's assertion that 'it is because genres exist as an institution that they function as "horizons of expectation" for readers and as "models of writing" for authors'.[6] The problem is finding a way of negotiating the work of genre as a structure of recognition necessary for the understanding of a text and its contexts and as a structure of exclusion, maintaining the status quo. The complication, even with this opposition, is that 'recognition' can itself be a conservative labelling which seeks to place a text in the structures of the already known, rather than risk difference or unfamiliarity.

Autobiography is particularly contested, and critics tend to be divided between tracing its history from Augustinian confession through to conversion narratives and spiritual autobiography, or linking its 'emergence' as a modern secular genre to the rise of the novel in the eighteenth century. It is not surprising that some critics wanted to affiliate autobiography to one or other of the 'recognised' genres. Thus autobiography, at times used to cast doubt on the fixity of generic classifications, has also served to reinforce them. For example, by establishing a *rapprochement* between autobiography, viewed in terms of its formal properties, and the putatively more secure category of the novel, critics felt able to remove the troubling ambiguity of the aesthetic status of autobiography, and at the same time reassert the substantial nature of literary kinds. Equally, of course, the *differentiation* between novel and autobiography can serve to shore up generic boundaries.

The question of autobiography's generic status, although debated most intensely in the last few decades, arose, as we saw in Chapter 1, in nineteenth-century discussions of autobiography with an attempt to map different types of autobiography on to the classical generic divisions – epic, dramatic and lyric. Such typologising has survived in more recent autobiographical theory – William Howarth's 'Some Principles of Autobiography' (1974), for example, divides auto-biography, defined as self-portraiture, into the types of oratory, drama and poetry.[7] William Spengemann's *The Forms of Auto-biography* classifies autobiographies into three types – historical, philosophical and poetic – in ways reminiscent of the typologies of Prickard and Simcox discussed in Chapter 1.[8]

More fundamental attempts to restructure literary classification *in toto* have played a significant part in the perception of autobiography as a literary genre. In *Anatomy of Criticism* Northrop Frye argued against a novel-centred view of prose fiction and for a theory of the novel as just one type of the broader genus 'fiction'. As Wallace Martin notes, Frye's book marked 'an important stage in the transition from theories of the novel to theories of narrative'.[9] Auto-biography is granted a central role by Frye, but is conflated with 'confession', which, along with the novel, romance and anatomy (which presents 'a vision of the world in terms of a single intellectual pattern' [p. 22]), is one of the four basic kinds of fictional prose which intermix to form a variety of combinations. 'The forms of prose fictions are mixed', Frye writes, in a sentence whose terms now seem extraordinary, 'like racial strains in human beings, not separable like the sexes' [p. 305].

Frye's primary and most important assumption about autobiography is that its 'history' is that of a gradual merger with the novel:

> Most autobiographers are inspired by a creative, and therefore fictional, impulse to select only those events and experiences in the writer's life that go to build up an integrated pattern. This pattern may be something larger than himself with which he has come to identify himself, or simply the coherence of his character and attitudes. We may call this very important form of prose fiction the confession form, following St. Augustine, who appears to have invented it, and Rousseau, who established a modern type of it. . . . After Rousseau – in fact in Rousseau – the confession flows into the novel, and the mixture produces the fictional autobiography, the Kunstler-roman and kindred types. [p. 307]

Following and extending Frye's account of autobiography as confession, Robert Kellogg and Robert Scholes, in *The Nature of Narrative*, defined autobiography as having 'two usual forms – the apology and the confession'.[10] Autobiography is defined in terms of its inwardness, 'the inward journey'; 'It is the Christian and especially the Augustinian approach to man and the universe which leads the way to psychology. Without Augustine we would never have had a Freud' [p.79]. The line from Augustine to Freud will be taken up in a rather different way by Michel Foucault and his followers in theories of the role of confession, the regime of power–knowledge, and the discursive production of the 'truth' of the individual subject.[11] In Scholes's and Kellogg's account, Augustine is important not because he 'inaugurates' autobiography as such but because his legacy to 'narrative artists' in general is a concern with self and character. Rousseau, they add, 'bequeathed to the realistic novel both the quest for a vision and the radically ironic nature of his own'. The importance of autobiography/confession is the subjective vision and quest for the self which are fruitfully extended to the novel, but in the process 'a clear distinction between the confession and the novel can no longer be sustained':

The convergence of the novel with the history, biography and autobiography has resulted not so much from impatience with the story-
teller's fantasy as from a modern skepticism of knowing anything about
human affairs in an entirely objective (non-fictional) way. Science seems
to have demonstrated that Aristotle's distinction between history and
fiction was one of degree, not of kind. All knowing and all telling are
subject to the conventions of art. Because we apprehend reality through
culturally determined types, we can report the most particular event not
only in the form of a representational fiction, assigning motives, causes,
and effects according to our best lights rather than according to absolute
truth. [p. 151]

In this account a fact–fiction distinction between narrative forms is
effaced and the significance of autobiography is perceived to be its
subjective/inward focus on the individual life which it shares with the
(modern) novel, whose key form (in the early work of James Joyce or
D.H. Lawrence) is in turn defined as the *Bildungsroman*.

Scholes's and Kellogg's definitions are taken up in a number of
critical studies of autobiography in the last few decades and, as we
saw in the case of James Olney and others, autobiography becomes
significant for the very reason that it confirms both fictionalism and
subjectivism. Fictionalism can take on a strongly ethical dimension –
'according to our best lights' – as in Susannah Egan's more recent
Patterns of Experience in Autobiography.[12] The autobiographer, Egan
writes, 'unable to lift anything out of life and into art without transforming it . . . creates . . . a fictive self to narrate the events of his life
and a fictive story to contain those events' [p. 66]. Egan uses Susanne
Langer's distinction between 'actual events' and 'virtual events' to
oppose referential and autobiographical 'truth': 'virtual events . . . are
qualitative in their very constitution and have no existence apart from
values, from the emotional import which is part of their appearance'.
Autobiographical value and (Richardian) poetic/emotive discourse
become one and the same.

The collapse or merging of autobiography into novel may be less
satisfactory for critics who wish, for whatever reasons, to retain a
sense of autobiography's distinctiveness. The few book-length
studies of autobiography written in the 1950s and 1960s tend to focus
on autobiography's proper appropriations of novelistic *form*, while
rejecting novelistic *fictionality*. One important example of this is
Wayne Shumaker's study, *English Autobiography: Its Emergence,
Materials and Forms* (1954).[13]

As a prelude to the discussion of modern autobiography,

Shumaker offers a history of the development of the genre. The perceived significance of 'private living' and individual experience as values in themselves is seen as a precondition of autobiography 'proper'. Shumaker's eighteenth century is marked by secularism, empiricism and the development of bourgeois subjectivity. 'An audience of curious citizens' encouraging the production of memoirs and autobiographies led to a greater awareness of the structuring of life-accounts and hence to the development of an autobiographical convention.

Shumaker's systems of classification stem both from a developmental model of history, cultural and literary, and a synchronic organisation of genre and modes. His approach displays the difficulties inherent in reconciling the tensions between historical and structural accounts of a genre; one aspect of this tension is the way in which a 'developmental' account tends to embody a value system in which 'higher' forms develop out of 'lower' ones. In this case, 'subjective' autobiography develops out of relatively unreflective memoirs, reminiscences, and *res gestae*, which continue to exist within the same literary system, but embody a less self-conscious, and therefore for Shumaker less valuable, form of expression.

Subjective autobiography, Shumaker asserts, finds its apotheosis in novelised form. Modern autobiography emerged alongside, although independently of, the eighteenth-century novel, but its development from the late eighteenth century onwards involved a borrowing of novelistic techniques. In the nineteenth century, subjective autobiography became primarily concerned with charting psychic and intellectual development; the philosophical determinism and naturalistic accounts of individuality and society underlying the autobiographies of the period are also locatable in the novel.

The (realist) novel alone is used as a possible comparative model. The affinity between novel and autobiography could be explained in generic and/or historical terms. On the one hand, they are morphologically similar as continuous prose discourses; on the other, they may be argued to share a common origin and to be subject to the same historical and cultural determinations. The problem is, of course, that the 'origins' of the novel have become a matter of as much, if not more, contention and debate as the 'origins' of autobiography. Shumaker pegs the development of autobiography to an account of the rise of the novel very close to that given by Ian Watt, in his highly influential study. As Watt's critics have pointed out, *The Rise of the Novel* in fact celebrates the triumph of formal realism, offering a history that makes the novel's rise 'the means by which the Western bourgeoisie fulfils its cultural manifest destiny'.[14]

More recent studies of the early novel, and narrative more generally, have pointed to the radical heterogeneity of its materials and to complex and shifting concepts of truth, fact and fiction. One aspect of auto/biography's history is the incorporation of 'non-fictional' literatures – conversion narratives, memoirs, biographies, histories, letters – into the novel form. As Wallace Martin notes: 'Jokes and short anecdotes are strung together as "jest biographies"; tales about rogues and their wanderings accumulate in the "pica-resque" novel, closely related to criminal biographies that mix fact and fiction. . . . Almost every factual narrative – history, biography, autobiography, accounts of travels – generates an eponymous fictional counterpart.' Victor Shklovsky argued that verbal materials keep shifting across the boundaries of factual/fictional kinds and thus can only be identified in relation to a general 'map of discourse' in a particular historical period.[15] Identification of this kind is by no means simple: many seventeenth- and eighteenth-century writers entitled their 'fictional' works 'histories', 'lives' or 'memoirs' in order to avoid the negative (and increasingly feminised) connotations of the generic marker 'novel' or 'romance'.

The complex identities of 'factual' and fictional' discourses must inevitably complicate any attempt to isolate 'autobiography', or 'pre-autobiography', in this period. Critics have, however, identified specific forms of eighteenth-century 'self-biography'. Felicity Nussbaum argues, in *The Autobiographical Subject*, that

> a rethinking of the ideologies of genre in the eighteenth century must include the recognition that eighteenth-century English diaries and self-biographies existed in multiple versions, seldom reached the public eye during the life of the author and often remained unpublished until later centuries. . . . An eighteenth-century serial autobiography, read through the ideology of genre, is the thing itself rather than a failed conversion narrative or an incipient realist novel. [pp. 28–9]

The overwhelming focus on form and unity in autobiographical criticism, as a number of feminist critics have noted, has been one of the main ways by which women have been kept out of the auto-biographical club. Nussbaum's researches also reveal how central serial and fragmentary autobiographical writings were to eighteenth-century constructions and questionings of identity in general.

The nineteenth-century novel, as Nussbaum notes, has been the dominant critical model for autobiography. Roy Pascal, whose *Design and Truth in Autobiography* I discussed in Chapter 4, focuses on the 'shaping of the past' in autobiography, the imposition of 'a pattern on a life', the construction of 'a coherent story' and, above all, the representation of a unique personality, 'a projection of the real self on the world'. Despite the autobiography's 'novelistic' features – its 'shapely' form, its organic sections, its ripe conclusion – 'it is free of the conventional exigencies of "literature" ':

> It needs no plot, no spurious liveliness, and can devote itself truthfully to its theme, the slow accumulation of experience and emergence of a character. Even if the autobiographer makes demonstrable errors in respect to himself and others, these still are true evidences of himself, and truer to human nature than the absolute knowledge that the novelist often pretends to. [p. 162]

Pascal asserts that the 'great autobiographies' had a major influence on the development of the nineteenth-century novel, particularly the depiction of character as 'becoming', but ultimately holds the two forms apart.

Critics such as William Spengemann and Jerome Buckley have charted autobiography's 'progress' into the novel form. The auto-biographical novels and *Bildungsromane* of certain modernist writers are presented as the culminating point of the autobiographical tradi-tion and any distinction between 'autobiography' and 'auto-biographical' is effaced or elided. One result of this move is a definition of autobiography as akin to the *Künstlerroman* – the story of the development of the artist – thus confirming the essential 'literariness' both of autobiographical form and of the identity of the autobiographer. It is less clear what happens, or is perceived to happen, to the autobiography–novel relationship after modernism. Cultural postmodernism, while endorsing fictionalism and conven-tionalism, has to an extent relativised the sphere of the 'literary' and thus troubled the concept of literary identity.

The elision of autobiography and novel seemingly releases critics from vexed questions of autobiography's referential status and the fact–fiction relationship in autobiography. Many, if not most, of the theorists I have discussed who wish to hold on to some concept of autobiography's referential status have turned to concepts of truth as the truth of the present, or the truth of consciousness, or the truth of memory. This view is occasionally questioned; Louis Renza, for example, suggested that the past of memory, being private and therefore essentially incommunicable, can hardly be said to constitute 'truth', objective or subjective, when recalled by the writer in the present and through the medium of language.[16]

The focus on the present of writing and on the past as recalled or reconstructed rather than lived is linked, as we have seen, to phenomenological emphases on presentness. It is also related to speech-act and act-based theories of literary production, in which the concept of the performative is central, though disputed. Tzvetan Todorov, for example, in 'The Origin of Genres', constructs a model of literary history in which literary genres 'have their origin . . . in human discourse'. The identity of autobiography, he writes, 'comes from the speech act which is at its base: to tell a story about oneself ': more generally, 'there is no abyss between literature and that which is not literature'.[17]

Other critics have used speech-act theories to define the nature of fictionality. Barbara Herrnstein Smith, for example, employing a distinction between 'natural discourse' and 'fictive discourse', asserts that 'the essential fictiveness of novels . . . is not to be discovered in the unreality of the characters, objects and events alluded to, but in the unreality of the alludings themselves'. The writer of fiction is 'pretending to be *writing* a biography while actually *fabricating* one'.[18] Smith appears to be suggesting that 'biography' is a species of 'natural discourse', which 'fictive discourse' will fabricate. I discuss the problems of speech-act models of fictive utterance for a theory of non-fictional 'literary' narrative at the end of this chapter.

In 'Autobiography as De-Facement' De Man expresses a weariness, articulated by other critics, over 'theories of autobiography': he sees one of the central problems preventing such theories going forward as 'the attempt to define and to treat autobiography as if it were a literary genre among others':

> Empirically as well as theoretically, autobiography lends itself poorly to generic definition: each specific instance seems to be an exception to the norm; the works themselves seem to shade off into neighbouring or even incompatible genres and, perhaps, most revealing of all, generic discussions, which can have such powerful heuristic value in the case of tragedy or of the novel, remain distressingly sterile when autobiography is at stake.

The attempt to confront the distinction between autobiography and fiction is, de Man suggests, more fruitful, though equally undecisive. He argues that the apparently 'referential' status of autobiography reveals the fictionality of all referentiality, and that although we assume that the life produces the autobiography, it is equally possible that the autobiographical project produces and determines the life. It appears, he suggests, that 'autobiography . . . is not a genre or a mode, but a figure of reading or of understanding that occurs, to some degree, in all texts'.

De Man's critiques of the work of Todorov and other 'formalist' theorists focus on their over-systematic approaches to texts and their non-conflictual accounts of rhetorical effects. Genette's assertion of the impossibility of deciding between fact and fiction in Proust's *Recherche* turns on the 'undecidability' of autobiography: 'It goes without saying, in the case of Proust, that each example taken from the *Recherche* can produce . . . an endless discussion of the novel as fiction and as reading of the same novel as autobiography. We should perhaps remain *within* this whirligig [*tourniquet*].'[19] De Man resists this account of 'undecidability' as a 'system of differentiation based on two elements'. To remain *within* an undecidable situation is 'certainly most uncomfortable, and all the more so in this case since this whirligig is capable of infinite acceleration and is, in fact, not successive but simultaneous'. In other words, it is rather too simple to 'resolve' the fact/fiction opposition in a model of the coexistence of mutually exclusive opposites; how long can one stay within a 'whirligig' before becoming nauseous? The fact that writers on and of autobiography have, in de Man's words, been all too ready to move 'from cognition to resolution and to action, from speculative to political and legal authority' suggests that the answer is 'not very long'. Unable to tolerate the ceaseless 'performativity' of language, autobiographical theorists turn language into speech-act – promise, contract, declaration of intent.

Todorov, in his work on the genre of the 'fantastic', made 'undecidability' into a generic property; the reader of the fantastic text (Henry James's 'The Turn of the Screw' is a central example) is caught, or 'hesitates', between a supernatural and a naturalistic explanation of inexplicable states of affairs (either the ghosts are real or the governess hallucinates them in her madness).[20] The text is only truly in the realm of the fantastic if the reader remains held between the two modes of explanation. The element of undecidability in Todorov's own account is between hesitation as a

textual property, or as an either/or produced by the reader's response, or both. Jonathan Culler sees this as a virtue of Todorov's
generic model: 'it captures an important aspect of texts and reading.
On the one hand, the responses of readers are not random, yet on the
other hand the interpretive orientation of a response is what gives
certain elements significance within a work.'[21]

Theories of reading, which were prevalent during the 1970s and
1980s, did not have as great an impact on autobiographical theories as
one might have expected.[22] De Man theorised autobiography as a
question of reading but, as we have seen, his account seems to allow
the reader nothing more than one of two kinds of 'transcendental
authority' – making the subject in his own image or forcing this
linguistic puppet to appear before the law and sign and testify to his
name, his identity and his story. Jonathan Loesberg, in a discussion of
Olney's *Autobiography: Essays Theoretical and Critical*, attempts to
show that all the problems that vex autobiographical theorists –
authority, intention, fact or fiction – are in fact the problems of
readers of autobiography and not writers, at least not until those
writers become the readers of their autobiographical works. Autobiographical theorists:

> are all involved in asserting genre to deny it, denying genre to assert it,
> because they all . . . separate the self from the autobiography which
> concerns it and thus assume that the problem of autobiography, as genre
> or as event, is the problem of an author writing. If . . . autobiography
> contains and is what it purports to convey, then it is pointless to worry
> what an author must attempt or achieve in order to attain the ends of
> autobiography. It is a mistake even to talk about ends and acts from the
> perspective of a writer if the text, consuming its own author, becomes
> what it wants to articulate. It is not a mistake to talk about any of these
> problems from the perspective of a reader, however.[23]

From the point of view of the writer, an autobiography cannot fail,
unless, as Jenny Uglow put it in a different context, it is about the
wrong person altogether – though what, she added, of *The Autobiography of Alice B. Toklas*?[24] Loesberg writes that 'it is the reader who
is forced to decipher issues of priority, intentionality, selfhood',
although he gives little indication of how we should react to this
apparent shifting of responsibility, or of how a more active role for the
reader of autobiography could be imagined. In a sense, of course,
intention has always been more of a problem for the interpreter than
for the intending person. Loesberg's point is that in the auto-

biographical act there is no gap between intention and result, just as the autobiographical self, he claims, does not pre-exist the act of representation. But it is not clear why Loesberg should wish to exclude so absolutely the possibility that, in Michael Sheringham's words, it is 'the writing of autobiography which, of itself, destabilizes and undermines fixity of intention ... the interaction of intention and execution never ceases to be at issue'.[25]

De Man emphasises the 'tropes' or rhetorical figures which make up autobiographical discourse, but deconstructive critics more generally have exploited the written nature of autobiography. Jean Marc Blanchard states that 'it is wrong to speak of *autobiography*. The only word that should properly remain is that of writing (*graphein*).'[26] Blanchard asserts that the element of writing in the term *autobiography* plays no explicit part in the denomination of any other literary genre: his judgement appears to be based on the assumption that autobiography *is* a literary genre, whereas biography is not. We have repeatedly encountered similar emphases on the origin and etymology of the term autobiography, which, in Blanchard's arguments and elsewhere, becomes a fixed point in the variable geometry of autobiography.

The deconstructionist argument also involves the bracketing of the question of the 'real self' ostensibly represented by the subject of the autobiographical text; this subject is of course constructed within the text. In a stronger version of this argument, the 'self ' is only discovered through its writing of itself and only exists as an effect of writing. One may question how far this ostensibly radical scepticism really differs from the idealist view of Gusdorf and others that the decentred self discovers itself in its acts of self-expression.

More recently, critics have been concerned to reclaim some concept of 'reference' for the autobiographical text, and hence to escape both the aestheticism of earlier positions and the self-reflexive discourse of deconstruction. This has rarely entailed, however, a return to an affirmation of the factual status of autobiography. Paul John Eakin, in *Fictions in Autobiography*, argues that 'fictions' – the stories that the individual constructs about his or her life and identity – are to be understood as the truth of that life or self: 'the self that is the center of all autobiographical narrative is necessarily a fictive structure'.[27] By this, Eakin does not mean, however, that the autobiographer creates a fictional 'persona'. Using theories of language acquisition and psychoanalytic accounts of 'identity-formation', he argues that narrative forms are a constitutive part of human identity – that we are, as it were, formed by narrative structures. The distinction between fact and fiction is therefore invalidated, because fact or reality shares the same form as fiction or narrative, while 'intention' is made identical with 'reference' – the biographical truth to which the autobiographer refers is his or her 'intention'. In his more recent *Touching the World*, Eakin makes a stronger claim for the referential dimensions of autobiography – often a matter of context and inference rather than assertion – while restating the extent to which 'fictions' reside in 'facts'.[28]

Eakin tends to use the terms 'narrative' and 'fiction' inter-changeably, invoking Peter Brooks's work on narrative structures and that of the historiographers Louis Mink and Hayden White, who have shown that 'narrative is a mode of cognition'[29] and argued for the fiction-making operation of the historical enterprise. In the 'new history', then, reality and fiction, history and autobiography, are no longer antithetical structures. White, for example, writes that we should overcome our 'reluctance to consider historical narratives as what they most manifestly are, verbal fictions, the contents of which are as much *invented* as *found* and the forms of which have more in common with their counterparts in literature than they have with those in the sciences'.[30] Peter Brooks, tracing the way in which, in Freud's case-histories, fantasies constitute events and origins are displaced, writes: 'tales may lead back not so much to events as to other tales, to man as a structure of the fictions he tells about himself'.[31] Jonathan Culler comments:

> By pursuing a narratological problem into non-literary realms, we dis-cover to what extent the case-history . . . is ultimately allied to the fictional. This shows the scope and functioning of the fictional in ways relevant to literary study itself. It also indicates a problem in the theory of fiction: when you leave fiction you discover fictions.[32]

Brooks also uses the term 'hypothetical construction' to describe both biography and fiction, and it is the category of the 'hypothesis' – the trying on or out of models – that may prove more enabling for a concept of autobiographical identity and story than the 'fictionality' Culler describes. Brooks's and White's work has proved extremely important for thinking about auto/biography, but I want to resist a falling back into the kind of fictionalism represented in the work of Northrop Frye, or Frank Kermode, for whom fictions are necessary constructs we live by to protect ourselves from the vicissitudes of an arbitrary world.[33] Indeed, a number of autobiographical theorists have turned to the work of Brooks, White and Paul Ricoeur because autobiography is now being inserted, or reinserted, not into fictionalism but into the history–memory nexus which has become such a dominant feature of contemporary work across the human sciences.

The philosopher Jay Bernstein, in a critical discussion of Habermas's account of psychoanalysis, has brought out the sense in which 'at bottom, psychoanalytic self-transformation is a form of theory-mediated autobiography'.[34] Discussion of autobiography has tended to polarise between an impossible demand for representational accuracy or its abandonment in a fictionalist position. If the purpose of modern secular autobiographies has been to reveal the

> identity of the narrating/narrated self . . . the common and consistent nervous reaction to this uncontrolled productivity has been to conclude that really autobiographies are not representations of a self in its travels throughout the world but art, creation, fiction. Psychoanalysis, theory-mediated autobiography, challenges this conclusion by revealing that the constitutively productive element of autobiography is but the consequence of the human temporal predicament when self-consciously realized in narrative praxis.

To write of external events, including the actions of others, is a different matter to writing about oneself: 'self-narration is the excessive truth of narrative form; autobiographical excess reveals the self as twisting free from form and universality even as it appropriates it to itself' [pp. 65–6]. An interesting implication of Bernstein's account is that the fictionalist reading of psychoanalytic or autobiographical narrative is no less enclosing than a representationalist one, and stems from an anxious need to control and contain that which exceeds form and threatens our conceptions of representability.

Michael Sheringham argues that autobiography is interdependent with 'prevailing view of narrative . . . any moves towards a rehabilitation of narrative's mimetic, heuristic or pragmatic functions are likely to support comparable shifts in the way autobiography is regarded'. Ricoeur's concept of the *entrecroisement* of history and fiction as the two primary narrative modes is of particular relevance to autobiography.[35] I would endorse this, while arguing that the history–fiction relationship must not be theorised yet again as a fact–

fiction dichotomy, nor should it lead to further disciplinary disputes in autobiographical theory. It is time that autobiographical theorists recognised that historians are not straw positivists and that auto-biographical narratives can illuminate the past as well as the present. Finally, I would argue that we need far more searching analyses of the ways in which the categories of fact and fiction, fiction and history, have and do operate. It seems appropriate to recall Raymond Williams on this point:

> The real range in the major forms – epic, romance, drama, narrative – in which this question of 'fact' and 'fiction' arises – is the more complex series: what really happened; what might (could) have happened; what really happens; what might happen; what essentially (typically) happened/happens . . . The range of actual writings makes use, implicitly or explicitly, of all these propositions, but not only in the forms that are historically specialized as 'literature'. The characteristically 'difficult' forms (difficult because of the deformed definition of history, memoir and biography), use a significant part of each series, and given the use of real characters and events in much major epic, romance, drama and narrative, the substantial overlap – indeed in many areas the substantial community – is undeniable.[36]

Inside out

In his discussion of Nietzsche, Derrida calls attention to the problems of traditional concepts of 'the life' and 'the work' in the lives of philosophers, referring to what he terms the border or line between 'the life' and 'the work' as the place of the text's *engendering*; it is neither outside nor inside:

> Between a title or a preface on the one hand, and the book to come on the other, between the title *Ecce Homo* and *Ecce Homo* 'itself ', the structure of the exergue situates the place from which life will be *recited*. . . . This place is to be found neither in the work (it is an exergue) nor in the life of the author.[37]

Derrida's arguments resist simple paraphrase, but I would point to the way in which this concept of the inside/outside not only picks up the issue of the 'contours' or 'borders' of texts, but bears on the longstanding problematic of the 'inside' and 'outside' of self or life in autobiographical criticism.

In 'The Law of Genre' Derrida debates a related issue, but one which relates more directly to Lejeune's concept of the auto-biographical pact.[38] The essay also points up a number of problems, not only in 'traditional' theories of genre but also in recent attempts to redefine the question of genre. His discussion bears interestingly on a number of the theories outlined in this chapter, not least because Derrida does not merely treat as metaphor the 'legal' status of generic rules; instead he explicitly interrogates what is meant by 'the law of genre'. Secondly, he relates this law to concepts of nature and history, arguing that these cannot be seen as simply opposed to one another. Thirdly, he looks at the status of generic labels as they appear within the book as object, a discussion which further complicates the attempts by critics like Elizabeth Bruss and Philippe Lejeune to 'fix' autobiography by asserting the designatory or referential status of the authorial address or the author's name.

Opening up the ambiguous status of genre in relation to laws of nature or non-nature, Derrida questions Genette's distinction between 'genres' and 'modes'. Genette argued that 'genres are, properly speaking, literary/or aesthetic categories; modes are categories that pertain to linguistics or more precisely, to an anthropology of verbal expression'.[39] In this account, the 'history' of genre-theory has involved a deformation of classical accounts of genres through the *naturalisation* of genres, projecting upon them the 'privilege of naturalness, which was *legitimately* . . . that of three modes'. In the Romantic era, Genette asserts, the system of modes is (incorrectly) interpreted as a system of genres. Derrida points to the way in which this account is dependent upon an opposition between nature and history which is itself an aspect of Romanticism, while the treatment of the Romantic era as a 'moment' in the history of genres is a legacy of 'the teleological ordering of history', simultaneously obeying a naturalising and a historicising logic. We remain, he argues, within the Romantic heritage as long 'as we persist in drawing attention to historical concerns and the truth of historical production in order to militate against abuses or confusions of naturalization' [pp. 57–8].

Derrida's primary concern, however, is less with the problematic of genre-history or theories of history than with the 'taxonomic certainties' implied by Genette's distinction between 'genres' and 'modes'. He demonstrates that the 'genre-clause', by which a text marks itself as belonging to a particular genre, is excluded from the genre or class of texts which it designates. For example, the designation 'novel', whether it appears in the form of a sub-title on the title-page or not, is not itself 'novelistic': 'the re-mark of belonging

does not belong'. Both inside and outside the work, 'along its boundary', the designation of genre 'gathers together the corpus and, at
the same time, in the same [very] blinking of an eye, keeps it from
closing, from identifying itself with itself '. Thus the genre-clause
both engenders 'genealogy' and 'genericity' and puts them to death,
is the condition of their possibility and their impossibility [p. 61].

Derrida does not wish to argue for the existence of a 'genreless'
text; every text, he asserts, participates in one or several genres. The
point is that this 'participation never amounts to belonging'. The
concept of the 'genre-clause' emerges, as I have stated, in Bruss's and
Lejeune's discussions, whether in the form of preface, title-page, or,
in Bruss's account, as internal signals of the autobiographical act. I
would argue that there are problems in perceiving these markers as
unproblematically indicative of generic status or as codifications of an
'autobiographical intention', and that these are in part exposed by
Derrida's account of the way in which the markers of genre are not
productive of a simple or single 'identity'. On the other hand, I would
also wish to query Derrida's claim that the genre-clause is always and
necessarily 'present' in a text, even if it has no 'actual' location. His
account of non-belonging, that is, logically depends on the postu-
lation that every text signals its belonging to a particular genre,
're-marks on this distinctive trait within itself '. While this is offered
initially as a hypothesis, it is imbued, through the force of the
argument which follows it and bases itself upon it, with the status of a
truth.

This hypothesis/truth is not investigated further; instead Derrida
turns to Blanchot to demonstrate how a text can 'transgress' the law
of genre. The title-page of *La Folie du jour* contains the genre-clause
'Un récit', but in different forms in the text's different occurrences,
sometimes with a question-mark, sometimes without. The appearance of the term 'un récit', within the body of the text, used to deny or
to put into question whether an account has been made, prevents us,
Derrida argues, from identifying 'un récit' as a mode:

> Faced with this type of difficulty . . . one might be tempted to take
> recourse in the law or the rights which govern printed texts. One might be
> tempted to argue as follows: all these insoluble problems of delimitation
> are raised 'on the inside' of a book classified as a work of literature or
> literary fiction. Pursuant to these juridicial norms, this book has a begin-
> ning and end, a title, an author, a publisher, its distinctive denomination
> is *La Folie du jour*. . . . Furthermore, on the inside of this normed space,

the word 'account' does not name a literary operation or genre, but a
current mode of discourse, and it does so regardless of the formidable
problems of structure, edge, set theory, the part and the whole, etc. that it
raises in this 'literary' corpus.

That is all well and good. But in its very relevance, this objection cannot
be sustained – for example, it cannot save the modal determination of the
account [*récit*] – except by referring to extra-literary and even extra-
linguistic juridical norms. The objection makes an appeal to the law and
calls to mind the fact that the subversion of *La Folie du jour* needs the law
in order to take place. [p. 68]

Derrida criticises those who seek to legitimate genre with reference
to the 'inside' of the book and/or by an appeal to public and external
sources of legitimation. Thus, again, he attempts to deconstruct the
inside/outside opposition, referring instead to the edges and folds of
textual processes. Through Blanchot, he moves from an account of
the law of genre as a set of interdictions which guard the 'purity' of
genres, to an assertion of its transgressive and disruptive force. It
might be useful to compare Derrida's arguments with Benedetto
Croce's statement that 'every true work of art has violated an established genre'. This statement would reinforce Derrida's assertion
that the law is essential to transgression: it must be in place for a
violation or transgression of its rules to occur. But in Derrida's
reading, the law itself is transgressive: the question of transgression is
not clear-cut. The law is not in place first to be subverted by a
magnificent act of transgression. Nor, to extend this argument, would
it be possible to assert the priority of nature, instinct or, indeed,
'autobiographical impulse', to a law which would constrain and
inhibit it. In this context, Blanchot's 'submission' to the law – 'The
law demands a narrative account' is Derrida's gloss on this [p. 64] –
would subvert the concept of an 'imperative autobiographical necessity', proposed, for example, by Eakin. The place of the demand, in a
Derridean reading, cannot be easily located in the interior of the
psychological person.

A further issue raised is that of the etymologies of the term 'genre',
which, Derrida notes, has a much larger semantic and etymological
range in French than in English, including within its reach 'gender':
'the question of the literary genre is not a formal one: it covers the
motif of the law in general, of generation in the natural and symbolic
senses, of birth in the natural and symbolic senses, of the generation
difference, sexual difference between the feminine and the mas-

culine genre/gender' [p. 70]. This conceptual link has been very important for feminist approaches to autobiography.

Once again, we see a number of familiar issues raised concerning the status of genre. Derrida, here and in *The Ear of the Other*, points to a problematic recurrent in autobiographical criticism: the relationship between 'inside' and 'outside', lives and works, text and *hors-texte*. We see throughout this chapter and elsewhere that attempts to 'define' the nature of autobiography are often derived from statements made from *within* autobiographical texts which are held to have a definitional function, or to operate as statements of intent.

These statements are also said to be in some way 'outside' the narrative, or at least capable of commenting or reflecting on it. Derrida subverts the Romantic concept that literature should include criticism, that the work should contain its criticism within itself as its own vital supplement. James Olney, for example, explains the 'late' development of autobiographical criticism by claiming that autobiography is a self-critical act 'and consequently the criticism of autobiography exists *within* the literature rather than alongside it'.[40] One implication of this statement, not pursued by Olney, is that autobiographical criticism is redundant. Just as the autobiographer is the only person truly qualified to speak about himself and his life, so he is the privileged interpreter of his own autobiographical endeavours. But it is important to distinguish this position from that of Lejeune and other critics for whom markers of generic identity or intention are conventional signs, subject to change and, presumably, contestation or parody. Lejeune's account of the spaces and borders in which authorship marks itself has some affinity with Derrida's redistribution of the autobiographical, despite their different emphases on the signs of authorship.

The inside/outside opposition in more traditional autobiographical criticism, the focus of Derrida's critique, also operates in relation to models of the self, in which, for example, psychological interiority as 'depth' is opposed to a public and 'exterior' self. An 'inside out' model of autobiography is prevalent in early twentieth-century discussions, giving the title to at least one lengthy critical study, E. Stuart Bates's *Inside Out* (1936–37) and two autobiographies, including Adrian Stokes's Kleinian account of his childhood.[41] The model of the 'inside out' expresses both the viewpoint of the self 'behind' the eyes looking out at the world, and the inversion of turning something inside out, the exposure of an 'inner' self. More recently, feminist critics, in particular, have taken up an 'inside/outside' model of autobiography. In relation to Simone de Beauvoir, for example, Leah D. Hewitt notes that 'the mobile borderlines between de Beauvoir's fiction and non-fiction, between internal and external concerns . . . have the potential to contest the specificity of the autobiographical genre . . . [an] unlimited interaction between "outsides" and "insides" '.[42] The current concern with the question of 'embodiment' in auto/biography entails an emphasis on corporeal borders and boundaries: Sidonie Smith, in *Subjectivity, Identity and the Body*, writes at length of the ways in which the 'corporeal' dimensions of women's autobiographies disrupt autonomous individuality.[43] She draws upon Judith Butler's account of the corporeal metaphors of identity, in turn drawn from the anthropologist Mary Douglas's highly influential work on bodily metaphors. Butler's account in fact warns against a too easy conflation of the actual and the metaphorical:

> Regardless of the compelling metaphors of the spatial distinctions of inner and outer, they remain linguistic terms that facilitate a set of fantasies, feared and desired. . . . Rather, the question is: From what strategic position in public discourse and for what reasons has the trope of interiority and the disjunctive binary of inner/outer taken hold?[44]

It would be interesting to pursue further the application of these spatial categories, 'inner' and 'outer', 'surface' and 'depth', to both autobiographical 'lives' and 'works', especially when we recall the body imagery so dominant in nineteenth- and early twentieth-century auto/biographical discourse and the correlation between introspection and anatomising.

Authenticating authorship

Lejeune, as we saw, grounded his early discussions of possible autobiographical devices in the following definition of the genre: autobiography is 'a retrospective prose narrative produced by a real person concerning his own existence, focusing on his individual life, in particular on the development of his personality'.[45] All situations of identification 'inevitably end up by cashing in the first person for a proper noun [name]', both in oral discourse, in which 'there is not full presence without naming', and in written discourse, where the *signature* designates the utterer.

The problems of autobiography must thus be considered in relation to the *proper noun* [name]. In printed texts, the whole utterance is assumed by a person whose *name* is customarily placed on the cover of the book, and on the flyleaf, above or below the title. In this name is summed up the whole existence of what is called the *author*; it is the only mark in the text of an indubitable 'outside-of-the-text', designating a real person. . . . By these words, I mean a person whose existence is legally verifiable, a matter of record . . . exceptions and frauds only serve to emphasize the general credence given to this variety of social contact.

An author is not just a person, he is a person who writes and publishes. With one foot in the text, and one outside, he is the point of contact between the two.[46]

The author, Lejeune states, is 'thus a personal name, the identical name accepting responsibility for a sequence of different published texts'. It is possible, he argues, that one only becomes an author with the publication of one's second book; for the autobiographer, in particular, the production of other, non-autobiographical texts constitutes his 'sign of reality' in the eyes of the reader – a reality deriving, Lejeune suggests at one point, from the list of his other works which is often to be found at the beginning of the book under the heading 'by the same author'. Thus the 'outside-of-the-text' is ambiguous in Lejeune's formulation; it seems to refer both to the public sphere of civic and legal identity, in which the author is a 'real person', and to the 'information' about the author which exists 'outside' the narrative or textual sphere, but inside the book as material object, providing a legitimation of the identity between author and narrator/protagonist, and of authorial status. It is the latter inside/outside opposition which Derrida exploits.

The 'outside-of-the-book' as the title-page is the location, for Lejeune, of the autobiographical 'pact'. In *L'Autobiographie en France* Lejeune wrote that we cannot distinguish between autobiography and novel on the basis of an internal analysis of the text; he now asserts:

This is true as long as the text is considered without the title page; when that is taken as part of the text, with the name of the author, then a general textual criterion is available: 'identity' between the names of the author, narrator and protagonist. The autobiographical contract [*pacte*] is the affirmation in the text of this identity, referring in the last resort to the *name* of the author on the cover.

The forms of the autobiographical contract [*pacte*] are quite varied, but they all manifest an intention to 'honour' the signature.[47]

Lejeune opens up a confusion by referring to the title-page as 'part of the text', in which case its claims to legitimate the textual 'inside' as an 'external' instance is surely problematical. This is also the case in his statement that 'identity' (between author and narrator) can be established through an *initial section* of the text 'where the narrator makes commitments to the reader by behaving as if he was the author, in such a way that the reader has not the slightest doubt that the "I" designates the name on the cover'. Later, he redefines the relationship between inside and outside, moving referentiality into a social dimension:

> When, therefore, we look for something to distinguish fiction from autobiography, to serve as a basis for the referent of 'I' in first-person narratives, there is no need to appeal to an impossible region 'outside-the-text': the text itself provides, on its outer edge, this final term, the proper name of the author, which is at once textual and indubitably referential. This referentiality is undubitable because it is based on two social institutions: the legal identity of the individual (a convention which is internalized by each of us from early childhood) and the publisher's contract; there is hence no reason to doubt the author's identity. [p. 21]

Ultimately, he claims, the guarantee that the autobiographical pact will not be falsely entered into lies in the fact that authors are incapable of giving up their proper names: 'it is impossible for the autobiographical vocation and the passion for anonymity to exist in the same being'. Lejeune's emphasis on the proper name derives from his desire to 'anchor' his theory of autobiography as a *contractual* genre, and to avoid both an approach to autobiography based 'on an externally established relation between the text and what is outside it' and one based solely on 'an internal analysis of the functioning of the text'. The author *as* proper name, 'with one foot in the text, and one outside' seemed the ideal way to give substance and an entry into 'that borderline area of the printed text which in reality *governs* all our reading'. At the close of the essay, Lejeune discusses the need for research into the historical dimensions of this 'contractual' space – 'author's name, title, subtitle, publisher's name, down to the ambiguous function of the preface' – and the codes by which it has functioned.

One of the most important aspects of Lejeune's work is his exploration of the relationship between *authorship* and *autobiography*. The author is the name of a person who takes responsibility for his published texts. Autobiography, a narrative recounting the life of the author, 'supposes that there is *identity of name* between the author (such as he figures, by his name, on the cover), the narrator of the story, and the character who is being talked about'. This identity constitutes 'the autobiographical pact' and creates what Lejeune calls 'the autobiographical space'.

Clearly, most of the claims Lejeune makes could be qualified, if not countered. His arguments assume too readily that an autobiographer is only so by virtue of his or her other publications. He suggests that an author's autobiography must appear subsequently to other works – that it cannot be a first work. I would argue, however, that Lejeune's discussion is of value as it relates to the question of authorship as a public role with a history, and that exploring this dimension of authorship does not exclude attention to writings outside this context. After all, Lejeune is one of the few theorists to have examined the worlds of unpublished life-writings, 'vanity press' publications and 'how-to' books on the writing of autobiography.[48]

Michel de Certeau reads Lejeune's account of the 'pact' as a comment on the institutional determinants of autobiographical credibility, the way in which the value of a discourse is secured by the status of its author. Autobiography is grounded 'not on the text itself, but on the conjunction between the author named by the text and his effective social place':

> This argument can be generalized: the accreditation of the author by his historical place generates the legitimation of a text by its referent. Reciprocally, an attitude of docility toward the norms of a community (learned or not) assures the possibility of the text's 'conformity' to the facts. Here, one does not believe in writing, but in the institution which determines its function. . . . The reality of this position renders credible the semblance of referentiality.[49]

'Referentiality', though it takes many forms in autobiographical theory, 'internal' and 'external', is a key generic desideratum. In de Certeau's reading, ' "conformity" ' to the facts' becomes a question of authorial status; the issue is complicated in the case of autobiography (in whose theorising 'coherence' concepts of truth have been dominant), but not invalidated.

Lejeune's 'Pact' essay and his other earlier work should be understood in relation to the debate around authorship which reached its zenith in the 1960s and 1970s. Roland Barthes's essay 'The Death of the Author' argues that the author, as authority and even God-figure, has to 'die' in order for writing to be born and, indeed, for the reader to come into his/her own: 'the birth of the reader must be at the cost of the death of the Author'.[50] Michel Foucault examines in a rather more measured way the history of the 'author-function'. In 'What is An Author?' he argues against what he sees as Barthes's recourse to a 'transcendental' concept of 'écriture'; we should wait and see what comes after the traditional concept of the author.[51]

The implications of this influential debate are ambiguous for autobiography. The 'death of the author' necessarily means the death of the autobiographer *qua* author. On the other hand, as we saw in the previous chapter, autobiography can itself be figured as thanatography, supporting, and indeed, enacting the author's death. It is biography and biographical criticism, which refers texts back to the lives of their authors, which are the focus of Barthes's critique. Biography remains very largely untheorised, while autobiography is increasingly celebrated as exemplary impossibility.

Lejeune does not refer specifically to Barthes's or Foucault's discussions of the cultural category of the author, but there are numerous parallels between their arguments and his. Foucault's essay is particularly relevant, in part because it directly addresses the issue of the relationship between proper name and author's name. Starting from John Searle's account of the role of the proper name as both description and designation, or in Searle's terms, 'identifying reference', Foucault argues that 'the name of an author is not precisely a proper name among others. . . . Its presence is functional in that it serves as a means of classification' [pp. 122–3].

> We can conclude that, unlike a proper name, which moves from the interior of a discourse to the real person outside who produced it, the name of the author remains at the contours of texts – separating one from the other, defining their form, and characterizing their mode of existence. It points to the existence of certain groups of discourse and refers to that status of this function within a society and a culture. The author's name is not a function of a man's civil status, nor is it fictional; it is situated in the breach, among the discontinuities, which gives rise to new groups of discourse and their singular mode of existence. Consequently, we can say that in our culture, the name of an author is a variable that accompanies only certain texts to the exclusion of others: a private letter may have a signatory, but it does not have an author; a contract can have an underwriter, but not an author; and, similarly, an anonymous poster attached to a wall may well have a writer, but he cannot be an author. In this sense, the function of an author is to characterize the existence, circulation, and operation of certain discourses within a society. [pp. 123–4]

Foucault's decentred account of the authorial centre points up the ambiguity in Lejeune's notion of the pact/contract. On the one hand, it can be seen as an actual, if implicit contract, 'proposed to the reader'; on the other, it can be taken as a structural feature of the literary system, an idea expressed by Lejeune when he refers to 'the global level of publication'.

Lejeune's arguments overlap with as well as departing from Foucault's. Lejeune obviously upholds the isomorphism between proper name and author's name which Foucault explicitly rejects and, presumably, would at least wish to claim that autobiography, as a *referential* genre, supports Searle's claim that 'we have the institution of proper names to perform the speech act of identifying reference'.[52] Foucault would without doubt have rejected this concept of referentiality, although a 'Foucauldian' approach to autobiography might include the idea that autobiographies serve a special function in legitimating authorship and organising an author's texts around this representation of the 'true self'. Lejeune follows Foucault in his account of the 'boundaries' of the text in which the author's name is located, although this is made more literal than in Foucault's concept of textual 'contours'. The two theories diverge over the issue of identity: as we have seen, Lejeune asserts the self-identity of the 'I' manifest in the inside and on the 'outside-of-the-text'; and between author, model, narrator and protagonist, albeit at a structural level. Foucault, on the other hand, refers explicitly to the non-identity of the utterances at different textual levels – for example, the preface and 'the body of the text' – in non-fictional as well as fictional discourse. The 'author-function', he writes, 'simultaneously gives rise to a variety of egos and to a series of subjective positions that individuals of any class may come to occupy' [p. 131].

Lejeune, in 'Autobiographie et histoire littéraire', sets out a project of research into the historical conditions of authorship and the changing relationships between authors and readers, and authors and publishers. Clearly he views the study of autobiography as giving a special entry into this history, which has strong parallels with Foucault's programme for further investigation of the 'author-function'. Foucault writes:

> This form of investigation might also permit the introduction of an historical analysis of discourse. Perhaps the time has come to study not only the expressive value and formal transformations of discourse, but its mode of existence: the modifications and variations, within any culture, of

modes of circulation, valorization, attribution and appropriation. Partially at the expense of themes and concepts that an author places in his work, the 'author-function' could also reveal the manner in which discourse is articulated on the basis of social relationships. [p. 137]

In Lejeune's account, 'the system of the author is the fundamental message that the autobiographical genre conveys'.[53]

Exploring the 'emergence' of the author as a category, Foucault discusses the tradition in which 'literary' discourse is acceptable only if it carries an author's name. In literary criticism, he argues, the traditional methods for defining an author 'derive in large part from those used in the Christian tradition to authenticate (or to reject) the particular texts in its possession'. The author's name, *contra* Lejeune, is insufficient as a marker of authenticity: 'In *De Virus Illustribus*, Saint Jerome maintains that homonymy is not proof of the common authorship of several works, since many individuals could have the same name or someone could have perversely appropriated another's name' [p. 127]. Modern criticism follows Christian exegesis in its emphases on unities or consistencies of themes, ideas, style and context as structures which authenticate authorship.

These arguments provide a context for some of the recurrent concerns in autobiographical discourse, not least the issues of deception and inauthenticity. Lejeune calls attention to the pheno-menon of apocryphal memoirs in post-Revolutionary France:

> the public was ravenous for memoirs on the *ancien régime*, which publishers tried to exploit by fabricating false memoirs. . . . The author of the deception imitates in its totality the autobiographical process, and while cheating in effect on the level of the contract, he respects the effect of unity inherent in the genre.[54]

Whether or not 'the effect of unity' is 'inherent' in the genre, it is certainly the critical criterion most frequently invoked. Unity must then be a double-edged sword: internal coherence allows for the bracketing of demands for external validation or verification pro-cedures (reference). On the other hand the effect of unity may be the most successful way of passing off a 'false' memoir as true.

In eighteenth- and nineteenth-century contexts, 'fraud' and, more generally, 'crimes of writing', are key concerns. Susan Stewart notes that:

> Within the eighteenth-century transformation of the literary market-place – the decline of patronage, the rise of booksellers, the advent of

mass literary production and copyright, the development of 'intellectual property' – lies a central set of questions regarding the relations among speech and writing, authorship, authenticity and audience.[55]

The transformation of the eighteenth-century concept of the writer involves the gradual detachment of the writer from his or her audience and a number of devices, including first-person narrative, are deployed both to reduce the gap between writer and public and to authenticate authorship. It is also, and relatedly, the question of narrative truth that is at issue. Michael McKeon has traced the diverse criteria employed – he takes as his example certain eighteenth-century travel narratives – to ascertain the truth and historicity of language. Original documentation can be forged. Eyewitness accounts are dependent on the objectivity of the observer. Style is an indication of the truthful character of the narrator – for example, plain style – but it can be mimed. As William Warner comments: 'once it has been transported from the space or time of its production, no text, whatever its aspirations to facticity and truth, can bear a mark in its own language that can truly verify its relation to something outside itself '.[56]

Critics agree on the importance, at the beginning of the eighteenth century, of the first-person autobiographical novel or memoir-novel. Lejeune argues, in *L'autobiographie en France*, that autobiography emerges out of the new form of biography represented by the autobiographical novel, and, more radically, that the emerging 'genuine' autobiographer imitates the pseudoautobiographer:

> authenticity began by being mimicked in the novel before being recuperated and interiorised by the autobiographers. The autobiographer could only become himself by imitating people who imagined what it was to be an autobiographer. This curious game of mirrors shows that sincerity is something learned, that originality is a matter of imitation, and that what is at issue is not the genius of certain individuals but a general transformation of the notion of the person through the appearance in a society of a new type of narrative. [p. 47]

Philip Stewart's study of the memoir-novel in early eighteenth-century France documents the concern at the way the historical record was being contaminated by fictional memoirs: Pierre Bayle wrote that those who combine the novel with history 'shed a thousand shadows on real history'.[57] We need to remember that the desire to keep fact and fiction separate has often stemmed from the ideological demand that history should not be contaminated by fictional productions. Bayle's suggestion that it might be necessary to constrain authors to choose between history and the novel (or to use brackets to separate truth from invention) is paralleled in England by Sir Isaac Bickerstaff's attack on apocryphal French memoirs:

> By this means several who are unknown or despised in the present age will be famous in the next unless a sudden stop be put to such pernicious practices . . . the most immediate remedy that I can apply to prevent this growing evil is that I do hereby give notice to all booksellers and translators whatsoever that the word *memoir* is French for a *novel*; and to require of them that they sell and translate it accordingly.[58]

Bickerstaff's diatribe exhibits an ambiguity between the snobbish distaste for memorialisation of and by the obscure (the Earl of Clarendon's 'dirty people of no name') and the entry of fiction into the historical record. These are linked, in fact, by the assumption that only people of quality are acceptable chroniclers of the times, a view that we have seen perpetuated in numerous discussions of autobiography, biography and history.

The other side of public anxiety about literary fraud is the writer's anxiety about abuses of his work. The classic expression of authorial anxiety is Rousseau's declaration of 23 January 1774. In view of the improper or 'disfigured' reprints of his work, Rousseau disavows all past and future works printed under his name 'as being either no longer his work or falsely attributed to him'. Geoffrey Bennington notes that Rousseau takes pains to sign the text which disavows his signature.[59]

As both Peggy Kamuf and Bennington have argued, following Derrida's extensive work on 'signature', a signature requires a counter-signature to guarantee it and thus fails to assure authenticity. Like Foucault, deconstructionist critics have attempted to undermine any relations of mutual support between signature, proper name, and other ostensible markers of authorial identity: 'What is called a signature, its trait or its contract, traces the disappearance [of the author] and marks the division of the proper name where it joins the text.' Kamuf adds:

> the demand to know who signs, the move to authenticate the signature, are gestures that Rousseau was, to a significant extent, the first to perform, and he performed them on 'himself' in somewhat the same way that Freud, the founder of another institution of self-reflection, had to perform his own analysis. . . . Doubling itself, the signature 'Rousseau' uncovers what must always divide it: it exposes the limit at which one signs – and signs again.[60]

While criticising Lejeune for failing to distinguish between proper name and signature, deconstructionists direct their more serious criticism at the concept of the proper name, seen as the 'keystone of logocentrism'. The 'proper name', Bennington asserts, is supposed to establish a direct link between language and the world by unambiguously designating a concrete individual – but in fact a proper name is always part of a system of oppositions and therefore part of 'writing'.[61]

The repetition of the act of signing, which is never sufficient to authenticate authorship or identity, is paralleled by the multiplication of the autobiographical 'I', dramatically illustrated in Rousseau's famous sentence in the *Dialogues*: 'It was necessary for me to say how, if I were another man, I would see a man like me.'[62] This 'surplus articulation ' of the 'I' articulates even as it undermines the fiction of the unified subject. In turn, it is the biographical subject, the 'totalising figure' of auto/biography, which conceals the 'essentially fictional resource at the source of autobiography . . . the fiction that the subject is the *same thing* as the words deployed to name experiences'.[63] In Kamuf's account, this 'fictional resource' invalidates the pact as Lejeune presents it.

The insistence on authenticity and sincerity in autobiographical criticism seems to reflect a continuing anxiety about authorship and attribution. At its most optimistic, the claim is that the problems of external verification can be overcome through the operations of internal truth as consistency or personal style. We recall Georg Misch's claim that 'autobiographies are not to be regarded as objective narratives'; truth is ultimately the truth of personality:

> In general their truth is to be sought not so much in their elements as in the whole works, each of which is more than the sum of its parts . . . even the cleverest liar, in his fabricated or embroidered stories of himself, will be unable to deceive us as to his character. He will reveal it through the spirit of his lies. Thus, in general, the spirit brooding over the recollected material is the truest and most real element in an autobiography.[64]

Anna Robeson Burr adopts a more suspicious approach to the literary institution. The spurious autobiography or memoir – 'the memoir as fiction and the memoir transposed by another hand' – is

> more subtly dangerous than the frankly spurious class. . . . Once thrown upon life, difficult to avow, impossible to recall, it lurks about the decent society of books like some base-born adventurer, communicating evil and

distrust. . . . When the original circumstance of its writing is forgotten, it becomes listed under biography in the libraries.[65]

The 'bastard' text seeks cover in the legitimate family of autobiography.

Questions of deception and authenticity emerge, in more or less overt forms, in a variety of recent autobiographical theories. We have become familiar with the invocation of Buffon's aphorism 'le style c'est l'homme'. In 'The Style of Autobiography', discussed in the previous chapter, Starobinski defines 'style' as the act of an individual, 'the fashion in which each autobiographer satisfies the conditions of the genre'.[66]

'Style', Starobinski argues, has been viewed as suspect in autobiographical writings implying 'a redundancy that may disturb the message itself':

> Not only (in this view) can the autobiographer lie, but the 'autobiographical form' can cloak the freest fictive invention: 'pseudo-memoirs' and 'pseudo-biographies' exploit the possibilities of narrating purely imaginary tales in the first person. . . . It is easy to conclude, under this traditional conception of style, that, in autobiography or confession, despite the vow of sincerity, the 'content' of the narrative can be lost, can disappear into fiction. . . . Style, as an original quality, accentuating as it does the importance of the present in the act of writing, seems to serve the conventions of narrative, rather than the realities of reminiscence. It is more than an obstacle or a screen, it becomes a principle of deformation and falsification.
>
> But if one rejects this definition of style as 'form' (or dress, or ornament), superadded to a 'content' in favor of one of style as deviation (*écart*), the originality in the autobiographical style – far from being suspect – offers us a system of revealing indices, or symptomatic traits. The redundance of style is individualizing: it singles out. . . . No matter how doubtful the facts related, the text will at least present an 'authentic' image of the man who 'held the pen'. [p. 75]

This gives further support to the idea of autobiographical 'truth' as the truth of the present – that is, of the person/author writing in the present – rather than of the past. 'Style' as individuation, in the theories of phenomenological critics, takes us nearer 'to the psychic uniqueness of writers'. The concern with literary style, however, also emerges outside these critical contexts. *Stylometry* is the science used to detect authorship, in legal–criminal as well as literary instances; it 'describes and measures the personal elements in literary or extempore utterances, so that it can be said that one particular person

is responsible for the composition'.[67] Like graphology and
fingerprinting, the analysis of style is an element in the identification
and recognition of persons. In scholarly contexts, style is crucial
'internal evidence' for authorial attribution. In *Evidence for Authorship*,
David V. Erdman writes, in an essay entitled 'The Signature of Style':

> granted that a writer's style is sometimes silent, it must be recognized that
> the test of style is always crucial, at least in the negative sense. There are
> styles that would rule out Marvell as author: others that would rule out
> Smart . . . no matter how impressive the external evidence.[68]

Style is signature, Erdman argues, the key to authorial identity and its
guarantee. Debates in the field of literary attribution over the relative
merits of 'internal' and 'external' attribution have striking echoes in
autobiographical criticism, in which the 'referential', external
dimension of autobiographical verification has been almost entirely
dispensed with in favour of 'internal' concepts of veracity. The
desiderata have become the 'authenticity' of the person; coherence
concepts of truth in which the truth is the whole; fictionality as a
higher order of truth; 'style' as the act of an individual and as
revelation and authentication of that individual.

These issues of textual authenticity are also an important element
in apparently formalistic discussions of the logical status of autobiographical discourse. Elizabeth Bruss's *Autobiographical Acts: The
Changing Situation of a Literary Genre* (1976)[69] makes creative and
convincing use of the concept of 'illocutionary action' developed by
philosophers of language, particularly Austin, Strawson and
Searle. Bruss argues that 'just as speaking is made up of different
types of action carried out by means of language [e.g. asserting and
commanding, promising and questioning], the system of actions
carried out through literature consists of its various genres'. As an
illocutionary act becomes explicable not by syntax but as an association between a piece of language and certain contexts, conditions and
intentions, so the style or structure of an autobiography 'cannot
explain what is at the heart of its generic value: the roles played by an
author and a reader, the uses to which the text is being put' [p. 5].

Autobiography could only come into existence in a literary community which recognised it as a 'distinct and deliberate undertaking';
this recognition was dependent on its being distinguished from other
illocutionary acts. There are problems in setting up isolated
definitions of autobiography: 'what autobiography is in part depends

on what it is not – on how it is related to and distinct from other kinds of activity available in its original context' [p. 7]. The nature of genres is variable, and cannot be understood outside symbolic systems. Thus while asserting that autobiography has gained or retained a generic identity, Bruss defines a number of potential sources of variation which any definition of autobiography needs to take into account.

One central aspect of Bruss's discussion is the decreasing need for autobiographers along the historical continuum, as the genre becomes more familiar, to provide internal signals of the act being performed. In recent texts, 'the title page or mode or publication alone may be enough to suggest its illocutionary force' [p. 10]. Bruss also discusses the changing perception of the opposition between fact and fiction; whereas for John Bunyan 'the distinguishing feature of autobiography is facticity', Vladimir Nabokov's autobiography suggests 'that no autobiographer ought to depict himself without first becoming aware of how much fiction is implicit in the death of a "self" ' [p. 18]. There is no intrinsically autobiographical form, but 'there are limited generalizations to be made about the dimensions of action which are common to these autobiographies, and which seem to form the core of our notion of the functions an autobiographical text must perform' [p. 10]. These generalisations constitute 'rules' which the text must satisfy in order 'to count' as autobiography.

The rules she outlines include the conditions that (1) the author claims sole responsibility for the creation and arrangement of his text, and the individual referred to within the text is 'purported to share the identity of the individual exemplified in the organization of the text'. This agent, independently of the text itself, 'is assumed to be susceptible to appropriate public verification procedures'. (2) Information and events reported in connection with the autobiographer are asserted to have been, to be, or to have potential for being the case – the audience is expected to accept these reports as true, and is free to 'check up' on them or attempt to discredit them. (3) The autobiographer purports to believe in what he asserts [pp. 10–11].

To this, Bruss adds that

> what is vital for creating the illocutionary force of the text is that the author purport to have met these requirements, and that the audience understand him to be responsible for meeting or failing to meet them. . . . Although centered largely on the responsibilities of the author, these rules also create the rights of the readers of autobiography and stipulate

the legitimate extent of the expectations allowed them. [p. 11]

Bruss and other formalist critics of autobiography may have opted for a legalistic vocabulary out of a desire to find a 'dispassionate' critical vocabulary and to avoid the apparently more value-laden arguments of earlier critics. One might also speculate that, given Bruss's general assumption that literature is subject to 'constitutive rules', a 'new' and essentially contestable literary genre will require a more explicit codification of these rules, just as new regimes originating from revolution or an independence struggle are more likely to draw up written constitutions than regimes ostensibly grounded in historical continuity.

Bruss's language also serves in part to qualify the absolute claims she makes; hence all we can ask of the autobiographer is that he 'purports' to be telling the truth and to believe in his assertions. It is unclear whether 'purporting' is a further illocutionary act – that is, a feature of specific autobiographical discourses, in which case it could not be said to pre-exist an actual text and to be a general condition – or whether it is an implicit generic condition to which the auto-biographer tacitly subscribes in choosing to write 'auto-biographically'.

In his article 'The Logical Status of Fictional Discourse', John Searle applied his theory of speech or illocutionary acts to the distinction between fictional and non-fictional writing.[70] He argued that 'there is no textual property, syntactical or semantic, that will identify a text as a work of fiction'. If we claim that fiction contains different illocutionary acts from non-fiction, we commit ourselves to the view that words do not have their normal meaning in works of fiction; the logical but absurd extension of this argument is that in order to understand a work of fiction we would have to learn a whole new set of meanings for all the words or elements it contains. Searle's answer to the problem is that what makes a text a work of fiction is 'the illocutionary stance that the author takes toward it, and that stance is a matter of the complex illocutionary intentions that the author has when he writes or otherwise composes it' [p. 325].

Searle argues that the writer of fiction 'pretends' to make assertions – pretence here does not imply an intention to deceive, but the act of 'engaging in a nondeceptive pseudoperformance' which, in the case of the novelist, constitutes pretending to recount to us a series of events. Thus 'the author of a work of fiction pretends to perform a series of illocutionary acts, normally of the representative type' [p. 325]. Secondly, the conventions of fictional discourse suspend the normal requirements which serve to establish connections between language and reality. The conventions of fictional discourse do not alter the meanings of words or other language elements, but 'enable the speaker to use words with their literal meanings without undertaking the commitments that are normally required by those meanings' [p. 326]. The existence of a set of conventions suspending the normal operation of the rules relating illocutionary acts and the world makes possible the pretended illocutions which constitute a work of fiction.

The difficulty for Bruss is that Searle does not allow for an area between fiction and non-fiction, or for a non-fictional discourse in which assertions or truth-statements are not necessarily primary. She in part negotiates this problem by altering the weight attached to degrees of 'contractual' obligation. Thus, the act of 'purporting' is used as a median term between authorial 'commitment' to a belief in the truth of an assertion (non-fiction) and the 'pretence' of making an assertion (fiction).

However, 'purport' – itself a term with two meanings – only becomes a median term if the meaning of 'pretend' is the one which Searle rejects: that is, pretending with the intention to deceive. Moreover, in autobiography, as theorised by Bruss and other critics, obligations exist in relation not only to truth-claims but to the question of personal, or legal, identity. The consequences entailed by the 'violation' of the constitutive rules of autobiography are realised, in her account, in the sphere of the public legal system:

> An autobiographer can be convicted of 'insincerity' or worse if he is caught in a premeditated distortion. On the other hand, when Clifford Irving claimed to be only the editor of an autobiography of Howard Hughes, having in fact written the manuscript himself without contact or authorization by Hughes, he was sentenced to prison for literary fraud. [p. 11]

If the legalistic metaphors employed by Bruss and other formalist critics have their basis in the concrete operations of the legal system, then the 'literary system' can hardly be said to function autonomously, and the 'rules' for the functions an autobiography 'must perform' place upon autobiographers not only contractual obligations but a form of legal protection; after all, how would it be

possible to prove or disprove that individuals '*purport* to believe in
what they "assert" '?

Thus the critical rehabilitation of 'authorial intention', to which
Searle refers, cannot be explained purely in terms of the repudiation
of New Critical tenets; it is clearly linked to the legal understanding of
the term, as in 'intention to deceive'. The critical move towards
legalism is not a new departure; I discussed similar approaches, albeit
made rather differently, in nineteenth- and early twentieth-century
criticism, and argued that the issue of sincerity became all-important
in early psychologistic and 'ethological' approaches, in which general
laws of human nature were to be adduced from autobiographical
texts. In the nineteenth-century periodical reviews the autobiographer's pretence to 'valid' knowledges illicitly gleaned, or to a
falsely assumed social status, was the subject of condemnation.
Bruss's example of a 'literary fraud' and its punishment indicates that
'popular' or 'sensational' autobiography continues to present
difficulties for the literary critic; generic 'rules' thus operate to
protect the 'serious' autobiographer and his or her audience from
association with 'inferior' or 'improper' productions, where the legal
system *fails* to do so. For example, an authorised ghost-written
autobiography would violate Bruss's generic laws on a number of
counts but, unlike the Hughes instance, would not violate legalities.
Bruss does not mention such acclaimed co-productions, or 'allo-
autobiographies', as Jung's *Memories, Dreams, Reflections* or *The Autobiography of Malcolm X*.

Autobiographical space

Lejeune's researches reveal that recent 'scandals' in France over
ghost-written and 'collaborative' autobiographies raise familiar
anxieties. He notes of the collaborative autobiography:

> It is not the inauthenticity of these books that people condemn, but the
> fact that they let the cat out of the bag. They cast suspicion, no doubt
> legitimately so, on the rest of the literature. On a certain number of
> points, autobiography by people who do not write throws light on auto-
> biography written by those who do: the imitation reveals the secrets of
> fabrication and functioning of the 'natural' product. . . . The division of
> labour between two people (at least) reveals the multiplicity of authorities
> implied in the work of autobiographical writing, as in all writing. [p. 186]

The role more properly played by autobiography in the system of the author and authorship is to confirm the status of the author: 'what the public consumes is the personal form of a discourse assumed by a real person, responsible for his writing as he is for his life' [p. 194].

Autobiographies and biographies have played a key role in 'organising' the literary system and maintaining the value attached to the category of the literary and to authorship. In an article on the Enlightenment's invention of a 'public image' for its writers, Jean-Claude Bonnet looks at the ways in which the 'phantasm of the writer', created in the imaginary or fictional space of the identification between writer and reader, has produced an institutionalisation of 'biographical space',[71] in which such identifications become a neces-sary complement to 'literary space'. This process of institu-tionalisation is illustrated in examples of a reader becoming witness to a writer's life: Boswell's biography of Johnson, Eckermann's conver-sations with Goethe. These 'executive' figures become, in Kamuf's words, 'the posthumous guardian(s) of the great writer's public image' [p. 108]. In a different context, biographies, autobiographies and memoirs, contemporary and retrospective, have been crucial in 'orchestrating' literary or artistic groupings, such as the Pre-Raphaelites and the Bloomsbury Group, confirming the individual identity, or indeed 'genius', of the writer or artist while consolidating an image of group identity.

We have seen, primarily in the example of Wordsworth, how nineteenth-century writers negotiated the fine but all-important line between the pursuit of literature as a trade and as a profession. Autobiography played a central role in this structure by identifying the public self with private experience. Many of the most popular and 'enduring' autobiographical texts serve to endorse conventional (post-Romantic) images of 'the literary' and 'the literary life'. Gosse's *Father and Son*, for example, represents the literary life as a vocation rather than a profession; the development of the self is made identical with Gosse's rejection both of the science and the religion of his father in favour of literary culture. In a number of episodes through-out the text, Gosse portrays the expansion of his world through literary influences and his perceptions of a secular Sublime. A com-mon theme in 'literary' autobiography is the divide between science and literature: the 'literary' autobiography has tended to represent the 'literary life' as natural rather than cultural, defined by opposition to the 'cold' world of fact and science which is portrayed as a threat to the natural poet, at least up to the point where the knowledge of his true vocation bursts upon him.

More generally, we see, in the autobiographies of writers in particular, that the autobiography contains various and, at times, competing definitions of 'literature'. The autobiography becomes a way of defining what literature is or should be and charting the course of the writer's relationship to the literary – as, for example, in André Gide's or Jean-Paul Sartre's autobiographical accounts of their childhood reading, the literary taste of the older generation and their own, earlier, misconceptions about literature, or in Anthony Trollope's representations of the writer as artisan. Autobiographical, authorial and literary spaces exist in complex interdependence with each other. The autobiography may also function to redefine the generic spaces of the literary. In his 'anti-autobiography', *Roland Barthes by Roland Barthes*, Barthes repudiates the life-as-biography and refuses to be a party to the autobiographical pact: 'It must all be considered as if spoken by a character in a novel' are the words that appear, in handwriting, on the page between the title-page and 'the body of the text', the 'signed' authorial directive (we assume) at odds with the fictional pact. In Barthes's autobiography, as in his theoretical work, 'literature' becomes 'writing', and 'to write' is presented as an intransitive verb: 'His place (his *milieu*) is language: that is where he accepts or rejects, that is where his body *can* or *cannot*.'[72]

One of the most important aspects of women's biographical and autobiographical productions is what they reveal of women's relationship to the sphere of the literary and to literary culture. Critics such as Mary Jean Corbett have explored women's autobiographical expressions of the conflict between femininity and literary work, conflicts which have clearly changed from the nineteenth century, which forms the focus of her study, to the present. The autobiographies of women writers may be continuous with their other writings, reinforcing their professional status, or they may be used to construct an image of the self in the private sphere: Mrs Oliphant, for example, wrote in and of her autobiography 'I need scarcely say that there was not much of what one might call a literary life in all this.'[73] In the twentieth century, and at the other extreme, Simone de Beauvoir used the five volumes of her autobiography to describe the making of the woman intellectual – every aspect of her experience contributes to this end. In other words, how and when does the woman writer become the Woman Writer?[74] There is still further work to be done on the ways in which women have used autobiographies to define, negotiate or contest their 'professional' identities as authors.

There are also, as I suggested at the opening of this chapter, important distinctions, as well as correlations, to be drawn between autobiographical and literary space. The autobiographies of many twentieth-century women writers, for example, have been overlooked or diminished, even by feminist critics, because they are not primarily concerned with literary culture, or are incommensurate with cultural images of the writer, or fail to exhibit the required degree of literary self-consciousness. There is immense scope for exploration of the ways in which women, and other marginalised groups, have used autobiographical writings as a way of writing histories that would otherwise be omitted from the records. In my next and final chapter I take up some of these issues in a discussion of new and alternative spaces in and for autobiography.

Notes

1 Jonathan Loesberg, 'Autobiography as Genre, Act of Consciousness, Text', *Prose Studies*, 4, 2 (Sept. 1981), 171.

2 Sidonie Smith, *A Poetics of Women's Autobiography: Marginality and the Fictions of Self-Representation* (Bloomington: Indiana University Press, 1987).

3 Linda Peterson gives an interesting account of the ways women were perceived as incapable of sustained and synthesising thought, and by extension autobiography, in 'Gender and Autobiographical Form: The Case of the Spiritual Autobiography', in *Studies in Autobiography*, ed. James Olney (New York and Oxford: Oxford University Press, 1988), pp. 211–12.

4 Nancy K. Miller, 'Women's Autobiography in France: For a Dialectics of Identification', in *Women and Language in Literature and Society*, ed. S. McConnell-Ginet, R. Borker, and N. Furman (New York: Praeger, 1980), p. 267. See also 'Changing the Subject: Authorship, Writing and the Reader', in *Feminist Studies/Critical Studies*, ed. Teresa de Lauretis (London: Macmillan, 1988).

5 Philippe Lejeune, 'Autobiography and Social History', in *On Autobiography*, ed. Paul John Eakin, trans. Katharine Leary (Minneapolis: University of Minnesota Press, 1989), p. 168.

6 Fredric Jameson, *The Political Unconscious* (Ithaca: Cornell University Press, 1981), p. 106, and Tzvetan Todorov, 'The Origin of Genres', *New Literary History* 8, 1 (autumn 1976), 163.

7 William L. Howarth, 'Some Principles of Autobiography', in *Autobiography: Essays Theoretical and Critical*, ed. James Olney (Princeton University Press, 1980), pp. 84–115.

8 William C. Spengemann, *The Forms of Autobiography: Episodes in the History of a Literary Genre* (New Haven: Yale University Press, 1980).

9 Wallace Martin, *Recent Theories of Narrative* (Ithaca: Cornell University Press, 1986). See pp. 31–9.

10 Robert Kellogg and Robert Scholes, *The Nature of Narrative* (New York: Oxford University Press, 1966), p. 73.

11 This is a central aspect of auto/biographical discourse which I have not been able to address in this book. For recent work on confession, primarily from Foucauldian perspectives, see Jeremy Tambling, *Confession: Sexuality, Sin, the Subject* (Manchester University Press, 1990); Dennis A. Foster, *Confession and Complicity in Narrative* (Cambridge University Press, 1987); Terence Doody, *Confession and Community in the Novel* (Baton Rouge and London: Louisiana University Press, 1980).

12 Susannah Egan, *Patterns of Experience in Autobiography* (Chapel Hill: University of North Carolina Press, 1984).

13 Wayne Shumaker, *English Autobiography: Its Emergence, Materials and Forms* (Berkeley and Los Angeles: University of California Press, 1954).

14 See William Warner, 'Realist Literary History: McKeon's New Origins of the Novel', *Diacritics* 19, 1, (Spring 1989), 65.

15 See Martin, *Recent Theories of Narrative*, pp. 42, 50.

16 Louis A. Renza, 'The Veto of the Imagination: A Theory of Autobiographical Form', in *Autobiography*, ed. James Olney, pp. 268–95.

17 See Todorov, 'The Origin of Genres', 169.

18 Barbara Herrnstein Smith, *On the Margins of Discourse* (Chicago University Press, 1979), quoted in Jonathan Culler, *Framing the Sign: Criticism and its Institutions* (Oxford: Blackwell, 1988, pp. 207–8).

19 Gérard Genette, *Figures 3* (Paris: Seuil, 1972), p.50.

20 See Tzvetan Todorov, *The Fantastic: A Structural Approach to a Literary Genre*, trans. Richard Howard (Cornell University Press, 1975).

21 Jonathan Culler, *The Pursuit of Signs* (London: Routledge and Kegan Paul, 1981), p. 59.

22 Of course, Philippe Lejeune's theories of the 'autobiographical pact', and his claim that he is considering autobiography from the point of view of readerly recognition, are to a significant extent reader-oriented. Feminist critics have also produced important work on female authorship and the reception of women's texts; see for example, Nancy K. Miller's work on autobiography and authorship.

23 Loesberg, 'Autobiography as Genre', p. 182.

24 Jennifer Uglow, 'Publicizing the Private', *Times Literary Supplement*, (17 October, 1980), 1166.

25 Michael Sheringham, *French Autobiography: Devices and Desires* (Oxford: Clarendon Press, 1993), pp. 13–14.

26 Jean Marc Blanchard, 'Of Cannibalism and Autobiography', *Modern Language Notes* 93 (1978), 668.

27 Paul John Eakin, *Fictions in Autobiography: Studies in the Art of Self-Invention* (Princeton University Press, 1985), p. 3.

28 Paul John Eakin, *Touching the World: Reference in Autobiography* (Princeton University Press, 1992), *passim*.

29 Eakin, *Fictions*, p. 134. See Louis O. Mink, 'History and Fiction as Modes of Comprehension', *New Literary History* 1 (1969–70), and Hayden White,

Tropics of Discourse: Essays in Cultural Criticism (Johns Hopkins University Press, 1978) and *The Content of the Form: Narrative Discourse and Historical Representation* (Johns Hopkins University Press, 1987).

30 White, *Tropics of Discourse*, p. 82.

31 Brooks, *Reading for the Plot: Design and Intention in Narrative* (Oxford: Clarendon Press, 1984), p. 277.

32 Culler, *Framing the Sign*, p. 203.

33 See Frank Kermode, *The Sense of an Ending* (New York: Oxford University Press, 1967).

34 Jay Bernstein, 'Self-Knowledge as Praxis: Narrative and Narration in Psychoanalysis', in *Narrative in Culture*, ed. Cristopher Nash (London: Routledge 1980), pp. 51–80.

35 Michael Sheringham, *French Autobiography: Devices and Desires* (Oxford: Clarendon Press, 1993), p. 23 and *passim*. See also the three volumes of Paul Ricoeur's *Temps et récit* (1983–86), trans. by K. McLaughlin and D. Pellauer as *Time and Narrative*, 3 vols. (University of Chicago Press, 1984–87).

36 Raymond Williams, *Marxism and Literature* (Oxford University Press, 1977), pp. 146–9.

37 Jacques Derrida, *The Ear of the Other* (Lincoln and London: University of Nebraska Press, 1988), p. 14.

38 Derrida, 'The Law of Genre', in *On Narrative*, ed. W. J. T. Mitchell (University of Chicago Press, 1981).

39 Genette, quoted by Derrida, in *ibid.*, p. 59.

40 Olney, *Autobiography*, p. 25.

41 See Chapter 2, n. 29 above.

42 Leah D. Hewitt, *Autobiographical Tightropes* (Lincoln: University of Nebraska Press, 1990).

43 Sidonie Smith, *Subjectivity, Identity and the Body* (Indiana University Press, 1993), esp. chs. 1 and 7.

44 Judith Butler, *Gender Trouble: Feminism and the Subversion of Identity* (New York and London: Routledge, 1990), p. 134.

45 Philippe Lejeune, 'The Autobiographical Pact', in *On Autobiography*, ed. John Paul Eakin, p. 4.

46 *Ibid.* p. 11; translation substantially modified.

47 *Ibid.* pp. 13–14; translation substantially modified.

48 See n. 34 to Ch. 5.

49 Michel de Certeau, *Heterologies: Discourse on the Other* (Minneapolis: University of Minnesota Press, 1986), p. 32.

50 Roland Barthes, 'The Death of the Author' in *Image, Music, Text*, ed. and trans. Stephen Heath (London: Fontana, 1977).

51 Michel Foucault, 'What is an Author?', in *Language, Counter-Memory, Practice* (Oxford: Blackwell, 1977), p. 52.

52 John Searle, 'Proper Names', in *Speech Acts* (Cambridge University Press, 1969), pp. 163–74.

53 Philippe Lejeune, 'Autobiography of Those who do not Write', in *On Autobiography*, ed. Paul John Eakin, p. 194.

54 *Ibid.* p. 187.

55 Susan Stewart, *Crimes of Writing* (Oxford University Press, 1990), pp. 3–4.

56 Warner, 'Realist Literary History', p. 67.
57 Quoted by Philip Stewart, *Imitation and Illusion in the French Memoir Novel 1700–1750: The Art of Make-Believe* (New Haven and London: Yale University Press, 1969), pp. 15/16.
58 Quoted by Stewart, *Imitation and Illusion*, p. 235.
59 Geoffrey Bennington, *Dudding. Des noms de Rousseau* (Paris: Galilée, 1991), p. 109.
60 Peggy Kamuf, *Signature Pieces: On the Institution of Authorship* (Ithaca: Cornell University Press, 1988), p. 26.
61 Bennington, *Dudding*, pp. 100–2.
62 *Rousseau judge of Jean-Jacques: dialogues* in *The Collected Writings of Rousseau: Vol. 1*, ed. R. D. Masters and C. Kelly (Hanover, NH: University Press of New England, 1990), p. 6.
63 Kamuf, *Signature Pieces*, p. 102.
64 Georg Misch, *A History of Autobiography in Antiquity*, trans. E. W. Dickes, 2 vols. (London: Routledge and Kegan Paul, 1950), vol. 1, pp. 10–11.
65 Anna Robeson Burr, *The Autobiography: A Critical and Comparative Study* (Boston: Houghton Mifflin, 1909), pp. 19–20.
66 Jean Starobinski, in Olney, *Autobiography*, pp. 73–4.
67 A. Q. Morton, *Literary Detection* (Bowker Publishing Co., 1978), p. 7.
68 David Erdman and E. G. Fogel, *Evidence for Authorship* (Ithaca: Cornell University Press, 1966), p. 47.
69 Elizabeth W. Bruss, *Autobiographical Acts: The Changing Situation of a Literary Genre* (Baltimore and London: Johns Hopkins University Press, 1976).
70 John Searle, 'The Logical Status of Fictional Discourse', *New Literary History*, 6, 2 (1975).
71 Jean-Claude Bonnet, 'Le Fantasme de l'écrivain', in *Poétique* 63 (Sept. 1985).
72 Roland Barthes, *Roland Barthes by Roland Barthes*, trans. Richard Howard (London: Macmillan, 1977), p. 53.
73 Margaret Oliphant, *The Autobiography and Letters of Margaret Oliphant: The Complete Text*, ed. Elisabeth Jay (Oxford University Press, 1990).
74 I owe this formulation to Carol Watts, who uses it in 'Releasing Possibility into Form: Cultural Choice and the Woman Writer', in *New Feminist Discourses*, ed. Isobel Armstrong (London: Routledge, 1992), p. 89.

7

Auto/biographical spaces

My final chapter broadens out from a predominantly literary critical and theoretical focus to a consideration of some of the new directions taken in auto/biographical theory, and in life-writings more generally. Throughout this book, we have seen that the autonomy and the separateness of autobiography as a category and a genre have been in large part maintained by a denial of its relationship to other forms, historical and literary. In the last decade or so, generic and disciplinary borders and boundaries have started to break down. The most interesting auto/biographical theory and practice are being written across traditional conceptual and disciplinary divides.

For example, critics have claimed for many years that autobiography could only be recognised for the important area that it is by being sharply demarcated from biography. The Victorians were castigated for their critical *naïveté* in defining autobiography as a sub-genre of biography. The debates around the 'new biography' in the early part of the century, which linked biography and autobiography, were largely forgotten, or presented as obsolete. In a critical and theoretical milieu where the self and its cognates – self-reflection, self-consciousness, self-alienation – were all-important, biography seemed to be largely irrelevant, as if reflection on another life (and the terminology is that of the 'father' of auto-biographical studies, Wilhelm Dilthey) could have nothing to say about subjectivity or the representation of a life in writing. Very recently – and the impetus has come primarily from feminist critics – the inadequacy of this conceptual divide has been clearly revealed and far more exciting conjunctures occur, showing how auto-biography and biography function together. Recounting one's own life almost inevitably entails writing the life of an other or others; writing the life of another must surely entail the biographer's identifications with his or her subject, whether these are made explicit or not.

Another important development is the growing affinity between auto/biography and oral history. Perhaps the most important impetus here has been from the study of working-class autobiographies, based partly on existing texts such as those documented in Britain, in *The Autobiography of the Working Class* (1984–),[1] and partly on projects to elicit and publish new works, such as those of the groups who came together in 1976 to form The Federation of Worker Writers and Community Publishers; these deliberately brought autobiography, seen in large part as a collaborative enterprise, up to the limits of oral history. Paul Thompson's *The Voice of the Past* (2nd edition 1988)[2] is one of the most important contributions to this field and to the integration of oral history and life stories into the study of history.

Theorists such as Jerome Bruner have emphasised the textual and narrative dimensions of oral history and other forms of oral discourse, while work on testimonial literature, cultural memory, and related genres has attenuated the hard and fast distinctions between oral and written forms which have predominated in recent decades. Bruner, for example, in his work with Susan Weisser, gives one of the most convincing analyses of oral and life histories in 'The Invention of Self: Autobiography and its Forms'.[3] Arguing that 'through auto-biography we locate ourselves in the symbolic world of culture', the authors assert that the textual status of life-accounting depends upon acts of conceptualisation rather than acts of speaking and writing alone: 'it is the form or genre of the reflexive act involved in self-consciousness that matters not the nature of the printout that ensues from it'. A crucial aspect is that of the 'family genre', and Bruner and Weisser produce a consensus model of life-narration: 'we early on learn how to invent our lives for the sheer necessity of getting on in the family.' Discussing the oral narratives produced by members of a particular family-group, Bruner and Weisser give the example of one self-accounting theme in the family's culture – the distinction between 'real world' and 'home': 'it is not just the theme but the language that locks them to the distinction. Their autobiographical accounts are drenched with metaphors of space and location, with locatives and spatial deictics ... each [family member] enters a communal genre of autobiography' (pp. 144–5]. Bruner and Weisser's work is an extension of genre and narrative theory into a dynamic and dialogic model of oral and life histories.

A dialogical conception of autobiography and identity is illustrated in two of the most innovative British autobiographies of the past decade. Ronald Fraser's *In Search of a Past*[4] and Carolyn Steedman's *Landscape for a Good Woman: A Study of Two Lives*,[5] are written at the intersections of biography and autobiography, case-history and social history, psychoanalysis and oral history. These texts use auto/biography to mediate, or perhaps to intertwine, theory and experience. Debate and discussion around these and other narratives have resulted in a sharper sense of the links between historical, psychoanalytic and literary representations – and of what is at stake in asserting their difference.

Fraser's autobiography was itself inspired by an earlier autobiographical project: Andre Gorz's *The Traitor* (1989).[6] Gorz's book stands out for its deployment of 'theory' (Marxist, psychoanalytic and existentialist) as a way of comprehending the self and its situation. Although at one level Gorz recounts the 'story' of his experiences – as the son of a Jewish father and a Catholic mother in anti-Semitic pre-war Austria and as an exile in Switzerland in his adolescence and early twenties – the narrative is partial and fragmented, and Gorz judges the value of his experience primarily in light of the question whether his 'condition' was 'subjectively' assumed or 'objectively' given.

Whereas Arthur Koestler, in his autobiography *Arrow in the Blue*,[7] argues that Freudian and Marxist theories were inadequate to explain the complexities of life, Gorz responds to any apparent mismatch between theory and experience with an ever more rigorous examination of his theoretical models. He does not simply assume that the theory is inadequate to explain the life – it might also be that the shape and meaning of the life, as he has represented it and narrated it to himself and/or to others, have been misconstrued. We should not, in any case, suppose that there is direct accord between the living of the life and the telling of it.

In this 'Sartrean' autobiography – for it is Jean-Paul Sartre's 'method' which is represented as the means of Gorz's salvation, and Sartre 'appears' in the text under the pseudonym 'Morel' – writing is said to be meaningful only in so far as it communicates and the self only becomes substantive when it recognises the existence of others. One of the most striking aspects of *The Traitor* is Gorz's use of pronominal forms to chart the move from alienation to a kind of self-affirmation. Gorz entitles the sections of the autobiography 'We', 'They', 'You' and 'I'. 'We', Gorz writes, 'consists for him in the ascetic accession of intellects to that abstract universality in which they can proliferate their theories and lose themselves in the anonymity of the generic' [p. 88]. 'They', the most narrativised part of the text, recounts those aspects of Gorz's childhood and adolescence in Austria and Switzerland 'relating to his exclusion from the world of men'. Gorz divides this section into 'Exclusion', 'Persecution' and 'The Impossible Nullity'. In 'You' (*toi*), he examines 'his reality as a person in relation to other persons', while the final section 'I', is not only written, at least in part, in the first person, but moves back to the 'beginning' of selfhood and forward to an intimation of a future.

The use of pronouns is further complicated by the shifting temporalities of the autobiography. *The Traitor*, in exemplary modernist fashion, reflects on the process of its own writing, though Gorz is perhaps less interested in linguistic self-reflexivity than in the problem of *Darstellung*, the representation of states of affairs. This issue is entwined with that of self-representation and the temporal perspective from which the autobiography is to be written. The autobiography's ostensible project – the move from an anonymous 'we' to a self-affirming 'I' – is not in fact invented, as a possible outcome of the book being written, until some way into the text. There is no sense of a secure standpoint from which the past can be recounted as something already known and complete, nor any obvious starting-point for the analysis. As in Freud's case-histories, the beginning, as a structure determining the shape of a life, is given a location, only to be undone as the analysis proceeds and pushed further and further back into the past, to the point where its real existence may even become unsustainable.

Gorz vindicates Sartre's 'progressive–regressive' method in presenting it as a means of his analytic (rather than psychoanalytic) cure. In the final section of *The Traitor*, Gorz analyses the ways in which his 'original complex' was confirmed by his 'original project' of 'nonidentification' [pp. 253–4]. Gorz's fundamental complex, he asserts, clarifies his other complexes; his insistence on changing languages from German to French, primarily 'in order to get rid of his mother tongue, a term whose meaning now explodes with all its force'; his taste for abstraction, also a foreign language; a tendency to 'irony' and 'treason' (the treason of the intellectual of the person constrained by roles to behave inauthentically, as in Sartre's claim in *Words* that 'I became a traitor and have remained one';[8] writing as a way of becoming anonymous and invisible. Once recognised, ' "the

complex of nonidentification" ... has drained like an abscess'
[p. 264] enabling him to 'hold on to life' instead of trying to escape
from it. The text thus enacts both analysis and cure.

The Traitor is still an important text, as a document of its time and
as an autobiography which breaks traditional moulds. Fraser's *In
Search of a Past* is a direct reworking of Gorz's autobiographical
project, keeping the framework of Marxist dialectics and
psychoanalysis as the two primary narrative and explanatory structures through which the self and history, the self and its history, are
explored and (incompletely) accounted for, but 'concretising' them in
specific contexts – the oral history interview and the psychoanalytic
session. Fraser interweaves accounts of his sessions with his analyst,
interviews with the servants on his parents' estate between 1933 and
1945, and conversations with his brother and his amnesiac father,
who has forgotten the past the son seeks to remember.

In Sartre's Foreword to *The Traitor*, dialogue is said to become
possible only when an authentic self can speak itself as a first person.
Fraser, in producing a version of Gorz's pronominal segmentings of
the text (We/They, She/He/It, You, We, Us/I) is also echoing
Gorz's representation of *The Traitor*'s movement toward authentic
identity and towards the possibilities of dialogue, with his putative
readers as well as the figures within the text. Gorz's narrative strategy
is to present the writing of *The Traitor* as the necessary condition for
the construction of an 'I'. By contrast, Fraser depicts the construction
of the 'I' as the condition for the writing of the autobiography.

In Fraser's foreword to *Blood of Spain*, his collection of oral
accounts of the Spanish Civil War, he describes the purposes of oral
history as the articulation of 'the subjective, a spectrum of the lived
experiences of people who participated in the events ... because of
the need to make a coherent totality, it may seem as though this book
is saying: this is "how it was". But no. This is how it is remembered as
having been.'[9] The selective and relative nature of historical truth
becomes more problematic in *In Search of a Past*, in which Fraser
requires oral history to serve a dual function. The servants he interviews are required to bear witness both to an historical past and to his
personal past. The failure, as Fraser perceives it, is that although the
oral historian can capture 'a part of reality', the self is denied its
meaning for itself. Fraser as oral historian brings his subjectivity into
the object of his study, but his 'witnesses', and history, refuse or are
unable to return an image of himself as subject. It is this image,

Fraser suggests, that this is to be sought through the processes of psychoanalysis.

The tension, and at times overlap, between historical and psychoanalytic explanation remains, however. When asked, in an interview given soon after the publication of the autobiography, how he envisaged the results of a successful search for a past, Fraser replied:

> A book that would have attempted to synthesize the social and the psychoanalytic. A book which would have been a finished object. A literary work instead of this desperate rummaging among the fractured objects of the past. A seamless totality; a work of art, in other words, dead before its birth.[10]

Much contemporary interest in autobiography – and the success of Fraser's and Carolyn Steedman's texts attests to this – is in the interrelation between theory and experience, the interplay of different voices, and the representation of the past as a complex and elusive terrain. Steedman[11] shares the concern with the relationship between the psychic and the social. The 'two lives' of the title are her own and her mother's, and the story is of a working-class childhood. She intertwines this story, and that of her mother, with broader historical and sociological interpretation, testing theory against experience, and experience against theory. But throughout her text there is also a conflict between the desire for autobiographical singularity, for a story which belongs only to the self, and the obligation of the social historian to produce an account which is representative. The autobiographical and the socio-historical project are in tension.

Distinctions between individualism and representativeness in autobiography have become central to discussion of oral histories and working-class life-writings. The Popular Memory Group differentiates between them in the following terms:

> Representativeness, moreover, is a feature of social positions that are understood to be shared and collective: the main feature of much autobiographical writing is to distinguish the author from the people and determinations that surround him. Such accounts belong not to the construction of 'popular memory' but to the reproduction and dissemination of 'dominant memory'.[12]

Steedman's autobiography exposes certain limitations in this position. In setting up the polarity between 'marginal' and 'dominant', rather than 'popular' and 'dominant' or, indeed, 'private' and public', she points up questions of power, control and exclusion as well as the issue of how the stories of lives lived on the margins are to be told at all, if the interpretative devices and narrative strategies of a culture are produced through dominant discourses. Her concern, she states, is with 'sad and secret stories', which are socially and historically determined, and yet are precisely not 'understood' to be shared and collective: the effect of exclusion from dominant myths, narratives and interpretative strategies is isolation, not a benign collectivism.

Unlike Fraser, Steedman does not incorporate psychoanalysis as therapy into the text, nor its concomitant, the figure of the auto-biographer/analysand moving, via the analytic dialogue, towards the fullness of autobiographical/analytic identity. In opposition to this progressive model, she asserts that the text is structured on the formal model of the Freudian case-history, incorporating dreams, memories and structural loopings. The specific case-history to which she refers is Freud's 'Dora'; as her own case-historian, Steedman borrows Freud's account of the fragmentary nature of the 'Dora' case history for her own narrative. The gaps and inconsistencies which Freud attempted to elide into a coherent narrative become for Steedman the necessary mode of articulation for lives lived on the social margins.

Steedman continues to explore the complex relationships between history-writing and auto/biography: like Julia Swindells, Regenia Gagnier and others, she is also constructing a history, or histories, of subjectivities, focusing, in her writings, on the significance of 'child-hood' as a post-Enlightenment concept and on the meanings and values attached to 'interiority', again closely related to the figure of the child, who comes to embody interior being, the self within. Redefining 'historical consciousness', Steedman has made class and gender questions central to auto/biographical study: she has also substantially contributed to a new interdisciplinary nexus which includes autobiography, biography, history and literature.

Feminism and autobiography

Autobiography has, as we have seen, played a central role in feminist thought, in articulating conceptions of subjectivity and of the relationship between individual and collective identity. The 'confessional' text of autobiographical self-revelation was a dominant form in the 1970s, with major feminist theorists such as Kate Millett redefining the autobiographical form in narratives which combined the close record of daily life with the thematics of feminist liberation and self-discovery. Texts such as Kate Millett's *Flying* (1974)[13] and *Sita* (1977)[14] retain an aspiration, in Rita Felski's words, to uncover 'an underlying buried self ',[15] although the anxious need to produce more and yet more narrative suggests that confession is indeed endless and that the 'self' cannot ever catch up with itself in autobiographical representation. Millett, one of whose heroines is Doris Lessing, whose *The Golden Notebook* she emulates, includes within her texts commentary on the efficacy of her journal project as a means of recording 'reality'. In *Sita* she writes, of her record of a love affair with another woman: 'And this whole notebook's unfair probably. And inaccurate. Too close, too intimate. It should be described as an experiment in charting and recording a relationship. Day to day. No one's ever done that' [p. 250].

Millett's has been criticised as an overly self-centred project. Other texts of feminist confession, such as Ann Oakley's *Taking it Like a Woman*[16] and Sheila McLeod's *The Art of Starvation*,[17] alternate the 'personal' with theoretical explanation or speculation, placing individual experience in the broader context of women's lives and experiences. One form taken by this combination of the individual story and the collective experience is the use of fiction within the autobiographical text. As Felski and others have noted, women autobiographers subvert the 'autobiographical pact' by including problematic or ambiguous signals which trouble rather than confirm the distinction between autobiography and fiction, or by making the 'proper name' ambiguous. Ann Oakley, for example, opens her autobiography with these words: 'Some of the characters in this book are real and some aren't.' The 'fictional' can become the space for more general identifications, or for the trying-out of potentialities and possibilities – what might have been, what could have been, what might yet be – or it can be a way of suggesting how much fiction is involved in all self-representations.

In various anthologies – for example, *Let it Be Told* (in which Black British-based writers discuss their experiences and their writing),[18] *Truth, Dare or Promise: Girls Growing up in the Fifties*[19] and *Fathers: Reflections by Daughters*[20] – the form gives a 'group' identity to the individual histories recounted. The structures of fiction, fantasy, autobiography and experience are often played across and against each other. In 'Our Lance' (in *Fathers: Reflections by Daughters*) Sheila Rowbotham includes an account of a consciousness-raising group in which the topic was women's relationship to their fathers. Women's stories, their sense of their experiences, were circulated here in a space outside writing, though not outside narrative: a space constituted in part by the cultural, social and political history of a post-1960s feminism. Rowbotham's published piece is a part of this cultural exchange of stories. A number of the narratives in the theatre collective Sistren's *Lionheart Gal: Life Stories of Jamaican Women*[21] are transcripts of oral testimonies. The oral and the written support rather than oppose each other.

A further important development is the writing of 'relational' lives and group biographies of women, often within lesbian contexts: examples of this growing literature are Shari Benstock's *Women of the Left Bank*,[22] Suzanne Raitt's *Vita and Virginia*,[23] and Whitney Chadwick and Isabelle de Courtivron's collection of essays *Significant Others*.[24] This trend is an aspect of the new interest in biography, discussed by Liz Stanley in *The Auto/Biographical 'I'*. Stanley argues that

> a distinct feminist autobiography is in the process of construction, characterized by its self-conscious and increasingly self-confident traversing of conventional boundaries between different genres of writing ... a distinct feminist biography is less well developed because innovations in form are less easily accomplished here than in autobiography; and thus such innovations will centre a social focus, a contingent and engaged authorial voice, a thorough-going anti-realism and a focus upon textual practice, innovations which will encourage active reading.[25]

Most recent work in and on feminist autobiography and biography shares a focus on issues of identity, now seen less as something to be disinterred or captured and more as something to be made, cultural and gender hybridity, embodiment, and the transgression of generic and other boundaries. The pervasive hybridity attributed to auto-biography – as we have seen throughout the preceding discussions of nineteenth- and twentieth-century auto/biographical discourse – has made it a crucial site for the exploration of new identities. A more cautious note might be struck here, though. Genres can be defined, as we have seen, as enabling structures of recognition as well as systems of containment and limitation. Before we celebrate the bonfire of controls, we might wish to think further about the possibilities for transformation and innovation of certain of the structures we have inherited.

Personal criticism

I referred in Chapter 5 to the recent development in feminist theory of what has been called 'personal criticism', which, in Nancy K. Miller's account, has developed in part out of recent feminist interest in autobiography and a more general feminist concern with the personal. An autobiographical moment is made central to the activity of criticism, thus both foregrounding the identity of the critic and reconceptualising the nature of criticism itself; in Miller's words, it 'entails an explicitly autobiographical performance within the art of criticism. Indeed, getting personal in criticism typically involves a deliberate move toward self-figuration, although the degree and forms of self-disclosure of course vary widely.'[26] The value of such self-figuration is endorsed by Nicole Ward Jouve:

> criticism must take autobiography into account. Only by daring to make the observing subject part and parcel of what critical observation is about, can criticism sail towards a three-dimensional land. . . . Just as the writing of autobiography has been, for so many women, the road toward selfhood, so writing criticism as autobiography may be the way to a fuller, more relevant voice.[27]

Autobiographical texts are engaging directly with theoretical accounts of subjectivity and history, while criticism and theory are calling for a recognition of the subjectivity of the theorist.

The challenge by women of colour and ethnic minorities to the exclusions and universalisms of white feminisms seems to have led, particularly in North America, to a wariness of collectivist claims and claims to general representativity – what Nancy Miller calls the incantatory recital of the 'speaking as a's' and the imperialisms of 'speaking for's'. The 'speaking as a's' stem also, however, from an identity-politics which, while it challenges 'bourgeois self-representation', produces, in Miller's view, an equally problematic concept of representativity. She is troubled by the demand that we should speak in the name of the group or groups we are said to represent in terms of class, gender, colour, and so on. Auto-biographical discourse is thus closely linked to (or arises from) an anxiety about 'speaking for others' as well as the problems of repre-sentativity – an 'identity politics', in this view, may also subordinate the individual.

Personal criticism is also said to go along with an increasing suspicion of the 'impersonality' and 'objectivity' of theoretical discourse; this is viewed as a pseudo-objectivity, in that it conceals the first person and denies the 'situatedness' of the person theorising. This call for a recognition of the subjectivity of the theorist is of course not a new one – in both philosophy and literary criticism there seems to be a cycle whereby subjectivity and objectivity are invoked in turn to compensate for each other's shortcomings. The current climate, at least in Anglo-American criticism, appears to have moved strongly towards the subjective pole: 'I prefer the gossipy grain of situated writing to the scholarly sublime', writes Miller. The particularity of 'the autobiographical act – however self-fictional' resists 'the grandiosity of abstraction that inhibits what I've been calling the crisis of representativity'[28]. Autobiographical or 'personal' criticism – like the study of autobiography – 'has in part to do', Nancy Miller writes, 'with the gradual and perhaps inevitable waning of enthusiasm for a mode of Theory whose authority – however variously – depended finally on the theoretical evacuation of the very social subjects producing it'.[29] This of course relates to the broader issue of whether or not deconstruction hindered the attempts of feminist thinkers to construct new identities. Personal criticism is in part an expression of the sense that, as Nicole Ward Jouve puts it, 'you must have a self before you can afford to deconstruct it' – though she adds that 'it is no easier to say "I" than to make theory'.[30]

Two primary emphases emerge in discussions of 'personal criticism': firstly, metaphors of the dramatic and the corporeal, and secondly, representations of 'conversation' and dialogue. Extensively and wittily employing the former, Miller writes that: 'the autobiographical act – however self-fictional – can, like the detail of one's (aging) body, produce this sense of limit as well: the resistance particularity offers to the grandiosity of abstraction.[31] Some of the emphasis on writing as a process also recalls earlier emphases, in *écriture féminine*, on women's writing as subversion, and it is undoubtedly important that women bring the personal into places in which it is constituted as inappropriate. The attempt to erase the gap between 'body' and 'writing' in 'personal criticism', in part through versions of the performance utterance, may also be, however, a more anxious gesture – a claim to an 'authenticity' which is linked to the forms of identity-claim or identity-crisis. The 'performative' (I am using the term loosely for the moment) becomes both an 'embodiment', a speaking-out of selfhood, and an enactment of 'situation' and 'position' which exploits the spatial and substantive metaphors of political affiliation ('This is where I stand on this issue'), while insisting upon the singularity of the self or body occupying a particular space.

In her recent book *Gender Trouble*, Judith Butler asserts that 'parody' – 'the parodic repetition of gender' – is the means by and through which the constructed nature of gender identity will be revealed and opened to subversive intent: 'I describe and propose a set of parodic practices based in a performative theory of gender acts that disrupt the categories of the body, sex, gender and sexuality and occasion their subversive resignification and proliferation beyond the binary frame'[32] – and beyond the limiting and coercive frame of compulsory heterosexuality.

Substantially working in a Foucauldian framework and critiquing the 'foundationalist reasoning of identity politics' [p. 142], Butler argues for a shift from a grammar of identity (which privileges being) to an account of 'doing gender' as a performative enactment. Here the concept of the performative appears to cover two different senses. Firstly, it exists in Butler's account as a form of ideological mystification in which 'doing' serves to confirm or compel gender as 'being' – identity is performatively constituted. 'The notion of sex as substance', Butler writes, is achieved 'through a performative twist of language and/or discourse that conceals the fact that "being" a sex or a gender is fundamentally impossible.' 'Gender is an enactment that performatively constitutes the appearance of its own interior fixity' [p. 21]. Secondly, the 'performative' and 'the performance' seem to become synonymous, or at least closely related, terms, and are discussed as radical ways of revealing the multiple constructions of gender identity and of opening up to 'the parodic proliferation and subversive play of gendered meanings'. Repeated references throughout the text to drag-acts and cross-dressing reinforce the image of the theatricality of gender, of the performance aspects of the performative, and of the corporeal basis of gender acts: 'Just as bodily surfaces are enacted as the natural, so these surfaces can become the site of a dissonant and denaturalized performance that reveals the performative status of the natural itself ' [p. 146]. The radical play of the performative is pitted against the essentialism of an identity-politics.

I now want to move to the second of the two related concerns in 'personal criticism' noted earlier – conversation, dialogue, and, more generally, 'linguistic subjectivity'. Nancy Miller writes:

> It was clear that feminist theory had arrived at a crisis in language, a crisis
> notably inseparable from the pronouns of subjectivity: between the
> indictment of the feminist universal as a white fiction brought by women
> of color and the poststructuralist suspicion of a grounded subject, what
> are the conditions under which as feminists one (not to say 'I') can say
> 'we'?[33]

The defensive note struck here points to an important factor in the
origins of personal criticism. Miller appears to be saying that this
crisis has in part been brought about by 'women of color' outlawing
the 'we'; a more adequate analysis would be one that recognised the
need for white as well as black feminists to address the problems of
homogenisation and universalism.

The concern with 'the pronouns of subjectivity' described by
Miller has become increasingly widespread in feminist and other
theory. In a recent discussion at the Institute of Contemporary Arts in
London, the American critic, Mary Ann Caws, the most impassioned
proponent of 'personal criticism', asked the question 'how will pronouns represent us?', and unlike Miller, is unambivalent about the
need to reclaim the collective pronoun: 'the saying of "we" is under
siege', she asserted, adding that 'I' and 'we'-saying allow us to
alternate between the individual and the collective. In Caws's rather
idealised model of reading, as in her recent book *Women of
Bloomsbury*, criticism becomes a conversation:

> It is around such an experiential generosity of community that characters
> in and out of the text may find themselves grouped, reading together,
> seeing together. Such criticism is the deliberate opposite of a cool science
> but is not in disregard of fact; it is composed of an unshakeable belief in
> involvement and in coherence, in warmth and in relation.[34]

Cynically, one might suggest that Caws is establishing the community, the 'we', in a safe place, answering the problems raised by
other groups about the constituents of the 'we' by proposing a
dialogue between (possibly) dead authors, fictional characters, personal critics and putative readers seen as critical companions and
sharers of the same values. With less scepticism, Caws's position can
be allied to Tania Modleski's persuasive claim that 'feminism can
only evolve through a process of dialogue ... symbolic exchange
between the critic and the women to whom she talks and writes'.[35]

Luce Irigaray's emphasis on the project of revealing 'who is
speaking, to whom, about what, with what means', in order to discover the subject and its relations with the other and the world seems

to have strong links with the preoccupations of personal criticism. It may be relevant in this context to note her *anti*-autobiographical stance. 'The transformation of the autobiographical "I" into another cultural "I" seems to be necessary if we are to establish a new ethics of sexual difference.'[36] Privileging the fictional, the fabular and the imaginary, Irigaray contrasts these with the autobiographical, which for her seems to be opposed to the innovation and transformation of ethics and aesthetics. I would argue that autobiography can and does partake of, in Irigaray's terms, the structures of the imaginary. I am interested, however, in the concept of the non-autobiographical 'I', the subject unencumbered by her story or history, a concept which is also current in personal criticism. Mary Ann Caws, for example, while not sharing Irigaray's suspicions of the autobiographical or biographical, describes personal criticism as characterised by 'a certain intensity in the lending of oneself to the act of writing', but argues that this 'participation in the subject seen and written about doesn't necessarily require autobiographical self-representation'.[37] In other words, the critic's self-situating need not be accompanied by a confessional act.

What is the status of this 'I' which is 'personal' and 'situated' yet not 'autobiographical'? 'Can we imagine', Nancy Miller asks, 'a self-representational practice – for feminism – that is not recontained by the preconstituted tropes of representativity?'[38] In this context, I would want to distinguish between the categories of 'speaking as a' and speaking for a' – given that 'speaking as a' is surely part of a model of situated knowledge which is invoked by most feminist critics. Furthermore, the distinctions Caws and others wish to make between the autobiographical, the confessional, the personal, the narrational, and so on, are not always clear-cut ones, nor is it always obvious where positional statement turns into autobiography.

The concept of the non-narrated but situated self was proposed in Domna Stanton's study of autobiography *The Female Autograph*, in which she removes the life, the 'bios', from autobiography in order to resolve or evade the apparently unresolvable problem of referentiality in the autobiographical text – in her words, 'to bracket the traditional emphasis on the narration of a 'life' and that notion's facile presumption of referentiality'.[39] In fact, this strategy seems closer to the current concern with the self who seeks to mark her presence but not necessarily to recount her history.

Aspects of this discussion need to be understood in relation to the concerns of feminist epistemology, one of the major currents in contemporary feminist thought, closely tied to debates around identity politics and situated knowledge. As Liz Stanley has noted, however, 'the links between feminist auto/biography and feminist epistemology remain under-discussed'.[40] Stanley argues for a concept of 'intellectual autobiography', by which she means that the feminist researcher should record the context-dependent aspects of her approaches and understanding: 'all knowledge is auto-biographically-located in a particular social context of experiencing and knowing', she states, while 'all autobiographies are theoretical formulations through and through' [p. 210]. While endorsing Stanley's assertion of the need for 'accountable knowledge', I would want to question her claim that feminist academics should 'reject the subjective/objective dichotomy, recognising instead that "objectivity" is a set of practices designed to deny the actual "subjective" location of all intellectual work' [p. 208]. Even if the positions from which we understand the world are necessarily 'subjective', can we not talk meaningfully about subjective perspectives on an objectively given world? The kinds of determinations which govern our knowledge are not always as readily known and available as Stanley suggests; knowledges, like identities, are complex, multiply given and, to use a well-worn phrase, 'overdetermined'. Sandra Harding has argued, in her important work on 'feminist standpoint theory', that we need more objectivity rather than less, a broader notion of objectivity grounded in but not confined to the positions of the marginalised. These are not necessarily, nor indeed usually, those of the theorists themselves.[41]

One major link between the disparate forms of discourse I have examined would seem to be the concept of the performative. The shared focus on the performative suggests certain common tendencies in the cultural field: the valorisation of personal histories, a stress on the positional, a certain anti-theoreticism, a sense of the importance of 'speaking out' as a way of authorising identity while at the same time identity is said to be performatively constituted rather than pre-discursive. Yet the performative is defined in a variety of ways: as experience/action opposed to theory; as de-authorising play and performance; as authenticating identity and positionality; as deceit, duplicity and self-referentiality; as an ethical discourse of commitment; as testimony. The radically different accounts of the performative invoked indicate the diversity, and perhaps incommensurability, of the conceptual approaches and intellectual or political contexts in which they arise. What counts (or should count) is not only that a story or a history is being recounted, nor even how it is told, but its varying content, contexts and import.

Autobiography and ethnicity

The United States is an obvious starting-point for any discussion of the complex relations between autobiography and ethnicity. Alongside the neo-Romantic emphases of an 'autobiographical studies' which affirmed a 'universal' consciousness, in fact based on European traditions of individualism and mythologies of subjectivity, a more grounded cultural and historical approach to autobiography developed in the field of American Studies. It has been argued that the Puritan tradition, combined with the isolation of the frontier and the need to create a new national identity, was particularly conducive to autobiographical writing. Although some of this analysis repeats familiar themes of self-consciousness and self-representation, and perhaps more alarmingly, the colonial myth of a virgin land, it has at least been open to questions of culture and identity raised by the ethnic diversity of the country itself.

The nineteenth-century slave narratives which were a crucial resource for white abolitionists and which were subsequently claimed to constitute 'the most uniquely American' autobiographical writing, 'created *sui generis* by the conditions of a racially and politically divided country', have more recently been taken up in a broader history of Black American resistance and its individual and collective expression in life-writing. Questions of authorship and authority, discussed in a general way in the previous chapter, arise with a special force in the case of slave narratives published under pseudonyms and/or with extensive editorial framing by white sponsors. For example, the first edition of Harriet Jacobs's *Incidents in the Life of a Slave Girl* (1861)[42] listed the editor but not the author and presented a pseudonymous narrator, Linda Brent. Anonymity was thought necessary to protect friends and relations still enslaved. Jacobs, whose identity was confirmed by Jean Fagin Yellin in the 1980s, wrote:

> Reader, be assured this narrative is no fiction. I am aware that some of my adventures may seem incredible; but they are, nevertheless, strictly true. . . . I have concealed the names of places and given persons fictitious

names. I have no motive for secrecy on my own account, but I deemed it kind and considerate towards others to pursue this course.[43]

Clearly, *pace* Lejeune, the autobiographical pact can coexist with anonymity, and there is a complex politics to these acts of framing and disclosure. The irony is that works rendered acceptable in the first instance by editorial appropriation were subsequently discounted as autobiographies for the very same reason. As Gwendolyn Etter-Lewis writes, in her study of oral narratives:

> most early autobiographies of African American women can be found in this gray area, this middle ground between subject (autobiography) and object (biography). These women arrived at autobiography through a mongrel form – the slave narrative, many of which were 'as told to' or ghost-written accounts. Dismissal of these texts because of their collaborative authorship would have permanently lost to obscurity crucial aspects of American history and culture.[44]

Beyond the obvious historical importance of these texts, their hybridity in fact anticipates the general opening-up of generic boundaries in recent years and a particular interest in the relationship between biography and autobiography, and auto/biography and ethnography.

Two major issues in discussions of black autobiography are, firstly, group or collective identity and secondly, authenticity and masquerade. African American life-writing has been seen by many critics as articulating a strong sense of community. In Stephen Butterfield's influential formulation, individual identity also involves 'ties and responsibilities' to the community;[45] much of this writing takes place against the background of political and social struggle in which group identity is sustained in part through writing. There is also a gender dimension here – Nellie McKay writes that women who escape from slavery stress family ties and support from both black and white women to a greater extent than men. After the Civil War, she suggests, 'the rhetoric of black men's and women's narratives moved closer together' as they were united by shared political goals. More recently, the politics of black autobiographical writing have become more diverse – although it retains its group identifications. For black women autobiographers, of course, engagement with feminism is often central.

Strong claims for the importance of autobiography for black women are made by bell hooks:

Though autobiography or any type of confessional narrative is often devalued in North American letters, this genre has always had a privileged place in African American literary history. As a literature of resistance, confessional narratives by black folks were didactic. More than any other genre of writing, the production of honest confessional narratives by black women who are struggling to be self-actualized and to become radical subjects are needed as guides, as texts which affirm our fellowship with one another. . . . Even as the number of novels by black women increase this writing cannot be either a substitute for theory or for autobiographical narrative. Radical black women need to tell our stories; we cannot document our experience enough.[46]

hooks's reference to the production of 'honest' autobiographical narrative resonates with debates over a major problem faced by earlier black writers – that of audience and authenticity. Slave narratives, if written to convert white readers to the abolitionist cause, demanded the production of a selfhood acceptable to a white audience. In her study of African American women autobiographers,[47] Elizabeth Fox-Genovese puts the issue of autobiographical 'authenticity' into question. She substitutes the concept of 'condition' for that of 'experience' as the source of this writing, taking 'condition' to include the circumstances of the writer's gender, race and geographical place, and, for two of the writers she discusses, Harriet Wilson and Harriet Jacobs, both the experience of slavery and the literary tradition of slave narratives. The tension within their autobiographies is that they were written for readers with some social influence; this would automatically have excluded black women. The literal truth of their writings is compromised, or subverted, by their ambiguous relationship towards their putative readers.

In Fox-Genovese's account of Zora Neale Hurston's *Dust Tracks on a Road* (1942), the 'core' of the writer's self becomes even harder to locate. In creating a 'statue' – an ideal self – Hurston finds a freedom from the self bound by the circumstances that would have denied her recognition as a writer. Her autobiography is 'a marvel of self-concealment', representing an ideal self unconstrained by 'condition'. Yet any attempt to locate the 'true' self of the writer underlying her social and literary strategies will come up against the ambiguous and troubled nature of what black female identity is – defined as it has been against norms composed by white, male culture.

Henry Louis Gates argues that the black autobiographical tradition involves 'the positing of fictive black selves in language, in a mode of discourse traditionally defined by large claims for the self. The self, in this sense, does not exist as an entity but as a coded system of signs, arbitrary in reference.'[48] As Nelly McKay comments, strategies of this kind may be a product of 'the powerlessness and vulnerability of the racial self', although Hurston, for one, 'refused to accept the oppression of blacks as a definition of her life'.[49] The fictional self, invoked in a variety of autobiographical theories, appears in these debates with a strongly political dimension; fiction is both a defence and a strategy of resistance. In recent black women's auto-biographies, the fictional self becomes a powerful device for self-description, as in Audre Lorde's *Zami: A New Spelling of My Name*, in which Lorde's renaming of herself as Zami allows for the construc-tion of a new identity.[50] As Claudine Raynaud writes: 'the first name, the *nom propre*, the signature on the title page will give way to the mythic name'. In Lorde's own words, Zami is 'a biomythography which is really fiction'.[51]

Contemporary interest in autobiography and new developments in autobiographical writing focus on the interweaving of fact, fiction and myth, and also that of ethnic identities and identifications. Maxine Hong Kingston's *The Woman Warrior*[52] has become a central text representing such imbrications; Kingston, a Chinese-American, narrates a childhood caught between conformity to American stan-dards and the power of her mother's stories and of the mythic legacies of China: 'To make my waking life American-normal, I turn on the lights before anything untoward makes an appearance. I push the deformed into my dreams, which are Chinese, the language of impossible stories' [p. 82]. As Michael Fischer writes: 'Non-Chinese are called ghosts, but for the American-Chinese children, ghosts are the bizarre fragments of past, tradition, and familial self-overprotectiveness that must be externalized and tamed.'[53] Lan-guage and languages represent both the possibility and the difficulty of identity: for many immigrants, the choice would seem to be between Babel and aphasia, too much language or too little. Tellingly, Hong Kingston's particular difficulty was with the letter 'I', the 'I' of autobiography:

> I could not understand 'I'. The Chinese 'I' has seven strokes, intricacies. How could the American 'I', assuredly wearing a hat like the Chinese, have only three strokes, the middle so straight? . . . I stared at that middle line and waited so long for its black centre to resolve into tight strokes and dots that I forgot to pronounce it.

Yet the Chinese 'I' also has its problems, for there is a 'Chinese word for the female 'I' – which is "slave" ' [p. 150]. Kingston's task, Fischer writes, 'is to construct or find images that are neither Chinese nor European. . . . Being Chinese-American exists only as an exploratory project, a matter of finding a voice and a style' [p. 210].

This trying-on of alternative identities is central to ethnic auto-biographies. In Fischer's words:

> Ethnicity is merely one domain, or one exemplar, of a more general pattern of cultural dynamics in the late twentieth century. Ethnic auto-biographical writing parallels, mirrors and exemplifies contemporary theories of textuality, of knowledge and of culture . . . Insofar as the present age is one of increasing potentialities for dialogue, as well as conflict, among cultures, lessons for writing ethnography may be taken from writers both on ethnicity and on textuality, knowledge and culture. [p. 230]

The concept of *métissage* or creolisation has been used by the Martinican writer and theorist Edouard Glissant to describe this interweaving of Western and indigenous cultural forms.[54] In *Auto-biographical Voices*, Françoise Lionnet describes *métissage* as opening up a defensible space for Third World writers:

> within the conceptual apparatuses that have governed our labelling of ourselves and others, a space is . . . opened where multiplicity and diversity are affirmed. This space is not a territory staked out by exclu-sionary practices. Rather, it functions as a sheltering site, one that can nurture our differences . . . [*métissage*] is the site of undecidability and indeterminacy, where solidarity becomes the fundamental principle of political action against hegemonic languages.[55]

This interweaving of identities is also an intertextuality and a crossing of generic boundaries. Cultural hybridity is now affirmed along with a breaking of traditional conceptions of the 'law of genre', bringing into the open the ways in which generic boundaries have also been racial boundaries – a point made by Derrida in his account of the taboo against generic 'miscegenation': 'as soon as genre announces itself, one must respect a norm, one must not cross a line of demarcation, one must not risk impurity, anomaly or monstrosity'.[56]

The difficulties, as well as the advantages, of straddling the border are powerfully explored in Gloria Anzaldúa's autobiographical text *Borderlands/La Frontera*:

> I am a border woman. I grew up between two cultures, the Mexican (with a heavy Indian influence) and the Anglo (as a member of a colonized people in our territory). I have been straddling the *tejas*-Mexican border

and others all my life. It's not a comfortable territory to live in, this place of
contradictions. Hatred, anger and exploitation are the prominent features
of this landscape.

   However, there have been compensations for this *mestiza*, and certain
joys. Living on borders and in margins, keeping intact one's shifting and
multiple identity and integrity, is like trying to swim in a new element, an
alien element. There is an exhilaration in being a participant in the
further evolution of humankind, in being 'worked' on.[57]

Alternating between the languages and forms of poetry and prose,
and addressing the gender ambiguity of her lesbian identity,
Anzaldúa also switches 'from English to Castilian Spanish to the
North Mexican dialect to Tex-Mex to a sprinkling of Nahuatl to a
mixture of all of these . . . [this] reflects my language, a new language
– the language of the Borderlands'. These borderlands are geographical, cultural, sexual, generic and linguistic.

   Anzaldúa also crosses the divides between 'fact' and 'fiction' and
the oral and the written; like Maxine Hong Kingston, she explores
the power of story-telling and myth-making. Utopia, too, is valorised
as a mode appropriate to the future-orientated dimensions of the new
autobiography. Rejecting, as Sidonie Smith writes, definitions of
autobiography as wholly retrospective or written under the sign of
death, as in deconstructionist accounts, postmodernist feminism
emphasises autobiography as a mode in which the self or selves are
made ready for the future: 'the autobiographical manifesto is a
revolutionary gesture poised against amnesia and its compulsions to
repetition. It is not quite anamnesis (or reminiscence) so much as a
purposeful constitution of a future history, the projection of
anamnesis into the future'.[58]

   Autobiography is now a key element in new understandings of
cultural identity and coalition politics. Yet many recent critics have
found the 'genre' of autobiography to be irrevocably tainted by its
Eurocentric, masculinist, individualist assumptions. Their critique
partially converges with the claims of some of the more traditional
theorists discussed in this book, that autobiography expresses the
individual self, the pure consciousness or the 'essence' of Western
humanity. The claim that autobiography is a Western genre is of
course refuted by researchers into autobiography in non-Western
cultures, who have also broken with the limiting, and culturally
self-serving, rules of the genre.

   We are back, then, with the question of the troubled naming of 'autobiography', with which this book began. Attempting to open up the modes of autobiographical representation, recent critics have coined neologisms intended to redefine, extensionally and intensionally, 'autobiography' away from the limits of its component parts, self-life-writing. The term auto/biography, which I have used throughout this book, is one such attempt to indicate the affinities between biography and autobiography as traditionally defined. Other critics have bypassed 'autobiography' altogether, overtaking it on the left, and focus instead on related 'outlaw genres' – including testimonial literature, oral narratives and ethnographies.[59] Contemporary debates in feminist and post-colonial theory have made autobiography a central topic, but it is now a centre which disperses towards its margins and its borders.

Notes

1 John Burnett, David Vincent and David Mayall (eds.), *The Autobiography of the Working Class. An Annotated, Critical Bibliography*, Vol. 1: 1790–1900 (Brighton: Harvester, 1984).

2 Paul Thompson, *The Voice of the Past: Oral History* (Oxford University Press, 2nd ed. 1988).

3 Jerome Bruner and Susan Weisser, 'The Invention of Self: Autobiography and its Forms', in *Literacy and Orality*, ed. David R. Olson and Nancy Torrance (Cambridge University Press, 1991), pp. 129–48.

4 London: Verso, 1984.

5 Carolyn Steedman, *Landscape for a Good Woman*, London: Virago, 1986.

6 London: Verso, 1989.

7 London: Hamish Hamilton, 1952.

8 Jean-Paul Sartre, *Words* (Harmondsworth: Penguin, 1984), p. 161.

9 Ronald Fraser, *Blood of Spain: The Experience of Civil War 1936–1939* (Harmondsworth: Penguin, 1981), p. 32.

10 History Workshop Group, 'In Search of the Past: *a dialogue with Ronald Fraser*', *History Workshop Journal*, 20 (autumn 1985), 175–88.

11 Steedman, *Landscape for a Good Woman*.

12 Popular Memory Group, 'Popular Memory: theory, politics, method', in *Making Histories: Studies in History-writing and Politics*, ed. R. Johnson, G. McLennan, B. Schwarz and D. Sutton (London: Hutchinson, 1982), p. 238.

13 New York: Ballantine, 1974.

14 New York: Farrar, Strauss and Giroux; London: Virago, 1977.

15 Rita Felski, *Beyond Feminine Aesthetics: Feminist Literature and Social Change* (London: Hutchinson Radius, 1989), ch. 3. Felski gives an excellent account of women's confessional writing.

16 London: Cape, 1984.

17 Sheila McLeod, *The Art of Starvation* (London: Virago, 1981).

18 Loretta Ngcobo, *Let It Be Told: Black Women Writers in Britain* (London: Pluto, 1987).
19 Liz Heron (ed.), *Truth, Dare or Promise: Girls Growing up in the Fifties* (London: Virago, 1985).
20 Ursula Owen (ed.), *Fathers* (London: Virago, 1983).
21 Sistren Theatre Collective, *Lionhart Gal: Life Stories of Jamaican Women* (London: Women's Press, 1986).
22 London: Virago, 1987.
23 Oxford: Clarendon Press, 1993.
24 London: Thames and Hudson, 1993.
25 Liz Stanley, *The auto/biographical I* (Manchester University Press, 1992), p. 255.
26 Nancy K. Miller, *Getting Personal* (New York: Routledge, 1991), p.1.
27 Nicole Ward Jouve, *White Woman Speaks With Forked Tongue: Criticism as Autobiography* (London: Routledge, 1991), pp. 5,11.
28 Miller, *Getting Personal*, p. xiii.
29 *Ibid.* p.2.
30 Ward Jouve, *White Woman Speaks*, pp. 7, 10.
31 Miller, *Getting Personal*, p. xiii.
32 Judith Butler, *Gender Trouble: Feminism and the Subversion of Identity* (New York: Columbia University Press, 1990), p. 92.
33 Miller, *Getting Personal*, pp. 74–5.
34 Mary Ann Caws, *Women of Bloomsbury: Virginia, Vanessa and Carrington* (New York and London: Routledge, 1990), pp. 2–3.
35 Tania Modleski, 'Some Functions of Feminist Criticism'; Or, the Scandal of the Mute Body', in *Feminism without Women* (New York and London: Routledge, 1991).
36 Luce Irigaray, 'The Three Genres', in *Philosophy in the Feminine*, ed. Margaret Whitford (Oxford: Blackwell, 1992), p. 148.
37 Caws, *Women of Bloomsbury*, p. 2.
38 Miller, *Getting Personal*, p. 98.
39 Domna C. Stanton (ed.), *The Female Autograph: Theory and Practice of Autobiography from the Tenth to the Twentieth Century*, 2nd ed. (University of Chicago Press, 1984), p. vii.
40 Liz Stanley, 'Feminist Auto/biography and Feminist Epistemology', in *Out of the Margins*, ed. Jane Aaron and Sylvia Walby (London: Falmer Press, 1991), p.204.
41 See Sandra Harding, 'Rethinking Standpoint Epistemology: "What is Strong Objectivity"?', in *Feminist Epistemologies*, ed. Linda Alcoff and Elizabeth Potter (New York and London: Routledge, 1993); *Whose Science? Whose Knowledge?: Thinking from Women's Lives* (Milton Keynes: Open University Press, 1991). See also Donna Haraway, 'Situated Knowledges: The Science Question in Feminism and the Privilege of Partial Perspective', in *Simians, Cyborgs and Women: The Reinvention of Nature* (London: Free Association Books, 1991).
42 Ed. Jean Fagin Yellin (Cambridge, Mass.: Harvard University Press, 1987).
43 Cited in Gwendolyn Etter-Lewis, *My Soul is My Own. Oral Narratives of African American Women in the Professions* (New York and London:

Routledge, 1993), p.161.

44 *Ibid.* p. 113.

45 Stephen Butterfield, *Black Autobiography in America* (Amherst: University of Massachusetts Press, 1974), p. 3.

46 bell hooks, 'Revolutionary Black Women', in *Black Looks. Race and Representation* (London: Turnaround, 1992).

47 'My Statue, My Self: Autobiographical Writings of Afro-American Women', in *The Private Self*, ed. Shari Benstock (London: Routledge, 1988), pp. 63–89.

48 Henry Louis Gates, jun., *Figures in Black: Words, Signs and the 'Racial' Self* (New York: Oxford University Press, 1987), pp. 119/123.

49 Nellie Y. McKay, 'Race, Gender and Cultural Context in Zora Neale Hurston's *Dust Tracks on a Road*', in *Life/Lines*, ed. Bella Brodzki and Celeste Schenk (Ithaca: Cornell University Press, 1988), pp. 181/188.

50 Trumansburg: Crossing Press, 1982.

51 Claudine Raynau 'A Nutmeg Nestled inside its Covering of Mace', in *Life/Lines*, ed. Brodzski and Schenk, p. 221.

52 London: Picador, 1982.

53 Michael M. J. Fischer, 'Ethnicity and the Post-Modern Arts of Memory', in James Clifford and George E. Marcus, *Writing Culture: the Poetics and Politics of Ethnography* (Berkeley: University of California Press, 1986), p.210.

54 Edouard Glissant, *Caribbean Discourse* (Charlottesville: University Press of Virginia, 1989).

55 Françoise Lionnet, *Autobiographical Voices. Race, Gender Self-Portraiture* (Ithaca and London: Cornell University Press, 1989), p. 5.

56 Jacques Derrida, 'The Law of Genre', in *On Narrative*, ed. W. J. T. Mitchell (Chicago and London: University of Chicago Press, 1981), pp. 51–77.

57 San Francisco: Aunt Lute Book Company, 1987, Preface.

58 Sidonie Smith, *Subjectivity, Identity, and the Body. Women's Autobiographical Practices in the Twentieth Century* (Indiana University Press, 1993), p. 182.

59 See the essays in *De/Colonizing the Subject: The Politics of Gender in Women's Autobiography*, ed. Sidonie Smith and Julia Watson (Minneapolis: Minnesota University Press, 1992). It could be argued that 'autobiography' is being repudiated precisely because it now appears to be too stable a form. It is kept in play through this shift to its transgressive homologues.

Bibliography

Abbott, H. Porter. 'Autobiography, Autography, Fiction: Groundwork for a Taxonomy of Textual Categories.' *New Literary History* 19 (1988) 597–615.

Abrahamsen, David. *The Mind and Death of a Genius*. New York: Columbia University Press, 1946.

Abrams, M.H. *Natural Supernaturalism: Tradition and Revolution in Romantic Literature*. New York: Norton, 1971.

Altick, Richard D. *Lives and Letters: A History of Literary Biography in England and America*. New York: Knopf, 1965.

Andrews, William L. *To Tell a Free Story: The First Century of Afro-American Autobiography, 1760–1865*. Urbana: University of Illinois Press, 1986.

Anon. 'Cowper's *Poems and Life*'. *Quarterly Review* XIV (Oct./Jan. 1816/17), 117–29.

—— Review of D'Israeli's *Miscellanies; or Literary Reflections*, *Monthly Review*, 2nd series, 29 (1797).

—— Review of *Memoirs of Life of Peter Daniel Huet, Bishop of Avranches, written by himself*. *Quarterly Review* IV (Aug./Nov. 1810), 103–11.

Anzaldúa, Gloria. *Borderlands/La Frontera*. San Francisco: Aunt Lute Book Company, 1987.

Arac, Jonathan. *Critical Genealogies: Historical Situations for Postmodern Literary Study*. New York: Columbia University Press, 1987.

Armstrong, Isobel. *Victorian Scrutinies: Reviews of Poetry 1830–70*. London: Athlone, 1972.

Armstrong, Isobel (ed.) *New Feminist Discourses*. London: Routledge, 1992.

Arnold, Frederick. 'How Every Man Writes his Own Memoirs.' In *Three-Cornered Essays*. London: Ward and Downey, 1886, pp. 174–99.

Arnold, Matthew. *Culture and Anarchy*. Cambridge University Press, 1932.

—— *Selected Essays of Matthew Arnold*. Ed. Christopher Ricks. New York: Signet, 1972.

Bakhtin, M.M. *The Dialogic Imagination*. Ed. Michael Holquist, trans. Caryl Emerson and Michael Holquist. Austin: University of Texas Press, 1981.

Baldick, Chris. *The Social Mission of English Criticism*. Oxford: Clarendon Press, 1983.

Barthes, Roland. *Roland Barthes by Roland Barthes*. Trans. Richard Howard. London: Macmillan, 1977.

—— 'The Death of the Author.' In *Image, Music, Text*. Ed. and trans. Stephen Heath. London: Fontana, 1977, pp. 142–8.

Bates, E. Stuart. *Inside Out: An Introduction to Autobiography*. 2 vols. Oxford: Blackwell, 1936/37.
Battersby, Christine. *Gender and Genius: Towards a Feminist Aesthetics*. London: The Women's Press, 1989.
Beaujour, Michel. *Miroirs d'encre*. Paris: Seuil, 1980.
Beer, Gillian. 'Virginia Woolf and the Body of the People.' In *Women Reading Women's Writing*, ed. Sue Roe. Brighton: Harvester Press, 1987, pp. 85–114.
——*Arguing with the Past*. London: Routledge, 1989.
Benjamin, Jessica. 'A Desire of One's Own: Psychoanalytic Feminism and Intersubjective Space.' In *Feminist Studies/Critical Studies*, ed. Teresa de Lauretis. London: Macmillan, 1988, pp. 78–101.
Benjamin, Walter. 'The Storyteller.' In *Illuminations*. New York: Harcourt, Brace and World, 1968, pp. 83–109.
—— *The Origin of German Tragic Drama*. Trans. John Osborne. London: New Left Books, 1977.
Bennington, Geoff. *Dudding. Des noms de Rousseau*. Paris: Galilée, 1991.
Benstock, Shari (ed.) *Women of the Left Bank*. London: Virago, 1987.
—— *The Private Self: Theory and Practice of Women's Autobiographical Writings*. London: Routledge, 1988.
Benveniste, Émile. *Problèmes de linguistique générale*. Paris: Gallimard, 1966. Trans. as *Problems in General Linguistics*. University of Miami Press, 1971.
Bernstein, Jay. 'Self-Knowledge as Praxis: Narrative and Narration in Psychoanalysis.' In *Narrative in Culture*, ed. Cristopher Nash. London: Routledge, 1980, pp. 51–77.
Bertaux, Daniel (ed.) *Biography and Society: The Life History Approach in the Social Sciences*. London: Sage, 1981.
Blake, Robert. 'The Art of Biography'. In *The Troubled Face of Biography*, ed. Eric Homberger and John Charmley, pp. 75–93.
Blanchard, Jean Marc. 'Of Cannibalism and Autobiography.' *Modern Language Notes* 93 (1978): 654–76.
Blanchard, Marc Eli. 'The Critique of Autobiography.' *Comparative Literature* 34 (1982), 97–115.
—— *On Leiris*. *Yale French Studies* 81. New Haven: Yale University Press, 1992.
Blasing, Mutlu Konuk. *The Art of Life: Studies in American Autobiographical Literature*. Austin: University of Texas Press, 1977.
Bonnet, Jean-Claude. 'Le fantasme de l'écrivain.' *Poétique* 63 (Sept. 1985), 259–77.
Braidotti, Rosie. *Patterns of Dissidence*. Cambridge: Polity, 1991.
Brée, Germaine. *Narcissus Absconditus: The Problematic Art of Autobiography in Contemporary France*. Oxford: Clarendon Press, 1978.
Brodzki, Bella and Schenck, Celeste (eds). *Life/Lines: Theorizing Women's Autobiography*. Ithaca: Cornell University Press, 1988.
Brooks, Peter. *Reading for the Plot: Design and Intention in Narrative*. Oxford: Clarendon Press, 1984.
Bruner, Jerome and Weisser, Susan. 'The Invention of Self: Autobiography and its Forms.' In *Literacy and Orality*, ed. David R. Olson and Nancy Torrance, Cambridge University Press, 1991 pp. 129–48.
Bruss, Elizabeth W. *Autobiographical Acts: The Changing Situation of a Literary*

Genre. Baltimore: Johns Hopkins University Press, 1976.

Buckley, Jerome Hamilton. *The Turning Key: Autobiography and the Subjective Impulse Since 1800*. Cambridge, Mass: Harvard University Press, 1984.

Burckhardt, Jacob. *The Civilization of the Renaissance in Italy* (1860), ed. Irene Gordon. New York: Mentor, 1960.

Burnett, John, Vincent, David and Mayall, David (eds). *The Autobiography of the Working Class: An Annotated, Critical Bibliography. Vol. 1. 1790-1900*. Brighton: Harvester, 1984.

Burr, Anna Robeson. *The Autobiography: A Critical and Comparative Study*. Boston: Houghton Mifflin, 1909.

—— 'Sincerity in Autobiography.' *The Atlantic Monthly* 4 (Oct. 1909), 527–36.

—— *Religious Confessions and Confessants*. Boston and New York, 1914.

Burt, E. S. 'Poetic Conceit: The Self-Portrait and Mirrors of Ink.' *Diacritics* 12, 4 (winter 1982), 17–38.

[Busk, Mary Margaret]. 'Autobiography.' *Blackwood's Edinburgh Magazine* CLIX, XXVI (Nov. 1829), 737–48.

Butler, Judith. *Gender Trouble: Feminism and the Subversion of Identity*. New York and London: Routledge, 1990.

Butler, Lord Richard. *The Difficult Art of Autobiography*. Oxford: Clarendon Press, 1968.

Butterfield, Stephen. *Black Autobiography in America*. Amherst: University of Massachussetts Press, 1974.

Cadava, Eduardo, Connor, Peter and Nancy, Jean-Luc (eds.). *Who Comes After the Subject?* New York: Routledge, 1991.

Campbell, Colin. *The Romantic Ethic and the Spirit of Modern Consumerism*. Oxford: Blackwell, 1987.

Cardano, Jerome. *The Book of My Life [De Vita Propia Liber]*. Trans. Jean Stoner. London and Toronto: J. M. Dent, 1931.

Carlyle, Thomas. 'Biography.' *Fraser's Magazine* (1832). Reprinted in Carlyle, *Critical and Miscellaneous Essays*. Vol. IV. London: Chapman and Hall, 1887, pp. 51-66.

—— 'Characteristics.' (1831). In *Critical and Miscellaneous Essays*. Vol. II. [*Thomas Carlyle's Works*, The Ashburton Edition, Vol. XVI. London: Chapman & Hall, 1887, pp. 193–227.

Caughie, John. *Theories of Authorship: A Reader*. London: Routledge, 1981.

Caws, Mary Ann. *Women of Bloomsbury: Virginia, Vanessa and Carrington*. New York and London: Routledge, 1990.

Chadwick, Whitney and de Courtivron, Isabelle (eds). *Significant Others*. London: Thames and Hudson, 1993.

Chase, Cynthia (ed.) *Romanticism*. London: Longman, 1993.

Chodorow, Nancy. *The Reproduction of Mothering: Psychoanalysis and the Sociology of Gender*. Berkeley: University of California Press, 1978.

Church, Richard. 'The Art of Autobiography.' *Cornhill* 171 (1960-61), 469–80.

Clark, A. M. *Autobiography: Its Genesis and Phases*. Edinburgh: Oliver and Boyd, 1935.

Clark, Samuel. *Self-Examination Explained and Recommended. In Two Discourses*. London, 1761.

Clifford, James. *The Predicament of Culture*. Harvard University Press, 1988.

Clifford, James L. and Marcus, George E. *Writing Culture: the Poetics and Politics of Ethnography*. Berkeley: University of California Press, 1986.
Clifford, James L. (ed.) *Biography as an Art*. Oxford University Press, 1962.
Coburn, Kathleen (ed.) *The Notebooks of Samuel Taylor Coleridge*. 2 vols. New York: Pantheon Books, 1957.
Cockshut, A. O. J. *The Art of Autobiography in 19th and 20th Century England*. New Haven: Yale University Press, 1984.
Coe, Richard N. *When the Grass was Taller: Autobiography and the Experience of Childhood*. New Haven: Yale University Press, 1984.
Collingwood, R.G. *An Autobiography*. Oxford University Press, 1939.
Connolly, Cyril. *Enemies of Promise*. Harmondsworth: Penguin, 1961.
Corbett, Mary Jean. *Representing Femininity: Middle-Class Subjectivity in Victorian and Edwardian Women's Autobiographies*. New York and Oxford: Oxford University Press, 1992.
Cox, Catherine. *The Early Mental Traits of Three Hundred Geniuses. Vol. II of Genetic Studies of Genius*. Stanford University Press, 1927.
Cox, James M. *Recovering Literature's Lost Ground: Essays in American Autobiography*. Baton Rouge: Louisiana State University Press, 1989.
Culler, Jonathan. *The Pursuit of Signs*. London: Routledge and Kegan Paul, 1981.
—— *Framing the Sign: Criticism and its Institutions*. Oxford: Blackwell, 1988.
Davies, Margaret Llewelyn (ed.) *Life As We Have Known It*, by Co-Operative Working Women. London: Hogarth Press, 1931.
De Certeau, Michel. *Heterologies: Discourse on the Other*. Minneapolis: University of Minnesota Press, 1986.
Delaney, Paul. *British Autobiography in the Seventeenth Century*. London: Routledge and Kegan Paul, 1969.
De Man, Paul. 'Autobiography as De-Facement.' *Modern Language Notes* 94, 5 (Dec. 1979), 919–30. Reprinted in *The Rhetoric of Romanticism*, pp. 67–81.
—— *Allegories of Reading: Figural Language in Rousseau, Nietzsche, Rilke and Proust*. New Haven: Yale University Press, 1979.
—— *Blindness and Insight*. Minneapolis: Minnesota University Press, 2nd ed. 1983.
—— *The Rhetoric of Romanticism*. New York: Columbia University Press, 1984.
—— *Wartime Journalism: 1939-1943*. Ed. Werner Hamacher, Neil Hertz and Thomas Keenan. Lincoln and London: University of Nebraska Press, 1988.
De Quincey, Thomas. *Confessions of an English Opium-Eater*. Ed. Greville Lindop. Oxford University Press, 1985.
Derrida, Jacques. *Of Grammatology*. Trans. Gayatri Chakravorty Spivak. Baltimore: Johns Hopkins University Press, 1976.
—— 'The Law of Genre'. In *On Narrative*, ed. W.J.T. Mitchell. University of Chicago Press, 1981.
—— *L'Oreille de l'autre: otobiographie, transferts, traduction*. Montreal: VlB, 1982. Trans. as *The Ear of the Other: Otobiography, Transference, Translation*. Lincoln and London: University of Nebraska Press, 1988, pp. 51–77.
—— *Glas*. Trans. John P. Leavey, jun. and Richard Rand. Lincoln: University of Nebraska Press, 1986.
—— *Mémoires: for Paul de Man*. New York: Columbia University Press, revised

ed. 1989.

—— 'To Speculate – on "Freud".' In *A Derrida Reader: Between the Blinds*. Ed. Peggy Kamuf. Hemel Hempstead: Harvester Wheatsheaf, 1991, pp. 518–68.

Diamond, Arlyn and Edwards, Lee R. (eds). *The Authority of Experience: Essays in Feminist Criticism*. Amherst: University of Massachusetts Press, 1977.

Dilthey, Wilhelm. *Der Aufbau der geschichtlichen welt in den Geisteswissenschaften. Gesammelte Schriften*. Vol. VII Stuttgart: B. G. Teubner, 3rd. ed. 1958.

—— *Selected Writings of Wilhelm Dilthey*. Ed., trans. and introduced by H. P. Rickman. Cambridge University Press, 1976.

—— *Poetry and Experience*. In *Selected Works*, vol. 5, ed. Rudolf A. Makkreel and Frithjof Rodi. Princeton University Press, 1985.

D'Israeli, Isaac. *Miscellanies; or Literary Reflections*. London: T. Cadell and W. Davies, 1796.

—— *Literary Character of Men of Genius*. London: Frederick Warne, 1822.

Doane, Mary Ann. 'Veiling over Desire: Close-Ups of the Woman.' In *Feminism and Psychoanalysis*, ed. Richard Feldstein and Judith Roof. Ithaca: Cornell University Press, 1989, pp. 105–41. Also in Doane, *Femmes Fatales: Feminism, Film Theory, Psychoanalysis*. New York and London: Routledge, 1991, pp. 44–75.

Dobrée, Bonamy. 'Some Literary Autobiographies of the Present Age.' *Sewanee Review* 64 (1956), 689–706.

Dodd, Philip. 'Criticism and the Autobiographical Tradition.' *Modern Selves: Essays on Modern British and American Autobiography*. Ed. Philip Dodd. London: Frank Cass, 1986, pp. 1–13.

Dollard, John. *Criteria for the Life History*. New Haven: Yale University Press, 1935.

Donato, Eugenio. 'The Ruins of Memory: Archaeological Fragments and Textual Artifacts.' *Modern Language Notes* 93 (1978), 575–96.

Doody, Terence. *Confessions and Community in the Novel*. Baton Rouge and London: Louisiana University Press, 1984.

Downing, Christine. 'Re-Visioning Autobiography: The Bequest of Freud and Jung.' *Soundings* 60 (1977), 210–28.

Eakin, Paul John. 'Malcolm X and the Limits of Autobiography.' *Criticism* 18 (1976), 230–42. Reprinted in *Autobiography: Essays Theoretical and Critical*, ed. James Olney, pp. 181-93.

—— *Fictions in Autobiography: Studies in the Art of Self-Invention*. Princeton University Press, 1985.

—— 'Narrative and Chronology as Structures of Reference and the New Model Autobiographer'. In *Studies in Autobiography*, ed. James Olney, pp. 32–41.

—— *Touching the World: Reference in Autobiography*. Princeton University Press, 1992.

Earle, William. *The Autobiographical Consciousness: A Philosophical Enquiry into Existence*. Chicago: Quadrangle Books, 1972.

Edel, Leon. *Writing Lives*. New York and London: Norton, 1987.

Edinburgh Review. 'Famous Autobiographies'. 214 (1911): 331–56

Egan, Susanna. *Patterns of Experience in Autobiography*. Chapel Hill: University of North Carolina Press, 1984.

Ellenberger, Henri F. *The Discovery of the Unconscious: The History and Evolution* of Dynamic Psychiatry. New York: Basic Books, 1970.

Ellis, Havelock. *Man and Woman: a study of human secondary sexual characters*. London and Felling-on-Tyne: Walker Scott Publishing Co., 5th edn. 1914.

—— *A Study of British Genius (1904)*. London: Constable and Co., 1927.

—— 'An Open Letter to Biographers'. In *Selected Essays*. London: Dent, 1936, pp. 108–17.

—— *Sexual Inversion. Studies in the Psychology of Sex*. Vol. II. Philadelphia: F.A. Davis, 1920.

Epstein, William H. *Recognizing Biography*. Philadelphia: University of Pennsylvania Press, 1987.

Erdman, David and Fogel, E.G. *Evidence for Authorship*. Ithaca: Cornell University Press, 1966.

Erikson, Erik. *Young Man Luther: A Study in Psychoanalysis and History*. New York: Norton, 1962.

—— *Gandhi's Truth: On the Origins of Militant Non-Violence*. New York: Norton, 1969.

Ermath, Michael. *Wilhelm Dilthey: The Critique of Historical Reason*. University of Chicago Press, 1975.

Etter-Lewis, Gwendolyn. *My Soul is My Own. Oral Narratives of African American Women in the Professions*. New York and London: Routledge, 1993.

Fassler, Barbara. 'Theories of Homosexuality as Sources of Bloomsbury's Androgyny.' *Signs: Journal of Women in Culture and Society*, 5, 2 (1979), 237-51.

Fekete, John. *The Critical Twilight*. London: Routledge and Kegan Paul, 1978.

Felman, Shoshana and Laub, Dori. *Testimony: Crises of Witnessing in Literature, Psychoanalysis and History*. New York and London: Routledge, 1992.

Felski, Rita. *Beyond Feminist Aesthetics: Feminist Literature and Social Change*. London: Hutchinson Radius, 1989.

Ferrarotti, Franco. *Histoire et Histories de vie*. Paris: Librairie des Méridiens, 1983.

Finney, Brian. *The Inner I: British Literary Autobiography of the Twentieth Century*. London: Faber, 1985.

Fischer, Michael M.J. 'Ethnicity and the Post-Modern Arts of Memory.' In *Writing Cultures*, ed. James L. Clifford and George E. Marcus, pp. 194–233.

Fleishman, Avrom. *Figures of Autobiography: The Language of Self-Writing*. Berkeley: University of California Press, 1983.

Foster, Dennis A. *Confession and Complicity in Narrative*. Cambridge University Press, 1987.

Foster, John. 'On a Man's Writing Memoirs of Himself.' In *Essays*. (1805). London: Bohn, 30th ed. 1863, pp. 1–66.

Foucault, Michel. 'What is an Author?' (1969). In *Language, Counter-Memory, Practice* ed. Donald F. Bouchard. Oxford: Blackwell, 1977.

—— *The Care of the Self: The History of Sexuality*. Vol. 3. Trans. Robert Hurley. London: Penguin, 1986.

—— *Technologies of the Self*. Ed. Luther, H., Martin, Huck Gutman and Patrick H. Hutton. London: Tavistock, 1988.

—— *The Archaeology of Knowledge*. Trans. A.M. Sheridan Smith. London: Routledge, 1989.

Fowler, Alastair. *Kinds of Literature*. Oxford: Clarendon Press, 1982.

Fox-Genovese. Elizabeth. 'My Statue, My Self: Autobiographical Writings of Afro-American Women.' In *The Private Self*, ed. Shari Benstock, pp. 63–89.

Fraser, Ronald. *Blood of Spain: The Experience of Civil War 1936–1939*. Harmondsworth: Penguin, 1981.

—— *In Search of a Past*. London: Verso, 1984.

Freedman, Diane P., Frey, Olivia, and Zauhar, Frances Murphy (eds). *The Intimate Critique: Autobiographical Literary Criticism*. Durham and London: Duke University Press, 1993.

Freud, Sigmund (with J. Breuer). *Studies on Hysteria* (1895). In *The Standard Edition of the Complete Psychological Works of Sigmund Freud*. London: The Hogarth Press and the Institute of Psychoanalysis (henceforth *SE*), II; Penguin Freud Library, Harmondsworth: Penguin (henceforth PFL), 3.

—— 'Screen Memories' (1899), *SE* III, 301–22.

—— 'Childhood Memories and Screen Memories', [1901] (1907). *SE* IV, 43–52; PFL 5, 83–93.

—— *The Interpretation of Dreams* (1900). *SE* IV–V; PFL 4.

—— *The Psychopathology of Everyday Life* (1901). *SE* VI; PFL 5.

—— 'Fragment of an analysis of a case of hysteria' ('Dora') [1901] (1905). *SE* VII, 1–122; PFL 8, 31–164.

—— 'Family Romances.' (1908/9). *SE* IX, 236–41; PFL 7, 217–25.

—— 'Leonardo da Vinci and a Memory of his Childhood' (1910). *SE* XI, 57–137; PFL 14, 145–231.

—— 'Psycho-Analytic Notes on an Autobiographical Account of a Case of Paranoia (Dementia Paranoides) (Schreber)' (1911). *SE* XII, 1–82; PFL 9, *Case Histories*, 2, 131–223.

—— 'A Childhood Recollection from *Dichtung und Wahrheit*' (1917). *SE* XVII, 145–57; PFL 14, 321–35.

—— *Beyond the Pleasure Principle*. In *On Metapsychology* (1920). *SE* XVIII, PFL 11, 271–338.

—— *An Autobiographical Study* (1925). Trans. James Strachey. London: The Hogarth Press, 1936.

—— *Moses and Monotheism* (1939). *SE* XXIII, 3–137; PFL 13, 239–386.

Friedländer, Saul. *History and Psychoanalysis*. Trans. Susan Suleiman. New York and London: Holmes and Meier, 1978.

Friedländer, Saul (ed.) *Probing the Limits of Representation: Nazism and the 'Final Solution'*. Cambridge, Mass.: Harvard University Press, 1992.

Froude, James Anthony. *Short Studies on Great Subjects*. 4 vols. London: Longmans, 1890.

Frye, Northrop. *Anatomy of Criticism*. Princeton University Press, 1957.

Gagnier, Regenia. *Subjectivities: A History of Self-Representation in Britain*. Oxford and New York: Oxford University Press, 1991.

Gallagher, Catherine. 'George Eliot and *Daniel Deronda*: The Prostitute and the Jewish Question'. In *Sex, Politics and Science in the Nineteenth-Century Novel*, ed. Ruth B. Yeazell. Baltimore: Johns Hopkins University Press, 1986, pp. 39–62.

Garber, Marjorie. *Vested Interests: Cross-Dressing and Cultural Anxiety*. New York and London: Routledge, 1992.

Garraty, John. *The Nature of Biography*. London: Cape, 1958.

Gates, Henry Louis, jun. *Figures in Black: Words, Signs and the 'Racial' Self*. New York: Oxford University Press, 1987.

Genette, Gérard. *Figures 3*. Paris: Seuil, 1972.

Gilbert, Sandra and Gubar, Susan. 'Ceremonies of the Alphabet: Female Grandmatologies and the Female Authorgraph.' In *The Female Autograph*, ed. Domna C. Stanton pp. 21–48.

Gill, W. A. 'The Nude in Autobiography.' *The Atlantic Monthly* 99 (1907), 71–9.

Gilman, Sander. *Jewish Self-Hatred: Anti-Semitism and the Hidden Language of the Jew*. Baltimore: Johns Hopkins University Press, 1986.

Glissant, Edouard. *Caribbean Discourse*. Charlottesville: University Press of Virginia, 1989.

Goethe, Johann Wolfgang von. *Dichtung und Wahrheit*. Trans. as *The Autobiography of Johann Wolfgang von Goethe*. Chicago University Press, 1974.

Goethe the Critic. Manchester University Press, 1960.

Goldberg, Jonathan. 'Cellini's *Vita* and the Conventions of Early Autobiography.' *Modern Language Notes* 89 (1974), 71–83.

Goodman, Katherine. *Dis/Closures*. New York: Peter Lang, 1986.

Gorz, André. *The Traitor*. Trans. Richard Howard. London: Verso, 1989.

Gosse, Edmund. 'The Custom of Biography'. *Anglo-Saxon Review*, VIII (March 1901), 195–208.

—— 'The Ethics of Biography'. (1903). Reprinted in *Biography as an Art*, ed. James L. Clifford.

—— *Father and Son*, London: Heinemann, 1909.

—— 'The Agony of the Victorian Age.' *The Edinburgh Review* 228 (July/Oct. 1918).

Greenblatt, Stephen. *Renaissance Self-Fashioning*. Chicago University Press, 1980.

Grosz, Elizabeth. *Jacques Lacan: A Feminist Introduction*. London: Routledge, 1990.

Gunn, Janet Varner. *Autobiography: Towards a Poetics of Experience*. Philadelphia: University of Pennsylvania Press, 1982.

Gusdorf, Georges. 'Conditions et limites de l'autobiographie'. In *Formen der Selbstdarstellung*. Berlin: Duncker and Humbolt, 1956. Reprinted in *Autobiography: Essays Theoretical and Critical*, ed. James Olney, pp. 28–48.

—— *La Parole*. Paris: Presses Universitaires de France, 1953. Trans. Paul T. Brockelman. Evanston: Northwestern University Press, 1965.

—— 'De l'autobiographie initiatique à l'autobiographie genre littéraire.' *Revue d'historie littéraire de la France* 75 (1975), 957–94.

—— 'Scripture of the Self: "Prologue in Heaven" '. In *Studies in Autobiography*, ed. James Olney, pp. 112–27.

Habermas, Jürgen. *Knowledge and Human Interests*. London: Heinemann, 1971.

Haight, Gordon S. (ed.) *George Eliot Letters*. Vol. VI (1874–77). New Haven: Yale University Press, 1955.

Halbwachs, Maurice. *On Collective Memory*. Chicago and London: University of Chicago Press, 1992.

Hamacher, Werner, Neil Hertz and Thomas Keenan, (eds). *Responses. On Paul de Man's Wartime Journalism*. Lincoln: University of Nebraska Press, 1989.

Haraway, Donna. *Simians, Cyborgs and Women: The Reinvention of Nature.* London: Free Association Books, 1991.
Harding, Sandra. *Whose Science? Whose Knowledge? Thinking from Women's Lives.* Milton Keynes: Open University Press, 1991.
—— 'Rethinking Standpoint Epistemology: "What is Strong Objectivity?" ' In *Feminist Epistemologies*, ed. Linda Alcoff and Elizabeth Potter. New York and London: Routledge, 1993, pp. 49–82.
Hart, Francis R. 'Notes for an Anatomy of Modern Autobiography.' *New Literary History* 1 (1970), 485–511.
Hartman, Geoffrey. 'Romanticism and Anti-Self-Consciousness' (1962). In *Romanticism and Consciousness: Essays in Criticism*, ed. Harold Bloom. New Haven: Yale University Press, 1970, pp. 47–56.
Heilbrun, Carolyn. 'Women's Autobiographical Writings: New Forms.' *Prose Studies* 8, 2 (1985), 14–28.
—— *Writing a Woman's Life.* London: The Women's Press, 1989.
Henriques, Julian, *et al. Changing the Subject: Psychology, Social Regulation and Subjectivity.* London: Methuen, 1984.
Hernadi, Paul. *Beyond Genre.* Cornell University Press, 1972.
Heron, Liz (ed.) *Truth, Dare or Promise: Girls Growing up in the Fifties.* London: Virago, 1985.
Hertz, Neil. 'More Lurid Figures'. *Diacritics*, 20, 3 (Fall 1990), 2–27.
Hewitt, Leah D. *Autobiographical Tightropes.* Lincoln: University of Nebraska Press, 1990.
History Workshop Group. 'In Search of the Past: *a dialogue with Ronald Fraser.'* *History Workshop Journal* 20 (autumn 1985), 175–88.
Hoggart, Richard. 'A Question of Tone: Some Problems in Autobiographical Writing.' *Critical Quarterly* 5 (1963), 73–90.
Holroyd, Michael. *Lytton Strachey: a Biography* (Harmondsworth: Penguin, 1971).
Homberger, Eric and Charmley, John (eds). *The Troubled Face of Biography.* London: Macmillan, 1988.
Hong Kingston, Maxine. *The Woman Warrior.* London: Picador, 1977.
Hood, Edwin Paxton. *The Uses of Biography: romantic, philosophic and didactic.* London: Partridge and Oakley, 1852.
hooks, bell. *Black Looks. Race and Representation.* London: Turnaround, 1992.
Howarth, William L. 'Some Principles of Autobiography.' In James Olney (ed.), *Autobiography: Essays Theoretical and Critical* (Princeton University Press, 1980), pp. 84–115.
Howells, W. D. 'Autobiography.' *Harper's Monthly* 107 (1904), 478–82.
—— 'Autobiography, a New Form of Literature.' *Harper's Monthly* 119 (1909), 795–8.
Hurston, Zora Neale. *Dust Tracks on a Road: an autobiography* (1942). London: Virago, 1986.
Irigaray, Luce. *Speculum of the Other Woman.* Trans. Gillian C. Gill. Ithaca: Cornell University Press, 1985.
—— 'The Three Genres'. In *The Irigaray Reader*, ed. Margaret Whitford. Oxford: Blackwell, 1991, pp. 140–53.
Jacobs, Harriet. *Incidents in the Life of a Slave Girl.* Ed. Jean Fagin Yellin.

Cambridge, Mass.: Harvard University Press, 1987.

Jacobus, Mary. 'The Law of/and Gender: Genre Theory and *The Prelude*.' *Diacritics*, (winter 1984), 47–57.

——— *Romanticism, Writing and Sexual Difference: Essays on* The Prelude. Oxford: Clarendon Press, 1989.

James, Henry. 'George Sand.' In *Selected Literary Criticism*, ed. Morris Shapira. Harmondsworth: Penguin, 1963, pp. 190–207.

James, William. *The Principles of Psychology*. 2 vols. London: Macmillan, 1890.

Jameson, Fredric. *The Political Unconscious*. Ithaca: Cornell University Press, 1981.

Jauss, Hans Robert. *Toward an Aesthetics of Reception*. Trans. Timothy Bahti. Sussex: Harvester, 1982.

Jay, Martin. 'Experience without a Subject: Walter Benjamin and the Novel.' In *The Actuality of Walter Benjamin*, ed. Laura Marcus and Lynda Nead, *New Formations* (20) 145–55, London: Lawrence and Wishart, 1993.

Jay, Paul. *Being in the Text: Self-Representation from Wordsworth to Roland Barthes*. Ithaca: Cornell University Press, 1984.

——— 'What's the Use? Critical Theory and the Study of Autobiography.' *Biography* 10, 1 (1987), 39–54.

Jelinek, Estelle (ed.) *Women's Autobiography: Essays in Criticism*. Bloomington: Indiana University Press, 1980.

——— *The Tradition of Women's Autobiography: From Antiquity to the Present*. Boston: G. K. Hall/Twayne Publishers, 1986.

Johnson, Barbara. 'My Monster/My Self'. In *A World of Difference*. Baltimore and London: Johns Hopkins University Press, 1989, pp. 144–54.

Johnson, Richard, McLennan, G., Schwarz, B. and Sutton, D. *Making Histories: Studies in History-Writing and Politics*. London: Hutchinson, 1982.

Johnson, Samuel. *The Idler* 84 (24 Nov. 1759). In *Works*: vol. II. New Haven: Yale University Press, 1959, pp. 339–42.

Jones, P. Mansell. 'The Paradox of Literary Introspection.' *The London Mercury* 32 (1935), 446–50.

Jouve, Nicole Ward. *White Woman Speaks with Forked Tongue: Criticism as Autobiography*. New York and London: Routledge, 1991.

Kamuf, Peggy. *Signature Pieces: On the Institution of Authorship*. Ithaca: Cornell University Press, 1988.

Kaplan, Cora. *Sea Changes*. London: Verso, 1986.

Kazin, Alfred. 'Autobiography as Narrative.' *Michigan Quarterly Review* 3 (1964), 210–16.

——— 'The Self as History: Reflections on Autobiography'. In *The American Autobiography*. Ed. A. E. Stone, pp. 31–43.

Kellogg, Robert and Scholes, Robert. *The Nature of Narrative*. New York: Oxford University Press, 1966.

Kermode, Frank. *The Sense of an Ending*. New York: Oxford University Press, 1967.

Koestler, Arthur. *Arrow in the Blue*. London: Hamish Hamilton, 1952.

Kretschmer, Ernst. *The Psychology of Men of Genius*. London: Kegan Paul, Trench, Trubner and Co. Ltd, 1931.

Krieger, Murray. *The New Apologists for Poetry*. Minneapolis: University of

Minnesota Press, 1956.

Lacan, Jacques. 'The mirror stage as formative of the function of the I'. In *Écrits: a Selection*. Trans. Alan Sheridan. London: Tavistock, 1977, pp. 1–7.

—— *Seminaires II*, 1954-55. *Le moi dans la théorie de Freud et dans la technique du psychanalyse*. Paris, Seuil, 1978. Trans. as *The Seminars of Jacques Lacan*, Ed. J. A. Miller: V. 2: *The ego in Freud's theory and in the technique of psychoanalysis 1954–55*. Cambridge University Press, 1988.

LaCapra, Dominick. 'The Personal, the Political and the Textual: Paul de Man as Object of Transference'. *History and Memory*, 4, 1 (spring/summer 1992), 5–38.

Landow, George P. *Approaches to Victorian Autobiography*. Athens: Ohio University Press, 1979.

Lang, Candace. 'Autobiography in the Aftermath of Romanticism.' *Diacritics* 12, 4 (winter 1982), 2–16.

Lasch, Christopher. *The Culture of Narcissism*. London: Abacus, 1980.

Leavis, F. R. *The Two Cultures: The Significance of C. P. Snow. Being the Richmond Lecture, 1962*. London: Chatto and Windus, 1962.

Lee, Sidney. 'A Statistical Account, (1885).' In *Dictionary of National Biography*. London: Oxford University Press, 1938, p. lxxviii.

—— *Principles of Biography*. Cambridge University Press, 1911.

—— *The Perspective of Biography*. Cambridge University Press, 1917/18.

Lehman, David. *Signs of the Times: Deconstruction and the Fall of Paul de Man*. London: André Deutsch, 1991.

Leiris, Michel. *L'Age d'homme*. Paris: Gallimard, 1946.

Lejeune, Philippe. *On Autobiography*. Ed. Paul John Eakin, trans. Katherine Leary. Minneapolis: University of Minnesota Press, 1989.

—— *L'Autobiographie en France*. Paris: Armand Colin, 1971.

—— 'Autobiographie et histoire littéraire.' *Revue d'histoire littéraire de la France* 75 (1975), 903-36. Trans. as 'Autobiography and Literary History', in *On Autobiography*, Ed. Paul John Eakin, pp. 141–62.

—— *Le pacte autobiographique*. Paris: Seuil, 1975.

—— *Je est un autre*. Paris: Seuil, 1980.

—— *Moi aussi*. Paris: Seuil, 1986.

—— *'Cher Cahier . . .'. Temoignages sur le journal personnel*. Paris: Gallimard, 1989.

—— *Le moi des demoiselles. Enquête sur le journal d'une jeune fille*. Paris: Seuil, 1993.

—— 'Autobiography and Social History in the Nineteenth Century.' In *On Autobiography*, Ed. Paul John Eakin, pp. 163–84.

—— 'The Autobiography of Those Who Do Not Write.' In *On Autobiography*, Ed. Paul John Eakin, pp. 185–215.

—— 'Teaching People to Write Their Life Story.' In *On Autobiography*, ed. Paul John Eakin, pp. 216–31.

Lentriccia, Frank. *After the New Criticism*. University of Chicago Press, 1980.

Lepenies, Wolf. *Between Literature and Science: The Rise of Sociology*. Cambridge University Press, 1988.

Le Rider, Jacques. *Le Cas Otto Weininger: racines de l'anti-féminisme et de l'antisémitisme*. Paris: Presses Universitaires de France, 1982.

—— *Modernité Viennoise et crises de l'identité*. Paris: Presses Universitaires de France, 1990.

Lewes, G. H. 'Recent Novels: French and English.' *Fraser's Magazine* 36 (1847), 686–95.

—— 'The condition of authors in England, Germany and France'. *Fraser's Magazine* 35 (March 1847), 285–95.

Lionnet, Françoise. *Autobiographical Voices: Race, Gender, Self-Portraiture*. Ithaca: Cornell University Press, 1989.

Locke, John. *The Second Treatise of Government*. (1690). Oxford: Blackwell, 1956.

Lockhart, James. 'Autobiography.' *Quarterly Review* XXXV (1827), 148–65.

Loesberg, Jonathan. 'Autobiography as Genre, Act of Consciousness, Text.' *Prose Studies*, 4, 2 (Sept. 1981), 169–85.

—— *Fictions of Consciousness: Mill, Newman and the Reading of Victorian Prose*. New Brunswick: Rutgers University Press, 1986.

Lombroso, Cesare. *The Man of Genius*. London and Felling-on-Tyne: Walter Scott Publishing Co., 1905.

Lorde, Audre. *Zami: A New Spelling of My Name*. Trumansburg: Crossing Press, 1982.

Lukács, Georg. *The Theory of the Novel*. London: Merlin Press, 1977.

MacCarthy, Desmond. 'Lytton Strachey and the Art of Biography'. In *Memories*. London: MacGibbon and Kee, 1953, pp. 31–49.

Macey, David. *Lacan in Contexts*. London: Verso, 1988.

McKay, Nellie Y. 'Race, Gender and Cultural Context in Zora Neale Hurston's *Dust Tracks on a Road*.' In *Life/Lines*, ed. Bella Brodzki and Celeste Schenk, pp. 175–88.

McKeon, Michael. *The Origins of the English Novel: 1600-1740*. Baltimore: Johns Hopkins University Press, 1987.

McLeod, Sheila. *The Art of Starvation*. London: Virago, 1981.

Mandel, Barrett J. 'The Autobiographer's Art.' *Journal of Aesthetics and Art Criticism* 27 (1968), 215–26.

—— 'Autobiography – Reflection Trained on Mystery.' *Prairie Schooner* 46 (1972–73), 323–38.

Manicas, Peter T. *A History and Philosophy of the Social Sciences*. Oxford: Blackwell, 1987.

Mansell, Darrell. 'Unsettling the Colonel's Hash: "Fact" in Autobiography.' *Modern Language Quarterly* 37 (1976), 115–32. Reprinted in *The American Autobiography*, ed. Albert E. Stone, pp. 61–79.

Marcus, Laura. ' "Enough About You, Let's Talk About Me": Recent Autobiographical Writing.' *New Formations* 1 (1987), 77–94.

—— 'Brothers in their Anecdotage: Holman Hunt's *Pre-Raphaelitism and the Pre-Raphaelite Brotherhood*.' In *Pre-Raphaelites Re-Viewed*, ed. M. Pointon. Manchester University Press, 1989, pp 11–22.

—— ' "An Invitation to Life": André Gorz's *The Traitor*.' *New Left Review* 194 (July/Aug. 1992), 114–20.

Marcus, Stephen. *Freud and the Culture of Psychoanalysis*. New York: W.W. Norton, 1984.

Marin, Louis. 'Montaigne's Tomb, or Autobiographical Discourse.' *Oxford*

BIBLIOGRAPHY   309

Literary Review, 4, 3 (1981), 43–58.
Martin, Wallace. *Recent Theories of Narrative*. Ithaca: Cornell University Press, 1986.
Martone, John. 'Augustine's Fate.' *Southern Review*, 23, 3 (July 1987), 597–8.
Mason, Mary. 'Autobiographies of Women Writers' In *Autobiography: Essays Theoretical and Critical*, ed. James Olney, pp. 207–35.
Maurois, André. *Ariel: a Shelley Romance*. London: Bodley Head, 1924.
—— *Aspects of Biography*. Trans. S. C. Roberts. London: D. Appleton & Co., 1929.
May, Georges. *L'autobiographie*. Paris: Presses Universitaires de France, 1979.
Maynes, Mary Jo. 'Gender and Narrative Form in French and German Working-Class Autobiographies'. In *Interpreting Women's Lives: Feminist Theories and Personal Narratives*, ed. The Personal Narratives Group, pp. 103–17.
Mazlish, Bruce. 'Autobiography and Psycho-analysis: Between Truth and Self-Deception.' *Encounter* 35 (1970), 28-37.
—— *James and John Stuart Mill: Father and Son in the Nineteenth Century*. New York: Basic Books, 1975.
Mehlman, Jeffrey. *A Structuralist Study of Autobiography: Proust, Leiris, Sartre. Lévi-Strauss*. (1912). Ithaca: Cornell University Press, 1974.
Meisel, Perry. *The Myth of the Modern*. New Haven: Yale University Press, 1987.
Meisel, Perry and Kendrick, Walter (eds.) *Bloomsbury/Freud: The Letters of James and Alix Strachey 1924–25*. New York: Basic Books, 1985.
Mellor, Ann. *Romanticism and Gender*. New York and London: Routledge, 1993.
Mercer, Kobena. 'Welcome to the Jungle: Identity and Difference in Postmodern Politics'. In *Identity: Community, Culture, Difference*, ed. Jonathan Rutherford. London: Lawrence and Wishart, 1990.
Mill, John Stuart. *A System of Logic*. Vol. II. London: Longmans, Green, Reader, and Dyer, 7th ed. 1868.
Miller, D.A. *The Novel and the Police*. Berkeley and New York: University of California Press, 1988.
Miller, J. Hillis. *Theory Now and Then*. Durham: Duke University Press, 1991.
Miller, Nancy K. 'Women's Autobiography in France: For a Dialectics of Identification.' In *Women and Language in Literature and Society*, ed. S. McConnell-Ginet, R. Borker and N. Furman. New York: Praeger, 1980, pp. 258–73.
—— *Getting Personal*. New York and London: Routledge, 1991.
—— 'Changing the Subject: Authorship, Writing and the Reader.' In *Feminist Studies/Critical Studies*, ed. Teresa de Lauretis. London: Macmillan, 1988, pp. 102–20.
Millett, Kate. *Flying*. New York: Ballantine, 1974.
—— *Sita*. New York: Farrar, Strauss and Giroux; London: Virago, 1977.
Minh Ha, Trinh T. *Woman, Native, Other: Writing Postcoloniality and Feminism*. Bloomington: Indiana University Press, 1989.
Mink, Louis O. 'History and Fiction as Modes of Comprehension.' *New Literary History* 1 (1969-70), 541–64.
Misch, Georg. *A History of Autobiography in Antiquity*. Trans. E. W. Dickes. 2 vols. London, Routledge and Kegan Paul, 1950. First published as *Geschichte*

der Autobiographie, 1907.
—— *The Dawn of Philosophy*. Ed. R. F. C. Hull. London: Routledge and Kegan Paul, 1950. First published as *Der Weg in die Philosophie*, 1926.
Mitchell, W. J. T. *On Narrative*. University of Chicago Press, 1981.
Modleski, Tania. *Feminism without Women*. New York and London: Routledge, 1991.
Moretti, Franco. *The Way of the World: The* Bildungsroman *in European Culture*. London: Verso, 1987.
Morton, A.Q. *Literary Detection*. New Providence: Bowker Publishing Co., 1978.
Nadel, Ira Bruce. *Biography: Fiction, Fact and Form*. London: Macmillan, 1984.
Neumann, Bernd. *Identität und Rollenzwang: Zur Theorie der Autobiographie*. Frankfurt: Athenaeum, 1970.
Neyraut, M. *et al. L'autobiographie. VIes Rencontres psychanalytiques d'Aix-en-Provence, 1987*. Paris: Les Belles Lettres, 1988.
Ngcobo, Loretta. *Let it be Told: Black Women Writers in Britain*. London: Pluto, 1987.
Nicolson, Harold. *The Development of English Biography*. London: Hogarth Press, 1927.
Nietzsche, Friedrich. *Ecce Homo*. Ed. and trans. Walter Kauffman. New York: Random House, 1967.
—— *The Gay Science*. Trans. Walter Kauffman. New York: Random House, 1974.
Noble, J. Ashcroft. 'The Charm of Autobiography'. In *Impressions and Memories*. London: Dent, 1895, pp. 36–45.
Norris, Christopher. *Derrida*. London: Fontana, 1987.
Nouvet, C. *Literature and the Ethical Question. Yale French Studies*, 79. New Haven: Yale University Press, 1991.
Nussbaum, Felicity. *The Autobiographical Subject: Gender and Ideology in Eighteenth-Century England*. Baltimore: John Hopkins University Press, 1989.
Oakley, Ann. *Taking it Like a Woman*. London: Cape, 1984.
Oliphant, Margaret. 'New Books (No. XV).' *Blackwood's Edinburgh Magazine* CXV (April 1874): 443–63.
—— 'Harriet Martineau.' *Blackwood's Edinburgh Magazine* CXXI (April 1877), 472–96.
—— 'Autobiographies' in *Blackwood's Edinburgh Magazine*: I. 'Benvenuto Cellini', (Jan. 1881), 1–30. II. 'Lord Herbert of Cherbury' (March 1881), 385–410. III. 'Margaret, Duchess of Newcastle' (May 1881), 617–39. IV. 'Edward Gibbon' (Aug. 1881), 229–47. V. 'Carlo Goldoni' (Oct. 1881), 516–41. VI. 'In the Time of the Commonwealth: Lucy Hutchinson – Alice Thornton' (July 1882), 79–101. VII. 'Madame Roland' (April 1883), 485–511.
—— *The Autobiography and Letters of Margaret Oliphant: The Complete Text*. Ed. Elisabeth Jay. Oxford University Press, 1990.
Olney, James. *Metaphors of Self: The Meaning of Autobiography*. Princeton University Press, 1972.
—— 'Some Versions of Memory/Some Versions of *Bios*: The Ontology of Autobiography.' In *Autobiography: Essays Theoretical and Critical*, pp. 236–67.

—— 'Autobiography: An Anatomy and a Taxonomy.' *Neohelicon* 13 (1986): 57-82.

Olney, James (ed.) *Autobiography: Essays Theoretical and Critical.* Princeton University Press, 1980.

—— *Studies in Autobiography.* New York and Oxford, Oxford University Press, 1988.

Owen, Ursula (ed.) *Fathers: Reflections by Daughters.* London: Virago, 1983.

Pascal, Roy. *Design and Truth in Autobiography.* London: Routledge and Kegan Paul, 1960.

Personal Narratives Group (ed.) *Interpreting Women's Lives: Feminist Theory and Personal Narratives.* Bloomington: Indiana University Press, 1989.

Peterson, Linda H. *Victorian Autobiography: The Tradition of Self-Interpretation.* New Haven and London: Yale University Press, 1986.

—— 'Gender and Autobiographical Form: The Case of the Spiritual Autobiography'. In *Studies in Autobiography*, ed James Olney, pp. 211–22.

Poe, Edgar Allan. 'The Facts in the Case of M. Valdemar.' In *The Complete Tales and Poems of Edgar Allan Poe.* Harmondsworth: Penguin, 1982, pp. 96–103.

Poulet, Georges (ed.) *Les Chemins actuels de la critique: Suivi d'un choix bibliographique établi et commenté par D. Noguez.* Paris: Union générale d'éditions, 1968.

Prickard, A. O. *Autobiography.* London: Rivingtons, 1866.

Pritchett, V. S. 'All About Ourselves.' *New Statesman and Nation* (26 May 1956) 601–2.

Pryce-Jones, Alan. 'The Personal Story'. In *The Craft of Letters in England*, ed. John Lehmann. London: Cresset Press, 1956, pp. 26–45.

Raitt, Suzanne. *Vita and Virginia: the Work and Friendship of Vita Sackville-West and Virginia Woolf.* Oxford: Clarendon Press, 1993.

Ranson, John Crowe. *The New Criticism.* Norfolk, Conn.: New Directions, 1941.

Raynaud, Claudine. 'A Nutmeg Nestled Inside its Covering of Mace.' In *Life/Lines*, ed. Bella Brodzki and Celeste Schenk, pp. 221–42.

Renza, Louis A. 'The Veto of the Imagination: A Theory of Autobiographical Form.' *New Literary History* 9 (1977) 1–26. Reprinted in *Autobiography: Essays Theoretical and Critical*, ed. James Olney, pp. 268–95.

Richards, I. A. *Principles of Literary Criticism.* London: Routledge and Kegan Paul, 1924.

—— *Poetries and Sciences. A Reissue of Science and Poetry*, (1926). London: Routledge and Kegan Paul, 1970.

—— *Practical Criticism.* London: Routledge and Kegan Paul, 1929.

Rickman, H. P. (ed.) *Wilhelm Dilthey: Selected Writings.* Cambridge University Press, 1976.

—— *Dilthey Today: A Critical Appraisal of the Contemporary Relevance of His Work.* New York: Greenwood Press, 1988.

Ricoeur, Paul. *Temps et récit.* Trans. K. McLaughlin and D. Pellauer as *Time and Narrative*, 3 vols. University of Chicago Press, 1984–87.

Riesman, David. *The Lonely Crowd: A Study of the Changing American Character.* New Haven: Yale University Press, 1950 (reprinted 1971).

Rinehart, Keith. 'The Victorian Approach to Autobiography.' *Modern Philology*

51 (1954), 177–86.

Rousseau, Jean-Jacques. *The Confessions*. Trans. J. M. Cohen. Harmondsworth: Penguin, 1953.

—— *Rousseau judge of Jean Jacques: dialogues*. In *The Collected Writings of Rousseau: Vol. I*, ed. R. D. Masters and C. Kelly. Hanover, NH: University Press of New England, 1990.

Russell, Bertrand. *The Autobiography of Bertrand Russell*. London: George Allen and Unwin, 1967.

Ryan, Michael. 'The Question of Autobiography in Cardinal Newman's *Apologia pro vita sua*.' *Georgia Review* 31 (1977), 672–99.

—— 'Self-Evidence.' *Diacritics*, (June 1980), 2–16.

Rycroft, Charles. *Psychoanalyis and Beyond*. London: Chatto and Windus, 1985.

Sartre, Jean-Paul. *Words*. Harmondsworth: Penguin, 1964.

Sauerland, Karol. *Diltheys Erlebnisbegriff*. Berlin and New York: Walter de Gruyter, 1972.

Schopenhauer, Arthur. 'On Women'. In *Studies in Pessimism*. London: Swan Sonnenschein and Co., 1891, pp. 105–23.

Searle, John. *Speech Acts*. Cambridge University Press, 1969.

—— 'The Logical Status of Fictional Discourse.' *New Literary History* 6, 2 (1975), 319–32.

Sennett, Richard. *The Fall of Public Man*. New York and London: W. W. Norton, 1992.

[Shand, A. Innes]. 'Contemporary Literature (No. V): biography, travel and sport.' *Blackwood's Edinburgh Magazine* CXXV (April 1879), 482–506.

Shapiro, Stephen A. 'The Dark Continent of Literature: Autobiography.' *Comparative Literature Studies* 5 (1968), 421–54.

Sheringham, Michael. *French Autobiography: Devices and Desires*. Oxford: Clarendon Press, 1993.

Shumaker, Wayne. *English Autobiography: Its Emergence, Materials and Forms*. Berkeley and Los Angeles: University of California Press, 1954.

Simcox, Edith. 'Autobiographies.' *North British Review*, CII (Jan. 1870), 383–414.

—— *Autobiography of a Shirt Maker*. (1876–). Unpublished ms, Bodleian Library, Oxford.

—— 'New Books'. *Fortnightly Review* 15, new series (Jan. 1874), 109–20.

Simons, Judy. *Diaries and Journals of Literary Women from Fanny Burney to Virginia Woolf*. London: Macmillan, 1990.

Simpson, David (ed.) *German aesthetic and literary criticism; Kant, Fichte, Schilling, Schopenhauer, Hegel*. Cambridge University Press, 1984.

Sistren Theatre Collective. *Lionheart Gal: Life Stories of Jamaican Women*. London: The Women's Press, 1986.

Smeed, J.W. *'The Theophrastan Character': The History of a Literary Genre*. Oxford: Clarendon Press, 1985.

Smith, Barbara Herrnstein. *On the Margins of Discourse*. Chicago University Press, 1979.

Smith, Paul. *Discerning the Subject*. Minneapolis: University of Minnesota Press, 1988.

Smith, Sidonie. *A Poetics of Women's Autobiography: Marginality and the Fictions of*

Self-Representation. Bloomington and Indianapolis: Indiana University Press, 1987.

—— *Subjectivity, Identity and the Body: Women's Autobiographical Practices in the Twentieth Century*. Bloomington: Indiana University Press, 1993.

Smith, Sidonie and Watson, Julia (eds). *De/Colonizing the Subject: The Politics of Gender in Women's Autobiography*. Minneapolis: Minnesota University Press, 1992.

Snow, C. P. *The Two Cultures and the Scientific Revolution* [The Rede Lecture, 1959]. Cambridge University Press, 1959.

Spacks, Patricia. *Imagining a Self: Autobiography and Novel in Eighteenth-Century England*. Cambridge, Mass.: Harvard University Press, 1976.

—— 'Stages of Life: Notes on Autobiography and the Life Cycle.' *Boston University Journal* 25, 2 (1977), 7–17. Reprinted in *The American Autobiography*, ed. Albert E. Stone, pp. 44–60.

Spengemann, William C. *The Forms of Autobiography: Episodes in the History of a Literary Genre*. New Haven and London: Yale University Press, 1980.

Sprinker, Michael. 'Fictions of the Self: The End of Autobiography.' In *Autobiography: Essays Theoretical and Critical*, ed. James Olney, pp. 321–42.

Stanfield, James Field. *Essays on the Study and Composition of Biography*. Sunderland: George Garbutt, 1813.

Stanley, Liz. 'Feminist Auto/Biography and Feminist Epistemology.' In *Out of the Margins*, ed. Jane Aaron and Sylvia Walby. London: Falmer Press, 1991, pp. 204–19.

—— *The Auto/Biographical 'I'*. Manchester University Press, 1992.

Stanton, Domna C. (ed.) *The Female Autograph: Theory and Practice of Autobiography from the Tenth to the Twentieth Century*. University of Chicago Press, 2nd ed. 1987.

Starobinski, Jean. *Jean-Jacques Rousseau: la transparence et l'obstacle*. Paris: Plon, 1957. Trans. as *Jean-Jacques Rousseau: Transparency and Obstruction*. Chicago University Press, 1988.

—— 'The Style of Autobiography.' In *Autobiography: Essays Theoretical and Critical*, ed. James Olney, pp. 73–83.

Steedman, Carolyn. *Landscape for a Good Woman: A Study of Two Lives*. London: Virago, 1986.

—— *Childhood, Culture and Class in Britain: Margaret McMillan, 1860–1931*. London: Virago, 1990.

—— *Past Tenses*. London: Rivers Oram Press, 1992.

Stein, Gertrude. *Everybody's Autobiography*. London: Heinemann, 1938.

—— *The Autobiography of Alice B. Toklas*. In *Selected Writings of Gertrude Stein*, Carl Van Vechten. New York: Random House, 1972, pp. 1–237.

Steinkraus, W. E. and Schmitz, K. L. *Art and Logic in Hegel's Philosophy*. Sussex: Harvester, 1980.

Stephen, Leslie. 'Autobiography.' *Cornhill Magazine* XLIII (April 1881), 410–29.

—— 'National Biography'. In *Studies of a Biographer*. Vol. 1. London: Smith, Elder and Co., Duckworth and Co., 1907.

Stewart, Philip. *Imitation and Illusion in the French Memoir Novel 1700–1750: The Art of Make-Believe*. New Haven and London: Yale University Press, 1969.

Stewart, Susan. *Crimes of Writing*. Oxford University Press, 1990.

Stokes, Adrian. *Critical Writings of Adrian Stokes*. Vol. 2. London: Thames and Hudson, 1978.

Stone, Albert E. (ed.) *The American Autobiography*. Englewood Cliffs, NJ: Prentice-Hall, 1981.

Strachey, Lytton. 'A New History of Rome.' *Spectator* 102 (2 Jan. 1909), 20–1.

—— *Portraits in Miniature*. London: Chatto, 1933.

—— 'Queen Victoria', in *Five Victorians*. London: The Reprint Society, 1942.

—— *Eminent Victorians*. (1918). Penguin, 1948.

—— *Elizabeth and Essex*. Harmondsworth: Penguin, 1971.

Sturrock, John. 'The New Model Autobiographer.' *New Literary History* 9 (1977), 51–63.

—— *The Language of Autobiography: Studies in the First Person Singular*. Cambridge University Press, 1993.

Swindells, Julia. *Victorian Writing and Working Women*. Cambridge: Polity, 1985.

Symons, A. J. A. *The Quest for Corvo: An Experiment in Biography*. London: Cassell, 1934.

Tambling, Jeremy. *Confessions: Sexuality, Sin, The Subject*. Manchester University Press, 1990.

Tayler, J. Lionel. 'The Study of Individuals (Individuology) and their Natural Groupings (Sociology)'. In *Sociological Papers*. Vol. III. London: Macmillan, 1907, pp. 105–40.

—— *The Writing of Autobiography and Biography*. Hull: printed for the author, 1926.

Taylor, Gordon O. *Studies in Modern American Autobiography*. London: Macmillan, 1983.

Thompson, Paul. *The Voice of the Past: Oral History*. Oxford University Press, 2nd ed. 1988.

Thwaite, Ann. *Edmund Gosse: A Literary Landscape*. London: Secker and Warburg, 1984.

Todorov, Tzvetan. *The Fantastic: A Structural Approach to a Literary Genre*. Trans. Richard Howard. Ithaca: Cornell University Press, 1975.

—— 'The Origin of Genres.' *New Literary History*, 8, 1 (autumn 1976), 159–70.

—— (ed.) *French Literary Theory Today*. Cambridge University Press, 1982.

Torgovnik, Marianne. *Gone Primitive*. University of Chicago Press, 1990.

Trela, D.J. 'Froude on the Carlyles: the Victorian Debate over Biography'. In *Victorian Scandals: Representations of Gender and Class*. Athens: Ohio University Press, 1992, pp. 180–206.

Trilling, Lionel. *Sincerity and Authenticity*. Cambridge, Mass.: Harvard University Press, 1971.

Uglow, Jennifer. 'Publicizing the Private.' *Times Literary Supplement* (Oct. 1980), 1166.

Vance, Eugene. 'Augustine's *Confessions* and the Poetics of the Law.' *Modern Language Notes* 93 (1978), 618–34.

Vico, Giambattista. *The Autobiography of Giambattista Vico*. Trans. T. G. Bergin and M. H. Fisch. Ithaca: Cornell University Press, 1944.

Vincent, David. *Bread, Knowledge and Freedom: A Study of Nineteenth-Century Working Class Autobiography*. London and New York: Methuen, 1982.

Walton, Izaak. *The Lives of John Donne, Sir Henry Wotton, Richard Hooker, George Herbert and Robert Sanderson.* World's Classics. London: Humphrey Milford and Oxford, 1927.

Warner, Marina. *Monuments and Maidens: The Allegory of the Female Form.* London: Picador, 1987.

Warner, William. 'Realist Literary History: McKeon's New Origins of the Novel.' *Diacritics* 19, 1, spring 1989, 62–81.

Watson, Julia. 'Shadowed Presence: Modern Women Writers' Autobiographies and the Other'. In *Studies in Autobiography*, ed. James Olney, pp. 180–9.

Watt, Ian. *The Rise of the Novel.* London: Chatto, 1957.

Webb, Beatrice. *My Apprenticeship.* 2 Vols. Harmondsworth: Penguin, 1938.

Weigel, Sigrid. 'Double Focus: On the History of Women's Writing.' In *Feminist Aesthetics*, ed. Gisela Ecker, trans. Harriet Anderson. London: The Women's Press, 1985, pp. 59–80.

Weininger, Otto. *Geschlecht und Charakter.* Vienna: Braumüller, 1903. Trans. as *Sex and Character.* London: Heinemann; New York: Putnam, 1906.

Weinstein, Arnold. *Fictions of the Self: 1550–1800.* Princeton University Press, 1983.

Weintraub, Karl J. 'Autobiography and Historical Consciousness.' *Critical Inquiry* 1 (1975), 821–48.

—— *The Value of the Individual: Self and Circumstance in Autobiography.* University of Chicago Press, 1978.

Wellek, René. *The Attack on Literature and Other Essays.* Brighton: Harvester, 1982.

Wells, H.G. *Experiment in Autobiography: Discoveries and Conclusions of a Very Ordinary Brain since 1866.* 2 vols. London: Gollancz, 1934.

Wethered, H. N. *The Curious Art of Autobiography.* London: Christopher Johnson, 1956.

White, Hayden. *Metahistory: the Historical Imagination in Nineteenth-Century Europe.* Baltimore: Johns Hopkins University Press, 1973.

—— *Tropics of Discourse: Essays in Cultural Criticism.* Baltimore: Johns Hopkins University Press, 1978.

—— *The Content of the Form: Narrative Discourse and Historical Representation.* Baltimore: Johns Hopkins University Press, 1987.

Williams, Orlo. 'Some Feminine Biographies.' *The Edinburgh Review*, 231 (Jan./April 1920), 303–17.

Williams, Raymond. *Marxism and Literature.* Oxford University Press, 1977.

Wilson, Elizabeth. *Mirror Writing: An Autobiography.* London: Virago, 1982.

Wimsatt. W. K. *The Verbal Icon.* Lexington: Kentucky University Press, 1954.

Winnicott, D.W. *Playing and Reality.* Harmondsworth: Penguin, 1971.

Wittgenstein, Ludwig. *Tractatus Logico-Philosophicus.* London: Routledge and Kegan Paul, 1922.

Woolf, Virginia. *Flush: a Biography.* London: Hogarth Press, 1933.

—— *Three Guineas.* London: Hogarth Press, 1938.

—— 'The Lives of the Obscure.' In *The Common Reader.* Harmondsworth: Penguin, 1938, pp. 116–32.

—— *Roger Fry.* London: Hogarth Press, 1940.

—— 'How Should One Read a Book?' In *The Second Common Reader.* Harmondsworth: Penguin, 1944, pp. 196–206.

—— *The Moment and Other Essays*. London: Hogarth Press, 1947.

—— 'Memories of a Working Women's Guild.' In *The Captain's Death Bed*. London: Hogarth Press, 1950, pp. 207–24.

—— 'The New Biography.' In *Collected Essays*. Vol. IV. London: Hogarth Press, 1966–67, pp. 229–35.

—— *A Writer's Diary*. London: Triad/Granada, 1978.

—— 'A Sketch of the Past.' In *Moments of Being*, ed. Jeanne Schulkind. London: Triad/Panther, 1978.

—— 'The Art of Biography.' In *The Death of the Moth*. London: Hogarth Press, 1981, pp. 119–26.

—— 'Memoirs of a Novelist.' In *The Complete Shorter Fiction*. Ed. Susan Dick. London: Grafton Books, 1991, pp. 69–79.

—— *Orlando*. World's Classics. Oxford University Press, 1992.

Wordsworth, William. *Letters of William and Dorothy Wordsworth. Vol. 1 – The Early Years – 1787–1805*. Ed. Ernest de Selincourt, rev. C.L.Shaver. Oxford: Clarendon Press, 1967.

—— *The Prelude*. Ed. J.C. Maxwell. Harmondsworth: Penguin, 1971.

—— 'Essays Upon Epitaphs.' In *Wordsworth's Literary Criticism*, ed. Howard Mills. Bristol: Classical Press, 1980, pp. 120–69.

Young, Robert M. 'Biography: the basic discipline for human science.' *Free Associations* 11 (1988), 108–30.

Index